P9-ARR-865

AWAKENING AMERICAN
EDUCATION TO THE WORLD

Awakening American Education to the World

The Role of Archibald Cary Coolidge, 1866-1928

ROBERT F. BYRNES

Theodore Lownik Library
Illinois Benedictine College
Lisle, Illinois 60532

University of Notre Dame Press

Notre Dame   London

370
.973
B995a

Copyright © 1982
University of Notre Dame Press
Notre Dame, Indiana 46556

Library of Congress Cataloging in Publication Data

Byrnes, Robert Francis.
Awakening American education to the world.

Bibliography: p.
Includes index.
1. Education—United States—History. 2. Inter-
national education—United States. 3. Coolidge,
Archibald Cary, 1866–1928. I. Title.
LA216.B92   370'.973   81-40451
ISBN 0-268-00599-0   AACR2

Manufactured in the United States of America

In Memory of

Laurence B. Packard
William L. Langer

Contents

Any serious fundamental change in the intellectual outlook of human society must necessarily be followed by an educational revolution.

Alfred North Whitehead

Non sibi sed nobis sed patriae.

Not for himself, but for us—the nation.

Inscription on Memorial to
Archibald Cary Coolidge
in Widener Library,
Harvard University

Preface

THE ORIGINS OF THIS volume lie in the 1960s, when my curiosity arose concerning the foundations of American colleges' and universities' expanded attention after 1945 to other peoples and cultures and to international affairs. I was able to supplement research in archives and libraries by discussions and correspondence with many men, most of whom are now dead, who contributed significantly to beginning that transformation in American education and outlook. Laurence B. Packard and William L. Langer, to whom this volume is dedicated, talked to me at length about Archibald Cary Coolidge and Harvard University during their years as undergraduate and graduate students. Robert F. Kelley and Robert J. Kerner, who studied under Coolidge; Edward Chase Kirkland, who was a student and graduate student in history at Harvard during Coolidge's years; and Philip E. Mosely and Ernest J. Simmons, whom Coolidge stimulated into interest in Russia when they were undergraduates, were also helpful. Three others who contributed to the founding of Russian studies in the United States, Jesse Clarkson, Harold H. Fisher, and Avrahm Yarmolinsky, were equally generous with their knowledge.

Others who worked with Coolidge at Harvard and who answered my queries included Reginald F. Arragon, Frederick B. Artz, Alexander Baltzly, Harold Deutsch, Dwight E. Lee, Sidney R. Packard and Mrs. Packard, Dexter Perkins, and Lawrence Steefel. Joseph R. Coolidge, IV, Lawrence Coolidge, Jr., John Crane, Bruce T. McCully, Frederick M. Kimball, and Father Mark H. Keohane were generous in their responses. Alfred F. Havighurst was most helpful in collecting information about Laurence B. Packard.

Harold J. Coolidge, Professor John Coolidge, J. Gardner Coolidge, and Oliver H. Coolidge assisted in locating family documents and in providing insights. The late Walter Muir Whitehill, whose wife was a niece of Professor Coolidge, in his conversations and splendid books helped me understand the Boston and Cambridge in which Coolidge lived and worked. Archibald Cary Coolidge, who was particularly close to his uncle, helped me get in touch with other members of the family and provided candid advice about my manuscript at various stages. The late Hamilton Fish Armstrong, who worked closely with Coolidge on *Foreign Affairs,* talked with me often about Coolidge and their joint work and gave me full access to their rich correspondence.

William Bentinck-Smith, whose *Building a Great Library: The Coolidge Years at Harvard* (Cambridge, Mass., 1976), illuminates Coolidge's achievements as Director of the Harvard University Library, was selfless in suggesting sources for this volume, in sharing judgments, and in reviewing an early manuscript. My wife and Robert Ferrell, my colleague in the Department of History at Indiana University, also made perceptive and useful comments about an early draft. The flaws and faults are my own.

I am happy to express my obligation to the staff of the Indiana University library and to librarians in many other institutions for their unfailing courtesy and helpfulness. The Harvard University Archives, an important resource for anyone interested in the history of American education, are so well organized and provide such convenient and comfortable arrangements that they serve as a model other American universities should follow in collecting materials and making them available. I am especially grateful to Harley P. Holden and his associates for their efficient and friendly assistance.

The secretarial staff of the Department of History of Indiana University was wonderfully efficient in typing the various drafts through which parts of this volume labored, and I appreciate their sympathetic understanding of my struggles.

The Office of International Programs and the Office of Research and Development of Indiana University enabled me to complete some of the travel necessary for my research. *Slavic Review* graciously granted permission to reprint materials which first appeared there.

It is a joy to thank the Rockefeller Foundation Study and Conference Center in Bellagio, one of the most beautiful sites in the world, for providing me a month in which to outline this volume, and the Netherlands Institute for Advanced Study, which offered ideal surroundings and good companions while I completed the first draft.

Completing the final touches on the manuscript in Gammarth, Tunisia seems especially appropriate, for this lovely part of the Maghreb was one of Coolidge's favorite places in the world.

Robert F. Byrnes

Part 1:
Introduction

1. American Education and the World

I PROPOSE IN THIS volume to describe the beginnings of research and instruction in American colleges and universities concerning the peoples and cultures beyond the United States and Western Europe. The years between 1890 and 1930 constituted an era of great change within the United States in world economic, political, and intellectual life and in international politics, and an exciting age in the history of American higher education. I shall concentrate upon the career of Archibald Cary Coolidge and the contributions this unassuming but imaginative and constructive teacher of undergraduates, director of graduate students, scholar, librarian, and editor made from 1893 until his death in 1928. Coolidge helped transform Harvard from a small New England college into one of the great universities of the world. The young men he trained and those with whom he worked in the war and peace efforts from 1917 to 1919 carried his ideas concerning research and instruction about other parts of the world into colleges and universities across the United States. His publications and lectures, the training he provided future diplomats, his contributions to New England organizations to increase knowledge and understanding, his help in founding the Council on Foreign Relations, and his service as editor of *Foreign Affairs* during its first six years helped to create the foundations and the interest in knowledge of other peoples and cultures which have distinguished American academic life in the second half of the twentieth century.

Coolidge lived from the end of the Civil War until just before the depression of 1929. In the summer of 1893, almost halfway through that period, Frederick Jackson Turner declared that the American frontier was closed. That fall, Charles Francis Adams left the Adams family home in Quincy, no longer a quiet town, for the privacy of Lincoln, further west in Massachusetts, and Alfred Thayer Mahan, whose *Influence of Sea Power upon History* and *Influence of Sea Power upon the French Revolution and Na-*

3

poleon together sold almost fifty editions, was lionized in England. In that same year, Coolidge (Harvard class of 1887), who was later to attract Turner to Cambridge from the University of Wisconsin, joined the Harvard faculty. Before he had completed his first year as an instructor, he launched a great change in American higher education by proposing that Harvard begin instruction in modern European history and on areas of the world beyond the United States and Western Europe, from which most of the American population and its cultures, traditions, and values had come. Acceptance by Harvard and then by other American universities of his thesis that the university should study the universe, not just the Western world, has contributed greatly to their intellectual modernization.

During the half century after the Civil War, the American people concentrated their intellectual and physical energies upon rebuilding their shattered nation and constructing the reality of an industrialized nation, unified in freedom. This occurred at the same time that the population continued to flow into unfilled, sometimes almost untouched, territories and that a wave of eager and ambitious men, women, and children from other parts of the world poured into the United States. Immigration constituted one of the principal sources of the country's rapid growth and vitality, but taxed its social and institutional resources: the immigrants usually had to learn a new language, adapt to a quite different society and sometimes resentful nativists, acquire meaningful work and a place to live, and begin to participate in a new and confusing life.

Agricultural production on both old and new lands by 1890 made the United States the leading producer of food in the world, with output so vast that it became a granary and breadbasket for many countries. Scientific-technical changes and the rapid growth of industry helped transform the economy and economic and social life at a rapid pace. These great transformations were carried forward by the railroads (the third transcontinental line was completed the year Coolidge entered Harvard) and by many new products, such as the telephone, the electric light, and the trolley car. By 1890 the United States had changed from an agricultural to a predominantly industrial country, from a rural to an urban society, dominated by a new class of wealthy industrial and banking barons. Millions of immigrants and sons and daughters of farmers piled into crowded industrial conglomerations. These developments twisted traditional, largely rural values and forced the United States from its cocoon of isolation into a nation inextricably engaged in the world economy and world affairs.

Political pressures, reflecting these transformations, led to reform movements designed to ensure the rights of blacks and whites, old settlers and new immigrants; to secure popular control of the political system at all levels; to weaken the political power of both the old and the new barons; and to make government ever more responsive to the needs of all Americans. These movements achieved monumental triumphs in expanding constitutional rights and in using accepted, peaceful instruments for political change at a time when economic, social, cultural, and intellectual foundations were shifting.

The unwanted and unexpected war with Spain in 1898, in one illuminating flash, thrust the United States into a prominent position in world affairs, just when the latest, and no doubt greatest, thrust of European expansion was overwhelming the peoples of Asia and Africa. American victory in this sudden war stunned Europeans, as well as Americans. The leap into empire and world power shed new light upon the emergence of the United States in world trade, just as the American role in the last year of the First World War demonstrated that the rising world power could harness its economic resources, manpower, and energy to significant participation in the political-military issues of Europe and the world. However, American foreign policy stumbled before the new responsibilities which arose at the end of the war. People and leaders fumbled their role and removed the United States from the position in world affairs which President Woodrow Wilson and many countrymen had envisaged during the months of American participation in the war and in the 1919 negotiations.

One of the many responsibilities of the American educational system is to enable those millions it touches to begin to comprehend other peoples and the way in which the histories of all become ever more closely intertwined. Foreign observers often find understanding the United States difficult because its institutional patterns differ from those of other societies. The American educational system is especially baffling because it reflects the decentralized, diversified economic and political pluralism of the United States. One of the wonders of the world, which has received little attention from even American historians, it puzzles and confuses others because of its varieties, absence of national standards, and great range in character and quality.

In the eighteenth and nineteenth centuries, as a country

which would today be called "less developed," the United States, or more accurately the American people, demonstrated extraordinary faith in and reliance upon education. The Puritans founded Harvard College less than twenty years after they arrived on this continent, and dozens and even hundreds of colleges and universities dotted the map by the last quarter of the nineteenth century, but the American people placed heaviest emphasis upon primary and secondary public schools. This concentration grew after the Civil War, in part because of the waves of immigration and the rapid growth of the population, and the public school system became one of the foundations and glories of the republic.

In the final third of the nineteenth and the early years of the twentieth century, interest in learning mounted rapidly and higher education expanded enormously, changed significantly in character, and improved greatly in quality. Turbulence and expansion between 1890 and 1910 in particular transformed the United States from a land of small colleges to a land that was becoming famous for its universities. The high priority given education, the desire that America become independent of Europe in education, rapid economic and population growth, the accumulation of wealth in the hands of men who saw investing in colleges and universities (rather than in churches) as a splendid way to ensure their remembrance, and the decisions of state legislatures after the Civil War to establish and to expand state colleges and universities made higher education a great national undertaking. It also became one of the dynamic parts of American intellectual life and a growing national "industry," no longer limited to or concentrated largely in the Northeast. The number of students in higher learning grew from 67,000 in 1870 to 156,000 in 1890 and 355,000 in 1910. (In 1938 it was 1,350,000; in 1948, 2,700,000 and in 1981 more than 11,000,000.) This growth was reflected in the expansion of faculties and then of learned societies and their journals, many of which were launched in the 1880s and 1890s.

The changing character of higher education during these years was even more important than accelerated growth. Because of the nature of the educational system, these revisions were by no means uniform in timing or character. In fact, some colleges in 1930 had not changed in character and quality since 1865. However, many changed dramatically. In this, Harvard, under President Charles W. Eliot, led the way by establishing an elective system of courses for undergraduates, breaking the grip of the

English college system and the monopoly exercised by theology, philosophy, the classsics, and mathematics. This loosening of curriculum weakened and ultimately almost destroyed the study of Greek, Latin, and some other fields of study and enabled the new sciences and, ultimately, the humanities and social sciences to share in an academic smorgasbord. The new emphasis upon the secular, practical world over piety weakened, then basically eliminated the grip of the clergy over higher education, and brought more laymen and new ideas into leading roles in the educational establishment.

Universities in the United States, and presumably elsewhere as well, are among the most conservative of man's institutions and usually respond slowly to social change. David Starr Jordan, one of the great educational innovators at the turn of the century, compared changing the curriculum to moving a cemetery. However, in this period of change, many institutions of higher education were becoming new carriers of culture, replacing those of Europe in providing training grounds for new leadership in business, the professions, and government and in exercising an important role in the process of "upward mobility," one of the principal characteristics of American society.

Harvard under Eliot after 1869 chose to recruit and select an ever larger percentage of its students from beyond Boston, Massachusetts, and New England. Widening these circles from Back Bay to the Bay area of San Francisco, and admitting the most promising and highly motivated young men of whatever background or class, helped make the university truly national and was an important step toward its becoming an international institution as well. The changing character of the student body, curriculum, and faculty enabled Eliot gradually to raise the standards of instruction and to place more emphasis upon research. Those institutions across the land that saw themselves as competitors of Harvard or who chose to follow its example benefited in the same way. Establishment of The Johns Hopkins University in 1876, primarily for research and for training graduate students; the foundation of Clark University in 1887 with the same goals; and the emphases other new private institutions, such as Stanford and Chicago, placed upon research and graduate work hastened the process of transforming both the established institutions and the ambitious new state universities.

Yale University awarded the first American Ph.D. degree in 1861. By the turn of the century, an ever increasing percentage of faculty members in the leading institutions possessed Ph.D. degrees, training graduate students was an accepted function of many universities, scholarship was recognized as a profession, and perhaps eight or ten American institutions were genuine universities. The dominance of European universities, especially those of Germany, in training young American scholar-teachers had been broken, and more young men received their advanced degrees in the United States than abroad. However, the closeness of ties, the respect and affection American scholars felt for Europe and the institutions in which they had studied, and growing recognition of international, even universal ramifications of knowledge led to increased cooperation and interdependence.

Before the last two decades of the nineteenth century, most American colleges ignored history: in 1880, Harvard had three historians, Princeton one, and Dartmouth none. Only distinguished amateur historians, such as John Lothrop Motley and Francis Parkman, had devoted attention to research and writing in history, even American history. In 1884, when the American Historical Association was established in upstate New York, only fifteen professors and five assistant professors of history had appointments in American educational institutions, and the majority of the forty-one founding members were scholarly amateurs. Anglo-Saxon Easterners, most of whom had received graduate training in Germany, launched the "great awakening in the American historical world." The first five presidents of the association had received their education in Germany, as had nearly half of the 600 members in 1895. Leopold von Ranke was elected the first honorary member at the association's third annual meeting, and obituaries of German scholars preceded those of Americans in the *American Historical Review* until after the First World War.

Research and instruction in history, as higher education in general, remained concentrated in the East until long after the First World War. When the *Review* was founded in New York City in April 1895, twenty-five of the twenty-six men involved were Easterners, and the twenty-sixth was to move from Cleveland to New Haven that fall. The association, until it met in Cleveland in 1897, held its annual meetings in the East, except for a special summer session at Chicago in 1893, at which Turner presented the paper which summarized his thesis about the significance of the frontier and its ending. The geographic center of its membership in 1906 was Pittsburgh.

The association and American interest in history grew rapidly, along with American wealth, power, and sense of national unity and purpose. In addition, secularism, the impact of Darwinism, and faith in science led many Americans to see in history an appropriate way to give meaning to life, or at least to provide some way to understand the swirling world of change in which they lived. Before the First World War, American universities had more than 300 graduate students in history. In its second year, 1885, the association had 287 members. By 1899 it had 1,200 members; by 1914, 2,913; and in 1928, when Coolidge died, 3,500.

As the number of professional historians grew, the critical spirit flowered, largely because of the scientific methods German scholars had emphasized. The annual meetings and the *Review* strengthened this approach, helped raise standards on a national basis, and created a spirit of confraternity important to any new profession. Historians began to acquire stature and influence as their numbers grew, and separate departments of history became a symbol of the profession's step toward independence and authority.

The original interest of American historians was naturally in Western European and American history and political institutions; indeed, the idea that "history is past politics" dominated. Most academic institutions and the *Review* divided history into ancient, medieval, and modern, until the 1930s; and the "new history" definition, that history is the study of man's every activity, was not widely accepted until that time. The changes in the American definition of the world and history which Coolidge and his generation introduced therefore represent an important shift, one which has deeply affected American education and the American view of the world.

At Harvard, the center of Coolidge's life, activity, and influence, his emphasis upon widening the university's horizons and upon quality helped change the Department of History from one that played a secondary role in the university into one that enjoyed a golden age and constituted for some years the outstanding group of scholars in history in the United States. His policies and standards affected other areas of the university as well, especially the library, which he helped make one of the finest university systems and collections in the world. He was one of the stellar group of scholars, under Presidents Eliot and A. Lawrence Lowell, who helped change the character of Harvard and put it in touch with the rest of the world. The Eliot and Lowell years thus made the university a part of "the great globe itself" and transformed Harvard from a New England college into a model or pacemaker for other institutions.

In many ways this creative man, who fully utilized his wealth and family position, was a predecessor of the great foundations in stimulating change in American universities. He played the role of Johnny Appleseed in training approximately fifty young men who helped introduce the history of Western civilization as the basic freshman history course. He launched research and instruction in modern history and in the history of other countries and cultures in colleges and universities across the country. Indeed, his definition of history spread rapidly as his graduates distributed themselves throughout the United States to teach about Russia, Latin America, China, Eastern Europe, and the Middle East. Some of those he trained became "theologians," productive research scholars who trained young professional historians in such major institutions as the University of Illinois, the University of California at Berkeley, and Stanford University. Others became "parish priests" and instructed undergraduates in large and small colleges across the land.

Coolidge launched this effort to modernize the university just when the war with Spain made the United States an important world state and created new responsibilities for its leaders. His work in identifying and helping educate young men for work in the Department of State assisted significantly in the creation of a professional Foreign Service. The research and advisory services he and those he trained performed after the United States entered the First World War helped lessen confusion at the peace conference in Paris. The work of scholars in Washington and Paris demonstrated to government officials the quality of mind scholars could bring to analysis of contemporary international problems. They also helped define the relationship between government and the academic community by showing that professors must function as independent analysts and critics when they assisted in times of national emergency.

Work in The Inquiry and in the American Commission to Negotiate Peace from 1917 to 1919 enlivened and deepened the interest of American historians in the need to expand attention to other peoples and to the outside world. It also led to Coolidge's signal effort to increase knowledge and understanding of the world and of international politics beyond the university, a function he had begun the year he joined the Harvard faculty, when he first wrote for the *Nation*. His six years as editor helped make *Foreign Affairs* the most influential American journal on international politics.

Each generation assumes that some kind of inevitability has shaped the society and the world in which it lives. Over centuries, historians have almost despaired at their failure to persuade their fellows that institutions do not grow automatically and that neither values nor libraries spring from the ground like mushrooms after a summer rain. The expansion and improvement of American higher education and the growth of public knowledge concerning other parts of the world have not been inevitable, as the failure of other countries to complete such changes demonstrates. Men and women, as much as circumstances, have helped shape and direct these changes. Except for the appearance of Coolidge at Harvard under immensely able presidents and propitious circumstances, interest in other cultures and countries might have begun in the heady years after 1898 and reflected some of the nationalism and imperialism that bubbled up at that time, with emphasis upon Latin America and East Asia. The most important founders might have been immigrants, who would have given a tone and quality to these studies quite different from that of the cool and dispassionate Bostonian. Sons of missionaries, delighted by their achievements in China or Africa, or annoyed by expulsion from these areas by aroused nationalists, would have provided different foundations. The founders might also have reflected some sense of New England cultural superiority, white Anglo-Saxon Protestant arrogance, or even the racist views quite common among the intellectual elite at the turn of the century (which survive today). Coolidge and others who helped launch this great change possessed different qualities and views and therefore exercised an influence which we assume today, but which might have been markedly different.

The awakening of American interest in the histories of other cultures and peoples surely derives to a large degree from changes within the United States and in American relations with other parts of the world in the last years of the nineteenth century. The nature of this transformation and its leadership also constitute part of "the flowering of New England," a consequence of the wider horizons of those years upon the Puritan inheritance and upon the Boston intellectual elite. Coolidge was a member of a self-assured family with roots in Massachusetts and Virginia, which also assumed that it belonged to a culture which included

Western Europe. This inherited tradition helped ensure that Coolidge as a scholar-teacher would nurture the new field of study in an international, even universal, framework and spirit rather than in a limited national view. Learning French and German as a youngster and other languages in and after college, and the habit of travel when the entire world was open to the intellectually curious members of the well-to-do help explain why Coolidge and other members of his generation were so eager to learn about foreign peoples and cultures.

Informed by his journeys in an age of empire and the visibly growing authority of a half dozen states, he saw that each people and culture possessed a particular historical foundation and that an observer must therefore view them in a dispassionate and nonpolitical fashion. Moreover, travel taught him to view each state and culture in both a regional and a world framework. His American inheritance helped him appreciate "the exploding desire for self-government" and the impact this worldwide phenomenon would one day exert upon all the great empires. Awareness that the world was "coming together" and stress upon seeing the world as a whole were particularly important in the formative years of American scholarship concerning foreign areas and peoples. They helped to limit overspecialization and parochialism. They emphasized basic factors, such as geography, population, and religion. They added a flavor of internationalism to all research and instruction. Above all, the movement which spread throughout the United States from Harvard emphasized qualities which placed a special stamp upon this new field of study: intellectual distinction; mastery of foreign languages; study and travel abroad (beyond the archives and libraries); and dispassionate and evenhanded knowledge and understanding.

In 1930, Americans were only beginning the study of other languages and areas of the world, but interest in and knowledge of other cultures were as great as in any of the major European states. Above all, Coolidge and those he trained established foundations of the highest quality, on which later generations have continued the unfinished work of assisting Americans to know and understand the other peoples with whom they share the world.

2. Boston, the Coolidges, and Harvard

ARCHIBALD CARY COOLIDGE was born at 145 Beacon Street in Boston on March 6, 1866, and died just a few houses away on January 14, 1928. He spent his entire life in Boston and Cambridge, except when he was abroad studying, working, or traveling. Boston played an important historical role in the American Revolution, and many during Coolidge's lifetime considered it the center of American culture and liberal aspirations. In addition, it was an important manufacturing and trading center. It competed with New York as a seaport and center of rail communications, although the decision of the Cunard Line in 1868 to make New York its American base signaled Boston's ultimate commercial defeat and decline. Many Bostonians of the generation of Oliver Wendell Holmes, and of his own (and George Apley's as well), considered Coolidge's native city the hub of the United States, and perhaps of the solar system, but Coolidge grew beyond this parochial view. Instead, he utilized the intellectual curiosity and the material resources of his class and city to acquire substantial knowledge of other cultures and countries and of world politics.

Boston changed rapidly after the Civil War. It grew from 170,000 in 1860 to 362,000 in 1880 and 561,000 in 1900—from a tightly packed seaport to a sprawling metropolis surrounded by thirty cities and towns. It gradually became two nineteenth-century cities rather than an eighteenth-century town. One was inhabited by native-born Americans, dominated intellectually by the self-styled Brahmins, a highly cultured elite. The other was composed of foreign-born Americans, most of whom were Irish, who may have formed "the most povery-stricken, illiterate, and improvident immigration that had ever set foot on American soil," and their progeny.[1] By the time Coolidge went to Harvard in 1883, "the other Bostonians" comprised about three fifths of the population, and by 1900 three quarters. The old Puritan city of Boston had become "the most Catholic city in the country."[2]

The Coolidges and other members of the Brahmin group had little knowledge of and few relationships with the Irish. The Coolidge family, like that of Charles Francis Adams somewhat earlier and Samuel Eliot Morison later, employed several Irish women as servants in its homes on Chestnut Hill in Brookline and on Beacon Street. These relationships—and occasional snowball fights and other such skirmishes between groups of boys of North and South Boston, or of Brattle and Mount Auburn streets in Cambridge—were usually the only associations the heirs of the great families had with the city's new majority.[3]

Most of "Cold Roast Boston" showed scant interest in local politics. Instead, they left this to the Irish, who in turn ignored them but acquired control of the police and fire departments in the 1870s, elected Hugh O'Brien the first Irish mayor in 1885, and for a century enjoyed almost complete control of the city's political life. Thus "while Yankees owned Boston, Irishmen ran it."[4] And thus later generations' Norman Casses felt confronted by "marauders, the representatives of that boisterous, crafty, and despised breed of latter-day Goths who had come to sack the city and had remained to enjoy their plunder."[5]

On the national scene Boston's great families gradually abandoned their leadership of responsible conservatism and reform to other parts of the country. In 1893, the year Coolidge joined the Harvard University faculty and Brooks Adams began *The Law of Civilization and Decay*, Barrett Wendell of Harvard lamented the decline of "their" Boston and New England: "We are vanishing into provincial obscurity. America has swept from our grasp. . . . I feel that we Yankees are as much a thing of the past as any race can be."[6]

The "proper Bostonians," who tended to live on Beacon Hill, were descendants of the families that had distinguished themselves in the creation of the United States and thereafter, for several generations, in commerce and business. By Coolidge's time, they constituted "the most homogeneous, self-centered, and self-complacent community in the United States."[7] Many who were most prominent in the last third of the nineteenth century were well-to-do, cultivated rentiers who lived on wealth created by their ancestors. Indeed, "inherited wealth had become the badge of the aristocracy."[8] Those in productive activities usually devoted their time to banking and brokerage rather than more demanding manufacture and trade. The most able and energetic had high personal qualities, "never praised or bragged," and were alert and useful citizens (like George Apley), often attaining quiet distinction in public service. John P. Marquand's "novel in the form of a memoir" about Apley, who graduated from Harvard the same year as Coolidge, provides a graphic account of the rentier class at its best.

Some Brahmin families during these Indian summer years contributed markedly to American culture, especially in literature, philosophy, and education. Descendants of the earlier ruling class in Coolidge's years provided Harvard many of its outstanding faculty and much of its intellectual and spiritual leadership. This small group endowed Boston with most of its museums, its orchestra and musical traditions, its architecture, and the foundation of its splendid system of parks. Their use of inherited wealth, leisure, and position inspired E.L. Godkin, who arrived from England after the Civil War and became an eminent editor of the *Nation*, to write that "Boston is the one place in America where wealth and the knowledge of how to use it are apt to coincide."[9]

Other Brahmin families, however, were provincial, even clannish; had "grandfather on the brain"; and deteriorated into stubborn members of a caste. They lacked the initiative and ability that distinguished their Salem ancestors in trade with the Far East. What Charles Francis Adams called a "lack of fresh outside air" helped make their Boston a stagnant and narrow place, whose great days belonged to the past.[10]

Such families, affronted by the changes that were undermining the system from which they benefited in an effortless way and creating a vastly different Boston and United States, turned in "aristocratic recoil" against their country in renewed reverence for England and English standards. Henry James was the exemplar of this group. Some Anglophile conservatives, such as James Russell Lowell and Henry and Brooks Adams, were so unable to accept the rapid economic and social changes the American republic tolerated that they retaliated meanly against other groups and races in outbursts of pessimism and racism.[11]

Archibald Cary Coolidge was born into a conservative but outward-looking Boston family (what the French called "notables") that traced its lineage in the commonwealths of Massachusetts and Virginia to the 1630s. His father, Joseph Randolph Coolidge, who was born in 1828 and died in 1925, was eighth in line from John Coolidge, one of the original proprietors of Watertown, Massachusetts. He was also a great-grandson of Thomas Jefferson, for whom his more famous younger brother,

Thomas Jefferson Coolidge, was named. The relationships which the Randolph and Jefferson names represent and the connection with Virginia played an important role in the family's views and activities. Joseph Randolph Coolidge and Thomas Jefferson Coolidge were, in fact, always called "Randolph" and "Jefferson." Their father, a harsh and unpleasant person, had engaged in trade with China with Augustine Heard and Company. Because of his long absences from home and his interest in European culture, he had his sons educated for eight years in Geneva and in a military school in Dresden, rather than in the United States. Randolph and Jefferson throughout their long lives maintained fluent command of French and German, considerable knowledge of Europe, cultivated habits, and interest in art. However, although their childhood experiences were similar and both graduated from Harvard College, the two were quite unalike.[12]

Jefferson Coolidge possessed many of the qualities traditionally associated with the vigorous and expansive years of the New England economy. An enterprising and successful businessman in trade with China, textile manufacture, banking, railroading, and a founder of the Old Colony Trust Company, he was a tactful, lively, and public-spirited member of the Boston community. He played an important role in creating the Boston and Brookline park systems, was American minister to France from March 1892 to May 1893, and served as a member of the Harvard Board of Overseers from 1886 to 1897. An intelligent collector of art and an active member of the Friday Club, which included James Russell Lowell, George Ticknor, Charles Francis Adams, and Louis Agassiz, he was active in the Massachusetts Historical Society, which James Ford Rhodes called "the oldest and wealthiest historical organization then in existence."[13] In 1898 he purchased and gave to the society 3,060 letters by Thomas Jefferson and 170 letters addressed to Jefferson. He was as aristocratic and strong willed as his brother and admitted an "incomplete acceptance of the democratic theory." He once declared that he belonged "to a superior class and that the principle that the ignorant and the poor should have the same right to make laws and govern as the educated and refined was an absurdity," but he was widely admired for his charm and sound judgment.[14]

On the other hand, Randolph Coolidge worked for only a year after he completed his education at Harvard in engineering and law. Rather than devote his time to commercial and financial enterprises and public service, he engaged in travel (largely in Western Europe), the study of geography and the Arctic, extensive reading of European literature, aiding select Boston charities, and ruling his wife and five sons.

Archibald Cary Coolidge's mother, Julia Gardner Coolidge, married her husband when he was thirty-two and she nineteen. A shy, plain woman, as deeply religious as he, she devoted her life to her family and her household. She was affectionate with her sons, treasured their letters, and remained close to them throughout their lives. One grandfather, a Peabody, had owned a hundred ships engaged in the East Indies trade. Her stories and those of her mother about life in Macao and other far-off cities constituted an important element of romance in her sons' lives. In 1884 her father, John Lowell Gardner, an immensely wealthy shipping and banking magnate, left her a considerable fortune (his estate was valued at $3,600,000), a handsome and elegant house at the waterside corner of Beacon and Berkeley streets, and an estate called Hillfields in Brookline, which sold in 1925 for about $500,000.[15]

All five Coolidge sons (Archie was the third) graduated from Harvard. With one exception, an inveterate traveler for whom Boston remained home base, they spent their lives in Boston or Cambridge. Two became Harvard professors. Three obtained substantial formal education abroad and spoke at least three foreign languages. All traveled widely.

The oldest son, Joseph Randolph Coolidge, Jr., graduated from Harvard in 1883. An amiable, serene, and unambitious man who enjoyed a happy married life, he soon learned that teaching Spanish at Harvard and banking did not excite him. He therefore continued his education for two years at the Massachusetts Institute of Technology, one year in Dresden and Berlin, and four years at the École des Beaux Arts in Paris, before he became a Boston architect. A responsible member of an endowed family, he was a prominent member of the Boston Chamber of Commerce, a generous contributor to charities, a trustee of the Boston Athenaeum for thirty-seven years, promoter of public libraries, and a vigorous supporter of the Boston Museum of Fine Arts.[16]

John Gardner Coolidge graduated from Harvard College in 1884 and devoted his indolent, fun-filled life to world travel, first class. He served intermittently in the diplomatic service from 1900 to 1919 (the first four years without salary) in South Africa, China, Mexico, Nicaragua, and France. The most renowned foreign correspondent of those years, Richard Harding Davis, thought his work under fire as a consular officer during the Boer War was outstanding. When John Coolidge resigned as American minister to Nicaragua in 1908, because he thought maintaining relations with dictator José Santos Zelaya inconsistent with the dignity of the United States, President Theodore Roosevelt termed him "an exceptionally able and efficient public servant."[17] However, before and after he married in 1909, he was a rich, unambitious American traveler, enjoying the fruits of his ancestors' work and thrift.

Harold Jefferson Coolidge, born in Nice in January 1870, completed his undergraduate study at Harvard in 1892 and graduated from law school in 1896. A dull, pompous man who organized family activities, he enjoyed a comfortable and easy Boston career in trust-property management.

The youngest son, Julian, graduated from Harvard *summa cum laude* in 1895, taught at Groton two years, and completed his education in mathematics at Oxford and Bonn. He joined the Harvard faculty in 1900, became an outstanding mathematician, and in 1930 was appointed the first Master of Lowell House. He told his fiftieth reunion class that he enjoyed "the fifty happiest years of any member."[18]

The Randolph and Julia Gardner Coolidge family in some ways resembled the New York Roosevelts and other families of established wealth. They lived in a simple and unostentatious way, with dignity and good manners, in the mansions Mrs. Coolidge inherited. They felt no envy of the very rich or deep concern for the poor, although their charities were generous. They remained Bostonians. The Jefferson and Randolph relationships with Virginia provided a sentimental, nostalgic touch to their otherwise conventional existence.

Grandfather Gardner, at his death in 1884, left each of the grandsons an annual income of $8,000 in trust—about two and a half times the salary of a full professor at Harvard at that time. In 1898 his son, John Lowell Gardner, left each of the young men, except John, $40,000. The four others then pooled and divided their money so that each, including John, received $32,000. Family correspondence indicates that the Coolidge sons were therefore able to live comfortable and unworried lives, particularly because of the financial skill of their adviser and Beacon Street neighbor, John F. Moors. They became moderately wealthy when their father died in 1925, dividing among them the considerable fortune of his wife, whose death occurred in 1921. After a career of travel and extensive gifts to Harvard University, Archibald Cary Coolidge at his death in January 1928 left an estate of more than $1 million, of which more than half went to Harvard.[19]

Randolph Coolidge was a faithful, even militant, Unitarian, for whom King's Chapel was the center of Boston. Perhaps because of his lonely experience in a severe Prussian-Saxon military school, perhaps because of the increasing deafness that afflicted him from the age of twelve, he was an impersonal, cold, and arbitrary parent. Handsome, autocratic, and vain, he so dominated his family that his wife enjoyed her own household budget only during her last years.[20]

The five Randolph Coolidge sons grew up under strict discipline, although their father was generous with them financially. Family life was spartan, marked by the absence of grace that a feminine presence often adds. According to family legend, his parents once informed Julian that he could have any dessert he wished on his birthday—then ate the ice cream he had requested as he watched, informing him that the promise applied only to desserts already in the house and that a servant had had to leave the house to obtain the ice cream.

The Coolidge boys also were brought up to be independent, able to live alone. John has described how he (like the others) went to school by himself, through the crowded streets of Boston, when he was four years old. The parents sent Archie to school in Virginia when he was nine and to six different private schools before he entered Harvard. Because his father was a militant Unitarian and no private school met his religious standards, their experiments did not consider one superior school, St. Paul's (Groton opened only in 1884), where he might have acquired the lifelong friends and sense of permanence obtained by some of his students, such as Joseph Clark Grew and Franklin D. Roosevelt.[21]

Even as young men, the Coolidge sons had no latchkey and they used the back stairs. They hesitated to stay away from home after midnight because they had to awaken a servant or their grim father, and they found it difficult to obtain permission to bring friends home. Throughout his life, the Harvard professor signed letters to his parents with his full name, Archibald Cary Coolidge.

Nevertheless, the Joseph Randolph Coolidge family was close and affectionate. The sons habitually visited their parents for Sunday night dinner. When they were abroad, they regularly wrote long letters which the parents read aloud at these weekly gatherings. The parents often traveled in Europe with their adult sons, and Archie journeyed on occasion with John and Julian. Archie as a young man acquired a reputation for brilliance, but none of his siblings resented being identified as "one of Archie Coolidge's brothers." His nickname, "the Doc," reflected the affection and esteem in which they held him. After Julian joined the Harvard faculty, Archie dined with him and his family on Thursday evenings. The sons remained close throughout their lives and their families often vacationed together.

The affection which marked the family circle did not reach beyond it. Archie's parents, known as "the scions of silence,"[22] chose to remain aloof from the class and even the clans to which they belonged and to provide, instead, a self-sufficient and somewhat isolated base for their sons. Their relationships with Jefferson Coolidge were cool and reserved, and they showed no interest in the strong Coolidge "Family Association." Except for Archie, they also remained aloof from Mrs. Coolidge's brother and his wife, the John Lowell Gardners, who lived nearby at 152 Beacon Street, even though "Mrs. Jack" had been a close friend of Archie's mother before the two women were married in 1860. Mrs. Gardner was celebrated in Boston history as Mrs. Jack Gardner, the art collector and creator of Fenway Court. In 1883, the summer before Archie entered Harvard, she and her husband, a director of the Chicago, Burlington, and Quincy Railroad, took him across the United States to San Francisco in a private railroad car. John Lowell Gardner in the 1890s provided Archie substantial financial support when he sought to improve the Harvard Library collection and to persuade President Eliot to add faculty appointments in new fields of study. Archie lunched often with "Mrs. Jack" and even took her to Harvard football games.

The Randolph Coolidges lived apart from Boston social and cultural life even after Beacon Street became their home in 1894, when Archie was twenty-eight and a member of the Harvard faculty. Perhaps because of the father's hearing disability, none of the family acquired the interest in the stage, the theater, or music which Henry Cabot Lodge and other Brahmin contemporaries enjoyed. Randolph Coolidge was an inactive member of three clubs: the Union and the Boston Art Clubs, both near his home, and the first American country club, in Brookline, of which he was a founder in 1882.

Randolph Coolidge's purchase of a summer home in 1893, a 350-acre farm on Squam Lake in New Hampshire, 134 miles from

Brookline (at that time a full day's trip), demonstrates the way he isolated his family from the Coolidge clan and from Boston society. Other members of his set owned places on the North Shore, in Beverly or Manchester, where Jefferson Coolidge maintained a summer estate, or in Cotuit on Cape Cod, where many Harvard administrators and faculty spent their vacations. Jefferson Coolidge had such a spacious summer home and so enjoyed entertaining that Baron Roman R. Rosen, the Russian ambassador, and many of his staff lived with him throughout the 1905 negotiations with the Japanese at nearby Portsmouth, New Hampshire.[23]

The Old Farm for thirty-five years was a second home for the Coolidge family, which often spent August, Thanksgiving, and the New Year holiday seasons on Squam Lake. The detailed record of those who visited the Old Farm from 1893 through 1928 shows that the family used it extensively, but that they invited few guests. Archie's graduate students and Harvard colleagues constituted by far the largest group of visitors. The five sons acquired the property from their father in 1908, and Archie added considerably to his share. In 1925 he was owner or part owner of 4,600 acres, including eight farms and eleven miles of road. When he was not abroad, he spent two weeks at Squam Lake late every summer, and he ordinarily visited it before and after his trips, as though it were a spiritual center. In 1919, though it seemed unlikely he would have descendants, he began construction of a monumental stone house, completed six months before he died of cancer of the spine.[24]

The Coolidge interest in Virginia demonstrated the family's independence or aloofness from Boston as much as did the farm at Squam Lake. It also reflected its concern for its Jeffersonian roots. Archie spent 1875-1877 at Shadwell, a private school administered by Charlotte Randolph, one of his aunts. As a boy, he became interested in the family hero, Thomas Jefferson, and in 1889 he sought to purchase Monticello, using $5,000 of his own money and seeking to borrow $30,000 from his father and other members of the family. In 1891 he sent his Harvard roommate to Monticello in another effort to buy the mansion. Later, he became an active member of the Monticello Association, an organization of descendants of Jefferson who took care of his grave. He was president of the association from 1919 through 1925 and almost always attended the annual sessions at the graveside.

In October 1898, Randolph Coolidge and four of his sons

purchased Tuckahoe, the seventeenth-century Randolph family estate of 600 acres on the James river, near the schoolhouse in which Jefferson had studied. They restored the house, and on April 19, 1900, arranged a reception for 400 distinguished Virginians, including the governor, an event which Archie proudly described to the Massachusetts Historical Society later that year.

All the Randolph Coolidges visited Tuckahoe often, Archie at least once every year. Sitting in the eighteenth-century gardens or walking through them while reading a favorite book were among his most satisfying pleasures. Because of the Tuckahoe purchase and the family roots, he became an active member of the Virginia Historical Society. He was particularly interested in the University of Virginia; he spoke at the installation of President Edwin A. Alderman in 1905 and at the centennial celebration of the university in 1921, and he gave the Barbour-Page series of lectures there in 1916. Thus Coolidge sought to combine the hardy Salem-Boston strain with that of aristocratic Virginia and to establish a second ancestral home.[25]

The life of the Randolph Coolidge family in Boston, the self-imposed isolation from other Bostonians on Squam Lake, and the emphasis on Virginia roots had a profound effect upon Archie and his brothers. Above all, they developed a different view of and relationship toward Boston and its role than did most of their contemporaries. The Coolidge boys grew up with very different relationships to members of their set, to the sea and seashore, to sport, and to many other ties to their region than did the Lodges, the Adamses, and the Morisons. Archie, for example, had little knowledge of birds or animals and could identify only one or two kinds of trees, although he vigorously supported programs for planting trees in the places where he lived or owned property. The athletic interests and abilities that most young Americans of his background obtained from playing with their fellows escaped him. He never learned how to sail or swim well. He played almost no baseball, rowed very little, and could not ride or snowshoe well. Walking in a strange way, with his toes pointed outward in "a kind of strut," he wore boots because he constantly kicked himself in the ankles. An awkward dancer, he remained clumsy throughout his life. His colleague and friend, George Santayana, wrote that Coolidge in physique and manner "seemed not quite normal, as if nature had put him together carelessly with insufficient materials, and had managed to make him go, but only by fits and jerks."[26]

Above all, Professor Coolidge was lonely and self-sufficient throughout his life, in part because of the way in which he was raised and the family's emphasis upon independence and even isolation. These qualities help explain why he turned to study of other cultures, as well as his reserved relations with family and colleagues (he did not succeed in establishing close relations even with his nieces and nephews). His reserve was such that he had many professional associates, but almost no close friends. He was extremely shy. After his death, the Department of History memorial noted that he was "almost pathetically modest." Foreign scholars, greatly impressed by his knowledge, understanding, and clarity of mind, were even more conscious of his humility.

The Harvard College that Coolidge entered in September 1883 had fewer than 1200 undergraduate students and about ninety faculty members, of whom fewer than twenty had a Ph.D. Henry Cabot Lodge called it a "school for Boston's elite," and others declared it "an extension of the Back Bay, small, snobbish, and dominated by the Unitarian clery."[27] It was then a third of the way through the presidency of Eliot, and its young men benefited from the elective system that Eliot had introduced. When Archie graduated in 1887, the only required courses were English composition and a modern language; even chapel was voluntary. Half of Archie's beginning class of 253 came from Massachusetts, forty from Boston alone, and two thirds of the undergraduate body were from New England; three quarters were graduates of private schools. Records of 40 percent of the class indicate that only four of that group were Catholics, although about 300 Catholics were undergraduates at Harvard in 1894.[28] The common freshman-year program ended in 1885, about the same time the college began to expand rapidly and social divisions began to appear between those from wealthy families and "others."

Archie enjoyed four happy years as an undergraduate. The college awakened him and became the center of his life. His examinations (the famous "bluebooks") contain clear and precise responses to his professors' questions. He graduated with highest honors in history, *summa cum laude,* and was a member of Phi Beta Kappa. His record won him permission as a senior to take History 12, the history of Europe since the seventeenth century, and Italian 4, Dante, although the two classes met at the same time. He was an intramural boxer and wrestler and a member of important clubs, such as Delta Kappa Epsilon ("Dickey"), Hasty

Pudding, and Alpha Delta Phi ("the Fly"). His four undergraduate years in Wadsworth 5 led to several lifelong friendships.
During twenty-eight of his thirty-five years as a member of the
faculty, he lived in a small suite of rooms in the Harvard Yard or
in a student dormitory in the Gold Coast on Mount Auburn
Street. He moved into the family home when his mother's death in
1921 left his father alone, and he purchased it in 1926, after his
father's death.[29]

The Harvard class of 1887 included three other men who had
an important effect upon American intellectual life. George
Pierce Baker, who came from Providence, Rhode Island, as a
member of the Department of English at Harvard from 1888
through 1924 and for the next decade at Yale, exercised a profound
influence upon American playwriting and amateur and professional theater. Baker's success and the renown achieved by some of
his students, especially Robert Benchley, Eugene O'Neill, and
Robert Sherwood, persuaded other educational institutions to
establish programs for playwriting and creative theater.

Bernard Berenson, who was born near Vilna in 1865 and
whose family moved in 1875 to East Boston, where his father was a
peddler, provided a different fillip. Berenson became "the world's
foremost connoisseur of Italian Renaissance art" and "arbiter of
taste, renowned authority on Renaissance painting, and oracle to
millionaire art collectors." He assisted Mrs. Jack Gardner in
building her art collection and was a close adviser to Joseph
Duveen, who arranged purchases of European art by other
prominent collectors. On his death, Berenson's Villa I Tatti near
Florence, one of the great art museums and libraries on art,
became the Harvard Center for Italian Renaissance Studies.[30]

Another member of the class, James Harvey Robinson, a
descendant of the Pilgrims, who came to Harvard from Bloomington, Illinois, contributed in a different fashion than Coolidge
to transforming instruction in history in the United States. At
Columbia University, he helped train a number of outstanding
historians, including Charles A. Beard, Carl Becker, Carleton
J.H. Hayes, and Arthur M. Schlesinger, Sr. Walter Phelps Hall of
Princeton University, himself a renowned teacher, called Robinson "one of the world's most distinguished teachers."[31] Robinson's textbooks made him one of the most significant populariz-
ers of history. He is best known, however, as the founder of "the
New History," as successful an assault against the emphasis on
constitutional and political history and names, dates, and crises as
that of Coolidge upon American and European history.[32]

When Coolidge graduated from Harvard College, Americans interested in obtaining advanced degrees traditionally undertook graduate study in Germany. One of Archie's Harvard colleagues, Bliss Perry, wrote that "us young fellows in the eighteen-eighties" were as sure that "Germany possessed the sole secret of scholarship" as George Ticknor and Edward Everett had been in 1814.[33] As late as 1889, Harvard on occasion selected a young faculty member by sending an outstanding student to Europe for two or three years of advanced training, before making the formal appointment. Two hundred young Americans were engaged in graduate work in Berlin in 1895, and only thirty in Paris. Moreover, Berlin was not the center for Americans: larger numbers went to Halle and Göttingen.

This tradition and the absence of professional training and adequate libraries in American universities almost dictated that Coolidge study abroad when he decided to obtain a Ph.D. in history. He spent two winter terms in Berlin and Paris, but chose to obtain his degree at Freiburg. His short thesis in 1892, "Theoretical and Foreign Elements in the Constitution of the United States," dealt with almost the same subject as that of Robinson two years earlier. The director of his studies was Professor Hermann E. von Holst, who sought to explain American democracy to Germans and who briefly acquired de Tocqueville's reputation as an interpreter of American history. The eight-volume translation of his *Constitutional and Political History of the United States,* published in Chicago between 1876 and 1892, gave him extraordinary influence in the United States. In fact, Johns Hopkins was only one of several universities that offered him an appointment before he joined the University of Chicago faculty in 1892.[34]

While studying in Europe, Coolidge asserted that "I shall always want to live in or near Boston." Correspondence between father and son reveals that both assumed he would one day be a professor at Harvard. Moreover, Eliot may have made an informal agreement with Coolidge about an appointment when Archie was still an undergraduate. In April 1890, Archie wrote from Paris that he hoped to become a Harvard professor but that he would be satisfied to attain that goal when he was thirty years old.

Study in Paris and Berlin and travel had demonstrated the advantage of having personal knowledge of the working of governments, particularly in helping one obtain "a look at the true inwardness of things." Coolidge also concluded that a few years in the diplomatic service would improve his training for an academic career, because "my interest in history has with time centered more and more on the present day, and most particularly on modern international politics." In fact, he indicated that a diplomatic career might attract him permanently: "After all, it is a great thing to be a Harvard instructor, but it is not the only thing in the world."

When he arrived in St. Petersburg on a trip in September 1890, Coolidge found that the American chargé d'affaires, George Wurts, had only a secretary to assist him and that he wanted a substantial home leave. Interested in diplomacy and eager to improve his Russian, Archie accepted appointment as acting secretary of the legation, with a commitment that Wurts would appoint him second secretary when Congress appropriated the funds. When Congress failed to act, Archie left St. Petersburg in March 1891 to continue his travels. In April 1892 he served for a month as private secretary of his uncle, Thomas Jefferson Coolidge, then American minister in Paris.[35]

After obtaining his Ph.D. from Freiburg, Coolidge returned to the United States, where "with much pleasure and gratification" he obtained appointment as secretary of the legation in Vienna. He arrived there on February 3, 1893, but returned to Boston two months later because of a "family matter of great importance": his fiancée, Corina Anna Shattuck, the twenty-year-old daughter of an outstanding medical doctor and editor, had broken their engagement.[36] Archie not only failed to change her mind, but resigned from the diplomatic service on April 21 and remained in Boston. Later that spring, Eliot wrote to Professor Edward Channing, chairman of the Department of History, inquiring whether Channing could use Coolidge in the department. Channing assented, the corporation appointed Coolidge an instructor on June 12, and he began his long career in education as the result of a young lady's unexplained decision.

The collapse of Coolidge's marital plans was a shattering blow (he told his favorite sister-in-law that he considered making use of a revolver). He translated several works of two Russian poets, Nicholas Nekrasov and Fyodor Tiutchev, that were marked by profound melancholy, gloomy descriptions of the Russian countryside, and such phrases as "I suffer still from anguished longing."[37] His relations with women thereafter were reserved and awkward. He was cordial and cheery with female members of the Harvard University library staff, but one member of the Order Department termed him "the most impersonal man she had ever known.''[38] When Widener Library opened in 1915, Coolidge as director sought to make it a male sanctuary, establishing a separate section of the main reading room for Radcliffe students and allowing them to study in the library after six o'clock only with his permission.

After 1893, Coolidge dedicated his time and energy to teaching and research, widening the horizons of Harvard and the American academic community, building a great library, helping make Harvard a great university, and advancing knowledge and understanding of the rest of the world and international politics among informed Americans. His fiancée's decision may have cost the United States an eminent diplomat, but it contributed to the transformation of American higher education and America's view of the world.

Part 2:

Coolidge the Historian

3. The Eternal Student and Scholar

COOLIDGE WAS A MAN of many skills, but his achievements as a scholar and teacher and his genius as an editor constituted the core of his work and reputation. Moreover, the qualities which exemplified his craft as a historian were essential factors in his success in selecting others to teach at Harvard, in training young men for positions in many other institutions, and in helping create a great library. The circumstances in which he lived and worked and his personal and professional qualities were particularly important for American education and public understanding because he helped shape research and instruction concerning the world and its affairs just as they were beginning in the United States.

Coolidge's curiosity concerning other parts of the world probably arose because he possessed an inquiring mind and grew up in a prosperous family, avid for knowledge of the world beyond Boston and accustomed to travel at a time when human affairs were changing rapidly. As a young boy, he was a voracious student of maps and engaged ardently in games involving history (especially wars) with his older brothers. Travel was an even greater stimulus than reading, for it began when he was only two and continued as a conscious learning experience throughout his life, in an age when moving around the world was much more difficult and less frequent than a century later. Commenting on this yen for travel and learning from it, his brother Julian remarked in March 1900 that Archie was "not the grubby studious kind of university professor." Santayana later recorded that Coolidge explained that he was making a trip to eastern Siberia "because I haven't been there yet."[1]

The Coolidges were inveterate travelers. Leisurely trips to Europe were frequent, practically annual, and two years after Archie was born, the family lived in western Europe for three years. While the Beacon Street home was redecorated, they roamed throughout Europe for eighteen months. They traveled so constantly that the Karl Baedeker guides were among the first books with which the boys became acquainted, and may have been the most important books Coolidge ever studied. They not only stimulated interest in seeing the world, but strengthened the concern for accurate information that became one of his characteristics.

The period of his most constant travel was from 1887 through 1893, when he combined graduate study in Paris, Berlin, and Freiburg with journeys throughout Europe and much of the world. He studied two of those six winters at the University of Berlin and two at the École des Sciences Politiques in Paris, which became bases for travel, often by bicycle, from the North Cape to southern Spain and from Wales to Ruthenia. After returning home in the summer of 1889, he toured the world for eight months, going by train across Canada and then through the Pacific to Japan, Indonesia, Burma, India, and Egypt, before resuming study. The summer of 1890 was consumed by journeys through Germany, Denmark, Sweden, European Russia, the Caucasus, Central Asia, and northern Persia. His mother toured Spain with him in the summer of 1892. Beginning in 1889, he was a frequent traveler in the Near East and North Africa, "the region I love best." The Balkans and Russia were especially alluring, and he made six trips to Russia. He made three extensive tours through Asia; the last, in 1905–6, included two months in the Philippines, where he arranged a secret meeting with insurgents.[2]

Western Europe, almost inevitably, was his base. In a letter to his mother in the autumn of 1909 he remarked that he was "running across" the Atlantic Ocean for the twenty-sixth time. Unlike most Easterners of that time, and even of later generations, he was knowledgeable about other parts of the United States and Canada, particularly Quebec and the Canadian Far West. In fact, he made at least four trips across the United States and three across Canada. He visited Alaska and Hawaii in 1897, and was especially well informed about the Upper South, the Midwest, and the West Coast.

Latin America had been "an important gap in my intellectual horizon of world politics," so he welcomed the opportunity to represent Harvard at the First Pan-American Scientific Congress in Santiago from December 1908 to January 1909. On the way, he spent a month in Spain and Portugal. Before crossing the Andes for the conference, he traveled for a month in Brazil and Argentina. After presenting a paper at the congress, he rode on horseback for a week in southern Chile to increase his knowledge of its geography and economic conditions. Visits to La Paz, Lake Titicaca, and Arequipa preceded his return to Harvard for the second semester, via Panama, Jamaica, and Cuba.[3]

Coolidge, a dedicated teacher, made most of his journeys in the summers and sabbatical years. At the same time, he was so convinced one could learn from seeing the world that he obtained a number of "travel leaves" without pay. These periods were spent in Paris and Berlin as a visiting professor, in traveling throughout North Africa during the spring semester of 1912, service in the Department of State in Vienna and Paris in 1919, and work for the American Relief Administration in the Soviet Union for six months in 1921 and 1922. His eagerness to learn about and from other parts of the world, especially in times of great upheaval, was such that he eagerly accepted invitations (which did not materialize) to serve the American Red Cross in Switzerland and Russia during the First World War and to direct an American Institute for Slavic Studies in Prague in the mid-1920s.

Exotic places, such as Angkor Wat, the Khyber Pass, the Klondike, Tibet, Mongolia, and Kashmir, attracted his special attention. He was eager to follow the steps of Lord James Bryce in climbing Mt. Ararat and in seeing Victoria Falls. He did not visit West or South Africa, Australia, or New Zealand, but he visited most of the other inhabited areas of the world. A letter to his father reveals that he spent Christmas in seven of the world's capitals— Paris, Berlin, Vienna, St. Petersburg, Moscow, Berne, and Santiago—as well as in such other important cities as Calcutta.[4]

Coolidge appreciated that knowledge of contemporary culture was important for anyone interested in international politics and that meeting writers and artists would be instructive. He visited Zakopane for six weeks in 1895, in part to talk with his favorite Polish novelist, Henryk Sienkiewicz. A trip to Arles in April 1907 to lunch with Frédéric Mistral increased his understanding of French literature and the power of regionalism. Similarly, chats with Ivan Mestrović in Boston and Zagreb improved his insight into the Balkans.

His excursions were long and leisurely, preceded by preparation that included study of histories, encyclopedias, almanacs, guides, and maps. Before he went to Spain and Portugal, he spent a summer reading about those countries. Extensive reviews of travel literature and histories of far-off lands for the *Nation* were of great benefit. Above all, the journeys occurred in circumstances conducive to learning. He crossed oceans not by jet, but by steamship. When he was young, he frequently traveled by bicycle. In 1902 he traveled twenty-two days via the trans-Siberian railroad from Moscow across Russia and then to Peking. Later, as in France in 1907, he bought a limousine and drove with a chauffeur. On other occasions he journeyed in primitive conditions and great discomfort. His first visit to Central Asia, in 1890, antedated the conveniences of later years. In the winter of 1905–6, an overland trip from Bangkok to Moulmein in Burma by foot, bullock cart, and poled flatboat, in very difficult circumstances, consumed more than two weeks.

This observant scholar acquired keen insights which were of greater value than factual data. Travel in particular helped him overcome ethnocentrism, revealed the impact of geography and climate upon historical development, gave a large and uncomplicated view of the universe, and helped place the roles of individuals and governments in perspective. His view that large territories and populations were more important in the age of world powers than before derives from long journeys by train across North America, Europe, and Russia. Seeing the areas and talking with the people most concerned helped him understand conflicts over boundaries and the roles religions play in shaping cultures and in cultural conflicts. Although he had no religious beliefs, his teaching and writing emphasized the contributions that religions made in the world. He did not talk or write of cultures or civilizations as such, but divided the world into political-cultural units, and used religion as the principal factor that separates units from one another. He made special efforts to visit places such as Lourdes. Long before most informed observers—even before the First World War—he saw the important role Islam would again play in world politics.

Carefully considered travel appeared to be the most effective way to learn about other peoples. The enormous changes in the world which he witnessed deepened and widened his curiosity. Seeing other countries, "an excellent corrective of book-bred ideas,"[5] provided a view of the world which deeply affected his teaching and those he trained. Acquaintance with libraries, archives, and scholars in other countries improved his teaching and research and helped him give sound advice to graduate students when they went abroad. He recognized, too, that travel extended the renown of the Department of History and Harvard by "carrying the university's flag" into distant areas.

Opportunities to meet the poor and dispossessed were rare, even though he sought them. Coolidge carefully observed rural areas (most of his trips were in regions which were not industrially developed), but met few peasants or workers. His relationships with scholars, politicians, and diplomats and his careful attention to the press gave him considerable insight into public opinion and local problems as leaders viewed them. Journalists were among his principal sources of information and understanding, and he became acquainted with a number of publicists in Paris in 1906 and 1907. He remained in contact with some, such as André Tardieu of *Le Temps* and Louis Aubert of the *Revue de Paris*, for the rest of his life, including the months they served in the French High Commission in Washington (in 1918) and at the Paris Peace Conference (in 1919).[6]

As a youngster who traveled often and who sought independence from others, Coolidge early learned the value of being able to speak and read modern foreign languages (he did not know Greek or Latin). While an undergraduate, he spent the summer of 1884 near Geneva improving his French, in which he became fluent, and the following year in Berlin and Vienna polishing his German. He learned Italian in college and Russian in the three years after graduation from Harvard. Academic work increased his determination to learn the important Western languages so that he could obtain access to a great wealth of literature and converse directly with men and women in other countries. He acquired substantial knowledge of Polish, Bulgarian, Swedish, and Spanish, as well as some Dutch and Portuguese. Although he had a good memory, acquiring command of languages required immense labor; in Cambridge, he often worked with a tutor an hour a day. Until he was over forty, he traveled with foreign-language books and dictionaries so that he could improve his linguistic competence.

In his view, every educated person should command two or three foreign languages. For those preparing for careers in diplomacy and teaching, mastery of several languages was essential. In 1924, Department of History colleagues learned he would oppose the appointment of anyone in modern European history who did not command Russian, French and German.[7]

Coolidge grew up in a cultivated family that paid high honor to learning and considered reading and informed discussion essential parts of life. As a boy, he was a voracious reader, concentrating (like many youngsters) on military history. Later he enjoyed browsing through the books in the library. Whenever he traveled by ship, he carried a trunkful of books, and replaced them when the vessel entered a major port. A family legend relates that his concern with improving the Harvard library began when he looked through its new books and periodicals after giving his History 1 lectures.

He was a compulsive reader in a variety of fields, particularly international relations, though apparently not of *belles-lettres*. Russian novels absorbed him in the 1890s, and late in life he turned to *Roderick Random* and *Tristram Shandy*, but "professional" literature received his concentrated attention during most of his adult years. Correspondence and records reveal that he consistently and carefully read about twenty journals, published for the informed public in four or five languages, in addition to the literature in his fields of professional interest, especially modern European, Russian, Asian, and diplomatic history. He was a consistent reader of three Boston newspapers, two New York papers, and the London *Times*. The Boston *Transcript* was mailed to him when he traveled.

Throughout his life he was endowed with enormous energy, as well as relentless curiosity and an inventive mind. Fearful he might become a dilettante like his brother John or a lazy Boston Brahmin like his father, he was impelled by a sense of *noblesse oblige* to make best use of his time and talent. He was a hard worker, forever busy, rising at 7:15 and often working until one o'clock in the morning. Serious, blessed with good health and a lack of frivolity, he frequently worked in the library on Saturday afternoons until 6:30, on Sundays and holidays, and even when he was unwell. As an assistant professor, he employed a secretary to maintain a "clean desk system." Years later, when he was a professor of history, Director of the Library, and editor of *Foreign Affairs*, he ordinarily responded to communications by return mail. During the last months of his life, when he was desperately ill, he kept up with matters in the university and in *Foreign Affairs* by inviting colleagues to his home on Beacon Street for dinner.

Ever the individualist, Coolidge participated only in social functions he judged of intellectual value or of utility to the university. He was a member of only four clubs: the Colonial Club in Cambridge, which was then in effect the Harvard Faculty Club; the Somerset Club in Boston; the Country Club in Brookline; and the Century Association in New York. He was active in two Harvard-Boston informal groups: the Saturday Club and the Tuesday Evening Club, and in the Massachusetts Historical Society. The Colonial Club was his social center, and he often invited students and visitors there for lunch or dinner. There too he joined foreign scholars and colleagues from other departments whom he found especially interesting, such as George Santayana of the philosophy department; Thomas Barbour, director of the Museum of Comparative Zoology; and Oric Bates, curator of African archaeology and ethnology at the Peabody Museum.

Coolidge's basic, enduring traits were well established by the time he arrived at Harvard in 1883, and his knowledge of the world and its languages was impressive even for a youngster from an informed and prosperous Boston family. His undergraduate education in an institution that was undergoing an exciting period of transformation and expansion stimulated his interest in history and in learning in general. Above all, it strengthened concern for orderly and accurate knowledge. Professors Charles Gross in European medieval history and Edward Channing in British and American history, both trained in Germany and new to Harvard in 1883, emphasized mastery of objective facts and clear, precise organization of political, diplomatic, and military history. Both required that their students make intensive use of Karl Julius Ploetz's *Auszug aus der alten, mittleren, neueren und neuesten Geschichte*. This famous handbook to European history, by an instructor in the French *gymnasium* in Berlin, went through seven editions within a few years of its publication in 1863, and twenty-eight editions by 1974. William H. Tillinghast, Harvard 1877, who spent two years in graduate study in Berlin before becoming a librarian at Harvard, translated the eighth edition as *Epitome of Ancient, Medieval, and Modern History* in the year Coolidge began his college career. Channing provided sections on modern English and American history for this edition, which became a kind of bible for Harvard undergraduates interested in history.

The Ploetz-Tillinghast volumes fascinated young Coolidge and helped direct his interest into the professional study of history. He required his undergraduate students to purchase and use the book in History 1, which he taught from 1893 through 1904, a tradition his successors continued. Those young men whom Coolidge trained as teaching assistants or whose theses he directed carried the *Epitome* with them into their courses in college and universities throughout the United States.*

Upon graduating from college, Coolidge decided to dedicate the next decade to learning, largely in Europe but in other parts of the world as well. This was not an unusual approach to an academic career, for Coolidge and the other well-to-do members of his generation had a different sense of time than later generations of American scholars. One of his closest colleagues at Harvard, Edwin F. Gay, spent twelve years in graduate study in Europe and obtained his Ph.D. when he was thirty-five.[8]

While a graduate student, Coolidge wrote that his goal was to become "a man of experience and cultivation, a man of the world in the broadest sense of the term." He rejected becoming a specialist and determined instead to acquire vast knowledge concerning all history and the contemporary world. One of his colleagues noted that he was "always a student," and another that he was "an intellectual huntsman, always riding to hounds." He was in many ways the last of the Victorians—like Walter Bagehot, "an amateur of genius." A New Englander with wide horizons, perhaps the first Brahmin professional historian, he saw learning as the new frontier. Even as a senior professor and librarian, he attended lectures on all kinds of subjects, from French symbolist poets to Central American archaeology.[9]

Determined to become a member of the international fraternity of those informed about world politics, Coolidge thought most scholars spent too much time in libraries and knew only what they acquired from books. He was eager to learn "how things were actually done."[10] He frequently visited Washington,

*The history of these volumes, as edited and revised by Tillinghast and later by scholars who worked closely with Coolidge, epitomizes rising American interest in history and the gradual expansion of that concern from the history of Europe to the history of the world. Tillinghast's translation went through twenty-four printings before 1905, reflected the latest and most competent scholarship, and devoted ever more attention to parts of the world beyond Europe. After Tillinghast died in 1913, the title was changed to *A Handbook of Universal History.* Harry Elmer Barnes, a colleague of Coolidge on *Foreign Affairs* from 1922 until 1925, in the latter year produced a thorough revision and added substantial material on the world since 1883. In 1940, William L. Langer, Coolidge's most outstanding student and his successor at Harvard, with the aid of a number of other scholars rewrote the volume and tried to make it "genuine world history." This *Encyclopedia of World History* has appeared in five ever larger editions, has been translated into other languages, including Arabic and Urdu, and has become a handbook for teachers and scholars throughout much of the world.

where a number of his students had become senior officers in the Department of State, to refresh his knowledge of international politics and of American and foreign statesmen. Before going to Paris as a visiting professor in 1907, he and Professor Barrett Wendell lunched with President Theodore Roosevelt. Before beginning the Berlin professorship in the autumn of 1913, he visited the capital, staying with Robert Woods Bliss, a former student in the Department of State, and enjoying long conversations with Secretary of State William Jennings Bryan and eminent statesmen and politicians, such as Elihu Root, Senator Henry Cabot Lodge, and the German ambassador, Count Johann von Bernstorff.[11] He knew outstanding scholars, politicians, and statesmen in many countries. Letters he wrote when he was a visiting professor in Paris reveal that he attended a dinner four or five nights each week. Edith Wharton called him "the retriever," because he brought many interesting French men and women to her home on the rue de Varenne. Responding to social debts in Berlin in January 1914, he filled five large rooms with a dinner for 100 at the Adlon.[12]

Travel and rigorous study helped make Coolidge an immensely learned man with unusually wide perspectives for that age, or any other. He commented easily and with authority on Ottoman history and that of the Balkan peoples, the Flemish-Walloon quarrel, Russian-Persian relations, the long history of North Africa, the colonies of the European powers, Canada, Yemen, Siamese politics, East African tribes, and the advantages and disadvantages of the metric system. He found factual errors in the manuscripts of the noted geographer, Isaiah Bowman. His last public lecture, at the Royal Institute of International Affairs in London in July 1926, provided a detailed historical background of the dispute between Chile, Peru, and Bolivia over Tacna-Arica and suggestions for resolving that complicated and critical quarrel, which is still unresolved. Hamilton Fish Armstrong noted, "In an age of specialists, he was one of the few who knew something about the whole history of the human race." Another associate, Walter Lippmann, declared that "perhaps his greatest work was to show that in an age of specialists, if a man is brilliant and hardworking and voracious enough, he can yet be a master in a whole field of thought and action."[13]

The works Coolidge published are only a small part of his effort to awaken Americans to the world. However, they were of considerable significance, their quality was high, they reached important groups just at the time American interest in other countries and cultures and in world affairs was growing, and they provided the recognition and foundations from which his other activities blossomed.

The most important of his three books was *The United States as a World Power*, published in 1908 in French and German as well as English. This was reprinted six times within the next decade, ten times before Coolidge died, and again in 1971, and was translated into Japanese in 1913. His second book, *The Origins of the Triple Alliance*, was the product of lectures given at the University of Virginia and at Northwestern University in 1916. A second edition appeared in 1926. The final volume, in 1927, was a collection of ten essays, three written between 1912 and 1920 and the others published in *Foreign Affairs* between 1922 and 1927.

Sixteen scholarly articles, dozens of professional reviews, and a flood of popular essays and reviews supplemented these volumes. Between 1893 and 1903, twenty-two articles appeared in the liberal journal, the *Nation*: four devoted to Russia, two to Poland, six to the Balkans, and the others largely to Southeast Asia and Africa. During the same period he contributed sixty-two book reviews. The *Nation* published eleven pieces in 1893 and eight reviews on Africa in 1897 and 1898 alone. From late 1919 through the summer of 1921, he published twelve leading articles in the New York *Evening Post*, edited then by his friend and colleague, Gay.

Coolidge edited three books, one a revision of Sir Edward Creasy's famous *History of the Ottoman Turks*, which he declared "one of the few books in English which deals with Turkish affairs" and which he brought up to date three times between 1907 and 1928. Another was a translation of the secret treaties of Austria-Hungary between 1879 and 1914, which Alfred F. Pribram had collected and published in Vienna in German and which excited Coolidge as soon as he met Pribram in May 1919. It included a narrative account of the Triple Alliance negotiations. The *Atlantic Monthly* and the New York *Evening Post* reprinted parts of this volume, which helped open the debate concerning the origins of the First World War. Editing *Foreign Affairs* occupied the last years of his life. His impact during the first six years of that distinguished journal's career was so profound that the high standards and the patterns he established in format and style, quality of paper, color of the cover, and the system of notices given new books still survive. He was, in fact, an immensely capable journalist and editor.

The goals and achievements of Coolidge and that generation of scholars were vastly different from those of historians several generations later. He lived in an era so near and yet so distant that even American historians may find judging his work fairly and placing it in proper perspective quite difficult. This is in part due to the different standards for published research, particularly in terms of quantity, that major institutions expected or required of senior scholars less than a generation after his death. Moreover, the principles and practices he established are so widely accepted that they seem absurdly normal, although even now they are rarely followed. Finally, his successors simply assume that the institutions and fields of study he created were always there or would have developed inevitably, with or without the insight and labors of his generation.

Especially in his first two decades at Harvard, Coolidge lived and worked in a university and professional atmosphere that discouraged specialized concerns and emphasized teaching, rather than research and writing as the instrument for professional success and for attaining intellectual distinction. Department lines and university structures were not so firm and rigid as they became: the Harvard Department of History became separate from Government only in 1911. Even then it was not the center of its members' intellectual and social activities; the institution as a whole was their realm. Moreover, the American Historical Association was founded only in 1884 and the *American Historical Review* began publication in 1895. The role of amateur historians therefore remained important in Coolidge's early years. Historians became a large, organized national group only later in the twentieth century. Scholars' concerns were therefore not so tightly concentrated on one subject or field as became common later.

By later standards of major universities, Coolidge's publications, like those of Lord Acton, were few, particularly for a scholar who taught at Harvard for thirty-five years.* An immensely informed scholar-teacher, he was a scholar who published because his main interest was in learning and teaching, rather than in participating in "the cult of the monograph and of the

*His colleague, Hart, an extraordinarily prolific writer, published 930 articles and completed, edited, or contributed to about 100 books in his long career at Harvard. See Carol F. Baird, "Albert Bushnell Hart: The Rise of the Professional Historian," in Paul Buck (editor), *Social Sciences at Harvard, 1860-1920* (Cambridge, Mass., 1965), p. 142.

research journal." In Santayana's words, he lacked the central dedication that "publishing" scholars must possess.[14]

During his first decade at Harvard, his major responsibility was teaching History 1. These years were also the richest for travel and for essays and reviews in journals for the informed public. Later he concentrated upon training scholars in a variety of fields and upon building Harvard's library because he believed his generation should devote itself to establishing the foundations for increasing American knowledge of history and of world affairs, rather than to cloistered research. This vision and interest in learning, in becoming a generalist rather than a specialist, help explain why he stimulated so many young men into advanced study in a great variety of areas of history.[15]

Traveling to increase knowledge and understanding had higher priority for Coolidge than publishing—but he forced himself to remain in the United States in the summer of 1907 to complete the manuscript of *The United States as a World Power*, which derived from a series of lectures in Paris the preceding winter and which was published the following year. However, opportunities to see other lands lured him away from four nearly complete manuscripts, each of which he could have prepared for publication in less than three months of intensive work. Thus, while preparing the Lowell Lectures on the expansion of Russia scheduled for late autumn 1902, on which he had completed a draft manuscript and had already published a summary analysis, he devoted the summer to a trip across European Russia, Siberia, and Manchuria to Peking, and thence home via Japan and Canada. A glorious trip around the world consumed the 1905-6 sabbatical year, when he might have completed his work on Suleiman the Magificent or Russian expansion. He applied the spring semester of 1912 to a trip through North Africa and his Christmas vacation to the Caribbean, although those periods and the summer of 1912 could have been used to complete his manuscript on France as a great power for the press. In 1921, rather than convert the 1920 Lowell Lectures on the new states of Central Europe into a book, he served the American Relief Administration in Russia.[16]

The paucity of Coolidge's published works also reflects his perfectionism. The training he received and the standards he created emphasized that one's research should be scientific, accurate, exhaustive, and interminable. His manuscripts testify to his canons and to the everlasting search for more information. In addition, writing about large subjects in recent multinational history, when this was new in American scholarship, was extremely difficult.

He could have produced much more of scholarly value, if he had completed four manuscripts and had devoted more effort to writing on other important subjects on which he was well informed. A volume on the origins of the First World War, on which his knowledge was vast, greatly tempted him. He gave a course and seminars on European diplomatic history before the war, directed a number of theses, and presented a series of lectures on the subject at the Lowell Institute in the fall of 1914 that attracted such attention that it was repeated in the spring of 1915. Throughout the 1920s he gave substantial attention to this issue, not only in essays in the New York *Evening Post* and in *Foreign Affairs* but also in teaching. However, he pressed a former student, Sidney B. Fay, to complete his study of the origins of the war, which Fay finally did in 1928.

Likewise, Coolidge could have produced important textbooks on the history of Russia, world politics, modern European history, or the history of the Balkans, all of which greatly needed such volumes. Until Sir Bernard Pares published his *History of Russia* in 1926, the only textbook available in English was the translation from French that Nathan H. Dole had made forty-five years earlier of part of the first edition of Alfred Rambaud's three-volume *L'Histoire de la Russie depuis les origines jusqu'à nos jours*. Coolidge possessed the knowledge, the ability to organize information, and the style for such a book, but neither that volume nor any other tempted him.

Coolidge saw himself as a scholar and teacher, a librarian, and an editor, not as a philosopher or reformer. He was optimistic by nature, but neither the idea of progress nor the belief that conditions were better or worse in his lifetime than in earlier periods attracted him. He never expressed nostalgia. For these reasons and because of his definition of a historian's craft, he created no conscious philosophy of history. He thought that the historian's principal obligation was to explain, and that judging or interpreting was of secondary significance. The German influence led American historians early in the twentieth century to "ask many questions, often of small subjects." Scholars of that age believed that determining with some certainty what had actually happened in the past was itself a great achievement. For them, historical truth lay in facts, in certain detail, not in exciting and spectacular generalizations or interpretations which might be fascinating but also were dangerous and misleading because they lacked solid foundations. Thus J. Franklin Jameson, by common consent one of the most distinguished American scholars at that time, declared that "the great task confronting historical scholars was to assimilate as many firmly established facts as possible, leaving their use to the scholars of the future."[17]

Coolidge's work as a historian was part of this pattern and reflected most careful and imaginative research and analysis. His work had a calm and considered touch, deliberately without drama, special pleading, or sensationalism. Serenity, good sense, and evenhandedness marked his writing in a confusing age of expansion, war, and political and social change. He simply sought the facts and objective understanding; his main service was to record, to explain, to analyze, with relentless honesty and objectivity. These attributes are especially evident in his writing and teaching about Russian history and politics, but illustrations of this and of his candor abound elsewhere as well. A 1902 review of Maxim Kovalevsky's *Russian Political Institutions* in the *American Historical Review* noted that Kovalevsky had omitted the Russian government's defense of its policies in Poland and Finland and was "biased in favor of parliament." Coolidge's reports from Murmansk, late in the summer of 1918, from Vienna in 1919, and from Moscow and Petrograd in 1921 and 1922 were models of calm objectivity. Indeed, if Wilson and other Allied leaders had studied the Murmansk reports carefully, they would have recognized Russian political realities and avoided entanglement in the Russian civil war. His last essay, in *Foreign Affairs* in October 1927 on Franco-British relations, was so fair that observers in both states praised it. President Raymond Poincare termed it "a model of perfect historical writing."[18] His last letter on December 27, 1927, just before he slipped into his final coma, was a remarkably dispassionate note to an old colleague, Raymond L. Buell, tactfully but candidly criticizing a manuscript Buell had submitted to *Foreign Affairs*.

Coolidge's work as an editor illustrates his emphasis on objectivity. In October 1922 he wrote the book-review editor that people would read him and the review with attention "as it becomes evident that your comment is not based on your own personal sympathies but on the ability, timeliness, and other qualities of representation in the work itself.... Praise or blame should not be affected by one's sympathies with the writer."[19]

He did not enter into political and social issues, even though he often had strong private views. His writings contain no information concerning his opinions on the Boston police strike, which made Calvin Coolidge politically important, or on the Sacco-Vanzetti affair, which troubled many Americans. An independent conservative, he was a Democrat as a young man, but later ordinarily voted Republican. He was critical of both parties and their candidates, never became a political partisan, and wrote no letters to politicians or newspapers about political issues. Hughes in 1916 and Harding in 1920 received his vote, but only after great soul searching and much internal debate. He did not join organizations interested in causes, such as the National Committee for the League to Enforce Peace in 1915 or the World Peace Foundation, although many colleagues joined them. In Santayana's words, he "never betrayed his deeper allegiance in politics and morals."[20]

Throughout the First World War, both before and after America's entrance, he remained reserved and judicious. Only slips in conversation told colleagues that he favored France after 1914, but he remained the scholarly observer and kept his beliefs private. Commending Secretary of State Charles Evans Hughes at his retirement as a clear-headed, patient, unemotional, and broad-minded public servant, he identified the virtues he considered most important for a scholar and public figure.[21]

All of Coolidge's work as a scholar-teacher and editor were marked by precision and accuracy, discipline and order, whether the subject was the amount of money the American government spent to expand and improve education in the Philippines or a delicate affair in international politics. He often checked the indices of books he reviewed to determine their accuracy. As editor of *Foreign Affairs*, he confirmed quotations from Kipling and translations from Taine and Dante. He paid close attention to spelling, was assiduous in reading proof, and proofread each issue after it was published to avoid future mistakes. In 1925 he sharply criticized the managing editor and the book-review editor for listing one book twice and for noting the number of pages incorrectly in one citation, because "it reflects on the whole magazine."[22]

For Coolidge, convinced that style was central to one's effort to attain objectivity, dramatic distortion was a cardinal sin. He devoted great attention to making his writing simple, direct, lucid, and without ornament. Even his letters were clear and free from confusion. A completely unpretentious person, he rarely used "I" or "we," and warned students and authors that use of "the first person pronoun should be kept to a minimum."[23] He wrote *The United States as a World Power* as though he were not an American but an independent, neutral observer, viewing the United States from outside. Garrett Mattingly wrote of Roger B. Merriman, Coolidge, and a number of their contemporaries, "Scientific historiography . . . made telling the truth about history and at the same time giving any kind of pleasure other than purely intellectual satisfaction a practically insoluble literary problem. . . . The only safeguard against unfairness, against distortion, is the neutral, colorless, painstakingly qualified style."[24]

Coolidge urged graduate students to remember that they were teaching and writing about human beings who did not differ greatly from age to age and that the human equation should remain central in their analyses. Their main goal was to understand, and each should "put yourself in [the others'] place" when studying other societies and periods of history. He was "fairness and impartiality personified."[25] This, and immense, well-ordered knowledge, help explain why his teaching and writing on international affairs received such respect.

For most American historians before and even after the First World War, as for the German and other European scholars who helped establish their approach to scholarship, history consisted largely of the record and analysis of political and diplomatic developments. Indeed, they devoted the bulk of their exertions to great empires and large states and their politics. Most members of his generation (but not his classmate, Robinson) considered economic and social history of peripheral importance, at most, although Coolidge recognized the impact of changes in transportation upon historical developments. He tended to neglect music, painting, and the other arts. Marx and other important intellectual leaders of the second half of the nineteenth century, and their ideas, received little attention. He considered socialism an important force in the twentieth century, but wrote little about it. His approach and his qualities and interests as a scholar led him to neglect intellectual history and the role of ideas, a position colleagues attributed to his belief that "he lived in a world of men, not of ideas." Indeed, "ideas are powerful in inverse proportion as they are abstract."[26]

For reasons which most careful analysis of the voluminous records do not enable us to fathom, personal ambition seemed utterly absent in Coolidge. He had no sense of mission, no desire for honor or power, no ambition to participate in political affairs or to achieve fame as a policy-maker or adviser in times of crisis. The security provided by an established family and ample financial resources may have contributed to this attitude. Growing up with a dominating father, a shy mother, strict discipline, and family affection combined with isolation from his extended family, class, and community, may help explain his reserve and modesty as well as the independence and self-sufficiency which also mark his life. The sense of personal dignity and the Napoleonic pose of the short, rotund professor, which impressed students and emerges from his photographs, as well as his purchase of fine clothes but never appearing well dressed, also reflect the circumstances of his upbringing, as well as the curious gap between his capabilities and his ambitions. His compulsive travel and relentless devotion to a great variety of functions suggest a lack of clarity concerning personal goals, but hardly explain it. Similarly, his unfinished manuscripts and years of devotion to the library (the least visible and least recognized service in an academic community) stand witness to his modesty and lack of personal ambition, but do not explain it.

In any case, craving for power or renown seems utterly absent, and silent and unrewarded service his goal. The old saying, that one of the necessary qualifications of a teacher is willingness to be forgotten, would have received his endorsement. Prestigious posts in government offered no attraction. He accepted a government position only in times of national emergency or when such activity might increase his knowledge and understanding and improve his abilities as a scholar-teacher. Even then, he sought and accepted positions involving service, especially research, instead of positions concerned with policy and power.

In short, Coolidge was a "Boston irregular" who emphasized independence, reserve, and service. His integrity, candor, and selflessness were also the product of sustained hard work and rigorous self-control. Deliberately and with effort, he grew away from—at least independent of—the class and the region into which he was born and from the attitudes of some members of that group toward the new business and manufacturing aristocracy. He did not resent the rise of the new economic groups edging the old Boston families (and New England) out of power and prominence. He did not participate in or even observe the classic

conflict between Beacon and State streets which had so impressed
Henry Adams a generation earlier, nor refer in his private letters,
teaching, or publications to business barons or big capital.
Boston's ethnic groups attracted neither his interest nor his
judgment. His open-minded, independent, and somewhat root-
less parents had helped make him a responsible conservative,
marked by the Puritan ethic and the self-assurance which secure
wealth and family pride can best provide. He had no institutional,
class, or regional loyalties, except to Harvard University, which
he saw as an institution destined to help lead other institutions in
an endless, cooperative quest for ever higher quality.

Neither his writings nor the voluminous records provide
evidence that he saw himself as the representative of an embattled
class or that he resented and resisted the success of New York in
overtaking Boston as the economic, perhaps even the intellectual,
motor of the United States. Perhaps the best testimony to his
generosity of mind and national spirit was his accepting, without
question, the preeminence of New York and its bankers and
lawyers over Boston and the cultured elite of Beacon Street and
Cambridge by his quick agreement to serve as editor of *Foreign
Affairs,* even though this meant daily correspondence with his
assistant in New York and frequent trips to that city.

4. Russia: Its History and Role

COOLIDGE AWAKENED AMERICAN historical scholarship and teaching to many areas of the world, but his first and most important contribution was founding the professional study of Russia in the United States. He taught the first course in Russian history. He helped establish instruction in Russian and other Slavic languages and literatures at Harvard, and created the base for Harvard's great library collection on Russia and the other Slavic and East European peoples. He trained the able men who succeeded him at Harvard, and many who introduced the study of Russia and other areas of the world into colleges and universities throughout the United States. The standards he set helped give Russian studies a stamp of quality and distinction at their formative stage.

Few Americans showed interest in Russia until the middle of the nineteenth century. Before Coolidge's birth, the first handful were attracted to Russian history and culture for reasons quite different from those that excited him: the abolition of serfdom, the attendant reforms, and the visit of the Russian fleet to New York in 1863. Similarly, romantic interest in the Russian peasants, in Slavophilism, and in escape from modern civilization—phenomena which affected Sir Bernard Pares, Maurice Baring, and many other European intellectuals and historians of Russia—did not touch Coolidge. His evenhandedness and his knowledge of Polish history prevented him from becoming a romantic Slavophil and from overestimating the significance of panslavism. Similarly, his conservatism and his belief that important changes in any society came slowly and gradually dissuaded him from joining those who admired Russia's revolutionaries. Sympathy and admiration for opponents of tsarist rule led him to arrange for men like Prince Peter Kropotkin and Paul Miliukov to visit Harvard and to give the Lowell Lectures in Boston.[1] However, he did not adopt their views of Russia. Above all, he remained aloof from Russian politics, before and after 1917.

Russia attracted his interest long before many Americans considered it a threat or even an enemy. Moreover, there is no evidence that Russian popular and official antisemitism or the Russian government's policy toward religious and political dissenters stimulated his attention. The flood of newspaper articles after 1881, when the Russian government allowed and even encouraged attacks upon Jews, and the flow of hundreds of thousands of Poles and Jews to the United States were not responsible for his interest. He was abroad when George Kennan's articles in *Century* and his 1891 book, *Siberia and the Exile System,* created a great stir by exposing the Russian government's treatment of political prisoners. He read the book later, but made no reference to knowledge acquired from it. When Coolidge traveled ten years later along the route Kennan followed in 1885 and 1886, he did not seek to visit the places Kennan described. So far as I can tell, Coolidge and Kennan never met.

None of his undergraduate courses touched upon Russian history or literature or any other aspect of Russian culture. Maxim Kovalevsky, on a visit to Harvard in 1881, noticed a number of books in Russian in the library, but learned that no one at the university could read the language.[2] No member of the faculty had an interest in Russia then—except, perhaps, Professor Francis J. Child in the Department of English, the "greatest living master in Anglo-Saxon," a renowned collector of ballads, and "the keenest, soundest, and most loved of American scholars." Child encouraged Jeremiah Curtin to collect Russian and other Slavic myths and folktales, applauded Isabel Hapgood for collecting and publishing Russian epic songs, and employed Leo Wiener in 1895 to translate ballads from Czech. His actions reflected a scholarly concern with folklore rather than interest in Russia or the Slavs, but they suggest that an international spirit existed at Harvard in the 1880s.[3]

No evidence has survived that the "Russian craze" which the novels of Count Leo Tolstoy and Fyodor Dostoevsky created among many educated Americans affected Coolidge until after he had begun graduate study in Paris, when they strengthened an interest which was already active. It is difficult to discover the reasons for his concern with Russia, rather than Western Europe, China, or some other part of the world. The Europe with which he was familiar no doubt lacked the attractive, exotic lure offered by Russia, the Ottoman Empire, and other areas then unknown to most Americans. Publication of the first Baedeker volume on

Russia the year Coolidge began his undergraduate studies, and the second edition when he started his graduate studies in Europe, may have provided a spark. In addition, the relationship of Russia with Europe at the height of Bismarck's career established a natural base for Russian studies. China probably did not become his first or central interest because it lacked this connection. Moreover, learning Chinese seemed beyond possibility. Above all, China was a weak and declining country, while Russia, like the United States, was emerging as a great power in a new age of world politics, marked by the expansion of Europe and the rise of world powers. His first articles on Russia dealt with its expansion and position in world politics, and one of his major (but unfinished) manuscripts was a study of Russian aggrandižement. Its first paragraph, an impressive description of the growth of Russian power, declared that "there is no other great country on the globe so widely feared at the present time."[4]

Coolidge began to study Russian in Paris in the winter of 1888–89, while he was attending the newly founded École des Sciences Politiques—before he made his first visit to Russia but after he had traveled widely in Europe. He studied Russian grammar on board ship on his trip around the world in 1889 and 1890, and made further progress when he spent six months in St. Petersburg and three months traveling in Russia in 1890 and 1891.[5]

The two winter terms in Paris, where he studied Russian language and literature with young Professor Paul Boyer, in the École Nationale des Langues Orientales Vivantes, and Russian history and institutions with Professor Anatole Leroy-Beaulieu, director of the École des Sciences Politiques and its professor of contemporary history, exercised a powerful influence upon Coolidge and his view of Russia. Boyer, a friend of Tolstoy, encouraged Coolidge to read Russian literature while he was learning the language. Short essays about Aleksei Tolstoy, Leo Tolstoy, Nekrasov, Tiutchev, and Turgenev in *Johnson's Revised Universal Encyclopaedia* in 1895 reveal considerable knowledge of both the major and minor works of these writers, as well as contemporary critical analyses of them.[6]

Coolidge in his teaching and research emphasized the role geography, climate, and religion have played throughout history, a stress he may have received from Leroy-Beaulieu and Alfred Rambaud, the two men who launched the scholarly study of Russia in France. In the École des Sciences Politiques, Coolidge

almost certainly studied Leroy-Beaulieu's publications, particularly his three-volume *L'Empire des Tsars et les Russes*, "an
encyclopaedia of Russian life and institutions." The first volume
appeared in 1881 and the third during Coolidge's first term as a
student in Paris. Coolidge entertained, and perhaps invited, this
French scholar to Harvard as a visiting professor in 1904, and
Leroy-Beaulieu wrote the preface to the French translation of *The
United States as a World Power*.[7]

Rambaud's classes and publications no doubt also influenced Coolidge in the period when his interest in Russia began
and its intellectual foundations were established. His principal
work, *L'Histoire de la Russie depuis les origines jusqu'à nos
jours*, was published in three volumes in 1877 and 1879 and
received international acclaim. Many of Rambaud's qualities and
views reappear in Coolidge. Rambaud, who lived in Russia
throughout the 1870s, believed scholars should reside for long
periods in the societies they studied, a position Coolidge emphasized. He knew several languages well, including Russian,
German, Greek, and Arabic, and stressed the importance of
mastering languages, as did Coolidge. His original scholarly
interest was in the Byzantine Empire, and he emphasized the
influence the Byzantine culture and political system exercised
upon Russia, a view the young American shared. A vigorous
advocate of French imperialism, especially in North Africa, he
wrote a study of Russian expansion. Here, too, Coolidge followed
Rambaud. Finally, in his teaching at Harvard, Coolidge made
extensive use of the twelve-volume *L'Histoire générale de IV ème
siècle à nos jours*, which Rambaud and Ernest Lavisse completed
between 1893 and 1901. Coolidge remained in contact with
Rambaud until the latter's death, and some of his closest French
friends, such as Louis Aubert, were students of Rambaud.[8]

Soon after his return to Harvard in the autumn of 1893,
Coolidge proposed a new course on the history of Russia. In
December 1895 he presented a paper at the annual meeting of the
American Historical Association which urged that Americans
cease their neglect of northern Europe and Russia. "Everything
connected with the development and conditions of such a mighty
Empire is obviously worth our attention," and the inhabitants of
Russia are "a gifted people destined to play more and more a
leading part in the history of mankind." Americans should study
Russia, Poland, and Scandinavia to increase their appreciation of
other societies and to learn that different systems of government

had developed over centuries among neighboring peoples because of "permanent" factors, such as geography, religion, and race.[9]

In 1894, Coolidge initiated undergraduate study of Russia with a one-semester course, Northeastern Europe, primarily on Russia, which in 1908 he converted into a full-year course on Russia. He was mainly responsible for the faculty appointments of Robert H. Lord, Robert Blake, and Michael Karpovich, which gave Harvard its first great strength in Russian history. In 1896 he persuaded President Eliot to endorse instruction in Russian, and pressed for the appointments of Leo Wiener and (later) Samuel Hazzard Cross in Slavic languages and literatures. These achievements, and Coolidge's role in building the university's great collections on Russia and Eastern Europe, made it the American pioneer in the study of the Slavic world.

After his first decade at Harvard, Coolidge transferred his emphasis as a teacher to training graduate students, in which he demonstrated remarkable skill. Indeed, his greatest ability was to identify and train scholar-teachers. From the beginning, he insisted that all specialists in Russian history master French, German, and Russian; emphasized that they should understand Russian society and culture; and required extensive and prolonged travel in Russia and throughout Europe. Many whom he selected and helped train introduced instruction in Russian history (and the history of other areas as well) in other colleges and universities. Those who helped make major universities such as the University of California at Berkeley and Stanford University research and instructional centers, or who began scholarly work in such fields as Byzantine and Polish history, were the most visible members of this great corps. Others whom Coolidge stimulated helped raise the level of competence on Russia and other previously neglected parts of the world in the Department of State by elevating professional standards and creating training programs which improved the quality of the government's work.

Coolidge's interest in Russia remained central throughout his life, even though other areas of the world and diplomatic history attracted him and the Harvard University Library, public service, and *Foreign Affairs* consumed more and more of his time. The First World War, the Russian revolution in 1917, the civil war and foreign intervention, his visits in 1918 and 1921 to 1922, and the debate in the 1920s about American policy toward Russia maintained his interest at a high level. In 1925 he wanted to serve a semester as the first director of the American Institute for Slavic Studies in Prague, judging that this would be a "cultural center of study for all the Slavic countries except Poland," that residence in Prague would give him a fair idea of "developments in Russia, and that he would learn a great deal from relations between Slavic and American scholars." In 1926 he and a young colleague, Walter R. Batsell, began work on a book describing the Soviet political system. In short, Coolidge remained fascinated by Russia from the time he began graduate studies until he died.[10]

Coolidge's knowledge of Russia, gradually and continually acquired, was deep. Travel constituted perhaps the most important source of information and understanding. Between 1890 and 1922 Coolidge visited Russia on six occasions, for a total of more than twenty-four months, from Murmansk to Kars and Samarkand, from Kiev to Khabarovsk—under the czars, in time of war and revolution, and under Soviet rule. His visits began with a week in St. Petersburg, a month in Moscow, six months in St. Petersburg as acting second secretary of the American legation, and more than two months traveling in European Russia, the Caucasus, and Central Asia to Samarkand and Bukhara. He spent the summer of 1895 traversing European Russia and Siberia on the trans-Siberian railroad, then under construction. On part of this journey he traveled with the chief construction engineer of the trans-Siberian. He took a freighter down the Ob to Tobolsk and Tiumen, and boated along the upper Volga. Irkutsk and Tomsk were among the cities about which he wrote during that excursion.

In the summer of 1898 he went to the Caucasus, where he climbed Mt. Ararat and visited fabled cities that had fascinated him, such as Erevan, Etchmiadzin, and Tbilisi. In 1902 he visited European Russia again, traveled for three weeks (with his brother John and Edwin V. Morgan) from Moscow to Peking via the trans-Siberian and its extension into Manchuria, and returned home via Korea, Japan, and Canada. He did not return to Russia until late in the summer of 1918, when he visited Murmansk and Archangel for three weeks on behalf of the War Trade Board. Finally, he spent five months in the winter of 1921–22 in Moscow and Petrograd, with a trip to Kazan, as chief of the Liaison Division of the American Relief Administration.

Just seeing the vastness and variety of Russia helped settle his view concerning the roles that location, size, and climate have played throughout Russian history. The Ural Mountains reminded him of New Hampshire, and thereafter he did not consider them a geographical barrier. On his first trip he compared Siberia to western Canada and the American West, and announced that it was a "land of promise destined before long to be the home of millions." The military position and fortresses of Kars gave him new comprehension of its significance and the character of the battles that Russians and Turks had fought for it. All the insights from his journeys helped him understand some of the basic problems Russian governments faced, their achievements, and their failures.[11]

In our age of jet travel, standardized international hotels, and Intourist tours through carefully selected areas of the Soviet Union, we must remember that Coolidge enjoyed a slower and freer age. He traveled by ship, train, boat, horse, bicycle, and springless cart in sections of Russia that tourists seldom visit. The excursions were leisurely, and he considered them vital, particularly because few publications provided the kind of information he cherished. He was a historian engaged in field work, not a scholar rushing from one city to another or a tourist being shepherded. He lived close to the people among whom he traveled, became acquainted with their lives and problems, and acquired some comprehension of the institutions and values—and even the landscapes—that shaped their lives. Moreover, his knowledge of Russian and other languages and his calm self-confidence enabled him to make tactful inquiries of senior officials and peasants concerning situations or issues which interested him.

Above all, Coolidge saw the Russian Empire over a period of more than thirty years in a great age of transformation: from Alexander III and Pobedonostsev through the work of Witte in launching industrialization, and the wars and revolutions that followed 1904 and 1914. He watched construction of parts of the trans-Siberian and trans-Caspian railroads. Irrigation, the planting of trees, and the introduction of ever more cotton fields helped shape his view of Central Asia. Seeing cities in various parts of Russia at different stages of their growth helped him appreciate the magnitude of economic and social change. Witnessing the transformations as they took place gave him a favorable impression of Russian achievements in newly acquired areas.

During his six months in the American legation in St. Petersburg, he met only minor officials in the Ministry of Foreign Affairs and other ministries. Travel in the 1890s provided acquaintance only with officials of the Ministry of Transportation and with a number of governors of provinces. He did not meet Alexander III, Nicholas II, or members of their families, or such men as Witte and Stolypin. His experiences were therefore unlike those of such other American observers as Andrew D. White and Senator Albert J. Beveridge, or of such British observers as Sir Donald Mackenzie Wallace and Sir Bernard Pares, who came to know a number of high court officials as well as men such as Tolstoy.

Coolidge's contacts with officials and cultural leaders were limited until the winter of 1921–22, when he worked for the American Relief Administration. At that time, he had extensive conversations with Leo Kamenev, head of the Moscow Soviet; Karl Radek, a leading member of the presidium of the Communist International; George Chicherin, Commissar for Foreign Affairs, and Maxim Litvinov, assistant commissar; and Christian Rakovsky, president of the Ukrainian Republic. His functions also provided extensive contact with middle-ranking Soviet functionaries, and he talked with the patriarch of the Russian Orthodox Church. Walking freely through Moscow and Petrograd and attending the opera, ballet, horse races, military reviews, and funerals of dignitaries gave him increased insight. He attended the Ninth All-Russian Congress of Soviets in December 1921, sitting in the diplomatic box in the Bolshoi Theater. Consular work educated him concerning developments throughout Russia, because the men and women who came to Moscow or who corresponded with him came from all parts of the country.[12]

Coolidge knew few citizens of the Russian Empire who were not Russians, except Georgians and Armenians whom he met on his trips to the Caucasus. His letters and publications, as well as his teaching, devoted little attention to national or religious minorities or to government policy toward them, until the essays he wrote during the First World War. His long manuscript on the expansion of Russia remarked that the discontented national minorities were sources of weakness, but he was confident that the White Russians and Ukrainians would become "indissoluble parts of the nation." He asserted that antisemitism existed almost everywhere, but devoted less than two pages to the position of the Jews. The section on Russian–American relations in *The United States as a World Power* was brief in its description of the autocracy and of American reaction to Russian policies toward minorities, although it condemned the forcible absorption of the

Uniates by the Russian Orthodox Church in 1875 as "impossible to defend from any modern standpoint of liberty of conscience."[13]

Coolidge knew scholars and librarians from Moscow and St. Petersburg to Erevan, Samarkand, and Tiumen. He visited libraries wherever he went—from Tomsk, where the university was celebrating its seventh anniversary, to Bukhara, where some collections were centuries old. A number of prominent historians, such as Michael Pokrovsky, Sergei V. Bakhrushin, Iurii V. Got'e, Alexander E. Presniakov, and Alexander A. Kizevetter, were acquaintances and friends. He provided them financial and moral assistance in their time of travail and urged the American Relief Administration to devote special attention to their plight. On his return to the United States, he sent food and medicine and launched a national campaign to send books. One scholar, Sergei P. Mel'gunov, whose family he had known since 1890, served as his book-purchasing agent until Mel'gunov left the Soviet Union for Czechoslovakia in 1922. Coolidge's acquaintance before Russia's great upheavals with such scholars as Michael Rostovtsev, the distinguished Byzantine specialist in St. Petersburg, who came to the United States after the revolution, encouraged him to assist Rostovtsev, Alexander A. Vasiliev, Baron Sergei Korff, and other "new Huguenots" when they reached this country.[14]

In his years of graduate study and travel in Europe, and later when he was a visiting professor in Paris and Berlin, Coolidge came to know many European specialists on Russian and Balkan history. Thus, in addition to the French scholars who helped introduce him to Russia and its history, the most important German specialists, particularly Theodor Schiemann, Anton Palme, and Otto Hoetzsch in Berlin, as well as Jovan Cvijić in Belgrade and Oscar Jászi and Henryk Marczali in Budapest, were friends.[15]

Reading about Russia provided him much, perhaps most, of his information concerning that country. He studied the "thick" journals as they arrived in the Harvard library. The important Russian historians of his time, such as V.O. Kliuchevskii, were among his basic sources, but most references in his publications and manuscripts cite French, German, and British studies, rather than Russian scholarship. He reviewed almost 100 important books published on Russia between 1894 and 1914, mostly written in Western languages.

Coolidge also acquired an enormous amount of information

and understanding from his work as a scholar-teacher and his professional activities. Like all teachers, he learned by teaching. Introducing courses and giving seminars forced him to define the important questions which Russian history poses. The work of men whose theses he directed increased his knowledge and understanding. Building the Russian collection in the Harvard University Library added knowledge, as did editing *Foreign Affairs*. Work for The Inquiry, a group of scholars that Edward M. House established in September 1917 to "collect material for formulating an American program" for President Woodrow Wilson, aided. His efforts in Vienna and Paris for the American Commission to Negotiate Peace and with the American Relief Administration in Russia in 1921–22 contributed insight which reading could not have provided. In short, the sources from which he learned about Russia were numerous and helped provide both the insight and the perspective he thought essential.

Coolidge was concerned with the need for accurate knowledge and balanced judgments about a country largely unknown to Americans, which would be of ever growing importance. Inculcation of a careful, evenhanded approach was particularly important because he created the academic base for Russian studies in their infancy in the United States. He felt no mission to protect Russia and had no particular affection for the Russian political system, but he concluded that the bias then developing might permanently distort the American view.

In Coolidge's opinion, the basic reason for Western ignorance and prejudice was the religious schism and the long political and religious conflict between East and West. which made the "Eastern Question," from Herodotus to Russian–British conflict in the Balkans, of profound importance. "In faith as in ideals, she [Russia] is the heir to the Byzantine Empire." Americans found it difficult to comprehend that empire, the role the Orthodox Church had played in Russian history, and "to appreciate the feelings of a people to whom country and creed are merely two aspects of the same idea." Most Western scholars were "not fair to the national Greek Orthodox Church, or to its source, the Byzantine Empire," in part because of the effect the Crusades, "two centuries and a half of misdirected effort," had had upon the West, the Orthodox East, and relations between East and West. Therefore, he devoted particular effort to building the library's collections on the Crusades and to adding specialists on the Eastern Orthodox Church and on Byzantine history to the Harvard faculty.[16]

The articles George Kennan published in the *Century* after 1887 and his 1891 book about the way in which the autocracy treated its political opposition exercised profound influence upon informed American opinion. In addition, the arrival in the United States of large numbers of Jews and Poles, fleeing national and religious persecution, brought another strongly anti-Russian influence to the intellectual scene.

Above all, British views and interpretations shaped American thinking about Russia when Coolidge began his career. Most of the Harvard faculty were profoundly pro-British, not only because of New England history and tradition but because it was fashionable to denigrate the new economic barons and the "vulgarity" of American social customs, compared to British culture. Most books about Russia came from England and represented the British view of the Russian political system and the collisions between the British and Russian empires. Coolidge believed these accounts of Russian power and policy exaggerated the threat Russia posed. Indeed, he thought most contemporary studies of Russia "offensively English" in tone and lamented that many Americans considered the Russians "mysterious, nay almost devilish" people.[17]

Coolidge's travels made him question the pro-British attitudes on international politics in the United States at the turn of the century. A visit to Siam in 1893 left him favorable to the French and critical of the British in their struggle for influence in Southeast Asia. The Boers and their "sacred if hopeless cause" won his sympathy, and he saw the Boer War as a war for independence and empire, "as old as Naboth's vineyard." While England was acting as a great power, he asserted that "a crime is a crime whoever commits it."[18]

Coolidge concluded that the American press and public support of Japan in 1904 had its roots in opinions that had developed in previous years. Articles and a widely reported talk to the Commercial Club in Boston on March 23, 1904, pointed out that the Russian Empire had been twice as large as that of the British a generation earlier, but in 1904 was smaller by a third. They compared the slowness with which Russia had withdrawn from Manchuria with Britain's remaining in Egypt after 1882, and noted that none of Russia's social problems "equal our negro problem." Trying to present "a temperate statement of certain aspects of the Russian side," he hoped that "the government and people of the United States while looking after their own interests will recognize the legitimate ones of others, treat both sides with scrupulous fairness in both word and deed, and remain on the friendliest terms with both." The headline of the Boston *Herald* account was "Prof. Coolidge Defends Russia."[19]

Coolidge made clear that he had no sympathy for the political system or culture of Russia, shaped "by history and circumstance," as those of the United States had been, and possessing the same justifications for existence. Americans should appreciate that their form of government was rare and that the Russian system was only one of the many different political structures that had developed for local reasons in other parts of the world. Alexander I, as a defender of law and order, "was in his way as much an idealist as the apostles of liberty," as his policy toward the Greeks during their revolution demonstrated. The conservative principles which Russia supported in the nineteenth century had as much justification as policies advocating revolutionary change in Europe. Moreover, a centralized bureaucratic government offered advantages, particularly "where the average of education and enlightenment is still low," because it "guides as well as restrains the masses."[20]

The view of Russian history which Coolidge held was remarkably consistent. He emphasized in 1900 that "Russians are men much like others, with the motives that are common to humanity, and use means chiefly determined by their circumstances." Russians "may have their own peculiarities, but they are neither particularly better nor worse than other people, nor in their foreign policy are they so much cleverer or endowed with so much more foresight." He ridiculed a volume that declared that "in many respects Russia is the most tolerant of all governments," and asserted that Russian history "should be viewed in just as cool and commonplace a fashion as that of any other country and its phenomena examined just as calmly. Under such treatment they lose any extraordinary character." A September 1922 article in *Foreign Affairs* on the new Soviet government and its policies, which won the approval of both Secretary of State Charles Evans Hughes and Lenin, repeated the substance of these statements, asserting that the Soviet rulers' assessment of Russian national interests and ways to achieve them reflected the history of Russia as well as their own beliefs.[21] Coolidge refused to accept prevailing popular images of Russians. He avoided attitudes which reflected paternal benevolence or contempt, admiration or disenchantment, hostility or evangelism.

Throughout his career, Coolidge believed one should study

Russia not as an isolated phenomenon but as a circle, so to speak, in a series of concentric circles. The first circle was Europe, because Russia was essentially a European state. Approaching Russia first through Germany and Scandinavia deeply influenced his view of Russian history, its relations with Europe, and its role in world politics. His first course on Russian history, and his analysis in general, emphasized the conflicts of religion and of ethnic groups. On the northeastern and northern boundaries of Europe, Russia played a central part in the long struggle between Germans and Slavs, which Coolidge considered an element in the expansion of Europe and in the ancient battle between Western Christianity and the Orthodox Church. This struggle was in part between two religious forces and the cultures they produced, and in part between two nationalities or groups of nationalities. Knowledge of these centuries convinced him that the panslav movement was unimportant because he saw "no necessary community of interests or of sentiments and ideals" between Russians and various other Slavs.[22]

Russia's position on the frontier of Europe, and as a frontier for Europe, led Coolidge to place its history in a Middle Eastern framework as well. His second new course, on the Eastern Question, analyzed the Balkans and the Middle East, religious and cultural struggles there between East and West, and the conflicting interests of Russia and other European states. Here again, travel helped shape the framework in which he viewed historical relationships.

The Balkans and the Middle East fascinated him, as they have many British and American scholars. The original lure came from travel, which gave him a sympathetic view of the Balkan peoples' achievements and aspirations and a curiosity about Constantinople which never waned. Reluctant to accept invitations to serve other educational institutions, in 1914 he quickly accepted appointment to the board of trustees of Robert College, just outside Constantinople. He remained active in its afffairs throughout his life, demonstrating particular interest in the library. He traveled more in North Africa and the Balkans than in Russia, and published more on those areas than on Russia. The detailed knowledge and insight he acquired from travel and reading is reflected in his several editions of Creasy's *History of the Ottoman Turks*.[23]

Coolidge wrote in detail about Serbian and Greek politics as early as 1893. He taught the course on the Eastern Question, in

alternate years, from 1896 until his last year at Harvard. Two of
the five papers he presented at annual meetings of the American
Historical Association were devoted to it: one analyzed the effects
of the Crusades and the other the positions of a number of states
toward Constantinople. By 1902 he had completed a long
manuscript on the life of Suleiman the Magnificent. Until the end
of his life, he hoped to complete a two-volume history of
Constantinople.[24]

Russia's policies in the Balkans and the Middle East, from
the time of Byzantium and the conversion of Grand Duke
Vladimir in Kiev, persuaded him to emphasize Byzantine influence upon Russia, particularly through Eastern Orthodoxy, the
accompanying political philosophy and system, and the continuing attraction and flow of ideas. For him, the Eastern Question
was "the eternal conflict of Europe and Asia" and the Ottoman
Empire's role in history "the last onslaught that Asia had made
upon Europe."[25]

Coolidge was convinced that knowledge of the peoples of
Eastern Europe and of the Eastern Question provided insight into
the history of Russia and of Europe, particularly of diplomacy:
"Anyone who understood what went on, past and present, at the
eastern end of the Mediterranean, would hold the key to European
affairs and to a good deal of world politics." The shape and
significance of the Eastern Question had begun to change in the
eighteenth century because of the almost simultaneous decline of
the Ottoman Empire and the rise of the Russian Empire. This led
him as early as 1894 to appreciate the dangers in the Balkans:
"The appalling element in the situation [Serbia] is the fact that
the condition of the Eastern Question, and of the relations
between the great powers, makes it always possible that the antics
of some irresponsible person or party may bring on the most
terrible war in the history of mankind."[26] Understanding this
explosive mixture led him and a number of his graduate students
to concentrate their research energies on various aspects of this
combination of forces in order to understand the dynamics of
international politics.

In part because of the range of his travel and the vast political,
economic, and social changes he saw taking place, Coolidge
viewed Russia in a world framework. The expansion of Europe,
the simultaneous growth of great new Russian and American
empires, the decline of the Ottoman, French, Austro-Hungarian,
and Chinese empires, and the appearance of what he described as

six world powers convinced him that the world setting was proper for the study of Russian history—indeed of the history of any great state. Americans would especially benefit from studying Russian history: it helped them not only understand another great country but the history of still other nations, such as China, where culture and creed were different from those in the United States. Those who comprehended Russian and American history could understand changes taking place throughout the world because both countries were young, arrogant, and large multinational states, each with its own form of government and attitudes toward race and religion, each an extension of Europe and, simultaneously, an opponent of Europe.

Coolidge was especially interested in the expansion of Russia, whose effects he saw in the Caucasus and Central Asia. Emphasis upon this aspect of Russian history antedated his interest in the expansion of Europe, but he saw the growth of its empire and its rise to great-power status as parts of a worldwide phenomenon. The series of lectures he gave at the Lowell Institute in November 1902 were devoted to the expansion of Russia. In 1900 he began working on this series; in 1901 he published an article on the subject; and he continued to work on a similar manuscript until 1907. Letters to friends indicated that the volume would be "philosophizing rather than narrating," but the manuscript is a long narrative description of Russian expansion until 1870. He began a new course in 1904 on the expansion of Europe since 1815, and no doubt planned to fit the history of Russian expansion into a study of European expansion.[27]

In his manuscript, as in his articles, reviews, courses, and public lectures, Coolidge emphasized that the expansion of Russia was continental, "along the lines of least resistance and most profit," that it involved remarkably little force or violence, and that it gave Russia the same sort of practical invulnerability the United States possessed. Russia's massive size tended to frighten other countries in an unjustified way. Moreover, its growth in the nineteenth century, particularly after 1890, had been less rapid than that of the British, or even of the German and American empires. The formation of the great Russian state resembled the same process which brought the unification of Germany and of Italy. Ivan the Terrible, an Oriental despot and a coward, played the same role as Cavour and Bismarck, in his case displaying "the culmination of the strong, unlovely qualities which have long distinguished the princes of Moscow, 'the gatherers of the Russian land.'" Yermak's activities resembled those of Cortez or Pizarro. The principality of Suzdal occupied the same position in the expansion of Russia and the formation of the Russian national state as Brandenburg did in the creation of a unified Germany. The Russian drive to the Black Sea was similar to American insistence upon control of the Mississippi River, and control of the Straits was for Russia "even more serious than a foreign-owned Panama Canal would be to the United States." Russian expansion in Central Asia and its ethics in that venture resembled American annexation of territory from Mexico and was "as legitimate as the British subjugation of India." The sale of Alaska to the United States proved that Russians were not "invariably distinguished by an indiscriminate land hunger." The Russian people from 1875 to 1878 were animated "by the same sort of unselfish enthusiasm as Americans in their war with Spain."[28]

In short, the expansion of Russia was much like that of other states. Indeed, it was especially admirable because Russia had fewer resources than the United States, its social organization discouraged the individualism that pioneering requires, and the Russian people "have always suffered from grinding poverty and over-taxation" and a barbarous and cruel system. Russians, unlike Anglo-Saxons, were not motivated by racial pride. On the other hand, they were more ruthless and dishonest.

Coolidge also suggested that the expansion of Russia, like that of the United States, was almost inevitable. A kind of manifest destiny, rather than rulers' decisions, economic pressures, or national ambition, explained it:

> The conquest of Turkestan (as it used to be called) was inevitable, sooner or later. No civilized modern state submits in the long run to a neighborhood of a jumble of barbarous principalities and tribes, unable and often unwilling to maintain order within their own boundaries or to prevent depradations beyond them. The Muscovite campaigns in Central Asia may have been due to political schemes of the time or to the ambitions of individuals, but at bottom they were brought about by perfectly natural causes, like the spread of British rule in India after it had once got a real foothold. Moreover, Russian expansion to the Pacific was as obvious and inevitable as was our own from an opposite direction.... It is inconceivable that Russia should not sooner or later have broken down the barrier and swept away the obstacles that separated her from the southern sea.[29]

A decade before the First World War he predicted that "the days of Persia as an independent nation are numbered" and that much of Persia would become part of the Russian Empire.[30] Coolidge also believed that Russian expansion had benefited most people brought under Russian control. "With the possible exceptions of Finland and Poland" and possibly of the people in the Baltic provinces, "all the regions which have passed under their [Russian] rule in this century have found it, whatever its faults, unquestionably superior to anything they had before known." Russian acquisitions in Central Asia and the Caucasus, like British subjugation of India, were "natural and inevitable processes when once the vigorous European communities had come into close contact with the decaying Asiatic ones. Both have meant the introduction of firm government, law, order, and equal justice in place of barbarous insecurity. Both have resulted in a gain for the civilization of the world." The Russian government in Turkestan was "incomparably better than anything the country has known for centuries, better, perhaps, than anything it has ever known." Some might not rejoice at living under Russian control, but Moslems in Algeria and India felt the same way about French and British control.[31]

Coolidge published little concerning Russia from the autumn of 1917 until after he returned to Harvard early in 1922. Even in 1920 and 1921, when he was contributing lead articles for the New York *Evening Post* on the consequences of the war, he made only two references to developments within Russia and to their influence elsewhere.

His first public comments on the Soviet system were untypical because they were passionate. A talk entitled "Jefferson and the Problems of Today," at the centenary celebration of the University of Virginia at Monticello in June 1921, described the system as a new despotism and oligarchy that had declared "ruthless war against all principles of true democracy." He saw "the red apostles of communism ... prepared to shed torrents of blood and if need be to stamp out civilization" in order to achieve the millennium throughout the world. These views concerning the system and its goals did not change; an article in *Foreign Affairs* in October 1925 on "Dissatisfied Germany" described Communist Russia as a connecting link between all discontents "in its remorseless campaign against the structure of modern society, eager to promote trouble anywhere and everywhere." However, the judgments were generally expressed in a dispassionate fashion.[32]

Coolidge worked in the Soviet Union as chief of the Liaison Division of Herbert Hoover's American Relief Administration from September 22, 1921, until February 1922. An appeal by Maxim Gorky on July 13, 1921, for "bread and medicine" led to the Riga Agreement of August 20, 1921, in which the Soviet government invited Hoover to provide food supplies and medical assistance. Hoover's invitation to serve as a "general political guide" for the Americans in Russia and the main liaison between the ARA and the Soviet government described a position "pretty much what I would have chosen if I had had the inventing." He had a double purpose, for he also wrote to Hoover, who was then Secretary of Commerce, and to Secretary of State Hughes concerning developments in Russia. However, his main function proved to be consular work, assisting hundreds of American citizens stranded in Russia to return to the United States.[33]

Coolidge's reports to the ARA and to friends in the United States concerning the new Soviet state were remarkably well informed and objective. Letters to Hoover, Hughes, Senators Hiram Bingham and Henry Cabot Lodge, and his parents noted that the Soviet government was in command, even though the Congress of Soviets had shown little enthusiasm. The Communist party had firm control over the army, and the secret police, the Cheka, was vigilant and cruel. The Communist leaders were "almost all men of unusual ability" and the "Internationale" was a fine, effective anthem. He saw Lenin as "a man of impressive power, and of determination, not to say ruthlessness," who excited genuine admiration and devotion, "although he was in many ways not a good speaker." Trotsky was a much more polished orator, but his influence was declining.[34]

Coolidge saw no visible threat to the Soviet system: "The economic ruin of the country" was so involved and desperate that no change of political system could help. The workers were disillusioned but loyal; the peasants were discontented but disorganized. The New Economic Policy was a strategic maneuver the government would reverse as soon as the Communists had resolved the most pressing economic problems. A talk at the Army War College on October 19, 1922 and an article in the first issue of *Foreign Affairs* that month emphasized that the economic situation was disastrous, that the "promised land" had become a hell on earth, and that Russia needed significant economic assistance. However, Coolidge saw no chance for overthrow of the system. Indeed, the Soviet leaders would establish a highly centralized government, rather than a loose federation, with the Communist party and its bureaucracy in control.[35]

For Coolidge, the spread of Soviet principles and institutions constituted a long-term threat to Europe, but he believed that Russian conquests on the Western frontiers were "never thoroughly welded to the rest of the Empire." The Soviet government resented the loss of Bessarabia, but considered regaining it less important than retaining the gold the Romanian government had entrusted to the tsarist government. Soviet leaders were not eager to recover control over Poland, or other territories with mixed populations, so long as the Poles behaved responsibly, because the Poles would constitute a persistent problem, as they had before the revolution. The Baltic states would retain their independence, and Coolidge saw no reason for the Soviets to threaten Finland. He therefore did not endorse a *cordon sanitaire*.[36]

In his view, the Soviet leaders, intelligent though they were, did not comprehend Western distrust of them. At the same time, the Soviet government would insist that other states treat it as an equal and accept its full participation in world affairs. Coolidge was convinced that Lenin and his followers would reassert Russia's position as a great power and that Russia would "make herself heard from in matters that interest her." Soviet policies at Rapallo and The Hague in 1922 indicated that Russia had resumed that position and that the United States had erred in not inviting the Soviet Union to the Washington Conference. In summary, Lenin and his colleagues were not "indifferent to legitimate national interests, even if she [Russia] is not now in a position to assert them effectively.... She will therefore not accept as valid any international arrangements concerning them made without her participation." Lenin underscored and circled this statement on the copy of *Foreign Affairs* Coolidge had sent him through Radek.[37]

Coolidge remained fascinated by "the vast and menacing enigma of Russia," and especially by the issue of United States' recognition of the Soviet government, under discussion throughout the 1920s. He recognized that the American public viewed the Bolsheviks "with unfeigned horror" and the regime they had established as "monstrous and unclean." He noted popular approval of Secretary Hughes's "firm, consistent and dignified" statement in March 1922 that the United States could not recognize the Soviet Union because its government did not respect the sanctity of life or freedom of labor and did not guarantee life and property, but did allow trade and encouraged "splendid unofficial charity." On the other hand, Russia existed "whether we like it or not," and the world would have to recognize the Soviet Union "sooner or later." The practical English had accepted "the decision of facts" by establishing trade relationships and recognizing the Soviet government. The United States, which most of the world considered "a rich Pharisee," would thus lose trade and opportunities to help the Russian people if it persisted in nonrecognition.[38]

On this subject, as on others, Coolidge acted on the conviction that his responsibility as teacher and editor was to provide as accurate an account as possible, describe the alternatives and the consequences fairly, and leave the decision to independent action. He faithfully described the arguments for and against American recognition of the Soviet Union (he did not reveal his own position, but he leaned toward recognition) and thus pointed out the paradox of the American position: "the self-appointed moral trustee, the benefactor who had dispensed such charity as no people before ever bestowed on another and at the same time the stern critic who declines to recognize the government she has been cooperating with in feeding millions of its people.... Shall we refuse to sell sorely needed farm instruments to the Russian peasants because we dislike the Moscow Soviet?... One cannot help wondering how much longer this policy can be continued... for Russia is too large a portion of the globe to be sent permanently to Coventry."[39]

As the principal founder of Russian studies in the United States, Coolidge exercised profound influence in awakening and then shaping American research and instruction on that country and its culture. Those specialists whom he trained, such as Frank Golder, and Robert J. Kerner, and many others who taught and wrote about Russia as an important part of the world, benefited from the depth of his knowledge, the perspectives and insights he had acquired from traveling, and his interest in factors other than the state system and Russian politics. Russian studies in the United States have profited from his stress on an imaginative search for information and understanding, as well as from his emphasis upon independent judgment and evenhandedness. His early training under French and German masters, his knowledge of Russian scholars and their work, and his reaction against the powerful flood of interpretations flowing into the United States from Great Britain placed a powerful stamp upon American scholarship. Above all, those whom he taught and those who read his work learned to think of Russia not as an exotic, curious phenomenon but as another European and world state, with characteristics just as natural as the characteristics Americans encountered in their own country and in Western Europe.

5. "The Coming Together of the World"

ONE OF COOLIDGE'S MOST important qualities, which helped place an important stamp upon a segment of American historical scholarship, was his ability to see the world as a whole and his making "the coming together of the world" central to his approach to the study of history. This characteristic was of particular importance at a time when graduate training in history in the United States was expanding from a very small base and when research and instruction concerning neglected areas and periods were beginning.

Teaching in a university that was growing and at the same time becoming one of the great universities of the world certainly helped Coolidge comprehend the significance of the changes he could see taking place. Similarly, living and working in a country that was bursting with energy and expanding also benefited him. These experiences in a country shaken by the Civil War, his residence in Germany during and after the age of Bismarck, and all his journeys helped him appreciate the central role of the modern nation-state and of minorities in states large and small. As William L. Langer demonstrated in masterful detail, the age of social Darwinism (at one level) and romantic and adventure literature (at another) helped young men like him, who read Robert Louis Stevenson, Rider Haggard, and Rudyard Kipling, to appreciate the magnitude of the transformations sweeping the world—particularly that "the tendency of social development was toward larger and larger units and that ultimately the world would be divided between the three or four fittest nations."[1]

Coolidge's writings and teaching constitute a record and analysis of that era of expansion, particularly when one considers that he described the changes as a contemporary and was one of the first Americans who wrote and taught about modern international history and relations. He demonstrated a great *forte* in viewing developments within individual states and continents in a world framework. Far earlier and more clearly than most statesmen or scholars, he began to appreciate the changing character of the era, "the opening up of the world," the new American role in world politics, and the growing desire for self-government everywhere, and to inject some understanding of these phenomena into American higher education and into the informed public.

In an age when intense nationalism and vast ignorance of other peoples often led to distortions of history and contemporary affairs, Coolidge was remarkable in recognizing the values of other cultures and in declaring them equal to those with which his students and readers were familiar. In the words of his Harvard colleagues, he had "what is more rare than an international mind, a multi-national mind."[2] He taught that all cultures and religions reflect the geography and historical traditions in which they developed and that no culture is grotesque to those who know and understand it. His editions of Creasy scrupulously reflected Creasy's spirit but removed Froissart's references to "barbarous customs" and omitted many "superfluous passionate phrases" because Coolidge was aware that all cultures encourage actions that seem outrageous to outsiders.

Above all, Coolidge recognized that imperialism helped cause its own end by stimulating "the exploding desire for self-government." The same forces which unleashed the expansion of Europe would bring about the unraveling of the great empires, help create new political entities, and make states and their peoples far more dependent upon each other than they had been before. As Langer wrote sixty years later, "imperialism's one great achievement was to open up the world and set all humanity on the high road to eventual association and collaboration."[3] All of his teaching and writing reflected these large views and helped begin the education of Americans to the world in which they lived and to the vast changes taking place.

The largeness of Coolidge's view of history, at a time when specialists were beginning to dominate American historical scholarship, was fortified by close attention to fundamental factors. Thus the state, a viable, legitimate, and essential part of the world's structure, the building block of political life and international politics, was central in his view. The state, the system of states, and nationalism were basic elements everywhere. Each state inevitably sought to defend its interests, beginning with the establishment and maintenance of national unity. Foreign policy therefore was "the result of practical consider-

ations." In 1894, and later in life as well, he observed that a
Chinese government would one day drive out foreigners. Fascism
was only "the most recent phase of the struggle to achieve Italian
unity—as an Italian and not as an universal movement,... in its
beginnings only the impulsive manifestation of the need for
strengthening the powers of the state in the face of social and
political disintegration"—particularly bolshevism and the national humiliation the First World War produced. The movement
and its policies, "awkward and brutal," deeply harmed Italian
influence abroad, and caused instability and disquietude in
European politics, but they were natural and even inevitable
developments. Similarly, the Soviet government's internal and
external policies in the 1920s represented its leaders' emphasis
upon the national state and that state's interests as they defined
them.[4]

Clashes were therefore inevitable among states. The rivalry
between France and Germany, the war between Russia and Japan,
and the efforts of Hungary and Germany to regain lost territories
after 1919 were reflections of the state system, facts of life, and
inexorable developments. Such conflicts were not necessarily
catastrophic.

For Coolidge, the nation-state rested upon a territorial
foundation, more essential in the twentieth century than before
because the power of the state "now rests on quantity, as well as on
quality." A state needed a defensible position, good soil, adequate
natural resources, and an attractive climate. He placed heavy
emphasis upon the role of geographic location and the power and
ambitions of neighbors. However, the growing dominance of the
great states did not make them "necessarily superior to the small
ones in civilization or more admirable in any way." He hoped
small countries would overcome the threatening "relatively
permanent factors" of position and territorial foundation and
remain independent, because their survival involved moral
principles essential to civilized political life, but he assumed that
some in unfortunate geographic locations would be absorbed.
Thus Belgium, "a state of recent and rather artificial origin" and
"predominantly French culture," was likely to disappear, as
would Montenegro and the Baltic countries. Japan's victory over
Russia in 1905 meant the incorporation of Korea into a Japanese
Empire that would continue to expand.[5]

The form of government and guiding political ideas had
lower priority for Coolidge than for most statesmen and scholars.

Every state needed an effective system of government and accepted political ideas, but he believed that most accounts of history and international affairs exaggerated the role of political systems and philosophies. Although his age was a time when most history was political, when political science was becoming an important discipline, and when history and political science were often combined into one university department (as at Harvard from 1895 to 1911), he wrote remarkably little about political institutions and values. A student in his Russian history course noted his declaration that forms of government reflected local situations and that "if Russia were a Republic, minorities would be just as badly off."[6]

Coolidge emphasized that forms of government varied in different parts of the world because of the effect permanent forces and history exerted, and that no government was superior in form to any other government. He endorsed and enjoyed constitutional and democratic government, but believed that the American political system was a consequence of history and tradition, received in good part from England and Western Europe, and that the rule of law and the democratic form of government would not spread throughout the world. His thesis in 1892 described the American founders as practical men who faced a concrete situation, not philosophers or politicians who dealt with abstract values which statesmen in other countries should accept. The American Constitution was "not to be a model system applicable to all places and at all times, but to suit the wants and ideas of the thirteen Confederated American States, to bring them together into a nation and to assure to them a great future. All this it had done."[7]

Another conclusion was that centralized government enjoyed some advantages over the American federal system, as well as some disadvantages. Its apparent superiority in providing law and order and an established conservative political system was important for underdeveloped countries that faced relentless pressure from more advanced or powerful neighbors. Americans would err if they made their government more highly centralized just to match apparently successful systems in other parts of the world. Other states that sought to adopt the American model, in violation of their history, would blunder in the same way.

Language was an especially important part of any culture, and the major languages played a significant role in creating national states and great empires. Collecting information on the role languages had played in imperialism was a hobby. He reflected upon which language would most likely emerge as the common world medium, concluding, after careful analysis of census data and the flow of history, that English was the most likely candidate, with French second. This did not indicate that English was superior to French, the foreign language he learned first which he called "a marvelous vehicle of human expression," but that it would have enormous consequences.[8]

The size and qualities of a nation's population were particularly important factors in international politics. Thus "the degree of civilization of the people of different nations, their industry, their habits of thrift, their skill, intelligence" are critical resources. The need for large numbers of people also made the birth rate and the fertility rate central. He studied census statistics, with particular emphasis upon birth and fertility rates and upon the size of each state's ethnic, national, and religious minorities, concluding that the young American republic and the ancient empires of Russia and China possessed advantages because of the size and rate of growth of their populations.[9]

Nationality and the relations among nationalities were also significant in national and in international politics. As a young scholar, Coolidge recognized that national minorities constitute a serious hazard for any state. Articles in the *Nation* on the Congo Free State in 1894 and on Hawaii in 1897 devoted attention to ethnic and religious groupings. In 1908, after the initial short historical chapter on formation and growth in *The United States as a World Power*, he titled the next chapters "Nationality and Immigration" and "Race Questions," issues which a contemporary book on the same subject, *America as a World Power, 1897-1907* (New York, 1907), by John H. Latané, almost totally neglected. His writings and lectures on European history, especially the Balkans, emphasized the crucial nature of the issues national and religious minorities created. Before the outbreak of the First World War, he foresaw no peace in Europe unless "consent of the governed" prevailed and unless national minority groups received essential freedoms. In 1919 and after, he advocated guarantees to minorities and asserted that no democracy could keep another people in subjection; for example, any Czechoslovak effort to restrict the liberties of Sudeten Germans would create strains and perhaps cause the downfall of Czechoslovakia.[10]

Ironically, recognition of the issues that minorities raised was most apparent in his analysis of the American political system. Indeed, appreciation of domestic issues in the United States deepened his understanding of ethnic conflicts everywhere and enabled him to see that many problems in the ever shrinking world are universal.

At the time he was becoming an important scholar-teacher, racist attitudes became prominent among some Boston Brahmins, hitherto immune from such infections.[11] He noted that the strength of antisemitism was rising rapidly among those he labeled "the upper classes." His brother John often wrote of "the lower races," used the word "nigger," and referred in a critical way to Jews as a group. Some of his students, such as Batsell and Kerner, were antisemitic in their private correspondence: the latter wrote in 1919 that "the international Jews" were plotting against the new Czechoslovak and Yugoslav states. William R. Castle, Jr., close to Coolidge as an undergraduate, Harvard colleague, and diplomat, wrote antisemitic letters. After President A. Lawrence Lowell learned in 1922 that the percentage of Jews had risen from 7 in 1900 to 21 in 1922, he proposed that Harvard establish a quota for Jewish students, but withdrew his proposal under criticism. Marquand's George Apley wrote to his son in New York in the 1920s that he did not consider New York an American city: "We have our Irish and you your Jews, and both of them are crosses to bear."[12]

Shortly after he retired as president of Harvard in 1909, Eliot, an enlightened conservative gentleman, declared that the Irish, Italian, and Portuguese Catholics "in Protestant Massachusetts" presented "the same race problem to that part of the country that negroes do to the South" and that the American North and West had "a racial suffrage problem...ever since the Irish began to arrive in this country, sixty years ago." Lothrop Stoddard, an immensely conceited member of a prominent and wealthy Boston family, who graduated from Harvard in 1909 and completed his Ph.D. work in 1914 under Coolidge's direction, was greatly concerned about *The Rising Tide of Color against White World-Supremacy*, the title of a book he published in 1920. Stoddard, a publicist for thirty years, wrote a number of popular volumes about the dangers "colored peoples" throughout the world created for whites. He saw the basic cause of revolutionary unrest as "a process of racial impoverishment, which destroyed the great civilizations of the past and which threatens to destroy our own." He opposed immigration. The Soviet Communists, "with Semitic leadership and Chinese executioners," were organizing "the last of a long series of revolts by the unadaptable, inferior, and degenerate elements" upon western Europe from Asia. The Nordic race must therefore "shake off the shackles of an inveterate altruism, discard the vain phantom of internationalism, and reassert the pride of race and of the right of merit to rule."[13]

Coolidge flatly rejected Stoddard's ideas and others like them. There is no evidence that he had any relations with Stoddard after the latter received his degree in 1914; no correspondence survives in the rich Coolidge archives, and Stoddard was one of the few who received a Ph.D. degree under Coolidge's direction whom he did not invite to contribute to The Inquiry in 1917.

Coolidge, of course, emphasized intellectual quality at the university and assumed that knowledge and those who possessed it would play important roles in any society. However, perhaps because of the low importance he assigned to ideas in historical development, social Darwinism and belief in Anglo-Saxon racial superiority, which obsessed many American intellectuals during his active years, did not affect him. He never wrote about Anglo-Saxons as such, and he did not consider Anglo-American relations special in any way. Indeed, he was not an admirer of the British. In 1925 he urged that the United States and Great Britain not cooperate closely lest they create fear of an Anglo-American bloc. He saw no common interest in preserving "white English-speaking races" or in picking up "the white man's burden." He either was not aware of or he rejected the view of such men as Sir Alfred Milner and Lord George Curzon, although he was an admirer of Rudyard Kipling.[14]

The Boston Irish received the ultimate compliment—or insult—because he ignored them at a time when many colleagues and friends were openly anti-Irish and to some degree anti-Catholic. Some of his students, including Robert F. Kelley and G. Howland Shaw, were Catholic. Others, such as Golder and Walter Lichtenstein, were Jews, a fact to which Coolidge paid little attention, except in private letters advising them about careers. He termed Charles Gross, under whom he studied as an undergraduate and of whom he was a close colleague for more than fifteen years, "our greatest historian." "Gross, born in 1857 of Jewish parents," but not "a Jew associated with the Jewish community," may have been the first Jew appointed to the Harvard faculty.

Coolidge was critical of the concerns of many of his class and generation about Jews, whom he considered not a nationality but "a people holding a certain religious belief." A speech in 1914 noted that prophesying is rash, "but as things are going now it would seem as if Jewish blood would be one of the strains in the composite America of the future, rather than that Jews will remain a separate element in the American people." A paper prepared at The Inquiry early in 1918 omitted the position of Jews in Romania as a problem which would be important after the war. His writings on Russia almost ignored the Jews. On the other hand, reports from Budapest in 1919 noted their prominent role in economic, intellectual, and political affairs under the Bela Kun regime, and that many observers referred to Budapest as "Jewdapest."[15]

However, the position and role of blacks in the United States raised critical issues for Coolidge, as they did for most of his class and generation. He reflected often and deeply about the blacks and about immigration as the world shrank, and he devoted many pages to blacks and their position in *The United States as a World Power*. A talk in Berlin just before the war concluded that "at the present day at least, all races are not of equal political value" and that blacks were inferior to whites. Blacks were not "mechanical," were "apt to be lazy, slovenly, and unprogressive," and were "more sexually passionate then the whites and less capable of self-restraint." On the whole, blacks lived better in the hot, rich flatlands of the South than elsewhere, though even there "they sometimes relax into indolence and even barbarism." Cities have a demoralizing effect because "they form a lowest class living under deplorable conditions, and the death rate as well as criminality among them is high." Their position in the United States was worse than in 1890 because the North had accepted the southern point of view and because most Americans did not consider blacks "a part of the sovereign people."[16]

Throughout his life, Coolidge like many other white Americans, was trapped between his judgment about a democratic society and his views concerning blacks and Asians. Study persuaded him that the United States would become "an English-speaking community, of mixed origin, but fused by common traditions, interests, aspirations, and language into one essentially homogeneous people." However, the presence of blacks and white attitudes toward them threatened these hopes "for harmony and a community of ideas." On one hand, "no people can be

expected to regard themselves permanently as inferior to others";
separation of the races was undesirable, and impossible to
achieve; and the blacks were obviously too numerous and deeply
rooted to expel. On the other hand, white Americans overwhelmingly opposed mixed marriages. His analysis of France and its
empire persuaded him that "a great conquering and ruling race
must keep itself unmixed if it is to retain its virtues" and that
"crossing of breeds too far apart is an undesirable thing." In short,
"proper treatment" of blacks was "a matter of momentous
importance for the future of the republic" that will "tax all the
wisdom in her statesmen and make every demand on the self-
control, not to say generosity, of her citizens."[17]

This issue also created serious problems for American
foreign policy. It complicated issues in the Caribbean, which
would probably become "an American lake," even though many
would oppose annexing islands where much of the population
was black. He was especially eager to have *Foreign Affairs* publish
articles on this issue. W.E.B. DuBois's "Worlds of Color," in
April 1925, impressed him as "one of the most interesting" essays
the journal had printed, although he "squirmed" under its
description of white treatment of blacks in Africa and at the
likelihood of worldwide revolt against the color line, which
DuBois termed the main problem of the twentieth century.[18]

In the last thirty years of Coolidge's life, immigration was
another intractable American political problem. He recognized
that many Americans resented the influx of groups from different
cultures and insisted that the United States should admit only
those who could speak and read English. For Coolidge, immigration from Europe raised no fear. These men and women came to
the United States highly motivated, eager to share its benefits. A
third of these foreign-born spoke English as a native language,
and a third of the foreigners in the United States had at least one
parent who spoke English as a native language. Public schools
and American politics tended to bring these immigrant groups
into American life directly. The Catholic Church helped "convert" many immigrants quickly in language as well as in ideas.
Finally, religion and nationality did not combine to create
problems in the United States, as they did in many European
states.

Chinese and Japanese immigration, however, raised complicated issues. Boston was the birthplace of the Immigration
Restriction League (in 1894), the first organized movement to

denounce America's traditional welcome to all European peoples. Coolidge's financial counselor, neighbor, and close friend, John F. Moors, was active in this league and became its head in 1899 and Lowell was a member.[19]

Coolidge devoted substantial attention to this subject, describing accurately the positions of those who opposed and those who favored such immigration and concluding, in 1908, that "there is no chance whatsoever that the United States will open its doors to unrestricted Chinese immigration." He ultimately supported those who urged controlled immigration from Asia, · even though this violated American standards and might push Japan into expansion and rivalry in the Pacific. Most Americans believed "Mongolians constitute an element which cannot be Americanized," which would lower living standards of the working class with whom they would compete, and which would gain control of the Pacific coast. Australia and Canada faced the same "obvious menace," and were responding in the same way. Indeed, the declining birth rate of the white race "in most of the civilized nations" suggested that its role was likely to decline and that of the colored races to grow. Just as families in the upper class die off and are replaced by more vigorous elements from below, so the white race might become "a sort of upper class, which will lose ground in numbers and yet be unable to obtain recruits from outside, as it rejects inter-marriage with people of another color."[20]

An observer and historian, not a theorist, Coolidge reached general conclusions about the expansion of Europe and the pressures for self-government in the colonies which would reverse that tide. Fundamentally, he judged that certain basic factors, beyond the control of peoples or their governments, were responsible for these important historical developments. However, strong leaders could help create great institutions and empires, while weaker men's decisions helped push the fortunes of states downhill. His own career of innovation and creation helped him understand the role individuals could play. His respect for Eliot and Lowell as builders of Harvard University reflects his views concerning the importance of able individuals at critical times, as did his remaining in contact with French colonial administrators whom he had met on trips through North Africa. Lectures to undergraduates revealed great admiration for Joan of Arc, Peter the Great, and Theodore Roosevelt. Builders of states, such as Bismarck, or expanders of empire, such as Catherine the Great

and Jules Ferry, were particularly significant.[21] His admiration
for Catherine was almost lyrical:

> There is something irresistibly attractive in her buoyant
> nature and high spirits, her generous impulses, her splendid
> courage, and her brilliant dreams. It is sometimes impossible
> to defend her, and yet it is not without reason that she has
> remained a national glory of the country of her adoption and
> come down to history as Catherine the Great. Her grasp of the
> situation, the simplicity of her aims, the variety of her
> methods, her art in playing off her rivals against each other
> bear the stamp of genius.[22]

Similarly, individuals and their decisions helped explain the
fall of states. In fact, he devoted almost as much attention to the
decline and fall of some empires as he gave to the rise of others and
the shrinking of the world. Thus, a number of turning points
helped explain the diminishment of France, principally the
decline of its population, or at least the stability of its population,
at a time when the population of rival states was growing rapidly.
The French government's refusal to allow Huguenots to move to
other parts of the empire deprived its lands of the population and,
above all, of the imaginative leadership that Puritans and other
dissident sects provided the British. Louis XIV wasted French
resources in the War of the Spanish Succession at a time when
France could easily have acquired control over Belgium, the
Netherlands, and the Rhine and become the most powerful
European state. The sale of Louisiana to Spain in 1763 and the
French decision to leave Egypt were disastrous decisions by
individuals.[23]

However, Coolidge considered the greatest age of European
expansion basically unplanned and inevitable, beyond the control of great states and individuals, the result of a series of
elemental, interrelated factors that affected all modern history and
that were ineluctably bringing the world together. These views on
the course of empire formed a thread that ran throughout his life.
An undergraduate paper on the French theater in the Age of
Romanticism concluded that "a great change in the history or
sentiments of a nation never depends entirely on the action of any
one force, is never due to any one cause, and is never totally
separated from kindred changes that are going on around it." An
essay in the 1890s, when he wrote a great deal about Armenia,
announced that the Ottoman Empire was "a moribund nation

with a disease for which there is no known remedy." Similarly, "the Russia of Peter the Great was what her history and circumstances had made her; the impetus he gave her was in the direction towards which she was already moving; and his own originality appears rather in his peculiar methods than in any particular novelty of his conceptions in themselves." Geography and inherited political institutions, habits, and experiences were fundamental. In short, "the chief cause of history appears to be history."[24]

His explanations of imperialism saw no relationship between forms of government and the outward thrust of the powerful states: the elements were more powerful than political systems. The theory that expansion is the work of political or economic groups or their leaders is ridiculous; planning is "a compliment we reserve to others" and statesmen, in particular, are not so far-sighted as some observers think. He ignored military forces, the often-celebrated virtues or glories of war, and the role of militarism. His writings include few references to war or to military actions. Moreover, "socialism offers no escape from the logic of this situation."[25]

Coolidge rejected the view that economic forces were responsible for imperialism, and in general ignored them. The Industrial Revolution and the economic and social developments of his lifetime received little attention, even though travel persuaded him that the principal motor in contemporary change was that "distance is... suppressed" by revolutions in transportation and communications. The European states contributed so significantly to the contraction of the world and benefited so greatly because the foundations created before the middle of the nineteenth century made Europe "the center, the starting point of outward impulse of any human progress, while Asia and America have been periphery, the distant opposite edges."[26]

Coolidge predicted that the twentieth century would be "the century of national imperialism," in which six great powers, "which are directly interested in all parts of the world and whose voice must be listened to everywhere," would dominate. Such states required not only natural resources, economic and scientific skills, and accepted leadership but large territories and population masses. Russia and the United States, in the long run, would become preeminent over the others.[27]

Next to Russia, the United States attracted his closest attention. In his view, American territory contained the soil, water, and other natural resources a great state requires. The United States enjoyed a temperate climate and splendid natural communications, which modern technology improved. Above all, its population demonstrated the industry, skill, and intelligence the people of a great state must possess. However, only the accident of war with Spain in 1898 forced the reluctant American people and their leaders to acquire an empire in the Pacific and to leap into the front rank of world nations. During the debate over empire that raged for two or three years after 1898, Coolidge remained aloof and inactive. The *Nation*, for which he wrote extensively from 1893 until 1905, was a consistent opponent of American expansion, as were many of his Harvard associates, including President Eliot, William James, Charles Eliot Norton, and Bliss Perry. Coolidge, who was not an enthusiastic promoter of American expansion, supported annexation of Hawaii and the Philippines after long thought about the complicated difficulties which lay ahead, whichever decision the United States made. Indeed, he agreed that most Americans did not know whether the Philippines were "islands or canned goods." However, once the decision to acquire them was made, "the Pacific era" had begun, the role of European states there would wane, and the Pacific would become "a sea of the Americans and the Asiatics."[28]

Coolidge concluded that America's appearance as a world power was as inevitable as the rise and fall of other states. American acquisition of the Panama Canal Zone was justified, and the United States would annex Caribbean islands, other than Cuba, roiling relations with Latin America in the process. The American government would intervene whenever developments threatened foreign property or American interests in Cuba, and instability in Mexico and throughout Latin America would also trigger American intervention. In addition, the Dominion of Canada was artificial, the "result not of natural forces but of historical accident." He declared it possible, though not likely, that "the great permanent forces of geography and nationality" and "modern economic forces" might in the distant future bring the United States and Canada together in one large North American state.[29] His 1908 volume ended with the statement that "greatness brings responsibilities" and the well-known quotation from Theodore Roosevelt: "We have no choice, we people of the United States, as to whether or not we shall play a great part in the world. That has been determined for us by fate, by the march of events. We have to play that part. All that we can decide is whether we shall play it well or ill."[30]

For Coolidge, imperialism implied no ethical, ethnic, or other superiority of one state over another. He did not assume the superiority of Western culture or advocate transforming the world with Europe as a model. He hoped, for example, that Siamese cultural, political and religious values would survive and that "Europeanization" meant simply the introduction of modern equipment and efficiency. Other peoples should not adopt American individualism, its political institutions, or its system of property holding. Indeed, efforts to introduce Western religions were destructive and dangerous. Missionaries were unselfish, and their help in alleviating suffering and advancing knowledge was noble, but they were "makers of endless trouble." He declared that "the coming of strangers to convert a people of ancient civilization from long-inherited beliefs with which they are satisfied is an impertinence in itself; . . . missionaries frequently lack tact, and by their meddlesomeness get into unnecessary difficulties, and . . . what good they have accomplished has been incommensurate with the money spent in doing it."[31]

Even though missionaries did more harm than good, the Age of Imperialism was on balance a blessing to colonial peoples. His 1906 tour led to a declaration that British East Africa was receiving the benefits of law and order from "a handful of honest, determined, and devoted white officials." A few years later, he concluded that "the verdict of posterity will be that the men who built up the Greater France of today are entitled to the gratitude of their countrymen and an honorable place in the estimation of the world." Americans used force in acquiring the Southwest, but the "region has been so developed as to become of much more value to mankind than it would have been had it remained the property of its former legitimate owners." His views of Central Asian territories brought under Russian control were similar.[32]

Coolidge foresaw the formation of continental and even regional organizations of states and considered this an inevitable tendency toward a unity of groups of peoples related by geography, blood, culture, language, economics, and above all history. In fact, according to Coolidge, the fourteenth chapter of Genesis was an "early instance of such a grouping." The rise of new, small states in Europe after the First World War was "fascinating and encouraging . . . and like a new dawn in history," but a large European unit was necessary to resist American capitalism and to strengthen the League of Nations. Russia and Britain, including the British Empire, should and would be part of the new European entity, but the United States would remain a separate and distinct power.[33]

Latin America, particularly because of the Monroe Doctrine, attracted special attention. One of the most able theses written under his direction was Dexter Perkins's in 1914, on the early reception European states gave the Monroe Doctrine. Perkins's memoirs indicate that Coolidge suggested the subject and demonstrated enormous interest in his work, before and after his thesis, because of his concern with Latin America and the doctrine, which he referred to as "the ark of the covenant." Its main purpose, to urge the European states to keep their hands off Latin American states, had been achieved for a century, but it had created fear and resentment throughout Latin America and was not "immune to the gentle perils of dissolution." In addition, European governments and Japan thought the American position ridiculous: the United States was deeply involved in European and Asian affairs, but demanded that other states remain aloof from Latin America. Finally, when most Latin American states joined the League of Nations, they destroyed the foundation of the United States' position in Latin America. Coolidge therefore assumed, in the 1920s, that a legitimate and responsible pan-American movement would gradually replace the doctrine, but he believed that it should include the United States and Canada. Latin America would play an increasingly important role in world politics, whether or not its states succeeded in forming some kind of alliance or organization. In particular, Brazil would play a world role and would soon occupy a more significant place than a state such as Italy.[34]

Coolidge anticipated no great clash of grouped states, empires, or civilizations. Such combinations created "chances of future conflicts on a gigantic scale," but this did not mean that the rise of great unions or great powers meant struggle was inevitable. However, they brought us "one step nearer to a world-wide fusion of international interests." He had deep faith in the ultimate emergence of such a community and saw the age of expansion and empire as one great step toward that.[35]

Experience in and after the First World War persuaded Coolidge that the United States was part of a visible international community and should "share in the vast work of reconstruction." Indeed, the "whole development of the last hundred years tended to emphasize the necessity of cooperation in all good works between nations as well as between individuals." Returning to some kind of isolation "looks like a desperate attempt to make water run uphill." However, he did not advocate that the

United States join the League of Nations, largely because he thought his obligation as a scholar and editor was not to endorse policies but to illuminate issues for informed citizens and for those Americans who had responsibility for reaching decisions. He was as critical of "rabid pro-League enthusiasts" as he was of those who strongly opposed the new organization.

However, in the mid-1920s Coolidge recognized that the League's work had been "unselfish and for the good of humanity" and represented hope for Europe. The United States should "come to terms with the League," because it needed a prosperous Europe and the European states could not reconstruct a peaceful order without harnessing the United States' energies. "Our days as 'the great and good friend of everbody' are over," and the United States, in a spirit of enlightened selfishness, should review its policies on war debts, rehabilitation, the World Court, and the League. But no clear public declaration concerning American participation emerged. At the end of his life, he concluded that Americans were less interested in joining the League than they had been in 1920.[36]

Coolidge thought that the imperialist powers' period of easy predominance would be short, principally because of "the exploding desire for self-government." As a scholarly observer, he recognized the elemental force of both great movements. Travel to Siam in 1889, and above all his visit to the Philippines in 1905, persuaded him of "the revolt of Asia": the Siamese, Filipinos, and Egyptians would press for independence and would seek to transform their countries into strong states, as the Japanese were doing. No question was "of more transcendent importance for the future of mankind than that of the capacity of the Asiatic and African races to work out their own salvation independent of foreign control." Almost a decade before the First World War, he praised the efforts of the French in North Africa, but noted that "the work of more than one generation" would inevitably lead to native self-government and probably independence.[37]

After the war, he recognized even more clearly that colonial peoples, newly conscious of their authority, were unwilling to have others rule them. Democracies such as France and the United States, which were ruling other people by force, were violating the principles on which their own governments rested. The Philippines would become independent of the United States before long, and "we shall hardly know the difference." The British Empire, "perhaps the most wonderful political achievement of

any people," by 1925 was "a menace to world tranquility" because
it controlled a quarter of the area of the world and a fifth of its
population. It also faced the inevitability of home rule: Egypt and
India, among others, were determined to leave. Later, he concluded that the British Commonwealth might survive as a loose
federation of independent states.[38]

The Western states, particularly the great powers, therefore
served as trustees whose role was to help those whom they ruled to
prepare for self-government. William Howard Taft impressed
him in 1905 because Taft accepted the slogan "the Philippines for
the Filipinos" and the American obligation to develop, educate,
and liberate the Filipinos. In fact, before the First World War,
Coolidge wrote: "The answer that the great Western colonizing
nations and modern democracy will give to this sudden impetu-
ous demand is one of the most interesting and gravest questions in
the world today." Colonial empires rested on insecure foundations, and providing good government was not sufficient because
"self-determination when it can be applied ought to come first as
a moral principle." His last letter declared that "what is going to
be the relation of the white man to the colored one in countries
where they both can thrive but not on even terms" is a "tremendous" subject.[39]

Part 3:

Helping Transform Harvard University

6. "Broadening the University's Horizons"

THE HARVARD COLLEGE TO which Coolidge returned as a faculty member in 1893 was much like that from which he had graduated in 1887, little more distinguished, except in age, than any other Eastern institution. Undergraduate life was somewhat primitive, and the university was just installing central heating and running water in the dormitories. Above the basement, some halls lacked central heating and plumbing until 1908. Most college buildings, including the dormitories, were inside the Yard. Some major buildings, particularly Widener Library, had not yet been constructed. In the 1880s, after Eliot gave assurances that the college would build no more undergraduate residence halls, some enterprising businessmen began construction of private dormitories on Mount Auburn Street, a block away from the Yard. These spacious and luxurious structures, which formed the Gold Coast, housed wealthy graduates of preparatory schools, such as Franklin D. Roosevelt, who spent four years in Westmorley Court.[1] Their existence symbolized the caste system and widened the social division. Henry Lee Higginson, who recognized the peril this presented, in 1899 gave the university $150,000 for its Union, which helped for a time to bring the various undergraduate elements together.

Neither the university nor Cambridge was especially exciting or stimulating in 1893. The population of Cambridge was less than 90,000. The subway connecting it with Boston was twenty years in the future. Contact between town and gown hardly existed, even though Harvard Yard was unfenced and the faculty lived within a ten-minute walk from the chapel, with Brattle Street their center.

Before the Civil War, James Russell Lowell saw the city as "essentially an English village," and Henry Adams wrote that "no one took Harvard College seriously." Adams remarked in the

89

1870s that Cambridge was about the dullest place in the world, "a social desert that would have starved a polar bear," and that "society was a faculty meeting without business." In the 1890s, one of Coolidge's students called it "a pleasant little town." A few years later, Norman Hapgood signaled the changes which had occurred in fact and in view, by declaring that he could not imagine "a place intellectually more attractive than Harvard."[2]

Harvard, under Eliot, from 1869 until 1909 was transformed from "an extension of the Back Bay" into a university with international pretensions. In the words of the university's historian, Eliot assisted it to grow "more rapidly and significantly than at any period since its foundation." The faculty, which felt unease and dissatisfaction when Eliot was named president, twenty-five years later rejoiced at his making Harvard a true university and placing it "among the great seats of learning of the world."[3]

Eliot was a clear, confident, forceful Unitarian and a great educational statesman whose dominance over the university was clear from the beginning. Until the 1890s he engaged only in "informal consulting," even with Harvard's most distinguished faculty members, when making new appointments. He concentrated upon the goal outlined in his 1869 inauguration address: "We mean to build here securely and slowly a university in the largest sense." His central concern was quality, and his guides were "liberty and diversity."[4]

Eliot and Eliot's Harvard became known in the history of American higher education for the diversity of the curriculum, the continually increasing freedom and responsibility the undergraduates received, and the university's development into a center for research and training young scholars. A principal instrument for this transformation was the elective system, gradually established in Eliot's first twenty years, which destroyed the tight core of required courses that had dominated undergraduate education at Harvard (and elsewhere throughout the United States) and provided a common culture and a sense of the inheritance of the past. This expensive system, "one of the most creative, and also one of the most destructive educational developments of the post-Civil War years," freed the faculty from routine tasks and allowed it to enrich the curriculum, especially as it pertained to the contemporary world, by adding courses which represented special and even competitive faculty interests. By the time Eliot retired, Harvard offered almost three times as many courses as a quarter century earlier (600 compared to 212) and the greatest variety of any American educational institution.[5]

The elective system raised the sciences and other new disciplines to equality with the established fields of study and led to the expansion and proliferation of departments as knowledge expanded. Above all, it presented Harvard the opportunity to improve the college and to become a genuine university. In the words of Eliot, "The largest effect of the elective system is that it makes scholarship possible, not only among undergraduates but among graduate students and college teachers."[6]

Harvard began to grow rapidly about the time Coolidge joined its faculty. The college enrolled about 1,000 students in 1890. A dozen years later, it had approximately 2,000 undergraduates, and the graduate school attracted some 300 more. When Eliot retired, after forty years as president, the university had about 4,000 students, of whom some 2,200 were in the college. Under Eliot, Harvard gradually raised admission standards and became more cosmopolitan and democratic by attracting students from public and private schools throughout the United States into an "aristocratic meritocracy." By 1909, about a quarter of the undergraduates received scholarships. Forty-seven percent of Harvard students then obtained their preparatory education in private schools, compared to 68 percent at Yale and 78 percent at Princeton. More than half of Harvard's undergraduates in 1912 were from New England, but the college had students from most of the states and from twenty-nine foreign countries as well. It had become a distinguished national and international institution, as well as the fifth largest university in the United States.[7]

Eliot's success in making Harvard a national center of strenuous undergraduate educational change in that age of optimism and expansion was matched by his achievements in raising the quality of the faculty and in creating a place for research and training graduate students. After he had been president fifteen years, only 19 of the 189 faculty members possessed Ph.D. degrees. The number of full professors rose from 66 in 1890 to 142 in 1912, and the total teaching staff from 217 to 774.[8]

Eliot also put his great authority to use by raising salaries, so that private income was no longer a factor for those who were interested in academic careers. Just before he became president, Harvard's financial situation was such that it was "not improbable" that faculty salaries would not be paid in full, yet the faculty raised no great protest. During his presidency, approximately a third of the faculty enjoyed substantial private incomes, from inheritance or marriage or both. Henry Cabot Lodge served without pay for a year in the 1870s and taught the following three years for $1,000 annually. Eliot in his first year raised the salaries of professors to $4,000 per year, assistant professors to $2,000, and tutors to $1,000.* Ten years later Harvard adopted the sabbatical system and established a pension program. Salary figures thereafter remained virtually unchanged for fifty years: the maximum salary in the Faculty of Arts and Sciences in 1919 was $5,500. The range for full professors rose to $6,000-8,000 the following year, when the Harvard endowment was $34 million (it had been $5 million in 1889).[9]

Eliot collected and retained an eminent faculty by emphasizing excellence in every aspect of the university's work. The faculty benefited too from teaching in an institution that was visibly becoming superior in every way and from a relaxed and informal system of administration. The catalogue arranged courses according to department only in Eliot's second year, when the college acquired its first dean and the university established a graduate studies program. This was placed under the graduate school in 1890, in the newly established Faculty of Arts and Sciences. Departments had a rotating chairmanship and held meetings only after 1891, and the faculty did not acquire its room for meetings until 1896.

Eliot emphasized research and publication and gradually dev>ted additional resources to graduate training. He was so successful that by 1900 Harvard, for the first time since 1878, awarded more Ph.D. degrees than its closest rival, Johns Hopkins. By 1904 the national reputation of the university was such that it produced more men with Ph.D.s who were graduates of other colleges than had completed their undergraduate work at Har-

---

*Leo Wiener, who became an outstanding Slavic scholar and linguist, joined the Harvard faculty in 1896 at age thirty-four at an annual salary of $1,000. In 1902, the mean salary for full professors at Harvard was $3,940, for associate professors $3,000, and for assistant professors $2,259. George Santayana, one of Harvard's great philosophers, received $2,000 per year in 1898, after nine years of service. (His room in Hollis, however, cost only $44 a year.) When he was promoted to full professor in 1902, his salary rose to $4,000. Even so, Harvard faculty members enjoyed salaries higher than those in most American colleges and universities. The Carnegie Foundation learned in 1908 that the average salary of a professor in the 100 leading American universities was $2,500, in the range of $1,350 to $4,800. See Carnegie Foundation for the Advancement of Teaching, *The Financial Status of the Professor in America and in Germany* (New York, 1908), p. vi.

vard College. Its progress and the success of other universities in establishing graduate programs produced a decline in the flow of young men to Germany for graduate studies. By the turn of the century, Coolidge and his colleagues urged their graduate students to undertake tours of European institutions, while they were writing their theses or after they obtained their Ph.D. degrees from Harvard, rather than obtain degrees in Germany. In 1909 American universities had 300 graduate students enrolled in history, compared to 30 in 1885.[10]

The new emphasis changed both the character and the attitudes of the university community. Santayana, a disinterested observer, was fascinated by the way each member of the faculty isolated himself so he could concentrate upon academic achievement. He described the faculty as "an anonymous concourse of coral insects, each secreting one cell, and leaving that fossil legacy to enlarge the earth." Twenty years later, Arthur M. Schlesinger, Sr., commented that faculty life in general was cellular, with each scholar maintaining limited relationships with colleagues and jealously guarding his privacy in order to concentrate upon research and writing.[11]

Interest in freedom, excellence, diversity, and nonconformity was so great that Santayana said Harvard was "willing to have any point of view, provided it was represented with distinction and good manners." In 1903, William James, Santayana's colleague in the Department of Philosophy, declared that scholars came to Harvard because "they have heard of her persistently atomistic constitution, of her tolerance of exceptionality and eccentricity, of her devotion to the principles of individual vocation and choice." As if to demonstrate this, when Coolidge inquired of the American minister to Czechoslovakia in November 1926 whether George Vernadsky spoke English well enough to teach at Harvard, he noted: "We do not care very much about his political opinions provided they are not too obtrusive."[12]

The most renowned departments when Harvard began its golden age were philosophy and English, which boasted of distinguished scholars and compelling personalities at a time when individuality was important for establishing a teacher's reputation. The Department of Philosophy included Josiah Royce, George Palmer, and Hugo Munsterberg, as well as James and Santayana. These five reflected the national and international character of Harvard, for they came from Massachusetts, New York, California, Spain, and Prussia. The Department of English included George Pierce Baker, Le Baron Russell Briggs (who was a beloved dean of the Faculty of Arts and Sciences from 1902 to 1925), George Lyman Kittredge, Charles Townsend Copeland, Charles Eliot Norton, Bliss Perry, and Barrett Wendell. Those who achieved special renown as nonconformists acquired famous nicknames; undergraduates referred to Francis J. Child as Stubby, to Copeland as Copey, to Coolidge as Archie, to Charles H. Haskins as Duke, and to Kittredge as Kitty.

The university's reputation for originality, independence, freedom, and the character of its faculty made it "the mecca of the disaffected young men who wanted to write" and help explain the number of literary and social rebels it attracted or produced in the ten or fifteen years before the First World War. These include Malcolm Cowley, Wallace Stevens, T.S. Eliot, E.E. Cummings, John Dos Passos, Eugene O'Neill, John Reed, Walter Lippmann, and Heywood Broun. In fact, almost the entire staff of the *New Republic* in 1914 had graduated from Harvard.[13]

Harvard's rise to preeminence among American universities and the quality of its faculty contributed to the faculty's sense of superiority, an often condescending attitude toward other educational institutions, and admiration for things European, from Plato and Dante and Donne to the French Symbolist poets. Van Wyck Brooks early in the twentieth century learned as an undergraduate that Americanism meant philistinism. Faculty views of Europe and the United States were such that Barrett Wendell's remark to an opening-class session was considered typical: "Gentlemen, this is a course in American letters; there is no American literature." Malcolm Cowley wrote that "the Eastern universities regarded themselves as trading posts beleaguered on the edge of Indian country, where they offered a stock of cultural goods to the younger natives. Almost all the goods had been freighted in from Europe." American literature was not considered respectable until after the 1920s.[14]

Transforming research and instruction in history was more difficult than in most other fields of study because American interest in history, even in history of the United States, was so low; only eleven professors taught history in the United States in 1880. Harvard established its first professorship in history in 1839, and had only one historian on the faculty as late as 1857. In 1875, when Edward Channing applied for a position, Eliot responded that Channing's ambition was "laudable," but he identified "only two colleges in this country within my knowledge where much is made of American history." Four years later, Eliot noted that "the great majority of American colleges ... have no teaching history whatsoever. ... In so old and well-established a college as Dartmouth there is no teacher of history, whether professor, tutor, or temporary instructor; while in so excellent an institution as Princeton there is only one professor of history against three of Greek"[15]

Twenty years before Coolidge joined the faculty, the college engaged three faculty members to teach history: Ephraim Whitman Gurney in classical history, Henry Adams in medieval European and American history, and Henry Warren Torrey in the history of Europe since the seventeenth century. The department began to offer the Ph.D. in 1873, after its members and the president had agreed that it had adequate faculty resources and library facilities for a select number of graduate students in American and West European history, medieval political history, and medieval institutions. Students formed a history club in 1885.

Progress was slow but impressive in quality. The careful national review that Herbert Baxter Adams made in 1885 noted that "Harvard now rivals German universities in the field of history. The American student no longer absolutely needs to go abroad for thorough instruction in European and American history. He can find it in Cambridge, Massachusetts. All the methods which characterize the most advanced history work and all the facilities for special research in libraries that a student could reasonably demand are in existence there."[16]

When Coolidge graduated, the department had five members, all of whom had joined within the previous decade and four of whom had received Ph.D.s in Germany. Charles Gross, who was not a graduate of Harvard College, was the first American historian to make a significant scholarly contribution in European history. Moreover, as Adams noted, Harvard's resources were not limited to the department and the library. The college librarian, Justin Windsor, widely recognized because of the eight-volume *Narrative and Critical History of America* he edited, was elected the second president of the American Historical Association in 1885. John Fiske, William Roscoe Thayer, Charles Francis Adams, James Ford Rhodes, Worthington C. Ford, and George Bancroft were among the able amateur historians who, attracted by Harvard, lived in Boston and Cambridge, and contributed to its reputation in history. Some, like Thayer, declined appointments elsewhere so they could remain in Cambridge. In later years, Bernard de Voto and others followed this tradition.[17]

When Coolidge arrived in September 1893, the Department of History and Roman Law was considered an "adjunct of other studies." The college catalogue first listed courses in history and in government separately in 1892. In fact the department was named the Department of History and Government in 1895 and became a distinct Department of History only in 1911.

Coolidge was appointed to assist Channing in History 1, a freshman course launched in 1879 on the history of Western civilization from the fall of Rome until the French Revolution, and to aid Silas Macvane in History 12, on Europe since the seventeenth century. In March 1894, after he had spent a semester in these two courses and had offered a special section in History 1 for students without knowledge of ancient history, the department assigned him responsibility for History 1, with other members to give approximately twenty lectures on subjects or periods on which they were particularly competent. He concentrated on this course for ten years because he considered it the foundation for all liberal education and a solid core for everyone interested in the origins of his country and in world affairs. He reorganized the course, increased its prestige, and expanded its enrollment. This framework survived at Harvard until after the Second World War and spread throughout the United States. History 1 not only established Coolidge's reputation as an undergraduate teacher, but it also excited in a large number of Harvard undergraduates an enduring interest in history and in reading and even in collecting books.*

In the new system, common for years in departments of history, Coolidge or a colleague lectured twice a week. The class divided once each week into groups of about twenty for brief examinations and map tests and to discuss questions which emerged from the lectures and readings. A carefully selected and instructed senior graduate student directed these sessions. In addition to the quizzes, Coolidge required two one-hour examinations each semester, a demanding three-hour final examination, and term papers. The course emphasized intensive use of

---

*A. Lawrence Lowell, a few years later, launched his career in a similar way, obtaining resounding success in Government 1, the elementary course in constitutional government.

maps, and freshmen purchased and used a famous (but small) German atlas, Friedrich Wilhelm Putzger's *Historischer Schul-Atlas zur alten, mittleren und neueren Geschichte,* or the English translation, published in 1903. Opposed to the use of textbooks, Coolidge required each student to use Ploetz's *Auszug aus der alten, mittleren, neueren und neuesten Geschichte* or the translation which his Harvard library colleague, Tillinghast, had published in 1883. He encouraged undergraduates to read widely from primary sources and from outstanding secondary works in English, French, and German, and he urged students to "go to the books." Many, like Franklin D. Roosevelt, of the class of 1904, whom Coolidge served as freshman adviser and to whom he gave a *B,* had their interest in reading stimulated by his example and by his injunction to use the library, which some called "his cathedral."[18]

To emphasize that the course was introductory and to stimulate students to read, Coolidge provided a bibliography for this course (and for all he taught), identifying interesting books and articles. At the end of the decade during which he directed History 1, its outline and bibliography formed a sixty-page guide, which must have persuaded freshmen that the study of history was a serious enterprise.

Coolidge's success as a teacher was considerable. History 1 enrolled 364 students in 1894 and 526 in 1901, in spite of its reputation for exacting standards, sustained, serious work, and good manners. A faculty committee study in 1902, which reviewed the increasing number of large courses and suggested ways of improving undergraduate teaching, discovered that most students found lecture courses valuable "because they opened large subjects of thought, or because they introduced many students to 'big men' in the faculty or even because they brought a large body of students together." Coolidge's successors with the course (Haskins, Roger B. Merriman, and Michael Karpovich) followed his system faithfully for a half century, throughout which History 1 remained one of the most popular and influential courses in the college.[19]

Coolidge's lectures provided the narrative framework for the course: "knowledge of the narrative is the indispensable foundation for everything else." Whether devoted to feudalism, Napoleon's expedition to Egypt, or the First Balkan Wars, they furnished historical and geographical perspective as well as factual information. He was deeply conscientious, introducing the results of recent research into his talks and never missing a class. His lectures tended to be factual and dry, but they were "thorough, exacting, and inspiring" and provided an admirable synthesis for the subjects. The class notes and bluebooks of his students (in the Harvard University Archives) reveal that his students were attentive.

Reserved and modest, Coolidge projected such a forceful style and authoritative presence that the Harvard *Lampoon*, the undergraduate humor magazine, published a burlesque of a lecture, caricaturing him as an educational Napoleon—a rotund figure, five feet six inches in height but imperious and forbidding in manner, perhaps calculated to conceal his shyness, so the caricature was accurate. He spoke with a lisp, could not pronounce the initial *r* in any word clearly, and talked with a rising intonation at the end of each sentence. These defects (if they were such) helped to rivet students' attention and give Coolidge some of the distinct character students expected of faculty members. Above all, he possessed the secret of exciting an urge to learn and opening vistas for further study.

Coolidge participated in sessions at the 1898 and 1901 meetings of the American Historical Association devoted to the introductory college history course. His vivid description of the course, its organization, and system of instruction therefore reached fellow historians through the national organization. The early recognition he won in the profession derived from his teaching.[20]

Throughout his career at Harvard, but in his first twenty years in particular, Coolidge devoted himself to undergraduate students, especially those who lived in his residence hall. He got along well with all kinds of people, but especially students. Lonely freshmen, and anyone who wished to share a late-evening beer while discussing history or international affairs, found his suites in Ware 15 and Randolph 4 (during his first five years and from 1898 through 1921) a kind of open house. Letters indicate he often invited one or two undergraduates for dinner. Long walks around Cambridge, with students interested in academic careers or the diplomatic service, particularly along the Charles River, were a special pleasure. His report for the twenty-fifth reunion of his Harvard class noted that he was an active member of "several undergraduate organizations." In a sense, dormitory life provided the relaxed warmth he had missed at home. As one student recognized, he was an informal house master, and almost became

a Mr. Chips. He never attained the legendary acclaim of Copeland, who carefully staged readings in his rooms in Hollis, but his
relations with students during his first two decades were very
close.[21]

A member of a prominent Boston family and an outstanding
student, aware that he was one of "the happy few," Coolidge had
joined the "best clubs" when he was an undergraduate. As a
member of the faculty, he helped undergraduates establish new
clubs and expand the system to those who could not obtain
admission to the ancient ones. During his first years as a faculty
member he was known as "the King of Clubs."[22]

Coolidge employed needy or interested undergraduates as
library aides and secretaries, and often engaged an undergraduate
or graduate student as an assistant or secretary when he traveled.
For example, Theodore F. Jones, who graduated from Harvard in
1906, wrote his thesis under Coolidge, and became professor of
history and director of the New York University Library on
University Heights, served as an assistant and secretary when
Coolidge was a visiting professor in France in 1906 and 1907.
Clarence L. Hay traveled with Coolidge to the Iberian Peninsula
and in South America the following year. Franklin Eddy Parker,
Jr., later an eminent New York lawyer, accompanied Coolidge to
northern Europe and Russia in 1918 on the mission for the War
Trade Board; to Vienna and Paris in 1919, when Coolidge served
the American Commission to Negotiate Peace; and to the Soviet
Union in 1921 and 1922, when Coolidge joined the American
Relief Administration. Two graduate students who later attained
distinction, Dexter Perkins and Robert J. Kerner, also served as
aides. Perkins accompanied Coolidge in 1912 on a trip through
northern Africa, and Kerner was his secretary during his visiting
professorship in Berlin in the winter of 1913-14.[23]

The construction and administration of Randolph Hall,
"the best of the private dormitories on the Gold Coast," illustrate
his interest in undergraduates and student life. Four Coolidge
brothers provided the capital for the 1898 venture. Randolph was
the architect, Harold the lawyer and financier, and Archie the
proctor. The dormitory was so attractive to students who could
afford luxury that the Coolidges enlarged it in 1908. After the
college began construction of more dormitories in 1912, Randolph lost its lure, and the brothers in 1916 sold it at half its
construction cost to the college, which in the 1930s made it part of
Adams House.[24]

All college affairs attracted him, from planting trees in the Yard to joining a group that kept the administration from building an unattractive fence around the Yard in 1900. In 1908, with other alumni, he contributed to the purchase of property between the Yard and the Charles River for later university use. This helped provide the land for the residential Houses that Lowell erected. He helped ensure that Widener Library face inward, to make the Yard a "park-like enclosure," to increase the sense of unity within the college, and to isolate the college (in a sense) from the outside world.[25]

Coolidge was an active member of the Committee on the Regulation of Athletic Sports from 1899 through 1905, a critical period because of the national wave of criticism of football, and served as chairman during the last year. Interested in improving the athletic plant, he helped arrange construction of the Newell Boat House and the stadium, as well as improve Soldiers' Field— then as now the main recreational area for undergraduates. He even accompanied the Harvard crew to New London and Poughkeepsie for the annual races from 1895 through 1898. He resented the "gentlemanly indifference" with which Harvard teams consistently lost, and he fought to instill a winning spirit. A supporter of professional instruction of undergraduates interested in sports, as of able teaching in any field, he nevertheless opposed the use of paid coaches, so that the teams would not become "an obedient tool of a highly-paid professional."

The department that Coolidge joined in 1893 offered only one course on modern European history, none on other parts of the world except Europe and the United States, and "no very clearly defined seminary work." Coolidge, convinced that every educated man should "know something at least about every other country in the world," concentrated on revising "the Anglo-Saxon view of the world" and pressed for instruction, then research, in many fields of historical inquiry, particularly those about peoples beyond the United States and western Europe.[26] He also dreamed of bringing together a group of outstanding scholar-teachers who would make Harvard the premier school for history in the United States and then in the world. This would help make Harvard a great university in every way, his ultimate goal.

One can appreciate the magnitude of his achievement in helping widen the horizons of Harvard, and then other institutions, by measuring the reluctance or opposition with which the historical profession met his efforts. The American Historical Association annual meeting in 1911 devoted a session to discussing whether European history was an acceptable field of study for American historians. Coolidge admitted the difficulties in obtaining materials and mastering the necessary languages for research and training on Europe, but pointed out the compensations and stimulation such work provided, particularly in new insights into American history. His advocacy concluded in typical fashion by noting that the United States owed a debt to others for their historical scholarship and should accept some responsibility for expanding knowledge of the history of Europe, of which it was a part.*

Coolidge, no parliamentarian, was not notably effective in faculty meetings, which he attended assiduously during his first few years but seldom during the last two decades. He was rarely active in meetings, often writing checks or reading correspondence while others orated. He was chairman of the department less than three years and never served as a dean. Even so, he was remarkably successful in helping to reshape the department, the college, and the university.

Fortunate circumstances within Harvard and his determination and skills helped make Coolidge an effective pioneer, and the small department provided a friendly atmosphere. Most of his colleagues had also studied and traveled in Europe. For example, the two senior members in American history, Hart and Channing, were far from parochial in training and interests. Hart obtained his Ph.D. in Freiburg and also studied in Paris, Berlin, and Vienna, and Channing toured Europe for a year after obtaining his Ph.D. at Harvard. They supported, or at least tolerated, his efforts because they recognized the need for enlarging and revising the curriculum. Even so, Hart's 1898 article in the *American Historical Review*, on "The Historical Opportunity in America," discussed only American history.

Even after Harvard grew in size, it remained a small institution, in which a man with Coolidge's family connections, lively nature, quality of mind and judgment, and energy could

---

*Three years after Coolidge's death, the American Historical Association Committee on the Planning of Research, chaired by Arthur M. Schlesinger, Sr., a member of the Harvard Department, and including two former Coolidge students, noted that "productive scholarship in the United States is concerned primarily with American history." *Historical Scholarship in America: Needs and Opportunities* (New York, 1932), p. vi.

exercise great influence. Throughout his years at Harvard, when the president not only retained final authority but often exercised the initiative on faculty appointments, Coolidge enjoyed close relations with Eliot and Lowell (who was a third cousin). Both encouraged him in every way. Eliot in particular shared his views, allowed him great responsibility, and supported him and those like him who sought to strengthen Harvard. Coolidge's authority was such that he occasionally made initial inquiries and even issued offers of appointment, within and beyond the Department of History, as though he were dean of the faculty. Above all, of course, the Eliot system of electives, the expansion of Harvard, and the determination of both Eliot and Lowell to make Harvard a great university provided ideal circumstances.

Finally, Coolidge showed shrewdness and ingenuity and used his own financial resources. He succeeded in transforming the department and the college, in part because his colleagues appreciated that he was interested in the entire university, not in promoting personal concerns. He was willing to undertake much of the work himself. Harvard added some new fields of study and appointments because he guaranteed the salaries for the first few years for some of those who joined the faculty. Working within the departmental framework, rather than trying to create new organizational arrangements, was essential wisdom, as was his concentration upon practical, visible goals and his leaving revision of colleagues' views to the changed atmosphere the new faculty helped to create and to the processes of time.

The initial step was enlarging the instructional program, first within the Department of History and then in other departments. Coolidge's first interest, a major one throughout his academic life, was expanding instruction and research on the history of Russia, on which he offered the first undergraduate course and first provided graduate instruction in the United States. The effort to transform the curriculum began when he obtained permission in the spring of 1894 to offer a one-semester course, History 15, on the history of northeastern Europe (defined as Denmark, Sweden, Poland, and Russia) from 1453 to 1795. This course, which met three times a week, was soon supplemented by History 25 for graduate students, which met once a week. In 1908, History 15 became a full-year offering and changed its title to "History of Russia." It remained the basic Russian history course at Harvard until after the Second World War. Even though his concern was with contemporary international politics, Coolidge emphasized the medieval and early modern periods because he was convinced of the need to understand the foundations of Russian history. He stressed the conflict between western Christianity and Orthodoxy and between the Germans and the Slavs, paying special attention to the Hanseatic League, trade, and the Baltic provinces.

In 1896 Coolidge offered the first course in the United States on the history of the Eastern Question, which alternated each year with the history of Russia. History 19, which began with Herodotus and the Punic Wars and which he continually revised and brought up to date, included a good deal of Asian history because of the role Turks and other Moslems played in Central Asia and East Asia. This became perhaps his most popular course, and it was one he gave most often, probably because of the fascination the Eastern Question, "as old as history," forever exercised upon him and because of his conviction that its study illuminated the entire history of Europe. History 19 attracted a number of young men into history as a profession. Many diplomats, including Joseph Clark Grew and William R. Castle, Jr., indicated that it influenced them to join the diplomatic service.[27]

The following year, Coolidge introduced History 20, European diplomatic history, and presented his first seminar. Three years later, he added an advanced course on this subject for graduate students, "Principles of Foreign Policy in Modern European History." European diplomatic history attracted his increasing attention because of the constant diplomatic crises that marked his time. He exercised profound influence upon American teaching and research in this field of study, through his own writings and those of men he helped train, particularly William L. Langer and Sidney B. Fay.

In 1904 Coolidge surrendered responsibility for History 1 to Haskins, because he wanted to concentrate upon enlarging the curriculum, training graduate students, and finding faculty for neglected areas. However, for the remainder of his career he presented the lectures in History 1 on the period since 1871, which constituted the last three or four weeks of the course. In 1904 he introduced still another course, History 30a, "The Expansion of Europe since 1815," with a related course specially designed for graduate students. Five years later, after devoting his sabbatical to a third trip around the world, he launched History 18, "The Far East in the Nineteenth Century," which he gave every two or three years and which introduced the study of Asia into the Harvard curriculum. Finally, after his return from the Paris Peace Conference, he instituted History 30b, "Europe from 1871 through 1914." Under Coolidge and Langer, who later taught it, this course became the most popular advanced undergraduate course in history at Harvard in the two decades before the Second World War.[28]

Comparing the Department of History in 1893 with the department two decades later reveals the magnitude of the achievements of Coolidge and his colleagues in transforming the department's character and curriculum. In 1893 the department offered Ph.D. degrees in three fields of history; by 1915 it had expanded to fifteen areas, including Russia and Eastern Europe, Europe since 1789, Spain, England, France, Germany, and Latin America, all due largely to Coolidge's efforts. Above all, new appointments he pressed and often financed gave the department the quality and breadth of interest which ensured its rise to distinction, and led other colleges and universities to introduce instruction on areas of the world and periods previously neglected.

Coolidge's first interest and primary concern was Russian history, and his second was modern European history. However, these were only parts of his vision of "broadening the university's horizons." In 1907, he persuaded Eliot to strengthen Harvard's resources in ancient Greek history by appointing William Scott Ferguson; in fact, Coolidge almost certainly paid Ferguson's salary during the latter's first five years on the faculty. He contributed more than anyone else to add instruction on Spain and Latin America to the curriculum. In 1902, he persuaded Eliot to add Spanish history and to appoint Roger B. Merriman, of the class of 1896, who had been an undergraduate student of his and whom he had encouraged to continue study in Germany and at Oxford University. Merriman was attracted to the study of history as a sophomore by Coolidge's "passion for disinterested research, his disciplined scholarship, and his high conception of his chosen profession."[29] Merriman's thesis at Oxford in 1902, and his first major work, was *The Life and Letters of Thomas Cromwell*, but the dramatic battles of 1898 and the rise and fall of empires captivated him, as they had Coolidge, and Merriman then devoted his scholarly career to Spanish history. In 1903 he presented the first course at Harvard on the history of Spain, and in 1914 the first seminar on Latin American history. Like Coolidge, Merriman was "a historian's historian." In the words of his most eminent student, Garrett Mattingly, "It would be hard to name many historical works written in our time which equal *The Rise of the Spanish Empire* in the combination of breadth, boldness, and symmetry of plan with the most patient, detailed critical scholarship in execution."[30] These four volumes, Merriman's powers as a teacher of History 1 and of Spanish history, and the imperial style in which he presided as master of Eliot House helped make him one of the towers of the Department of History and of Harvard until his death in 1945.

Merriman had no particular scholarly interest in Latin America, and Harvard delayed expanding its instructional and library programs in that area until Coolidge was certain that his student, Hiram Bingham, Latin American curator from 1903 until he went to Yale in 1908, was not going to direct Yale University into Latin American studies. He then launched a careful drive to create a strong library on Latin America and to begin instruction in Latin American history. With the assistance of Ambassador Edwin V. Morgan, a friend and former graduate student, he persuaded Robert Woods Bliss, a student of his in the class of 1900, to give $125,000 for a chair in Latin American history and economics. Coolidge first secured the appointment of one of his outstanding students, Julius Klein, who received his Ph.D. in 1915, and then arranged for visiting professors from Latin American countries. Harvard then appointed a man he believed appropriate, Clarence Haring, who had worked as a discussion leader with Coolidge in History 1, had obtained his advanced degree at Oxford, and had taught at Clark University for ten years. Haring helped make Harvard a center in Latin American studies, although the university's achievements in this area have been modest.[31]

Coolidge had a special concern with Asia, which attracted much attention in Cambridge and Boston because of nineteenth-century trade, missionary activity in China, and excitement about Chinese and Japanese art, which the Museum of Fine Arts demonstrated as early as the 1870s. Mrs. Jack Gardner was particularly interested in Japanese art, which was strongly represented in her collection in Fenway Court. The commercial and art interests together persuaded the university to begin instruction in Chinese in 1879, but this lasted only three years.

A program Coolidge chaired at the American Historical Association's convention in 1907 urged increased attention to

Oriental history and politics, and he was one of the founders of the East Asian Society in Boston that same year. In 1909 he introduced the first course at Harvard on Asian history, and he vigorously advocated a university course on Chinese and Japanese art in 1914 and 1915, "probably the first formal course in Eastern art at an American university," which survived only two years. In 1921 he was embarrassed to teach Asian history, "but it seemed to me so shameful that Harvard should not have some instruction that I have filled the place as best I could." His will left Harvard funds for a chair "in modern European or Asiatic history."[32]

In 1923 Coolidge obtained funds from plumbing magnate Charles R. Crane for a five-year lectureship in Asian history. Unsuccessful in persuading Stanley K. Hornbeck to accept the position, rather than join the Department of State, he arranged temporary appointments, as he had earlier in Latin American history. Beginning in 1925, he participated in a series of meetings that led to establishment of the Harvard-Yenching Institute three years later. In 1927, after gradually enlarging the library collection on China and Japan to 6,000 volumes in Western languages, he appointed a special librarian for that field. These steps created the foundations on which John K. Fairbank and Edwin Reischauer built when they joined the Harvard faculty in 1937. Fairbank that year revived the course on Asian history. Two years later, he and Reischauer began their celebrated full-year course on the history of East Asian civilization, which has had profound influence at Harvard and throughout the United States. In short, as a review of Asian studies at Harvard made clear in 1976, "the beginnings of instruction in the history of East Asia can be traced to one man, Archibald Cary Coolidge."[33]

Coolidge's interests were not restricted to areas beyond the United States. Thus Lowell agreed that Coolidge no longer need serve on university committees when he became director of the Harvard University Library in 1910. However, he became an active member of the Committee on Degrees in History and Literature, established in 1911 to promote study by undergraduates in those related fields. Convinced that American history as taught at Harvard had an East Coast emphasis and neglected the West, he induced Lowell in 1909 to add a position in Far Western history by offering to pay the salary of Frederick Jackson Turner through 1915. He then persuaded Turner to leave the University of Wisconsin for Harvard.[34]

Coolidge introduced the study of Russian and other histories and of Slavic languages and literatures at Harvard at both the undergraduate and graduate levels. The base he created was sound because he recognized the proper priorities, beginning with undergraduate education, foreign-language instruction, faculty resources, and a library, before he launched a graduate program. He also emphasized the critical importance of historical roots, starting with Byzantium for Russia, and he placed the study of all histories in an international framework. One of his last letters, written to Sir Bernard Pares on December 2, 1927, noted proudly that Harvard that fall listed nineteen one-semester courses on Russia, taught by nine different faculty members. In 1928, Harvard's combination of faculty, program, and library re-sources, all of high quality, made it the largest and most important institution in the United States for research and instruction concerning Russia and other peoples and areas that had been utterly neglected thirty-five years earlier.

Coolidge's teaching, of course, launched this process, and the next advance came in 1910, when he became director of the library and persuaded Lowell to appoint Lord, who had just completed his Ph.D. work to teach the Russian history course Coolidge had had to abandon and to add a new one on German history. The son of an Illinois country doctor, Lord graduated from Harvard in 1906. He spent 1908 to 1910 in Vienna, Berlin, Warsaw, and Moscow on his thesis: a study of Austrian policy and the second partition of Poland, published in 1915, and published again in Polish translation in Warsaw in 1973. Lord, a brilliant man of enormous knowledge and an astute and demanding director of graduate students, who was "admired, not loved," became the outstanding American scholar on Poland and helped train many others in Russian and Polish history.

Lord was Coolidge's deputy on The Inquiry and occupied an important position in the American delegation at the Paris Peace Conference, where he was chief of the Division of Polish Affairs and President Woodrow Wilson's principal adviser on Polish issues. He was a member of the Commission on Polish Affairs and of every major committee that dealt with Polish problems in 1919. It is "generally conceded that he worked out most of the boundaries eventually assigned to Poland by the Peace Confer-ence." A strong Wilsonian, a fervent believer in self-determin-ation, a firm opponent of Prussian and German militarism, and a militant supporter of the League of Nations, Lord was also an ardent defender of Polish interests. Unlike Coolidge, he took strong partisan positions. Thus he opposed a plebiscite in Upper Silesia because he believed the Germans would win, but he endorsed one in East Prussia, where he was convinced the Poles would triumph.[35]

In the winter of 1926–27, when Lord decided to become a Catholic priest, Coolidge helped make the senior appointment that ensured superior instruction in Russian history at Harvard for the next thirty years. After learning that George Vernadsky did not speak English well, he invited Michael Karpovich to Harvard for the spring semester of 1927 to substitute for Lord. Karpovich, who came to the United States in 1917 as the secretary of Boris A. Bakhmetev, ambassador of the Provisional Government of Russia, had taken graduate work in Moscow and St. Petersburg but had not completed his degree. During the war he met one of Coolidge's students, Golder, in Petrograd. Karpovich became acquainted with Coolidge in the fall of 1917 in Washington, and Coolidge arranged that he lecture in the spring of 1918 on the situation in Russia.

Coolidge in 1926 wrote that Karpovich "is not Lord, but he is not unpromising." From the beginning of his service at Harvard as a tutor, then as successor to Haskins and Merriman (in charge of History 1), and later as the faculty member responsible for Russian history, Karpovich exerted profound influence. He directed more than thirty Ph.D. theses in Russian history, including many by men who became leading scholars in every part of the United States. His work for the Russian Student Fund, the Humanities Fund, and the Chekhov Publishing Company helped hundreds of exiles from Russia, just as his editorship of *Novyi Zhurnal* from 1941 until 1956 created a bridge between generations of Russians who came to the United States and between American and Russian culture. A humanistic liberal, Karpovich possessed many of the same qualities as Coolidge, particularly the dispassionate view of history and of other peoples and cultures. Until after the Second World War, he refused to teach the history of Russia after 1917, because he believed he could not view it fairly.[36]

When Coolidge died in January 1928, the university appointed his most brilliant student, Langer, who had substituted for him on occasion and whom Coolidge admired greatly and considered "rather raw-boned and aggressive," to his position in the Department of History. Fay, another Coolidge student, joined

Harvard in 1929 to teach Lord's course in German history. Thus, directly and indirectly, Coolidge helped give Harvard the great strength in Russian and modern diplomatic history that had been one of his goals.

Langer's influence proved deep and profound. A member of the class of 1915 who had taken no history as an undergraduate, he obtained his Ph.D. in 1923, after study in Leipzig and Vienna and travel throughout Europe, particularly in the Balkans. Interested primarily in modern diplomatic history and a traveler in the 1920s (as Coolidge was throughout his life), Langer learned Russian at Coolidge's insistence. Indeed, until Karpovich was appointed to replace Lord, Langer hoped for the appointment in Russian history. He continued Coolidge's European diplomatic history course as well as that on the Eastern Question. After the Second World War, he cooperated with two colleagues to expand the latter into a full-year course. A truly great historian, Langer was the outstanding scholar of European diplomatic history on the thirty years before the First World War. With Everett Gleason, he later described, with equal care, the background of America's entrance into the Second World War. His many important contributions include the twenty-volume *Rise of Modern Europe*, which he edited, and which at the time he died (in 1977) had an average sale of 50,000 copies per volume, largely to faculty members and students.

Langer possessed the same intellectual qualities as Coolidge, and his range of interests, and asserted that his "whole career hinged on this man." He provided graduate students rigorous intellectual training and stimulated their highest abilities on the subjects of their choosing. His lectures and publications on modern European history provided the same clear "tour of the horizon" as Coolidge's, and colleagues noted that Langer ended sentences with the same rising inflection as Coolidge. He added a strong concern for economic, social, intellectual, and cultural history. Like Coolidge, Langer trained young men and women in new fields of study to teach throughout the country. He also served the United States government effectively during crisis, in his case in the Second World War and the Korean War.[37]

Coolidge was intensely interested in contemporary affairs, but he understood the importance of religion and of the age-old religious differences that separated Russia from its Western neighbors. He therefore urged and assisted the university to make two important appointments in 1920. One brought George

LaPiana from Italy to the Department of History and the Divinity School, in which he gave courses on the history of the Greek Orthodox Church. The other was in Byzantine history, which many American historians consider exotic even in the 1980s but which Coolidge judged essential even before the First World War. In this appointment, which brought Robert Blake into the faculty, first as a tutor and ultimately as professor of history and Coolidge's successor as director of the Harvard University Library, Coolidge showed his usual foresight and resolution.

Blake graduated in 1908 from the University of California at Berkeley, where one of Coolidge's closest friends, Henry Morse Stephens, encouraged him to continue at Harvard.[38] He mastered twelve languages, and on occasion taught Georgian and Armenian. Coolidge persuaded Blake to combine these skills and interest in early history to pioneer in Byzantine and early Slavic history. He even brought Charles Diehl, the outstanding Byzantine scholar, from Paris as a visiting professor in the fall of 1911 to assist in Blake's instruction. At Coolidge's suggestion, Blake went to Coolidge's institutions in Germany, Freiburg and Berlin, and spent a year in St. Petersburg with Michael Rostovtsev. After obtaining his Ph.D. in 1916, he returned to Russia and spent four years in Petrograd and Tbilisi before joining the Harvard faculty in Byzantine, medieval Slavic, and Near Eastern history. An immensely learned man, Blake became the first American specialist in Byzantine studies, and also helped launch scholarly work on Ottoman history. He built the base on which Harvard's eminence in Byzantine studies rests, not only in Cambridge but also in the Center for Byzantine Studies at Dumbarton Oaks in Washington.[39]

From the time he began his career at Harvard, Coolidge sought funds for an appointment in Slavic languages and literatures and a competent instructor. He published his translations of Russian poetry in January 1895 to persuade Harvard alumni that the university should begin instruction in Slavic languages and literatures. In 1896 he located Leo Wiener, "a nonacademic scholar of arresting mental alertness," persuaded his uncle, John Lowell Gardner, to contribute Wiener's salary of $1,000 annually from 1896 through 1900, and persuaded the corporation to appoint him. This appointment, the first in Slavic languages and literatures in the United States, launched Wiener's Harvard career, which lasted thirty-five years and gave the university high-quality instruction and continuity in Slavic languages. Gardner died shortly after he made the agreement, so Coolidge, his father, and friends paid Wiener's salary until 1904, when the corporation assumed it. In 1898 Wiener received funds from Coolidge for a summer trip through Europe, the Balkans, and European Russia to advance his research and to purchase books.[40]

Wiener was a remarkable man and a great philologist. Born in Bialystok in 1862, he arrived in New Orleans in 1880 with fifty cents. After he tried to establish a Fourierist colony in Louisiana, he taught in a high school in Kansas City and then at the University of Missouri. He came to Boston in 1895 with his wife and son, Norbert, the future genius in cybernetics. When Coolidge discovered him, he was engaged in part-time occupations at the New England Conservatory, Boston University, and the Boston Public Library; he also worked on the Merriam-Webster dictionary and as a translator of ballads from Czech for Child, and was publishing scholarly articles on philology. Wiener first undertook to catalogue Slavic books and pamphlets that Coolidge had purchased in Leipzig (and given to the library) and to teach him Polish.

A "prodigiously learned man" of rare linguistic ability, whom Coolidge considered a "Russian Irishman," Wiener was an "essentially quarrelsome man" in "a state of active warfare with others in his profession." He was about as different from Vladimir Nabokov's celebrated teacher of Russian, the pathetic yet dignified Pnin, as a mortal could be. Small (only five feet, three inches tall), alert, and impatient, and a scholar by nature rather than by training, Wiener introduced instruction and research in Slavic languages and literatures and, at the same time, published an astonishing number of works in a variety of fields. He knew forty languages and taught Russian, Polish, Old Church Slavonic, Czech, Bulgarian, Serbo-Croatian, Slavic philology, and popular courses on Russian literature (in translation). He helped build Harvard's Slavic and Yiddish collections. Within twenty-four months, he translated and published the works of Leo Tolstoy in twenty-four volumes for an honorarium of $10,000, ten times his annual salary from Harvard at that time. These translations were reprinted almost seventy years later.[41]

Wiener's interest in things Slavic declined after the First World War. Before Wiener's retirement in 1930, Coolidge in January 1927 arranged the appointment and paid the salary of Wiener's most brilliant pupil, Samuel H. Cross, a specialist in

Slavic philology and medieval literature, who was especially attractive because he "had done many things and lived in many places." A Harvard graduate in 1912, Cross received his Ph.D. in German literature in 1916, after studying in Graz, Freiburg, Berlin, and St. Petersburg. He taught German briefly at Western Reserve University, before spending three years in the army. After working six years as commercial attaché in Brussels and The Hague and as chief of the European Division of the Bureau of Foreign and Domestic Commerce in Washington, he entered business in Boston and continued research on medieval chronicles in the evenings,until Coolidge persuaded him to begin his career at Harvard with a history of the western Slavs.

Cross served originally as an instructor in German and was chairman of the Department of Germanic Languages and Literatures from 1935 to 1939. He continued the work that Coolidge and Wiener had begun at a time when only nine American universities taught Russian. (Twenty-one had done so at the end of the First World War.) He enlarged the group that taught Russian at Harvard, particularly by adding Ernest J. Simmons to the faculty in 1930, after Simmons had studied two years in Moscow. An extremely able scholar in medieval Russian literature, Cross also helped create the basic national organizations that serve those interested in Slavic languages and literatures and Slavic studies in general.[42]

Coolidge was one of the founders of Harvard's Bureau of International Research, established in October 1924 to foster research "of an international character in the social sciences." One of the first research centers in the social sciences and humanities, it helped provide support for research by Langer and other Coolidge students, as well as other Harvard faculty members (particularly Bruce Hopper, Merle Fainsod, and Timothy A. Taracouzio), on the Soviet Union. Coolidge was most responsible for the bureau's first grant ($50,000 from the Laura Spelman Rockefeller Memorial Foundation for five years) and was an active committee member of the bureau until he died. He played the same role when the university established the Harvard University Press in 1913, and served as a syndic of the press until his death.[43]

Establishment of the Harvard Graduate School of Business Administration also owes something to Coolidge. Impressed in the 1890s by the École des Sciences Politiques, he encouraged such graduate students as Dexter Perkins and Samuel Eliot Morison and such future diplomats as Franklin M. Gunther and Leland Harrison to attend the Paris institution. In 1899 he proposed that Harvard establish a School of Political Science and Administration to help train diplomats, consular officials, and officers for administration of America's new empire. John W. Burgess, similarly influenced by the Paris institution, succeeded in establishing a School of Political Science at Columbia University, but Eliot rejected Coolidge's suggestion. Coolidge advanced it again, through the Faculty of Arts and Sciences, in 1906, but Eliot thought such a graduate school too narrow and restrictive. Moreover, replacement of the personal and family responsibility of the old hereditary firm by "corporate selfishness" had persuaded him that the university should instead begin professional education for businessmen. He and the Harvard Corporation in March 1908 created the Graduate School of Business Administration. Coolidge was consoled; his close friend Gay served as the school's first dean from 1908 until 1919.[44]

Coolidge was convinced that Harvard professors should travel to improve their knowlege and understanding and to advance the reputation of Harvard abroad. In 1904 he helped persuade James Hazen Hyde (of the class of 1898), president of Equitable Life Insurance Company, to finance an annual Harvard visiting professorship at the Sorbonne and in several French provincial universities. Hyde, who worked with Coolidge as an undergraduate in the Cercle Français, and who even then granted the university money for books and for bringing French scholars to Harvard, lived in France after 1905 and supported this program until the Second World War. Coolidge in 1906 and 1907 was the third participant in the series, following Wendell and Santayana. He also taught at Berlin in the winter term of 1913–14, and may be the only American scholar who has taught in both these cities.[45]

Bringing distinguished foreign scholars to Cambridge as visiting professors to "increase the fresh air" and stimulate the faculty concerning ideas and techniques appearing elsewhere was another Coolidge tactic. Those whom he helped attract included Diehl, in 1911 and again in 1917; Josef Redlich of Vienna, who visited in 1910 and again in 1922; Father Aurelio Palmieri from Italy just before the First World War; H.W.V. Temperley, Harold Laski, Graham Wallas, George Trevelyan, and G.K. Webster from England at various times; Alfred Pribram of Vienna in 1927 and 1928; Manoel de Oliveiro Lima from Brazil in 1915 and Ernesto Quesada from Argentina in 1917; and Anatole Leroy-

Beaulieu, André Tardieu, René Doumic, Henri Lichtenberger, Abbé Ernest Dimnet, and Louis Aubert from France on different occasions between 1904 and 1922. All these men helped provide Harvard faculty and students some of the knowledge and insights Coolidge thought essential and returned home impressed by Harvard's qualities. Above all, they helped win recognition for Harvard abroad and placed the university in an appropriate international setting. They thereby assisted in the emergence of Harvard as a national leader of educational advance and its transformation from a small New England college into a research and instructional center with a deserved worldwide reputation.[46]

7. "Civilization's Diary":
The Center of the Great University

BOOKS FASCINATED COOLIDGE. Book stores everywhere attracted his careful study. Throughout his career, browsing among new books or examining volumes on subjects in which he was interested provided special pleasure and stimulated ideas and inspiration. Whether in Tomsk or in Budapest, he visited the library to examine its physical plant, collections, and catalogue system. The differences his early travels in Europe revealed between the Bibliothèque Nationale, the Prussian State Library in Berlin, and the crowded old library in the Yard led him to concentrate on that part of Harvard's foundations as soon as he joined the faculty. Growing interest in other peoples and in international affairs increased his determination to expand the university's book collection.

On a trip around the world in 1906 he wrote long letters from Calcutta and Bombay to Haskins about his vision of a great Harvard library, with detailed comments on more than a dozen areas on which the university should make "a respectable showing." He outlined steps the library should take (at his expense) to enlarge its French collection and reorganize its classification system, "a harmless, if futile, whim."[1] From the time he was appointed at Harvard but especially after 1910 when he became director of the library, it was a central cause. For him, a library was "not a charnel house filled with the bones of dead ideas, but rather a garden in which they might be made to germinate and grow and bear fruit, each after its kind."[2] The library was always in his mind, whether he was in Cracow or in Kenya, and he lavished energy, funds, and creativity upon it. Some colleagues observed that it occupied the place that families filled in their lives and that they might properly term it "the Harvard Coolidge Library." When Harvard awarded him an honorary degree in 1916, President Lowell declared that "every colleague owes [him] a debt of gratitude as foremost among living administrators of libraries for scholars."

In his view, every library's first and most basic problem was to define its public and to meet its readers' needs in space, facilities, staff, and collection. Earlier than most scholar-librarians, he realized that each library has a different purpose from every other library and that these goals constantly change. For an educational institution with aspirations for eminence, the library was the indispensable base. While "a library does not make a university, a great university today cannot exist without a good library of its own or within reach."[3]

His studies persuaded him that Harvard enjoyed a splendid opportunity to emerge as *the* university in the United States and to become one "with the great schools of the old world." Ambitions for Harvard and its library were especially high because "more is expected of the first university in America. It is there that every man should naturally turn first." Harvard must therefore accept the leadership and burden of greatness in library collections as well as in faculty and establish standards for other American universities to follow.[4] At the dedication on June 24, 1915 of Widener Library, Coolidge defined his goals: "We aim to make the library the glory of Harvard, to have it add to the fame and the influence of the university." He went on—to hope that "the ever increasing value of its collections and the opportunities for the use of them will draw scholars from near and far and send them back enthusiastic over what they have found and grateful to the name of Harvard."[5]

When Lowell became president in 1909 the library constituted a critical problem. Moreover, Lowell had learned as a member of the faculty that the then librarian, William Coolidge Lane, a gentle, courteous, and neat antiquarian, lacked vision, force, and influence with the faculty to direct the necessary changes. The system was thoroughly disorganized, and though central in theory, had little influence over the eleven department and school libraries. The main building, Gore, was so crowded, even in 1894, that 15,000 volumes were stored in the basement of the chapel. At the turn of the century, Eliot considered discarding infrequently used volumes, rather than seek space and money for storage. In 1910 the library had 543,000 volumes, crammed in every corner of the building, and 50,000 volumes were stored elsewhere. The faculty had no studies, the library provided no reading rooms for undergraduate or graduate students, and the stacks constituted a serious fire hazard.

The classification system and the catalogue represented even more serious problems. Several systems of cataloguing had developed since the Civil War, but the library had no university union catalogue. Coolidge estimated that at least 75,000 volumes were not in the public catalogue and that 200,000 were unclassified or defectively classified. The subject catalogue was disorganized and fundamentally useless. The library cards were smaller than those that the Library of Congress and the John Crerar Library had adopted in 1901 and that were becoming standard throughout the country. Thus the library needed a unified system of classification and cataloguing, a gigantic program to catalogue or recatalogue thousands of volumes, and a mammoth effort to convert its library cards into the same size as those of the Library of Congress.[6]

The book collection, Coolidge's principal concern, had tripled in thirty-five years. Still, the library in 1910 had only $31,500 for purchasing and binding books, of which the university contributed only $18,000. Moreover, the total expended for administration was about $80,000, of which less than $25,000 was for salaries. The Boston Public Library at that time spent more than eight times as much as Harvard on staff salaries.[7]

Lowell in November 1909 named Coolidge chairman of the Library Council, founded in 1867 to establish general library policy, which consisted of the president, the librarian, and six faculty members appointed by the corporation at the president's recommendation. Coolidge, who had become a member of the council in 1908, was an ideal appointment, not only because of contributions he had made to improving the library in the previous fifteen years, but also because of his enthusiastic interest in the library and his knowledge of other institutions. His admiration for German libraries was great, and his contributions at Harvard reflected much he had learned about purpose and organization there. Lowell especially valued his high standing in the faculty and among alumni, crucial because the sensitive and alert faculty might resist change, and his willingness to accept responsibility and not bother him with minor questions.

Coolidge accepted appointment under conditions that Lowell quickly granted, beginning with administrative power over the Harvard College Library and supervisory authority over the university's other libraries. Lowell dropped Lane from the council and added particularly able faculty members. He also agreed that the corporation would appoint a Library Council secretary, whom Coolidge would nominate and pay. Finally,

Coolidge resigned as chairman of the Department of History and reduced his teaching obligations to one course and one seminar each year. Lowell, in turn, awarded the department an additional appointment, Lord, in Russian and German history.

The new chairman quickly demonstrated vision and vigorous administrative ability. After he presented a comprehensive analysis, "looking back and ahead," at the first meeting he chaired, in January 1910, the council persuaded Lowell and the corporation to authorize a management review of the library's organization and administration. Even before this review had been completed, in November 1910 Coolidge persuaded Lowell to name him director of the Harvard University Library in order to increase his nominal authority over the other libraries, particularly those of the Law School and the School of Medicine, which cherished their independent positions. The Law School, for example, sought to sell to the college those volumes in its collection that had no relationship to law. In relations with these libraries, Coolidge demonstrated such tact that their councils soon accepted him as a member. The steady improvement of the library system and the quantities of books purchased for each library persuaded all that a "federal" system was useful and created such a spirit of local self-government within a federal system that the Harvard arrangement became one of the marvels and models of the library world. When he died, the faculties of the Schools of Law and Medicine expressed deep and warm appreciation of his services. The Medical School Library Committee called him "the University type of a Professor" and "a refreshing link" with Cambridge.[8]

Within the library administration, Coolidge was "a generous and thoughtful commanding officer." The appointment at first affronted some professional librarians, including Lane, but good sense and dedication soon overcame this resentment. The staff learned that "he cared more for this library than anything else in the world."[9] He not only provided vision and leadership but shared responsibility, from discussing major policies to moving books from the old library to the new. These qualities, his devotion to the library, buoyant enthusiasm, and visible satisfaction from seeing the collection grow and the system improve helped stimulate colleagues throughout the library to ever greater effectiveness.

Coolidge inherited and selected able assistants and gave them full support and independence. Refusing to pose as a professional librarian, he attended only one American Library Association annual meeting, in nearby Swampscott in June 1921, where a talk, "The Objects of Cataloguing," a paper of considerable sense and erudition, increased the respect professional librarians had for him.[10]

Coolidge identified space, the catalogue and classification system, and the collection as the major elements that needed attention. He worked throughout his years as director on these three issues, but concentrated in the first five years on establishing a simple classification system and reforming the catalogue, fundamental but essentially dull chores which he considered the most controversial aspects of the changes he introduced.

The conviction that a library catalogue "takes an honorable place among the agencies that contribute to the progress of our civilization" was central to his system of priorities. Experience indicated that most subject catalogues were too complicated, that faculty members made little use of them because they relied, instead, on bibliographies and professional journals, and that simplicity and good sense should serve as guidelines. Establishing an effective but simple classification system, on parts of which he had worked since 1894, he benefited from the work Wiener had done when cataloguing the first collection of books Coolidge had purchased on Russia and from that which Walter Lichtenstein and other graduate students had established for the publications on Germany that Coolidge had given the university after 1903. The director went through the catalogue slowly and patiently with staff members and graduate students as they created the new system. Reclassification, creation of a formal dictionary union catalogue, and making both the public and the official catalogues complete were basically finished before the move into Widener Library in 1915, but the work continued beyond Coolidge's death. Indeed, one of his very last letters was to an assistant librarian about the system of classifying books on Russia before and after 1917.[11]

The decision that most impressed those who used the library was made in 1910, to introduce the same size cards as the Library of Congress had adopted in 1901. In his first year as director, Harvard purchased and filed 470,000 copies of Library of Congress cards and 70,000 cards from the John Crerar Library. By 1915 the staff had inserted the new cards, had punched and inserted 1,500,000 old Harvard library cards into the new catalogue, and had begun the tedious work of typing and printing copies of the old cards. Coolidge had copies printed of the more important of the small Harvard College Library cards for which the Library of Congress had no card, persuaded twenty-four other libraries to subscribe to this series, and defrayed all costs that the consortium did not meet. He also paid for typing cards for titles that were not printed. By August 1913, 121,000 titles and perhaps 360,000 cards had been printed and inserted into the catalogue. This operation continued even after Coolidge's death because of the vast number of titles involved.

His interest in building the collections was as natural as his concern for the catalogue was remarkable. Acquisitions policy rested on several important principles. First, the library should be designed to serve "today's students and tomorrow's scholars." The university should create a library collection and faculty before establishing an instructional program, particularly a graduate program: "Every venture into a new area of scholarship and teaching has to be backed up with library materials."[12] The university should establish and follow a careful system of priorities in purchasing books. Because of its other obligations and the costs involved, the library should purchase and catalogue all materials regularly available for instruction in English and in other Western languages, while donors, friends, and alumni should provide research materials for graduate programs, especially in new fields of study and in other foreign languages. Coolidge, until late in his life, discouraged donors from contributing expensive rare books, although he gratefully welcomed all collections, because rare books occupied a low priority. Special collections, on the other hand, "constitute the strength and glory of a great library."

Second, Coolidge appreciated that he was enlarging Harvard's collections at a most opportune time. He felt a permanent sense of urgency concerning purchase of materials and adopted the principle "Buy first, and find the money afterwards." The university should obtain all the books it could, because "there never will be so favorable a time again," and delay would only increase the magnitude of the problem in later years. He sometimes envisioned "an unending stream pouring down in almost terrifying waves of knowledge upon the library shelves from every nation of the globe."[13]

Finally, libraries should cooperate in purchasing books in new fields of study. Harvard should remain the preeminent institution, with the finest library, but he was eager to work with other institutions for the common welfare, as in printing the Harvard University library cards and in creating a National Union Catalogue in the Library of Congress. He advised the University of Chicago and Yale University concerning the strengths and weaknesses of the approaches Harvard adopted. He invited other institutions to join Harvard in financing an agent to purchase books in Portugal and Spain in 1911 and 1912, and throughout Latin America in 1914 and 1915, and he was generous and understanding in dividing the volumes.[14]

In 1911 Ernest C. Richardson, librarian of Princeton University, published the *Union List of Collections on European History in American Libraries*, which listed the published series of documents on European history and identified American institutions that possessed full or partial sets of each series. Coolidge, who discovered that Harvard had somewhat more than 60 percent of these sets, sent Lichtenstein to Europe to acquire full series of those it lacked, and increased Harvard's holdings from 1,267 to about 1,900 of the 2,205 sets that Richardson had identified. Coolidge forwarded Richardson a list of the errors Lichtenstein had discovered in his tour, so that the second edition would be even more accurate and helpful than the first. He then urged American librarians to assist in publishing that edition.

In addition, Coolidge and a number of wealthy alumni were generous contributors to the expensive effort involved in compiling *The Union List of Serials in the United States and Canada,* "by far the most important cooperative undertaking which has been produced by American libraries." Richardson proposed this in 1913, work began in 1922, and the first edition appeared in 1927. This immense volume (1,588 pages) listed the 75,000 serial publications in the world and identified the issues or numbers available in each American library. Few volumes are of more value to scholars in the humanities and social sciences then this and its later editions.[15]

Coolidge demonstrated uncanny insight in identifying the principal areas of study on which future scholars would focus and was perceptive and rigorous in locating and obtaining materials. Wherever he was, he sought books, investigated bookstores, and talked with scholars about private collections, using his thorough knowledge of the Harvard library to help complete gaps. As visiting professor in Paris in 1906 and 1907 and in Berlin in 1913 and 1914, he purchased volumes in French and German history. While in Vienna for five months in 1919 for the American

Commission to Negotiate Peace, he acquired 4,000 volumes on the history of Central and Eastern Europe. Similarly, his "chief amusement" in Moscow in 1921 and 1922 for the American Relief Administration was purchasing books, including 1,000 volumes on Russian law and 2,500 volumes on the theater. Lucius Beebe has recorded the unfounded legend that Coolidge rushed to Budapest to purchase 50,000 volumes when Bela Kun seized power in 1919 and decided to sell the major Hungarian libraries.[16]

Coolidge's first concerns were Slavic and Balkan, where Harvard acquired a leadership it has never lost among American universities. When he returned to Cambridge in 1893, the university had fewer than 2,000 volumes on Russia, and he was the only faculty member who could read Russian. But Harvard was not unique; the Library of Congress in 1901 had 569 volumes in Russian and 97 volumes in Polish, plus uncatalogued volumes the Smithsonian Institution had obtained through exchanges. In 1907 a Krasnoyarsk businessman, Gennadi V. Yudin, sold the Library of Congress 80,000 volumes (in 500 crates) at a low price, as a step toward closer relations between Russia and the United States and a contribution to "the world of science." However, the Library of Congress established the Slavic and Central European Division as an acquisition, reference, and bibliographic center only in 1951, and it did not catalogue these volumes until the 1950s and 1960s.[17]

Similarly, the great days of the Slavic collection of the New York Public Library lay ahead. This library had 1,300 volumes on Russia in 1889, when it founded the Slavonic Division in response to a petition hundreds of recent immigrants from Russia had signed. It did not grow substantially until Avrahm Yarmolinsky was appointed chief in 1918 (he served until 1955). Its heart lay in the 9,000 volumes Yarmolinsky purchased in the Soviet Union and the 700 volumes he acquired in Poland on a trip from April 1923 through September 1924, thirty years after Coolidge had begun to build the Harvard collection.[18]

The Hoover Institution began its library in 1919, when Herbert Hoover gave Professor Ephraim D. Adams of the Stanford University Department of History $50,000 to purchase books, documents, journals, and newspapers in Western Europe. Hoover persuaded General John J. Pershing to help Adams by providing fifteen soldiers who had academic experience. In this way, using food ships returning empty to the United States for transportation, Adams began the Hoover collection on European history and on war and revolution.[19]

The entire Slavic section of the Harrassowitz bookstore in Leipzig, which he visited on his way to Siberia in 1895, was Coolidge's first gift to the Harvard library. It contained 1,371 titles, at a time when Harvard possessed about that number of volumes in Slavic history and added about 15,000 volumes a year to its holdings. Coolidge presented these books to the university, helped create a catalogue classification system, and employed Wiener to catalogue the volumes. The following year he added 415 volumes and 180 pamphlets on Russia. In 1899 he began the Polish collection with a gift of 300 volumes. The next year he purchased the Alexander Lombardini collection in Slovak history and literature, which Wiener had discovered on a trip to Eastern Europe. Coolidge had begun to purchase books on Slovak history in the 1890s, and this addition—123 volumes and 1,567 pamphlets— gave Harvard a collection in the 1950s, "without parallel on this side of the Atlantic and one that could almost certainly never be assembled again." As late as 1969, this purchase constituted about 20 percent of Harvard's collection on Slovakia.[20]

By 1901 Harvard had 6,100 volumes on Russia and the Balkans. Coolidge continued to add collections, the literature of the Social Revolutionaries and the Nihilists, the nineteenth-century "thick journals," the records of the Duma, government publications, volumes of railroad statistics, law, and theater and art. Late in life, he began to direct attention to Poland and then to Czechoslovakia, which he had virtually ignored while concentrating on Russia. Until he died, he purchased and paid for cataloguing virtually all volumes that the university acquired in the Slavic field. Almost all the 30,000 volumes in Harvard's Slavic collection in 1934 were Coolidge gifts.[21]

As in the Department of History, where the course on the Eastern Question followed that on Russia, interest in the collection on the Balkans and the Near East followed that on Russia. These purchases began in 1899, when Coolidge and his father purchased 445 volumes from the library of Charles Schefer in Paris on relations between Turkey and Europe in the sixteenth and seventeenth centuries. The following year, Coolidge, his father, and friends gave the university the Paris library of Count Paul Riant: 7,649 volumes of chronicles and other sources and 1,200 pamphlets on the Crusades and the Latin East. This collection cost $10,735, of which Coolidge contributed $3,750. It was then "the most valuable which the Library has ever received" and constituted a fourth of the volumes Harvard acquired in 1900. Within two decades, three Coolidge students, Theodore F. Jones,

Lichtenstein, and Albert H. Lybyer, completed theses on Otto-
man history based on the Schefer and Riant collections, and John
K. Wright one on geographical knowledge during the time of the
Crusades.[22]

In 1928, when Coolidge died, the Harvard collection on the
Ottoman Empire consisted of 7,000 volumes. Most of these were
in English, but in 1915 Coolidge began to purchase books in
Turkish and Arabic and to create a separate catalogue for them
and for volumes in Persian. Harvard's collection in 1960 was "the
most complete and valuable collection in the United States of
western language books on Ottoman history and literature."[23]

Study and travel in Germany naturally stimulated Coolidge's
interest in the history of that country and its immediate neighbors. In 1903, when Harvard had about 1,000 volumes on German
history, he promised to add at least 10,000 volumes in honor of the
visit of Prince Henry of Prussia to Harvard and the opening of the
Germanic Museum (now the Busch-Reisinger Museum of Germanic Culture). This effort "to make Harvard a center for study of
all that is highest and noblest in German civilization" began with
the purchase of the private library of Professor Konrad von
Maurer in Munich, a collection of 2,700 volumes and 2,900
pamphlets, largely on the history of Bavaria and the Rhineland.
He then gave employment and responsibility to Lichtenstein,
who worked twelve years at Coolidge's expense, purchasing and
cataloguing Slavic, West European, and Latin American volumes.
He sent Lichtenstein to Germany to complete the Hohenzollern
collection and to buy books in Scandinavian, Dutch, and Swiss
history. In fourteen months this remarkable young man obtained
11,000 volumes from 300 bookstores in Germany and Central
Europe for only $8,622. Coolidge then appointed him honorary
curator of the Hohenzollern Collection, a post he held until 1919.
As assistant in charge of European collections, he established a
classification system for these volumes and helped catalogue
them. The two men then transferred their knowledge of classification to the material Coolidge and others were purchasing on
British, French, and Italian history.[24]

Coolidge rejected Lichtenstein's suggestion that Harvard
employ a permanent purchasing agent on the Continent. However, Lichtenstein made other prolonged trips to Europe, and one
through Latin America, to purchase books, on all of which
Coolidge paid his salary and travel expenses. He accepted
appointment in 1908 as librarian and associate professor of

history at Northwestern University, but spent most of the period through 1914 on leave from Northwestern, working for Harvard or for a consortium of university libraries that Coolidge had assembled.[25]

Harvard by 1914 possessed almost all the German historical periodicals and its library was second only to the Prussian State Library on German history and culture. These materials naturally included many on Germany's neighbors, especially the Netherlands and Switzerland. Coolidge devoted much time and energy in the first decade of the twentieth century trying to persuade the Iselins and other American families of Swiss origin to contribute to a Swiss collection. In the 1920s he sought to induce Edward Bok and others of Dutch descent to give $100,000 toward a collection in Dutch history in honor of John Lothrop Motley, who graduated from Harvard in 1831. Scandinavia fascinated him throughout his life, and he named Henry Goddard Leach, one of his History 1 discussion leaders and a leading spirit of the American-Scandinavian Foundation for thirty-five years, curator of the Scandinavian History and Literature. These endeavors were not notably successful, but the university's resources on Switzerland and the Netherlands grew because of his purchases. The American-Scandinavian Foundation used the Harvard library in 1921 when it selected the 500 most important books in English by Scandinavians and about Scandinavians.[26]

France was as close as Germany to Coolidge's interests. In 1906 he gave the university $1,000 as a matching grant for works on French local history. The following year he purchased a splendid collection of 165 newspapers, 10,000 volumes, and 30,000 pamphlets on the French Revolution from Count Alfred Boulay de la Meurthe. Later he gave other volumes on French poetry. In 1931 some of his friends purchased the library of Professor Alphonse Aulard, 3,500 volumes and pamphlets on the French Revolution, as a gift in his memory.[27]

From Germany and France, Coolidge turned to the Iberian countries and Latin America. In 1911 he purchased the library of Marquis de Olivart on Spanish history—8,000 titles, particularly strong in law and international law—for $11,500, although he had expected to pay $25,000. He began collecting works on Portugal in 1923 by persuading a neighbor and student in the class of 1906, Ambassador John B. Stetson, Jr. (whose stepfather was a Portuguese nobleman), to serve as honorary curator of the Portuguese collection, a position he filled for thirty years.[28]

Latin America greatly interested him. From 1903 through 1908 he employed another graduate student, Hiram Bingham, later professor at Yale and senator from Connecticut, as curator of the Latin American collection. When Coolidge visited Chile in 1908 and 1909 as a representative of Harvard and the United States to the First Pan-American Scientific Congress, he and his secretary, Clarence L. Hay (Harvard 1908), acquired for $5,505 the 4,000-volume private library of Louis Montt, the national librarian of Chile. This collection was especially strong on Chile, Peru, and Argentina. Later, Coolidge sent Lichtenstein through Latin America for fourteen months on a trip from which Harvard, Yale, and other universities benefited. Lichtenstein purchased about 9,000 volumes for Harvard at a cost of slightly more than $17,000. Harvard at that time had the strongest Latin American collection in the United States, and its law school became "the only place in the world which has a complete collection of the codes and statutory laws of all the independent South American states."[29]

China, Japan, and Siam attracted much attention. By 1910, largely through purchases he and his father had made, the library had 1,000 books on China and was "perhaps the best working library [on China] outside of Washington." After 1909, his brother Harold contributed annually to the Chinese and Japanese collection. When Edward Henry Strobel (Harvard 1877) died in January 1908, after six years as adviser to the king of Siam, Coolidge persuaded the king and other officials to give $2,000 for books on Siam. The following year, he inspired Strobel's Harvard class to establish a library fund for world politics in his memory. Coolidge added a specialist for Eastern Asia to the library staff in 1927, when Harvard had 4,526 volumes in Chinese and 1,668 in Japanese. His will provided the library $200,000, and the residual sum after his specific bequests, primarily for "the purchase of works on European, Asiatic, and African history and government, or works descriptive of the political and economic conditions of the people of those continents."[30]

The United States was not neglected. Coolidge worked closely with Frederick Jackson Turner and Mrs. Alice Hooper in creating the Harvard Commission on Western History as a memorial to her father, Charles Elliott Perkins, who had built the Chicago, Burlington, and Quincy Railroad. This commission was active from 1911 until 1920, with funds Mrs. Hooper contributed annually, and bought more than 1,000 books on western United States history. Coolidge provided a room in

Widener Library for the collection, appointed an archivist, sent him to Salt Lake City in 1914 to purchase a collection on the Mormons, and encouraged alumni, particularly those in the West, to contribute materials and funds. However, Turner was not an aggressive supporter of this drive. Lowell feared it alienated western institutions—and understood too late that it might increase interest in the university among western alumni. Finally, the war concentrated American concerns on other parts of the world, so this program waned in Turner's last years at Harvard. However, both Turner and Mrs. Hooper recognized that Coolidge was one member of the Harvard faculty "whose horizon was not limited to his own region." Indeed, Mrs. Hooper was convinced that he deserved much of the credit for transforming Harvard into a major institution, which Eliot and Lowell ordinarily received.[31]

It is difficult to determine the magnitude of Coolidge's imaginative collecting and benefactions before his final bequest, because so many gifts were discreet, even anonymous. For example, in 1905 he quietly organized a small group of friends of Harvard and of Professor Charles Eliot Norton to purchase Norton's library for the university for $15,000. His contributions to the library approximately equalled his salary from 1893 through 1928. He bestowed a total of more than $100,000 for the purchase of books alone. In his last three years, he gave $16,400 for books and $11,000 for administration. In some years, Coolidge's gifts constituted more than 20 percent of the new titles added, and the dollar contribution was half the amount the university made available for book purchases. The library budget in his last year as director was only $250,000 and the fund for books was $70,000, so his contributions were very important indeed.*

In addition, he contributed substantial funds for cataloguing. During his first five years as director, he supported reclassifying and recataloguing thousands of volumes and the introduction of standard Library of Congress cards. He paid the salary of the secretary of the Library Council and employed a number of graduate students to assist in library work, as cataloguers, curators of collections in which they were particularly interested, or purchasing agents abroad. His salary in 1919 was alloted to raising salaries of members of the library staff. His annual grants

*Harvard University Library's total operating expenditures were $1.7 million in 1949, more than $9 million in 1969, and $19 million in 1979.

for administrative support in the 1920s were at least $3,000. While defending the Library budget request to the comptroller in 1922, he pointed out that he paid the salary of his secretary, although the university was responsible for his stationery, postage, and library telephone bill.[32]

Coolidge did not enjoy asking others to contribute to the library. Moreover, those who responded positively often requested support for *their* favorite charities. Consequently, the secretary of the Library Council corresponded with graduates and friends of the university, while Coolidge approached only his family, former students, and close friends for purchasing special collections and for assisting generously in other ways. For example, his father not only gave $3,500 for Ottoman studies in 1899 but helped to buy the Riant collection the following year and contributed thereafter to the Arctic and Antarctic collections. Coolidge's brother Harold purchased extensively in the Asian field, and his uncle, John Lowell Gardner, not only contributed the salary of new faculty members but gave substantial funds for library purchases. Another uncle granted $1,000 a year for books on Italy.

Even before 1910, Coolidge persuaded friends of Harvard to make annual gifts (from $10 to several hundred dollars) for purchases in fields of interest to them—from Finnish folklore to medieval cities to the history of chemistry. Late in his career, he established a small, informal organization, Friends of the Harvard University Library, which contributed to the collection. The leading spirit of this group became Franklin Eddy Parker, Jr., of the class of 1918, who had traveled with Coolidge on trips between 1918 and 1922 and who made substantial gifts in eighteenth-century English literature.[33]

Above all, Coolidge encouraged many students to collect books. Some became great benefactors. Stetson, a collector of Portuguese, Brazilian, and medieval French literature, as well as Oscar Wilde, in 1926 gave Harvard 600 editions of works by Camöens and in 1927 spent $75,000 for the Fernando Palha collection, 10,000 volumes and 30,000 pamphlets on Portuguese history and literature. Bayard L. Kilgour, Jr. (Harvard 1927), whom Coolidge and Blake had interested in Russia, began to collect books while a student of Coolidge, made his first trip to the Soviet Union while an undergraduate, and in 1956 presented Harvard a substantial collection of manuscripts and first editions of Russian poets and novelists. Robert Woods Bliss (Harvard

1900), a close friend of Coolidge as an undergraduate and throughout his diplomatic career, became interested in Byzantine history and culture, in large part because of Coolidge. The Dumbarton Oaks Library and Center for Byzantine Studies in Washington, which had 14,000 volumes when he and Mrs. Bliss presented it to Harvard in 1940, serves as a monument to Coolidge as well as to Mr. and Mrs. Bliss. James B. Munn, of the class of 1912, was secretary of the Library Council in 1916 and 1917, when he completed his Ph.D., and then served on the Visiting Committee. He and his father became outstanding donors in the field of English literature of the sixteenth and seventeenth centuries. They presented books worth $60,000 in 1926 alone.[34]

Persuading students who became diplomats or businessmen to strengthen the library in fields of their interest and to help meet emergencies was another successful tactic. Edwin V. Morgan (Harvard 1890), who completed his career in the Foreign Service by serving twenty years as American ambassador in Brazil, gave $2,500 each year for purchases on Latin America and made other substantial gifts as opportunities and needs arose. Ellis L. Dresel, a classmate of Coolidge, assisted in building the collection on German drama, especially when he was in Germany as United States High Commissioner after the First World War. William B. Phillips (Harvard 1900) purchased books on the city of London, and another diplomat, Leland Harrison (of the class of 1907), was interested in Bolivia and Colombia.[35]

August von Lengerke Meyer of the class of 1879, a neighbor on Beacon Hill, was also generous. When he was American ambassador in Rome, from 1902 to 1905, he agreed that presenting books on modern Italian history would assist his mission. Later, when he was ambassador in St. Petersburg, he supplied Harvard with official Russian publications. Julius Klein, who wrote a thesis in Castilian history under Coolidge for his Ph.D. degree, was especially helpful when he was assistant secretary of Commerce and had many business friends in Latin America. J.P. Morgan, Jr. (class of 1889), an overseer and a member of the Library Visiting Committee, gave $2,500 annually for books, especially in English poetry, and assisted when crises arose at the end of the budget year. He also paid for the desks, chairs, and lamps for studies and carrels in Widener Library when that great building opened.[36]

Coolidge's influence extended throughout the American library world, not only because of his achievements at Harvard but because he educated and excited Lichtenstein and other graduate students on the role of university libraries, their needs, and programs for enlarging and administering them. Many published useful bibliographies; some became librarians. Golder became the first director of the Hoover Institution. His purchases while he was in the Soviet Union in the 1920s created the foundations for the great Hoover collection on Russia. Lichtenstein served as librarian at Northwestern University for more than ten years, before becoming a successful Chicago banker. Jones was a professor of history and director of the University Heights Library of New York University for thirty years, with such distinction that Harvard awarded him the D. Litt. in 1951. Most of those whose graduate work Coolidge directed, such as Robert J. Kerner at Berkeley and Albert H. Lybyer at Illinois, became strong supporters of the library in their institutions, and Lord was for sixteen years a trustee of the Boston Public Library.

Harvard's most obvious need, when Coolidge became director of the library in 1910, was space. Within a year after his appointment, he outlined a long-term program and had architects prepare plans for a new building. Lowell was especially interested in constructing dormitories and laboratories, but Coolidge helped persuade him, and the corporation as well, of the central role of the library. Lowell and Coolidge in January 1912 began to discuss ways of obtaining the several million dollars necessary for this building with wealthy Harvard alumni, such as J.P. Morgan, Jr., and Joseph Choate.

The tragic death of Harry Elkins Widener (Harvard 1907) on the *Titanic* in April 1912 presented the opportunity they required. An avid collector of rare books, in part because of Coolidge, Widener had left his collection to the university, as soon as it provided a proper place. Within a month of Widener's death and announcement of his will, Lowell and Coolidge had arranged that a copy of the library plans be in the hands of Widener's mother. Lowell, with assistance from Coolidge and Stetson, a close friend of Harry Elkins Widener and one of Mrs. Widener's closest advisers, persuaded her to provide a library building as a memorial, a generous and magnificent gift of about $4 million.[37]

Widener Library, one of the world's great library buildings, was designed by Horace Trumbauer. It dominates the Yard and is the physical and spiritual center of the university. Its imposing entrance helps provide both grandeur and serenity to the Yard, for its physical characteristics are most impressive. Coolidge described it to the donor in 1920 as "unrivalled facilities in a magnificent setting." The reading rooms, the organization of the stacks, the seventy faculty studies, and the 300 carrels for graduate students were arranged to stimulate learning. They have made Widener a base and a center for research and instruction at Harvard and a model for other university library buildings in the United States.

In his years at Harvard, Coolidge "kept before the University and its friends a complete idea of the Library and its possibilities." Through his work with the faculty and the administration (particularly Lowell), he helped make the library an essential part of the university organization, an achievement many other institutions have not yet matched. He not only created a great library building, which is his "most conspicuous monument," but provided a splendid organization, administration, and classification and cataloguing system. Widener became the center for research and study and an intellectual symbol of the university. The skill with which Coolidge anticipated future needs of the collection and the library as a whole acted as a magnet that has helped Harvard attract and retain scholars. When Coolidge died, the library was the fifth largest in the world, and occupied "an assured position among the great libraries." The Harvard model of the federal library system and the quality of the entire library have inspired, perhaps even forced, other American institutions to follow Harvard's example.

Part 4:

Awakening the United States

8. Transforming American Higher Education: From Harvard to America

THROUGHOUT HIS LIFE, Coolidge was "far more interested in the production of scholars than in the product of scholarship itself."[1] The period during which he taught History 1 and trained large numbers of senior graduate students to teach were critical for instruction in history in the United States. He helped train more than fifty young men of high ability to introduce that freshman course as it was taught at Harvard, from Bowdoin College to the University of California at Berkeley, and in Canada as well. His colleagues—Haskins, Merriman, and Karpovich—continued the History 1 system for almost half a century and helped spread it further and deeper.

Probably even more important than History 1 and to some degree inseparable from that contribution was the launching of high-quality graduate training on areas and cultures which American higher education had neglected. Scholar-teachers, whom he helped train and encouraged to travel, changed the horizons of American historical scholarship and transformed the spirit of higher education by introducing courses on areas and periods new to American colleges and universities. Moreover, many students of these men became teachers and scholars, so that the character of the transformation Coolidge and others helped launch gradually spread deeply throughout the educational system.

Coolidge established high intellectual standards for those who undertook graduate work under his direction. He paid no attention to origins or social backgrounds, "welcomed talent wherever he found it," and had only one prejudice, "for intellectual distinction." Stoddard, who descended from an old New England family, was a son of the "most famous of travel lecturers." Langer's widowed mother raised her son (and his brothers) by maintaining a boarding house, while Kelley's father was custodian of the Jamaica Plain High School for thirty-four years. Golder and Lichtenstein emigrated to the United States, the first from Russia and the second from Germany. They were Jews, while Kelly was a Catholic. Blake and Klein came from Berkeley, on recommendation of his friend Henry Morse Stephens, while others, such as Frank Nowak and Dwight Lee, studied at the University of Rochester under Laurence B. Packard, whom Coolidge had trained.[2]

Resisting the departmentalization of information or "the vertical pillars of knowledge," Coolidge insisted that students understand the culture of the peoples they were studying. Geography, climate, demography, government, and religion received substantial attention in his courses and writings. Russia was part of Europe, and part of Russia was part of Asia, so he required that future scholar-teachers who specialized on Russia understand the wider European, Asian, and international frameworks of which their subjects were a segment. The Balkan peoples were just as important and probably even more interesting to him than their eastern or western neighbors, and they deserved just as careful study as the Russians and the French. Those whom he trained in European history studied the Bulgars as well as the Dutch, and those in Latin American or Asian history studied other areas as well.

His seminar, held in Room J on the top floor of Widener Library, which put "unrivaled knowledge and understanding" and information concerning bibliography, libraries, and archives at his graduate students' service, played a central role. He raised great expectations and inspired maximum effort; many recalled the "electrical atmosphere" he created. His comments on examination papers and manuscripts and on preparation for teaching careers were tactful but candid, and he remained interested and helpful long after the students left Harvard. Fourteen years after Coolidge died, George Rupp wrote in the preface to his major scholarly volume: "No one who came under the influence and moved within the circle of Professor Coolidge remained the same man afterwards; he encouraged his students to develop their own peculiar enthusiasms and personalities while he furnished them with every kind of facility and support." More than forty years after he completed his graduate work, Langer declared that Coolidge "never wavered in his interest and never hesitated to sacrifice his time in discussion and suggestion."[3]

Coolidge treated his young colleagues as equals, encouraging each to select his own thesis subject rather than work on one which contributed to Coolidge's research. Some undertook to complete studies he had begun, such as the rule of Suleiman the Magnificent, the Ottoman effect upon the Reformation, and the expansion of Russia. He urged students to work with other scholars. To ensure that they had additional insights, particularly those that foreign scholars might provide, and to encourage work in new fields, he was ingenious in bringing scholars from other countries into the Harvard community, especially the Department of History.

The 1909–10 seminar demonstrates the freedom of choice he gave and the range of his knowledge that benefited those he trained. The five theses that emerged from this seminar, which he hoped would concentrate on European history since 1878, dealt with an aspect of Spanish economic and social history from the thirteenth until the nineteenth century, Austria at the end of the eighteenth century, seventeenth-century France, the Monroe Doctrine in 1823, and the French Revolution in San Domingo.[4]

Coolidge was concerned that all graduate students in history travel and study abroad, whatever their special interest. He encouraged them to remain abroad as long as possible, rather than rush home to complete theses and obtain positions. Some graduate students were wealthy and could afford extensive travel; others he assisted, quietly and unobtrusively, through funds he gave the department for fellowships and through invitations to travel with him as secretaries or aides. He served on the Harvard Committee on Fellowships and Scholarships from 1907 until his death in order to promote graduate students' travel. He used his influence to obtain bourses in Berlin and Paris, particularly in the École des Sciences Politiques, and wrote letters of introduction to scholars he knew in many countries.[5]

Every student who received a Ph.D. under Coolidge's direction spent at least one year abroad, and some spent three. Clearly, travel stimulated those whose major interests were in English history or the American West but who had a minor concern with modern European, diplomatic, East European, or Russian history. It helped them introduce instruction in fields such as Russian history in institutions such as Brown, Colorado, Northwestern, and Wyoming, which were eager to initiate courses on neglected areas but unable to appoint a specialist.

Coolidge was conscientious, giving his graduate students' theses the benefit of his knowledge and perspective. Scrupulous in reading theses his colleagues directed, he commented on six manuscripts in the spring of 1923. He urged his young colleagues not to publish findings hastily, but first complete research in all archives and libraries and widen their knowledge and perspective. Dexter Perkins, who had a distinguished career as a specialist on American foreign policy, especially the Monroe Doctrine, published his first book thirteen years after he completed a dissertation on that subject. As a final discreet but immensely important service to the department and its graduate students, Coolidge after 1896 provided funds for the Harvard Historical Series, assisting colleagues and graduate students to put their work into print.[6]

It is difficult to discover precisely how many graduate students wrote theses under Coolidge's direction and impossible to determine how many young historians he deeply influenced.* The records of the Department of History frequently lack precise data concerning the scholar who directed a thesis, and often even the dissertation and the author's memoirs do not provide information concerning which faculty member directed a study and which served as readers.

However, his impact is evident. Only two theses were completed before 1900 in the fields in which Coolidge was interested. In the following twenty-seven years, the department produced 122 Ph.D. theses, of which forty-one were in American and twenty-three in English history. In the three fields in which Coolidge accepted major responsibility, the department turned out thirty-four: five in Latin American history, twenty on modern Europe, and nine in "East European and Asiatic history." Ten of the thirty-two theses completed between 1909 and 1916 were written under his direct supervision. Throughout his career, he directed a total of twenty-three theses: two on Germany or Central Europe, two on Eastern Europe, one on Byzantium, four on the Near East, three on Russia, one on Spain, two on France, one on Latin America, one on China, and five on European and one on American diplomatic history.[7]

The effects of classroom careers, books and articles, and other educational labors are difficult to define, but his impact upon American study of other areas and peoples was considerable. Men whom Coolidge helped train produced a significant proportion

*The bibliography (pages 250 ff) identifies the men whose graduate work Coolidge directed or helped direct, the titles of their theses, and the year in which they received their Ph.D. degrees.

of the seminal first books and articles concerning the areas and periods of history for which he was creating new interest and resources, and of course the men and women these Coolidge scholars trained have helped create the flood of scholars who now nourish American knowledge and understanding.*

Two or three illustrations of the role his students played in the years after the First World War demonstrate the importance of those whom he helped launch. When the American Historical Association in 1919 appointed six men to edit its first *Guide to Historical Literature* (a useful, annotated bibliography that was published twelve years later), two of these six were men whose theses Coolidge had directed. Ten of the twenty-nine section editors, including those on Germany and Central Europe, Russia, Eastern Europe, Asia, Africa, and Oceania, completed their graduate work with him. In 1925, more than half of those teaching Russian and Eastern European history in the United States had been his students. On the other hand, a university such as Cornell, which for one reason or another did not appoint young men Coolidge had trained to its Department of History, was late in introducing courses on Russia and Eastern Europe and on other neglected areas. Although a number of the Cornell faculty had played an important role in founding the *American Historical Review* in 1895 and the university was one of the leading institutions in history in Coolidge's years, it did not introduce Russian history until 1936, when Philip E. Mosely arrived in Ithaca. Mosely (Harvard 1926), as a freshman in History 1, had written a paper on the Russian revolutions in 1917 and went on to become one of America's best-informed and wisest scholars of Russian history and politics.[8]

Many who studied with Coolidge published important books that earned them renown within the historical profession and that increased knowledge of neglected areas and periods. For example, three who together taught in New England colleges for more than a century and who were among the outstanding American teachers of history, Richard A. Newhall of Williams, Laurence B. Packard of Amherst, and Sidney R. Packard of Smith, in 1928 initiated a series of twenty-eight volumes for History 1 or Western Civilization courses that remains popular. Four of the first eighteen volumes were devoted to the history of the Slavs, and

---

*The bibliography lists a few of the important and interesting books Coolidge students published.

other volumes dealt with the Crusades, the geographical basis of history, explorations, Spain, Iran, Africa, the Far East, and imperialism—areas on which Coolidge had helped launch research and instruction.[9]

Those who studied with Coolidge and who served as discussion leaders carried the courses, the Coolidge system, and often his habits with them. Their work reflected the "breadth of reading and the depth of knowledge" (as well as the sense of excitement) he conveyed about areas then on the frontiers of knowledge. Almost all followed his emphasis on trying "to teach students to acquire facts and to organize them." Most required that their students use books he had prescribed, so Ploetz's *Epitome of History*, Putzger's *Atlas*, and Einhard's *Charlemagne* were read by freshmen throughout the nation. The grueling examinations at Simmons, Iowa, and Washington State resembled those in History 1 at Harvard. Some, like Fay at Dartmouth, used his course outlines, readings and maps, examination questions, and even his course numbers and titles. Many adopted techniques he used which are now customary, such as providing a printed outline. Some adopted his vigorous style and even his mannerisms.

Thus Packard, whose "remarkable gift as a teacher" Coolidge had recognized early, was an inspiring instructor at the University of Rochester for twelve years and at Amherst College for thirty. He organized History 1 at both institutions and at Amherst introduced courses on modern European and Asian history. His classroom and seminar styles were unique, but Coolidge was visibly his model. The effect was tremendous: normally, 90 percent of the freshman class enrolled in his History 1 course, which more than half of Amherst's living alumni had taken when he retired in 1955. He possessed "an intellectual enthusiasm so vital, a critical standard so demanding of independent judgment based on solid facts, and so strong a devotion to truth that he invigorated the entire community and stirred generations of students." More than a hundred whom he taught undertook graduate work in history, and many were as influenced by Packard's "forceful and masterly lucid presentation" as Packard had been by Coolidge.[10]

Scholars whom Coolidge trained introduced "Western Civ" and courses on areas new to American students in every part of the country, except the South and Southwest. Indeed, a map identifying the institutions in which these men introduced instruction would reveal that they spread from Harvard throughout most of the United States.* In the East, they taught in the so-called Big Three, Harvard, Yale, and Princeton, as well as the "Little Three," Amherst, Wesleyan, and Williams. They introduced his courses and view of the world in such institutions as Boston University, Bowdoin, Brown, Bryn Mawr, Dartmouth, New York University, Pennsylvania, Pennsylvania Military (now Widener) College, Rochester, Simmons, Tufts, and Union. At Harvard, where Coolidge had ensured appropriate attention to the subjects with which he was concerned and had trained or helped appoint Blake, Langer, Lord, and Karpovich, Bruce Hopper became the first specialist on Soviet politics in the Department of Government. A Coolidge favorite who was a fighter pilot in the First World War, Hopper studied at Oxford for two years and traveled around the world for three years before beginning graduate work. At Coolidge's urging and through his support, he spent 1927 to 1929 in the Soviet Union as a fellow of the Institute of Current World Affairs.[11]

Others helped change the patterns of instruction in other institutions in the Boston area. At Simmons from 1906 until 1912 and at Tufts for the following fourteen years, Arthur I. Andrews taught History 1 and courses on Russia, the Eastern Question, modern European history, and East Asia. The Tufts *Bulletin*'s description of Andrews's course on Russia closely resembles that of Harvard for Coolidge's course. In the 1920s, Andrews introduced a course which had the same title as a Coolidge book, The United States as a World Power. George Steiger, who had taught in Shanghai for thirteen years and whose 1923 Ph.D. thesis dealt with the Boxer Rebellion, provided instruction in Asian history at Simmons from 1921 through 1952 and produced three widely used textbooks on Asia. Frank Nowak, whose 1924 thesis dealt with Polish foreign policy under King Stephen Batory, taught History 1 and Russian history at Boston University for more than forty years.[12]

*The information in the following pages concerning the young men who went from Harvard to other colleges and universities to launch courses similar to History 1 and instruction on modern history and on previously neglected areas comes from the sources identified, as well as from the Harvard University Archives and the archives and records of many other educational institutions, newspapers such as the New York *Times*, and professional journals. I also made intensive use of biographical aids to collect the data.

Clark University (Worcester) engaged at least one Coolidge-trained member in its Department of History through the first seventy years of this century, and sometimes three. George Blakeslee, who began teaching modern history and international relations in 1903 and remained active at Clark until 1948, introduced Asian history and international relations and was one of those most responsible for stimulating academic interest in East Asia. Blakeslee, who studied at Oxford, Berlin, and Leipzig before obtaining his Ph.D. in 1903, traveled extensively as a young scholar, particularly through Russia, Latin America, and the Far East. He was an able popularizer, for twelve years edited the *Journal of Race Relations* (later the *Journal of International Relations*), was president of the World Peace Foundation for sixteen years, and helped found the Institute of Pacific Relations. He was also a senior advisor to the Department of State on Far Eastern issues during the early 1930s and again from 1942 until 1952. Those whose theses he directed at Clark included four men whose publications and teaching helped significantly to increase American knowledge of diplomatic and modern world history: Samuel Flagg Bemis, F. Lee Benns, Forrest Pogue, and Leften Stavrianos.

Langer began his teaching career at Clark in 1923 and in four years launched courses in Russian, East European, diplomatic, and modern European history. Dwight E. Lee, whose thesis dealt with British policy in the Eastern Question in 1878, continued this program at Clark for more than four decades.[13] Similarly, Fay introduced History 1 and the Coolidge system at Smith College, after he had taught that course for twelve years at Dartmouth. Newhall did the same at Williams College, after he had taught at Yale for five years. In the 1920s, Fay and Sidney B. Packard combined to launch a course in Russian history, which they had taken at Harvard, and Fay also introduced a course on the Slavic peoples, although he was a specialist in German history and Packard a medievalist. Robert H. George, a specialist on medieval England, learned sufficient Russian history from Coolidge and Lord to teach it for more than thirty years at Brown. Dexter Perkins cooperated with Packard at Rochester, until Packard left for Amherst (in 1925), and devoted almost half a century to instruction in the history of Latin America, modern Europe, and diplomatic history at Rochester and Cornell.[14]

In the Midwest, Lybyer taught four years at Oberlin College and thirty-one years at the University of Illinois, introducing

History 1 and courses on the Eastern Question and the Ottoman Empire. The History 1 outline he used in his first year was a reproduction of that with which he had become familiar at Harvard, and Lybyer introduced few changes in subsequent years, except for adding occasional titles to the bibliography. His 1913 book, *The Government of the Ottoman Empire in the Time of Suleiman the Magnificent,* was the first scholarly volume by an American on Ottoman history, and he directed the first American thesis on Armenian history. In 1914 he published the *American Historical Review*'s first article on Ottoman history, and for thirty years he was the *Review*'s principal book reviewer on the Middle East.[15]

William Stearns Davis, who attained fame and wealth as a historical novelist, launched History 1 and the Eastern Question at the University of Minnesota in 1909, where others whom Coolidge trained supported his innovations. Mason Tyler taught the history of Russia and of the Near East from 1911 until his death in 1923. His successor, Lawrence Steefel, continued Russian history, added Ottoman and modern European history, and directed the Scandinavian Area Program until his retirement in 1959. At the State University of Iowa, Chester W. Clark in 1935 introduced Russian and European diplomatic history, after teaching at Princeton with Henry R. Shipman, who had launched History 1 and Russian history there in 1905. Colin B. Goody-koontz, who completed his degree in 1921 under Frederick Jackson Turner on the missionary movement in the American West, taught Russian history at the University of Colorado from 1921 until he retired in 1954. Others Coolidge had trained carried out similar responsibilities at Beloit, Miami (Ohio), Missouri, Northwestern, Washington University, Washington State, Western Reserve, Wisconsin, Idaho, and Wyoming.[16]

Coolidge's role in helping two institutions on the West Coast become centers on Russia, the Balkans, and modern diplomatic history is particularly illuminating. At Stanford University, Golder in 1920 became the first professor of Russian history and the first director of the Hoover Institution. He had studied briefly at Bucknell and spent three years teaching Aleuts in Alaska, where he became interested in Russia, before he graduated from Harvard in 1903. He obtained his Ph.D. in 1909 with a thesis on one of Coolidge's major themes, Russian expansion. By the time the United States entered the war in 1917 Golder had taught at the University of Missouri and Washington State and had published a book on Russian expansion and a *Guide to Materials for American History in Russian Archives,* the fruit of research in Petrograd and Moscow in 1914 and 1915. He visited Russia again in 1916 and 1917, and presented a fascinating eye-witness account of the March revolution at the annual meeting of the American Historical Association the following December. In December 1923, after twenty months in Russia, he described the early years of the New Economic Policy to the association.

Golder took advantage of his work in Russia with Hoover's American Relief Administration to enlarge the collection of the Hoover Institution. On a visit (from August 1921 to May 1923), he purchased 25,000 books and 60,000 pamphlets and obtained the library of Paul Miliukov. He aided Russian scholars by shipping food and sent 100,000 volumes to Soviet libraries. He ensured that the Hoover Institution become more than a library by publishing valuable collections of documents and by launching research programs on Russia and the revolutions. Grants he obtained from the Laura Spelman Rockefeller Memorial Foundation in 1925 and 1927, for establishing what he called the Soviet-American Institute for the Study of the Russian Revolution, were the first two awards an American foundation made for Russian studies.[17]

The impact of Coolidge on the University of California at Berkeley was even more impressive, for students and friends of his introduced History 1 and helped that institution begin the second Russian studies program in the United States, in the 1930s and 1940s the largest and strongest on both Russia and the Balkans. One instrument of this progress was George R. Noyes, a Harvard graduate in 1894 (*summa cum laude* in classics), who obtained his Ph.D. in 1898 with a thesis on Dryden but was attracted to Russian studies by reading Tolstoy and studying with Coolidge and Wiener. With aid and encouragement from the former, Noyes in 1898 went to St. Petersburg for two years to learn Russian and develop competence in Russian literature.*

*Ernest J. Simmons, a student and graduate student in English literature under George Lyman Kittredge (as Noyes had been thirty years earlier), was like Noyes impressed by Coolidge and "things Russian." A prolific scholar, stimulating teacher, and imaginative organizer who greatly expanded American study of Russia and its literature, Simmons began to study Russian as a Harvard undergraduate in 1925, but completed his thesis in 1928 on "A History of the Folktale and Its Theories," before going to Moscow in 1928 and 1929 on a traveling fellowship.

When President Benjamin Ide Wheeler in 1901 decided to introduce Russian studies at Berkeley, Noyes became an instructor in English and in Slavic philology. He had only fifteen or twenty students a year and was the sole member of the department until 1917, when Berkeley added Serbo-Croatian and Old Church Slavonic to the Russian, Polish, and Czech courses that Noyes had begun. An able, devoted, and deeply loved teacher, he labored at Berkeley for forty-two years to establish its strong Department of Slavic Languages and Literatures and to ensure the position of Russian studies there. His work on The Inquiry reveals both the paucity of American specialists on Russia and the Balkans in 1917 and 1918 and Noyes's understanding of affairs other than literature. He remained a specialist in English literature, editing Burns, Dryden, and Congreve, but he also directed five Ph.D. theses in Russian literature, wrote reviews for the *Nation* and other journals, translated thirteen Alexander Ostrovsky plays into English, and helped introduce the work of Adam Mickiewicz, Zygmunt Krasinski, and Juliusz Slowacki into the United States.* The Polish, Lithuanian, and Czechoslovak governments honored him in the 1930s for spreading knowledge of their cultures.[18]

Noyes's strongest supporter throughout his first twenty years at Berkeley was Stephens, a close friend of Coolidge, who came to Cornell University in 1894 from Oxford, where he had received a First in history at Balliol, and from a career in journalism. One of the founders of the *American Historical Review* in 1895, a member of its board of editors from 1895 until 1909, and president of the American Historical Association in 1915, he was attracted to Berkeley by Wheeler in 1902 to introduce modern European history, and became Wheeler's closest friend and adviser. As Sather Professor in 1902, chairman of the department, and later dean of the College of Arts and Sciences, he helped make the Department of History and the Russian program at Berkeley among the strongest in the United States. He introduced the Coolidge History 1 course at Berkeley in 1905 and arranged instruction in Russian history in 1902. He usually spent his

---

*Noyes was the first chairman of the Committee on Slavic Studies, which the American Council of Learned Societies founded in 1938 to bring together specialists from several disciplines to promote instruction and research on the Slavic world. His immediate successors in this important role were Samuel H. Cross and Philip E. Mosely, who also began to study as undergraduates with Coolidge.

Christmas holidays at President Lowell's and he used Harvard as a standard. Through Coolidge and Lowell, he kept informed of programs and ideas at Harvard and in the East, and he arranged that Harvard faculty members (including Coolidge and Samuel Eliot Morison) teach in the Berkeley summer school.[19]

Like Coolidge, Stephens recognized the necessity of a strong library. In 1905 he played the central role in persuading Wheeler and the regents of the university to spend $150,000 (then 30 percent of Berkeley's annual budget for instruction) to purchase the Herbert Howe Bancroft collection. These 60,000 books and other publications on the history of the Far West were significant in Berkeley's development into a great university.

Stephens resembled Coolidge in other ways in which he promoted research and instruction concerning neglected areas of the world. He organized a meeting of the American Historical Association in July 1915 in San Francisco, Berkeley, and Palo Alto, devoted to the Pacific Basin and American policy there. These three days, which attracted Theodore Roosevelt and 150 scholars, increased cooperation among the institutions in the Bay Area and stimulated interest in the Pacific and the Far East.[20]

Kerner, a Coolidge student, completed the transformation of Berkeley as a center for Slavic studies after his arrival in 1928. The son of a Chicago journalist of Czech origin, Kerner was persuaded by Coolidge in 1910 to continue graduate studies at Harvard rather than the University of Illinois. He obtained his Ph.D. in 1914, after studying in Prague, Vienna and Paris. He taught for fourteen years at the University of Missouri and was prominent in The Inquiry in 1917 and 1918 and in the American Commission to Negotiate Peace in 1919. His graduate school classmates considered him pontifical and "a bit grim," and his colleagues in The Inquiry thought him dogmatic and "not unprejudiced" because of his aggressiveness on behalf of Slavs and occasional intemperate charges against those who disagreed. "Of active temperament," he was a most productive scholar and a "colorful and dramatic lecturer" in Russian and central European history. During his three decades at Berkeley, he gave several hundred public lectures and directed more than thirty Ph.D. theses. Above all, he provided the leadership and boiling energy that helped vault Berkeley into its major position in Russian and East European history in the United States.[21]

Coolidge's range and style of instruction also spread to Canada. Charles E. Fryer worked two years as an assistant in

History 1, received his Ph.D. in English history in 1906, and spent thirty-six years at McGill University in Montreal, where he introduced Asian and modern European history. Reginald G. Trotter, who became "one of the main architects of Canadian historical and political studies," completed a Ph.D. thesis on the Canadian Federation, in which Coolidge had long had an interest, that became "the standard work of reference" as soon as it was published. After teaching for several years in a preparatory school in California and for five years at Stanford University, Trotter enjoyed twenty-seven productive years at Queens University in Kingston, Ontario. He contributed to widened horizons by publishing a volume on the British Empire and Commonwealth in the Berkshire Series, which his friends Newhall and the Packards edited. He organized four conferences on Canadian-American relations, which brought together scholars, politicians, and statesmen from the two countries to discuss the world in the 1930s and the roles their countries together should play.[22]

Not all of Coolidge's graduate students expanded knowledge and understanding through work in colleges and universities. Joseph V. Fuller (Harvard 1912), who worked in The Inquiry and the American Commission to Negotiate Peace, transformed his 1921 thesis on Bismarck as a diplomatist into a fine book and taught briefly at the University of Wisconsin and at Berkeley. Then he became chief of the Research Section of the Department of State, where he edited volumes of documents on United States foreign relations during the First World War. Klein, who had benefited from research in Germany, France, and Spain, made his 1915 thesis into an excellent volume, *The Mesta: A Study in Spanish Economic History, 1273–1836*, which the Harvard University Press published in 1920 and which was translated into Spanish in 1936. Klein in 1917 left his assistant professorship at Harvard to join the Department of Commerce, where he became assistant secretary in 1929. After the 1932 election, he became a successful scriptwriter and movie producer, but continued to review books for the *American Historical Review* and retained an interest in strengthening the Harvard library.[23]

Waldo Leland, who wrote his M.A. thesis in 1902 and worked two years as an assistant in History 1, left graduate study in 1903 for a career in three professional organizations that have played important roles in American intellectual life. Leland worked for thirty years in Washington under J. Franklin Jameson, who was managing editor of the *American Historical Review* from its inception in 1895 until 1901 and again from 1909 until 1928, directing the association and the *Review* from the offices of the new Bureau of Research of the Carnegie Institution of Washington. Leland served as secretary of the association from 1909 until 1920. From 1924 until 1946, he was the secretary of the new American Council of Learned Societies, which brought the professional associations of those interested in humanities together for common purposes. Leland helped organize and edit the *Dictionary of American Biography,* published a number of valuable guides to archives, helped make the National Archives the greatest American documentary collection, and was especially active in bringing American scholar-teachers into contact with European colleagues in conferences and for joint research. He was elected president of the International Congress (then Committee) of the Historical Sciences in 1938, the first American so honored.[24]

John Kirtland Wright, who received his B.A. from Harvard in 1912 and his Ph.D. in 1922, wrote his thesis with Haskins, Coolidge, and others on the geographic knowledge available in Western Europe at the time of the Crusades, using the Riant collection, which Coolidge had helped purchase. He served as librarian of the American Geographical Society from 1920 until 1937, transforming the research catalogue (as Coolidge had at Harvard), and was director of the Society from 1937 until 1949.[25]

After Harvard and its students (as they spread around the country), Coolidge's second inner circle was his profession and its principal instrument, the American Historical Association, founded in 1884 to encourage "the exchange of ideas and the widening of acquaintance, the discussion of methods and original papers." Coolidge attended almost every annual meeting of the association for thirty-five years, presented papers in five sessions, participated in four other programs, served twice on program committees, was chairman for two luncheon meetings, and gave generously to the endowment fund. He published three articles in the *American Historical Review* and served on the executive council of the association and on the board of editors of the *Review,* using these offices to help increase the association's attention to areas of the world American historians had previously ignored.

The association and its journal originally concentrated on the ancient world and medieval and early modern Europe. Of the nearly 400 articles the *Review* published in its first twenty years, hardly a dozen pertained to history after 1815. Fewer than that were devoted to the world beyond Europe and the United States.

The *Review* added sections for books on the Far East and India and on modern Oriental history only in 1919. As late as October of that year, it published an article, "The Diplomatic Preliminaries of the Crimean War," by Bernadotte E. Schmitt, later president of the association, which used no Russian sources or secondary works.[26]

Coolidge in 1895 presented the first paper on Russian history given at an annual meeting of the association. The association's annual report for 1895 printed it, as did the *Review*'s second volume in October 1896. In that year, when no heading referred to a part of the world other than Western Europe and the United States, the *Review* established a "Northern and Eastern European" heading in its "News and Notes" section.

In 1910 Coolidge commented on a paper on sources of information concerning the Crusades, for which his purchases of materials for the library qualified him. Seven years later he organized and chaired a session at the annual meeting that urged American historians to increase their attention to Oriental history and politics. In 1911 he participated in a program on European history as a field for American research. Five years later the annual meeting heard his detailed and enlightening analysis of the interests of Turkey and its neighbors in claiming Constantinople when the war ended, as well as the problems each "solution" would raise or revive. In 1920 he provided a similarly illuminating examination of the collapse of the Hapsburg Empire.[27]

Coolidge served as the *American Historical Review*'s principal commentator on volumes written in French, German, and Russian on Russian and East European history from 1897 until 1910. These twenty-three reviews, which reflect his knowledge, fairness in judgment, and wide perspective, made available to historians information about studies published in other countries on Russia and the Balkans.* After 1910, Coolidge encouraged the *Review*'s editor to invite young men who had recently obtained their degrees, such as Fay, Golder, Kerner, and Lord, to review books on the Slavic world, and each contributed approximately one review annually for the next fifteen or twenty years.

When Coolidge was a member of the *Review*'s board of editors (from 1920 to 1924), it published six articles on Russia and the Balkans, as many as during its first twenty years. These

---

*The bibliography lists the books Coolidge reviewed for the *American Historical Review*.

included essays by Henryk Marczali in Budapest and Alexander
Presniakov in Moscow. Other articles and reviews enabled
Russian scholars, newly arrived in the United States, such as
Rostovtsev and Alexander A. Vasiliev from Petrograd and Baron
Sergei A. Korff from Helsinki, to participate in the association's
work. One of Coolidge's main services was easing admission of
these men and others, such as Karpovich, into the American
academic community and their absorption by the profession.
Thus the association and American scholars began to extend their
vision beyond the United States and Western Europe. Paul
Miliukov, an outstanding Russian historian, gave papers at the
annual meetings in 1900 and 1904, and Argentine, Brazilian, and
English scholars participated before the First World War. Men
from Berlin, The Hague, London, Oxford, Oviedo, and Paris
attended the silver anniversary meeting in 1909. The *Review*
published its first article by a foreigner, Pierre Caron of Paris, in
1908, and Argentine, Belgian, British, French, Mexican, and
Russian scholars had contributed papers by 1914. Only one
American, William Roscoe Thayer, attended the International
Congress of the Historical Sciences in Rome in 1903, but
seventeen went to Berlin in 1908 and twenty to London in 1913.[28]

The first meeting of American historians who were interested
in Russian and East European history helped to dramatize the
progress made in that field, define the principal needs, and
underline the wisdom of working with scholars in other countries, especially the Soviet Union and England. Coolidge helped
organize this luncheon session at the association conference in
Richmond on December 30, 1924, which brought together about
150 men and women from twenty-nine universities (twenty from
the East, six from the Midwest, and three from the Far West),
many high schools, and embassies and government departments
in Washington. Coolidge served as chairman, but Kerner and
Andrews made the arrangements. Sir Bernard Pares, director of
the School of Slavonic Studies of the University of London,
traveled through the United States in the summer of 1924,
lecturing in thirteen colleges and universities, teaching at the
summer session at Berkeley, and presenting a series of talks at the
Institute of Politics in Williamstown in order to create interest in
cooperation with English scholars and their journal, the *Slavonic
Review*. Rostovtsev, who taught at the University of Wisconsin,
gave the principal paper, "The Main Lines of Development of
Modern Historical Research in Russia." Other papers, by Robert

Seton-Watson of the University of London ("The Future of Slavic Studies") and by Golder ("The Present Status of Historical Studies in Russia"), noted "the profound indifference and ignorance" of their fellow citizens. The commentators were Samuel Harper of Chicago, Kerner of Missouri, and Geroid T. Robinson of Columbia. After the luncheon, Seton-Watson gave lectures at the University of Chicago, in six eastern universities, and to a number of organizations especially interested in Russia and Eastern Europe or in international affairs.[29]

The 1924 program, the participants, the list of those present, and the tours of Pares and Seton-Watson show that the study of Russian history had spread throughout the United States and interested many nonspecialists, but the luncheon represented the peak of interest and organization among American historians interested in Russia and Eastern Europe until after the Second World War. Then and again in 1927, Coolidge blunted the effort to launch an association of scholars interested in Slavic studies, even as an affiliate of the American Historical Association, probably because he worked best as an individual rather than through an organization. Moreover, while Kerner and the other activists saw him as the natural head of the group, he was already overburdened with functions.

Most American historians who were interested in Europe, including Russia, had done research in Paris, Berlin, and Vienna, as well as in the Slavic capitals. The conference brought them together with British scholars, whom they had ignored.* Pares had begun publication of the *Slavonic Review* in 1922, hoping it would become the "organization of all those who have Slavonic sympathies or interests or who have desire to promote good relations between the English-speaking and Slavonic worlds." In part because of the correspondence that led to this luncheon meeting, the journal added three Americans, Harper, Kerner, and Lord, to its editorial board. Langer published his first article in the *Slavonic Review* and many American scholars thereafter published their research in this British journal. *Le Monde slave* did not have an essay by an American until after 1934.[30]

---

*Coolidge was a member of the Anglo-Russian Literary Society before 1900, had invited a number of British scholars to Harvard before 1914, and had cooperated with British colleagues in Paris in 1919, but his principal relationships (and those of his colleagues and graduate students) were with scholars on the Continent. He met Pares only in 1924.

9. The Scholar and the Government: The Coolidge School for Diplomats, and Government Service

DURING THE YEARS BETWEEN the Civil War and the First World War, the size and quality of the Department of State reflected American indifference to the rest of the world and to foreign policy. The American people concentrated their energies on internal issues, particularly reconstruction after the Civil War, expanding to the frontiers, absorbing millions of immigrants, the agricultural revolution, industrialization and urbanization, and making the government ever more responsive to the popular will. In the late 1880s, the New York *Sun* even suggested that the Foreign Service "had outgrown its usefulness . . . and ought to be abolished."[1] Washington conducted foreign affairs in such relaxed fashion that President Theodore Roosevelt wrote the United States minister in Japan in 1905 through the regular mail in a White House envelope. Three years later, when the department was divided into sections for the first time, the Near Eastern Division included Germany, Austria-Hungary, Italy, the Balkan countries, Russia, Egypt, Ethiopia, and Persia.[2]

The size of the Department of State reflected the role it played. In 1902 it had a total of 210 employees, of whom 35 were diplomats, 135 were clerks, and 40 were messengers and custodians. In 1914 it employed only 208. By the end of the war, the total had more than doubled, to 440. In 1928 the department employed 614 in Washington alone. It had grown by 1979 to about 3,700—but this figure did not include the International Communication Agency and the Agency for International Development.[3]

The American ambassador in London in 1907, Joseph H. Choate, directed three American secretaries and three English clerks, plus army and navy military attachés and their clerks. In

1979, after reductions in the previous two decades, the London embassy employed 870 men and women and that in Paris 1,140, including military attachés and foreign national employees.[4]

The diplomatic and consular service was naturally smaller than the department. In 1851 the thirty-one legations engaged a total of about 50 persons. Thirty years later, the United States administered thirty legations and allowed only twelve to employ a secretary at government expense. By 1890 the number had increased to 41 and the department permitted ministers in twenty-seven legations to employ a secretary at government expense. In 1893 the United States established its first embassies, in London, Paris, Rome, and Berlin. The diplomatic service grew from 107 in 1901 to 167 in 1907, largely because Congress agreed to increase the number of secretaries, but declined to 121 in 1914: 41 chiefs of mission, 61 diplomatic secretaries, and 19 foreign-language officers. In 1979 the Foreign Service had 6,800 members in Washington and throughout the world.[5]

The curricula of colleges and universities reflected the same national indifference concerning the world beyond America's borders. A 1906 poll revealed that few universities offered courses on other parts of the world and that no university offered one on international relations or politics. In December 1915 the Commissioner of Education and the Director of the Consular Service in the Department of State learned that not one of twenty-five leading universities offered a course on world affairs.[6]

The quality of those sent abroad when Coolidge was young was low. Lloyd Griscom, later accredited to Tokyo and Rome, was disgusted to learn in the 1890s that the American minister in Venezuela, a former mayor of Burlington, Vermont, was an alcoholic and drug addict and had spent at least one night drunk in the Caracas jail. A report characterized American envoys as "effete, intellectual, and snobbish." A scholarly study of American foreign policy during those years declared that the Foreign Service consisted of "honorary ambassadors, inexperienced ministers, and underpaid subordinates."[7]

Like the services of other countries, the American diplomatic corps during Coolidge's lifetime (and for many years thereafter) constituted a socially exclusive and isolated guild. It consisted largely of wealthy, conservative Christian graduates of private eastern universities, attracted by its apparent life of ease and the opportunity to escape from one's family, to travel, and to serve the nation in a comfortable way. They referred to themselves as "The

Family" and often despised those who displayed interest in American foreign policy. Joseph Clark Grew (Harvard 1902), who became "the model professional diplomat of his generation," declared the service a place for "young men of means seeking a few years in world affairs and European society before settling down to serious occupations." His biographer has pointed out that one-third of Americans who served in Europe between 1898 and 1914 were graduates of Harvard, two-thirds had graduated from Harvard, Yale, Princeton, or foreign universities, and a large proportion had attended private schools as well. When Grew was in Berlin, from 1914 to 1916, that small embassy included nine Harvard graduates, four of whom had studied at Groton.[8]

Appointments almost always reflected political connections, and amateur ministers recruited unpaid diplomatic secretaries among families of friends or political associates. When Coolidge sought appointment as minister to Constantinople in 1900, he obtained letters to President William McKinley from his uncle, Thomas Jefferson Coolidge, who had been minister to Paris in 1892 and 1893; his cousin, H.P. Gardner, a Massachusetts legislator; Senator Henry Cabot Lodge; and President Eliot. Francis M. Huntington-Wilson, who enjoyed a private income of $10,000 and who decided to join the diplomatic service when he graduated from Yale in 1897, secured appointment as second secretary of legation in Tokyo after his father had visited the two senators from Illinois and talked with McKinley. Griscom, whose father was a railroad magnate, secured his secretarial position in London through Senator Marcus A. Hanna of Ohio and the senators from Pennsylvania. Congressman John Jacob Rogers, who sponsored the Foreign Service Reorganization Act of 1924, told the House of Representatives in January 1919 he was startled "at the complete lack of consideration given to merit, ability, or useful experience" when the department made appointments. He noted that fifty-one men had been named ambassadors or ministers since March 1913, that only two had had diplomatic experience or been secretaries, and that the two experienced men had been posted to Colombia and Haiti.[9]

Inadequate remuneration helps explain why those who served were wealthy. American diplomatic salaries in the two decades before the First World War were half those of the British. Archie's brother John served as a secretary in Peking from 1902 to 1906 at no salary. Phillips worked his first year without pay and then received a salary of $1,800. Grew received no remuneration when he began service as deputy consul general in Cairo in March 1904 and after three months as an apprentice was given $600 a year. At that time the third secretary of the embassy in St. Petersburg received $1,200 a year and the first secretary $3,000. When Grew's salary was $3,000 but he required $15,000 a year for his family, his five servants, and their travel, income from a trust fund and an allowance from his mother enabled him to live comfortably. Oscar Strauss reported that his salary as minister to Constantinople at the turn of the century "barely covered my house rent" and that his appointment involved personal expenditures of about $40,000 a year. Griscom had seven servants when he was minister in Teheran in 1901. When he became ambassador to Rome in 1907, his salary was $17,500, and rent for his residence, the Drago Palace, was $15,000. The staff of nineteen, entertainment, and other costs a father and representative abroad had to bear required that he and his wife use their private wealth to support a national enterprise.[10]

Congress in 1906 for the first time granted the Department of State funds for its officers to travel to their posts abroad. After 1918 it enabled the department to pay for transporting an officer's family and household goods. Even in the 1920s, the salaries of diplomatic secretaries ranged from only $3,500 to $4,000, about that of an assistant professor at a major university. Castle (Harvard 1900), a student and friend of Coolidge, who came from a "feudably rich" Honolulu family and attained high posts in the department, "did not regard the increase of diplomatic salaries wise" and believed that "no man who was not possessed of a large income should be admitted to the diplomatic service." Hugh Gibson agreed: "If salaries were raised the jobs would be sought by a bunch of incompetents with political pull."[11]

The Department of State provided no instruction for new diplomatic officers or secretaries before they assumed their duties. Few visited Washington before beginning their work abroad. However, improvements occurred slowly in the diplomatic service and in its spirit, and the character of those who enlisted helped create a professional *esprit de corps*. Presidents Theodore Roosevelt and William Howard Taft strengthened this improvement when they introduced the merit system. Roosevelt issued an executive order in 1906 that applied the merit system to selection and promotion in the consular service and in the diplomatic service below the rank of chief of mission.

/Theodore Lownik Library
Illinois Benedictine College
Lisle, Illinois 60532

The Foreign Service Reorganization Act of 1924 introduced significant changes. It amalgamated the diplomatic service and the consular service, established the Foreign Service School, provided training before a new officer went abroad, and encouraged study programs for those interested in serving outside Europe and Latin America. Forty-two young diplomats between 1932 and 1941 received training in Far Eastern languages, seven in the languages of the Near East, and nine in Russian.[12]

The emergence of the United States as a world power and the excitement of world politics stimulated Coolidge's interest in government service, as well as in increasing his knowledge. As a graduate student, he considered a diplomatic career, and he might have become a diplomat if he had been ten years younger in 1898. In 1908, President Taft considered appointing him Secretary of State, and Lowell recommended him to President Wilson in June 1915, after William Jennings Bryan resigned. However, after 1893 he apparently abandoned interest in a diplomatic career. Even after the exciting months in Vienna and Paris in 1919, he hastened back to Harvard.

Nevertheless, service abroad was welcome when it promised to help him "know the real world" and add realism to teaching. On learning in March 1900 that Oscar Strauss might resign as minister to the Ottoman Empire, he sought the appointment, telling his brother Julian that he wanted "two or three years in Constantinople to get first hand knowledge of the Eastern Question." Service on the Aaland Islands Commission in 1920 would have attracted him, except for his mother's serious illness. He was pleased to serve with the private American Relief Administration in the Soviet Union in 1921 because he "hankered for a little more experience in government." Becoming the first director of the American Institute for Slavic Studies in Prague in the mid-1920s, a private research organization which would have been in the American Embassy, attracted him. He prized visiting his old students, both in Washington and in embassies abroad, and studied the promotion lists carefully to follow their careers. When editor of *Foreign Affairs*, he used his relationships with men in Washington and posts around the world to acquire information about current developments and to make informal approaches to foreign leaders, such as Mussolini in Italy and Hjalmar Branting, Sweden's first Socialist prime minister.[13]

The importance and the limitations of American representation abroad were clear to him. He noted that the apparent glitter of living overseas and the social relations one enjoyed in Western Europe in particular attracted many, but that few who entered were well informed or interested in international politics. He thought diplomatic service was a good career choice for a commonplace, second-rate fellow, but not "a real man's job." Just before 1914, he wrote that most officers led dull and unimportant lives, many of the most promising quickly resigned, and a number (particularly in the Far East) were "a disgrace to the country they represent." In November 1926 a nephew, considering a career, learned that his uncle thought the Foreign Service part of a "circle of foreign diplomats which is pretty much the same all the world over and who form a little band of much pretence and tiresome uniformity wherever they are." Indeed, he felt "a bit sorry" for an officer who "has really good brains."[14]

Experience and knowledge of international politics persuaded him that diplomacy was important, but not an "occult science," and that the best foundation for a career in the diplomatic service was a liberal arts education, "with particular attention to such subjects as commerce, geography, and languages," especially French, German, Spanish, Italian, and Russian (in that order). Such a program was superior to that of a professional school, in particular one that the government might establish. In 1899 and again in 1906, he urged Harvard to establish a school for diplomats and others who were to serve abroad, along the lines of the École des Sciences Politiques. Twenty years later, he strongly opposed the suggestion that Tufts establish a special school for diplomats, and he resisted the establishment of its school by The Johns Hopkins University.[15]

Early in his career, Coolidge decided that he could help raise the quality of the Foreign Service by exciting intelligent, civilized, and wealthy young men whom he judged talented and ambitious and by helping to arrange their appointment. One of his main contributions to widening American horizons and improving the quality of American participation in international politics was establishment of an informal school for diplomats for students who considered public service a responsibility of the rich and well born. Evidence is clear that he helped rouse, educate, and obtain appointments for more than twenty Harvard graduates interested in international affairs and possessing some mastery of foreign languages, and whom he considered sensible but not so intelligent or ambitious that they would be frustrated by work in the Department of State. Friends in the service received recommendations for those he felt met his standards, such as Franklin Gunther (1907), John Gilman D'Arcy Paul (1908), and Nicholas Roosevelt (1914). He suggested Grew as a private secretary to Edwin V. Morgan in Korea and then to Morgan's brother, Fred, in Egypt.* Similarly, he recommended Leland Harrison (1907) to the American minister in Tokyo, launching a career which included Harrison's serving as an assistant secretary of state and as ambassador in four countries. Coolidge corresponded with these men, followed their careers, visited them, and suggested other students when they sought secretaries. At every point in the 1920s the Department of State had at least one Coolidge student at the assistant secretary or undersecretary of state level.[16]

The careers of a handful of men demonstrate the impact this produced. One of his closest friends and the "dean of the American diplomatic service" in the 1920s was Edwin V. Morgan, the son of an Aurora, New York, merchant who graduated from Harvard in 1890 and whom Coolidge considered "probably the best man in our diplomatic service." Morgan traveled for two years before returning to Harvard as an assistant to Coolidge in History 1 while he obtained an M.A. degree. He studied in Berlin the following year, at Coolidge's suggestion, and traveled with him to Tomsk in 1895 and to Hawaii and Alaska in 1897. After teaching at Adelbert College in Cleveland for three years, he was appointed secretary to the American member of the American-German-British Commission to Samoa. He became minister to Korea in 1905, but served most of his career in Central and South America. Ambassador to Brazil from 1912 through April 1933, he so enjoyed Rio de Janeiro that he resided there after his retirement. Morgan was not only a jovial, knowledgeable, and effective representative, but a strong friend of Harvard. He helped the library increase its collection on Latin America by substantial annual gifts, by identifying private collections available for sale, and by assisting in arranging purchases.[17]

*Grew continued this system of appointing as private secretary a proper young man recommended by an academic friend. In 1932, when a nephew withdrew from this post, just as the Grews were to sail for the American Embassy in Tokyo, Grew telephoned Endicott Peabody, rector at Groton, who recommended J. Graham Parsons (Yale, 1929). Parsons at first received no pay, but Grew on the way to Japan gave him $50 a month. This later became $100 a month and remained so until 1936, when Parsons passed the examinations and entered the Foreign Service. See J. Graham Parsons, "From Wall Street to the Ginza," *Foreign Service Journal*, LVI (1979), 9, 35-37.

The class of 1900 produced three outstanding diplomats, friends of Coolidge while undergraduates and throughout their careers, whom he helped enter the diplomatic service. Robert Woods Bliss was director of the Division of West European Affairs in 1920 and became minister in Stockholm and ambassador in Buenos Aires before retiring in 1931. Bliss in 1913 endowed a chair at Harvard in Latin American history and economics, and he and his wife used their immense wealth to assemble a remarkable collection of pre-Columbian art. In 1940, they gave the university Dumbarton Oaks (and his library) as the core for the Center of Byzantine Studies.[18]

Castle was particularly close to Coolidge, not only as an undergraduate but also when he taught, edited, and administered at Harvard, from 1904 to 1917. He often visited the farm on Squam Lake, and Coolidge stayed with Castle or with Bliss when he was in Washington. Coolidge served as an usher at Castle's wedding in 1902, and Castle, who was a pall bearer at Coolidge's funeral, provided useful information and advice when Coolidge was editing *Foreign Affairs*. He was President Hoover's "most intimate foreign policy adviser," assistant secretary of State for Europe from 1927 until 1929, then served as ambassador to Japan (where Grew took his place), and became undersecretary of State in 1931.[19]

Phillips, a neighbor of the Coolidge family on Berkeley Street, studied with Coolidge when he was an undergraduate, and Coolidge recommended him to Ambassador Choate in London in 1903. Phillips, in turn, arranged a position for John Coolidge in the American Embassy in Paris in 1914. A proper Bostonian, whom Henry Adams greatly admired, Phillips was close to Franklin D. Roosevelt, whom he had come to know at Harvard. Assistant secretrary of State from 1914 to 1920, he apparently conceived the idea of creating the group of experts called The Inquiry that Edward M. House, special assistant to President Wilson, established in September 1917 "to collect material for formulating an American program" concerning the issues that would arise at the peace conference. After serving as minister to the Netherlands, undersecretary of State from 1922 to 1924, ambassador to Belgium, and minister to Canada, Phillips was made undersecretary of State by Roosevelt in 1933 (succeeding Castle) to take on the administrative and entertainment responsibilities that Secretary Cordell Hull disliked. He served as ambassador to Italy from 1936 until 1941, when he opened the

headquarters of the Office of Strategic Services in London. Later
he was political adviser to General Dwight D. Eisenhower and
Roosevelt's personal representative to India.[20]

Perhaps the most important diplomat whom Coolidge
helped launch was Grew, also a Boston neighbor. Completing
Groton two years after Phillips, Grew graduated in 1902 from
Harvard, where he too was a friend of Roosevelt, traveled around
the world for eighteen months, and studied French in Tours.
Attracted into diplomacy by wanderlust, dislike of his father's
wool business, the call of public service, and Coolidge's course on
the Eastern Question, Grew enjoyed a most satisfying career,
which began with a clerkship in the consulate in Cairo in 1904.

He served at every rank in the diplomatic service, twice as
minister in Copenhagen and Berne, and twice as ambassador in
Ankara and Tokyo. He participated in two international conferences: in Paris in 1919, where he was secretary of the American
delegation, and in Yalta in 1945. He was twice undersecretary of
State: 1924 to 1927, when another Coolidge student, Robert E.
Olds (Harvard 1897), succeeded him, and in the last two years of
the Second World War. Grew's position in the embassy in Tokyo,
for almost ten years after 1932, and his work with Roosevelt on
Japanese affairs throughout the war gave him influence on
American policy in the Far East.[21]

Two illustrations from the class of 1915 demonstrate the
impact of Coolidge upon the department's personnel policy and
training program and the virtual control his students exercised
over the Division of Foreign Service Personnel, the Board of
Examiners, and the Board of Review for much of the time between
the two world wars. G. Howland Shaw, who came from an old
Boston and Harvard family, completed Groton before becoming a
member of the class of 1915, in both cases a year later than Sumner
Welles. He obtained an M.A. in history with Coolidge before
joining the Department of State in 1917. There he became closely
associated with Grew, accompanying him to Paris in 1919 and
serving with him as counselor in Turkey after three years as chief
of the Near Eastern Division. Shaw and Castle dominated the
Division of Foreign Service Personnel and the personnel board of
the department from 1924 to 1927, as Olds and Grew had the
previous three years. In fact, these men and other Harvard
graduates—Harrison (1907), Frederick Sterling (1898), Bliss, and
Welles—filled the important personnel offices, the Division of
Foreign Service Personnel, the Board of Examiners, and the Board

of Review throughout the 1920s and much of the 1930s. Shaw in the 1930s dominated the Board of Examiners, which exercised great influence over new appointments. He served as chief of the Division of Foreign Service Personnel from 1937 to 1941 and for the next three years as assistant secretary of State and chairman of the Board of Foreign Service Personnel.

Shaw also helped shape the department program for improving the quality of Foreign Service officers. Under Grew, he established in Ankara "a small school of advanced study in Near Eastern affairs." Like Coolidge, he believed that Foreign Service officers should know the language and culture of areas to which they were assigned and should be trained to provide analytical, interpretive, and speculative essays on the circumstances and policies of the countries in which they served, as well as careful, objective reports. In short, Shaw helped strengthen in the Foreign Service the scholarly approach to international affairs.[22]

Robert F. Kelley also influenced professional training and raised the standards of the service. A freshman at Harvard from West Roxbury High School, where he learned Latin and began to study French and German, Kelley joined no Harvard clubs but became a member of Phi Beta Kappa. Coolidge encouraged him to learn French, German, Italian, and Russian and to concentrate on Russian history and literature while an undergraduate. He used these languages (and Latin) in the paper he wrote in December 1914, "The Union of the Principalities," for Coolidge's course on the Eastern Question and in his 180-page senior thesis, "The First False Demetrius."[23]

Kelley received a Sheldon Fellowship upon graduation, spent the next academic year traveling in Western Europe and trying to reach Russia for research, then returned to Cambridge, where he began work on the diplomatic history of the Crimean War. He did not complete his Ph.D. degree, but served in the army from 1917 until 1922, the last three years as assistant military attaché to Denmark and Finland and in Riga as a member of the American Military Mission to the Baltic Provinces. In December 1922 he passed the consular examination, and later transferred to the Foreign Service. Kelley became a member of the Division of East European Affairs in September 1923, and as its chief (from October 1925 until May 1937) advised four secretaries of State, Hughes, Kellogg, Stimson, and Hull, on Soviet affairs. He opposed recognizing the Soviet Union in 1933 and appointment of William C. Bullitt as the first ambassador. His reserve concerning American policy toward the Soviet Union was such that Roosevelt in 1937 incorporated his division into the Division of European Affairs, which had only one Russian specialist during the critical years before the Second World War, and had Kelley appointed counsellor of the embassy in Ankara, where he replaced his classmate, Shaw, and renewed interest in Byzantine history encouraged him to become a coin collector. The American Numismatic Society, to which he willed the 1,155 gold and silver coins he collected in the Anatolian countryside (including one for each Byzantine emperor and empress), in 1976 assessed their value at $500,000.[24]

The only member of the Division of East European Affairs in 1925 who had a graduate academic background, Kelley created a fine library in the division and wrote articles for Coolidge in *Foreign Affairs* that analyzed Soviet census statistics and administrative arrangements. He wanted to give the department "the best informed Foreign Office in the world on developments in the Soviet Union, Soviet relations with other countries, and Communist activities in furtherance of their world revolutionary aims," and to develop "a corps of Russian Language specialists in the Foreign Service." He assigned young officers to schools in Paris or Berlin to study Russian and the Russian area, insisting that they take no courses on recent history. Of the six men Kelley chose between 1928 and 1931, George Kennan and Charles Bohlen became outstanding specialists on the Soviet Union.[25]

In addition to encouraging young men in Foreign Service careers, assisting their training, and helping them enter the diplomatic service, Coolidge served the government during the First World War and in the negotiations that followed. Like Coolidge, those from the academic community who had knowledge and understanding of other parts of the world and international politics made important contributions in 1917 and 1919 to the policies of a government new to the world scene. After the peace, they returned to their campuses with increased knowledge of world realities. Their teaching and research helped waken the academic community and transform the nature of American higher education.

As soon as the United States entered the war, Coolidge became a member of the research committee of the volunteer National Board for Historical Service and of the New England Group for Historical Service, which consisted of professors and others who gave talks in army camps explaining the war and why the United States had become involved. His first official involvement in the war effort was with The Inquiry, which House established early in the fall of 1917 to link research with policy. From late spring until December 1918 he was a special assistant to the secretary of state and studied conditions in Russia for the War Trade Board. His most important contribution, and that from which he and his academic colleagues learned most, was to the American Commission to Negotiate Peace, to which he devoted almost five months in Vienna and more than three months in Paris in 1919. In all his government service he followed principles which were at the core of his life and work, which influenced those he advised as well as those he educated, and which helped establish a pattern for the relationship between the scholar and the government.

First, he was convinced that scholars should avoid participation in political groups and partisan positions on issues of moment. The scholar's function—his obligation—was to provide accurate and evenhanded information to students and fellow citizens. A scholar, like any citizen facing an issue which requires decision and action, must ultimately reach a judgment, but he was obliged to form conclusions only after he had completed the most searching and careful inquiry. Above all, he should explicitly separate the information he presented from his own conclusions and accurately and fairly describe the judgments others reached. Thus, until the United States entered the war, Coolidge avoided taking a public position on the war and on the men, states and conditions responsible for it. He even insisted (in 1915) that the *American Historical Review* not identify him as the reviewer of a book on the origins of the war.[26]

Coolidge reflected deeply upon the problems the peacemakers would face in Central and Eastern Europe after the war and wrote informative and reflective papers before America's entrance. Three essays he published before 1917 were remarkably objective descriptions of the issues and of the principles and policies which might prevent such horrors and give all peoples secure rights—tenets he advocated persuasively, but often without success, in Vienna and Paris in 1919. One essay outlined the origins of the system of alliances that had helped bring on the war. Another described the complicated problems involved in creating a Europe that would give reasonable satisfaction to all national groups and outlined the boundary changes likely to occur if the Central Powers or the Allies should win. The third essay analyzed the history of Constantinople, and the claims of a number of states to it, as a sample of the problems the peacemakers faced.[27]

Coolidge emphasized that establishing secure and accepted boundaries could "never be solved in a manner agreeable to all parties concerned" because geographic and ethnic lines often overlapped, as in Alsace-Lorraine and Macedonia. Ethnographic studies demanded immense care because the data were elusive, contradictory, and fragile and because most scholars were biased in one way or another. For many, language constituted the determining factor, but defining the primary or "first" language was difficult. Moreover, some languages had been imposed. Claims of historical possession were important, but they too collided, especially in areas where Germans and Slavs were intermingled. Some groups, such as the Sorbs and Slovaks, were so few in number that they could not establish viable independent countries, whichever group of states triumphed. In addition, the war had exacerbated tensions. In short, "the ideal state does not and cannot exist in Central Europe." The victors should create new organizations to accommodate the troublesome small groups and should seek to establish boundaries "in [the] least wrong places."[28]

Above all, "in as many cases as possible the settlement shall be based on broad grounds of human rights and legitimate interests which will content those who profit by them, while not appearing too unjust to the rest of the world. . . . In the Europe of the future, as far as may be, no people and especially no great people shall be forced to live in a manner to which it cannot be expected to resign itself." Statesmen must consider the wishes of national minorities when establishing frontiers, all unions should be voluntary, and the existence of the defeated should not be made intolerable. While demands for historical unity deserved consideration and the Czechs, for example, had a reasonable claim to an independent, self-governing state which included all Czechs, making a state such as Czechoslovakia "permanently dependent upon a wrong done to another people" would be "awkward and dangerous."[29]

Coolidge was convinced that peaceful resolution of the delicate, deeply felt boundary problems could be ensured only if all treaties "should be accompanied by a guarantee of essential rights to national minorities, a guarantee signed not only by the states concerned but by all parties to the treaty of peace." He sent a memorandum in January 1918 to House, with copies to his superiors in The Inquiry, on "certain frontier questions." This emphasized that recognizing consent of the governed as a central principle, with concessions to economic and geographical requirements, "would tend to make the most lasting and satisfactory peace." Two months later he told Walter Lippmann that The Inquiry should prepare a policy statement for House and Wilson on protection for all minorities. On March 10, 1919, he wrote to Paris from Vienna: "What is needed is a binding declaration on the part of the Allied Powers which will tranquilize apprehension and will serve as some sort of guarantee of the future." His paper, "The New Frontiers in Austria-Hungary," emphasized the guiding principle of self-determination: "The nearer we can come to forgetting the past and to applying equal treatment, the better it will be and the firmer the foundations for the future." These statements so impressed his colleagues that David Miller of the American Commission to Negotiate Peace instructed Grew, the commission's secretary, to press for insertion of guarantees in all treaties.[30]

The initiative for The Inquiry apparently came from Phillips, although Wilson or House may have conceived the idea of using scholars to provide information and help define principles for government policy. Its primary function was to identify the major problems, assemble basic information, and present the summary arguments for and against the principal proposed solutions. Its members used their training, knowledge, and research methods to prepare papers which included historical information, current facts and statistics, and maps. The evidence they provided concerning the issues within Europe and their causes helped define the problems the peace conference discussed and therefore influenced decision making. The Inquiry's "impact on Wilson and Americans cannot be underestimated," for it provided "the foundations of American territorial policies throughout the peace conference" through the quality of the data and the ideas it provided Wilson.[31]

The Inquiry, technically, was attached to the Department of State, but it was in fact autonomous and reported directly to House. President Sidney E. Mezes of the City College of New York, House's brother-in-law, was director; Lippmann was secretary; and Isaiah Bowman, director of the American Geographic Society and leading geographer of his time, was the executive officer. Headquarters were in New York in the American Geographic Society building on upper Broadway. The staff grew from 35 in January to 126 in October 1918. By the time Wilson and his advisers left for Europe in December 1918, The Inquiry had completed 2,000 reports and 1,000 maps, which filled three army trucks. Twenty-three members of The Inquiry accompanied Wilson to Paris, assigned to the Divsion of Territorial, Economic, and Political Intelligence of the American Commission to Negotiate Peace.[32]

Coolidge, one of the first scholars invited to join, was the unpaid director for Eastern Europe, which included Austro-Hungary, Russia, and its western frontier areas. This division dealt basically with suggesting arrangements in Central Europe that would satisfy the nationalities who lived in tangled juxtaposition with each other and that would lay foundations for a reasonably permanent peace. Coolidge proposed that the unit be called "Questions of Nationalities." His appointment was in many ways ideal because Coolidge's travel, research, and teaching and establishing a great library had provided splendid training. In fact, Widener Library served as the division's base.

Coolidge prepared a model outline report on the peoples and areas with which the division was concerned. After House approved the sample on Poland on November 17, 1917, he completed nine other outlines, identified scholars for each people or area, persuaded them to participate, assigned research projects, and made suggestions concerning issues and sources. He directed the work of ten scholars at Harvard and of others scattered throughout the United States and accepted personal responsibility for some of the most complicated issues, such as Transylvania, the Dobrudja, and Macedonia.

The division included ten men who had obtained their Ph.D.s with him: Andrews, Blakeslee, Fay, Golder, Kerner, Lord, Lybyer, Shipman, Steefel, and Tyler. In fact, all those in The Inquiry who wrote reports on Russia had studied with him. Eight other members of the Harvard faculty or men who had obtained their degrees from the Department of History contributed. In addition, Constantine A. Chekrezi, a Harvard senior who was a native of Albania, and three natives of Central and Eastern Europe participated. The contribution the group made to The Inquiry was immense, particularly when one recalls the confusion of that time, the lack of reliable and organized information on problems whose shadows were just becoming apparent, and American ignorance of and inexperience with the many issues that arose in Paris.[33]

The work of The Inquiry demonstrates how little information was readily available and how few specialists the United States possessed on Central and Eastern Europe. In 1920, only eighteen American historians had received Ph.D. degrees for theses on Russia and Central and Eastern Europe. Fay, whose specialty was German history, prepared the basic papers on the Baltic. Chekrezi submitted the reports on Albanian frontier problems with Yugoslavia, Italy, and Greece, as well as a book on Albania (published in New York in 1919), based on these papers and his Harvard senior thesis. Samuel Eliot Morison, who became an outstanding scholar in American colonial history but had taken Coolidge's course on the Eastern Question and had taught such a course at Berkeley in the summer of 1914, wrote a 563-page paper on Finland, another on Italian policy toward Albania, and a third with Noyes, a specialist in Slavic literatures, on railways in the Balkans.[34]

Coolidge left The Inquiry in May 1918, turning over his post to Lord, and became a special assistant to the Department of State. After two weeks in Washington, he went to London, where he stayed with H.G. Wells and had long talks with Lord Robert Cecil, Arthur James Balfour, Lord Northcliffe, and Austen Chamberlain concerning British knowledge of the situation in Russia and British policy. He spent three weeks in Stockholm and another three weeks in Murmansk and Archangel "to study and report upon economic and social conditions in Russia" for the War Trade Board, before returning to Montreal, from whence he mailed a report on September 28. His hope to return via Vladivostok indicates his interest in seeing as much of Russia as possible and the confusion and ignorance in Washington concerning Russia in the summer of 1918.

His brief visit to northern Russia led Coolidge to agree completely with a memorandum of Felix Cole, consul in Archangel, who argued against Allied intervention. The Allies had unclear goals, and the Russians with whom they were working were weak and divided and lacked spirit. Providing food to Russia should constitute the primary American policy, and Coolidge considered Murmansk and Archangel ideal ports for such shipments, for assisting the Bolsheviks against the Germans, and for postwar trade. This analysis of the strengths and weaknesses of the Allies and their friends in northern Russia reflects the objective quality he always sought. The proposal concerning aid may have led to the War Trade Board's establishing a Russian Bureau on November 5, 1918, but the variety of demands facing policymakers at that time helps explain why this bureau was not active and why these realistic views of the situation in Russia were ignored.[35]

Coolidge's most important government service was with the American Commission to Negotiate Peace. He had hoped and planned to serve as a reporter or observer in the Balkans during the peace negotiations, and his first orders, on November 16, 1918, assigned him there. However, the Department of State sent him to Berne and then to Vienna on December 26, 1918, after Wilson and House had recognized the need for an independent intelligence network "to observe political conditions in Austria-Hungary and neighboring countries" and to provide policymakers in Washington and Paris accurate information for reaching decisions that would advance American interests and establish bases for a lasting peace.[36] He was in Vienna from January 5 until May 22, 1919, except for trips to Budapest and Prague and for a week in Paris late in March to report on the Hungarian revolution. His group forwarded 285 reports to Paris, with great masses of documents, concerning developments in Austria, Hungary, Czechoslovakia, and northern Yugoslavia.

Coolidge possessed substantial knowledge concerning the peoples on whom he reported. His sympathy and affection for Germany and Germans had roots more than a quarter century old, and his Harvard work had increased his understanding of German history and culture. He had bicycled through Hungary, Bohemia, Moravia, and Slovakia as a graduate student and he had returned often to these lands and to Poland. The Hungarians' history and "lively sense of national significance" had attracted his admiration when he first studied the Ottoman Empire and Suleiman the Magnificent. An 1893 essay comparing the Czechs and their history to the Irish showed sympathy for both those peoples.

Whatever his affections, Coolidge's reports were as accurate and objective—as calm, cool, and clear—as the articles he wrote in his Cambridge study. He spent most of his time in Vienna and forwarded "investigative reports" directly concerning the turbulent situation and the factors which would interest a policymaker in Paris or Washington: food supplies, prices, unemployment, the police and the *Volkswehr*, political groupings and policies, the covert activities of Italy and other interested states, and the effects that developments outside Austria produced. His own views were carefully labeled. Estimates of possible developments outlined the likely alternatives and offered his judgments and those of colleagues as well. Although privately critical of the "Tower of Babel" in Paris, he did not allow this attitude to affect his reporting. Above all, he remained out of politics, avoiding the error committed by Lt. Colonel Sir Thomas Montgomery-Cunninghame of the British Military Mission in Vienna.

Coolidge exercised care in selecting his eighteen colleagues. Three had been his graduate students. A geographer was vital, so he chose Lawrence Martin, professor of geography from the University of Wisconsin. Another was a military officer, Lieutenant Colonel Sherman Miles, a graduate of West Point in 1905 who had experience as an observer in the Balkan Wars and at the Russian front in 1916. Philip Marshall Brown, professor of international law and diplomacy at Princeton, who had been a diplomatic secretary in Constantinople and American minister to Honduras, and whom Coolidge had met when Brown used the Ottoman collection at Harvard, was another member.[37]

The staff in Vienna was organized in precisely the same way as the division in The Inquiry, receiving clear instructions and full freedom. Coolidge forwarded reports to Paris as he received them, summarizing them on occasion and sometimes commenting, frankly but fairly, concerning his disagreements with their data or interpretations. He encouraged Miles to send reports directly to Paris from the Dalmatian coast. Similarly, he allowed Brown to remain in Budapest for two months after Bela Kun and Hungarian Communists had seized control. Brown established cordial relations with Bela Kun, whose vitality, maturity and poise impressed him; telephoned Vienna two or three times each day; and served as a kind of "unofficial intermediary" between Bela Kun and the diplomats in Paris. Coolidge on occasion disagreed with Brown's analyses and proposals, particularly that Bela Kun serve as an intermediary between Lenin and the Allies, because this would strengthen the communist position in Hungary. However, Coolidge forwarded everything to Paris because Brown was "a man of mature years and sound judgment and some experience in revolution." Above all, he defended him against the Paris charges that Brown was a "pinko."[38]

In the same way, Coolidge transmitted the reports of Kerner. He allowed him to send memoranda directly to Wilson, although the Vienna staff believed Kerner "prejudiced towards the Slavs" and his reports "Czech ones to all intents and purposes." Coolidge defended Kerner as a trained scholar, with energy, ability, and the necessary languages for serving effectively in Carinthia and in Czechoslovakia.[39]

The Vienna group demonstrated initiative and imagination in locating sources of information. The staff traveled to see the territories that were being discussed and to hear the conflicting views of those who lived there and of their leaders. They analyzed seventeenth-century maps which described the population distribution at that time and studied cemetery headstones to review changes in the generations before 1914. They attended political meetings and rallies. The hundreds of documents sent to Paris included speeches of political leaders, party programs and other official papers, statistics concerning prices and the economic situation, and newspapers. Coolidge talked at length with Michael Karoly, leader in Hungary during the early months of 1919, and with Czech President Thomas G. Masaryk, Foreign Minister Edouard Benes, and their colleagues in Prague. He interviewed policemen, political leaders, newspaper and journal editors, bankers, businessmen, clergymen, workers, and miners. He found time to study important scholarly volumes on the issues they faced and he reported the information and judgments of scholars, those whom he had known as well as those whose judgment he valued because he had read some of their published work. These included Josef Redlich and Joseph Schumpeter in Vienna (Schumpeter was minister of finance in the spring of 1919) and Oscar Jászi, Marczali, and Count Paul Teleki in Budapest. Foreign representatives in Vienna, particularly the Swiss, who had a more objective point of view than most other diplomats, constituted especially important sources. When the Austrian delegation went to St. Germain to discuss the peace treaty, Coolidge wrote thoughtful summaries of the character and views of these representatives, each of whom he knew.[40]

Wilson and his associates in Paris ordinarily considered the materials from Vienna carefully, but it is impossible to measure the influence the reports exercised, except in special cases. In general, they helped to calm the men in Paris. They hastened the dispatch of food trains to Vienna and blocked proposals to send Allied troops in the spring of 1919, which would almost certainly have led to long-term disasters. In some cases, the information and judgments Coolidge and his group transmitted influenced decisions concerning boundaries. Generally, however, the statesmen ignored the data and views of these scholars, partly because the political leaders were so ignorant of the facts they had to master, partly because they reached decisions so quickly, partly because political factors often overruled basic facts and principles. Thus the reports from Vienna and Budapest did not persuade Allied rulers to apply the Fourteen Points to the territories Hungarians had ruled. The uncontested information from Vienna, that three million Germans lived in areas the Czechs claimed, did not reach Wilson, or at least impress him. He did not realize that Germans resided in these territories until after Czechoslovakia had been created. Similarly, he believed that Upper Silesia was "unmistakably Polish," although about 80 percent of the population was German. Above all, of course, Wilson and the other Western statesmen had to recognize that their powers were severely limited, whatever the accuracy of the reports Coolidge and others forwarded.[41] Ultimately, they recognized or endorsed the situation that followed the collapse of the Austro-Hungarian monarchy, because the new states seized territories their peoples had long wanted and because the Allies did not have the strength or will to insist upon other arrangements.

Harold Nicolson in the British delegation, who served on the Committee on Czechoslovak Frontiers, described Coolidge's reports as "the sole source of reliable information" from Central Europe and was baffled that no one paid attention to "the sane and moderating words" of such a "humane and brilliant man." Others, working under great pressure in Paris, considered the Vienna reports too historical—"learned disquisitions on the Pragmatic Sanction." Some, who do not understand the reporting function such a mission plays and who assume that transmitting a report concerning a point of view indicates sympathy for that position, have criticized him for forwarding "massive" descriptions of the views of Germans who lived in Bohemia. Others thought him overgenerous in delivering the views of the Czechs.[42]

In his reporting about Austria, Coolidge provided detailed information and described the alternatives the Allies faced: complete political and economic independence, membership in a Danubian federation, or union with Germany. Care and candor marked the analyses of the advantages and disadvantages each solution offered. He concluded that Austria could not survive as an independent state and that the Allies should encourage formation of a Danubian federation or allow *Anschluss* with Germany. Recognizing that France would prevent *Anschluss*, he pressed for federation "as a political necessity for the peace of the world, for without it, the various small states of eastern Europe will inevitably be filled with mutual jealousy and rival aspirations. We shall have the story of the Balkan Peninsula over again."[43]

So far as Austria was concerned, the second most serious issue rose from the dispute that began in January 1919 between Austrians and Slovenes over the Klagenfurt Basin in southeastern Carinthia. A territory inhabited in part by Germans and in part by Slavs for a thousand years, Carinthia had enjoyed economic and cultural unity in the Austrian Empire. It was of critical importance to Austria, which was losing other territories, but its Slovene minority sought it for the new Yugoslavia. Coolidge considered this conflict a test case for the principle of self-determination and an early probe of the Allies' principles and resolution. His recommendation stated flatly: "In this case the principle[s] of self-determination and language do not coincide, and it is the principle of self-determination which should be observed."

The Carinthian issue was also significant because Coolidge and his colleagues established a provisional demarcation between Austrians and Yugoslavs when armed conflict broke out in January 1919. After Miles, Lieutenant F.R. King, Martin, and Kerner completed a ten-day investigation, Coolidge on February 10 forwarded the recommendation (of the first three men) for a line which ended the fighting, separated the Yugoslav and Austrian forces, and provided what he described as "the most just as well as the most practical solution." This action upset the American Commissioners Plenipotentiary in Paris because the Coolidge staff had become "more deeply involved than they should have allowed themselves to be" and because settling boundary disputes was the joint responsibility of all the Allies. At the same time, they rejoiced that the fighting had ended, reprimanded Coolidge mildly, and referred the dispute to the Technical Committee. The Council of Ten decided in June 1919 to divide the area into two zones, with a plebiscite in the disputed A zone on October 20, 1920. This demonstrated that Coolidge and his group had been correct in defining the line of demarcation, for more than three-fifths of the residents voted for union with Austria. Austrian Chancellor Karl Renner graciously thanked Coolidge and his group for their work.[44]

In the Tyrol, south of the Brenner Pass, Paris rejected

Coolidge's views. On January 9, 1919, he had pointed out that the frontier must be satisfactory with regard to language and geography and must recognize as German an area Germans had inhabited for centuries. He emphasized the profound historical importance Austrians and all German peoples gave this territory, "small in area, population, and economic value but endeared to them by its beauty and its romance, the one bit of Germany in a southern clime, a land of legend and of history, the home of the Minnesingers in the Middle Ages and of Andreas Hofer, who led the heroic struggle for independence against the French." Indeed, "it is inconceivable that this population would ever submit or become reconciled to Italian rule." However, the statesmen in Paris assigned the area to Italy, in violation of the Fourteen Points, because of Italy's strategic defense claim, "which belongs to an order of ideas which we trust will soon begin to be obsolete," and because of Italian political pressure.[45]

On Burgenland, or German West Hungary, a territory of 22,000 square miles inhabited by 389,400 people, reports from Vienna influenced the solution. These papers demonstrated that Germans had inhabited the area for generations, that it served Vienna as a kitchen garden, and that the Viennese considered it a protective barrier against the Hungarians, particularly after the Bolshevik revolt in the spring of 1919. Coolidge's report and recommendation of May 11, 1919, supplemented by his appearance before the Commissioners Plenipotentiary on May 26, led to a decision granting Austria the area.[46]

Coolidge exercised some influence on Allied policy toward Hungary but had little effect on the decisions concerning Hungary's boundaries. His reports from Budapest between January 15 and January 20 were "the first known documents emanating from a non-military authority recording conditions in post-armistice Hungary." They admirably summarized the confused state of the city because of the war and the dismemberments Hungary feared, the weakness of the middle class, and the prominence of radicals in political, economic, and intellectual life. He found Karoly attractive, sympathetic, "well-educated, experienced, and broad-minded." He summarized accurately, and generally agreed with, Karoly's description of the Hungarian position and of the consequences failure to recognize "the great and legitimate grievances" of the Hungarians would produce. A factual account described the enthusiastic, if belated, Hungarians' acceptance of the right of self-determination and their almost worshipful reliance upon Wilson to save Hungary from the effects of its decades of folly. The report estimated, early in January, that a national Communist revolt would overthrow Karoly if the Allies did not apply the Fourteen Points to territories Hungary had ruled. This description of Hungarian views was so precise that the Hungarians' presentations in Paris simply reiterated positions Coolidge had already outlined.

In Coolidge's view, an established state in Central Europe should receive prior consideration when statesmen were making judgments in a period of confusion and uncertainty. Hungary should therefore retain Transylvania and the Banat, which Germans, under Hungarian rule, had long occupied, as well as Ruthenia. The Paris Conference should not dismember Hungary without plebiscites: the new Hungarian leaders asked only that the Allies apply the right of self-determination to Hungarian territory as they proposed to do elsewhere. A fair vote would prevent the emergence of another Ulster or Alsace-Lorraine, while "to compel what has since a thousand years been an unified country" to accept such losses "would be only to condemn it to a future of hatred and strife with every probability of violent outbreak before many years had elapsed."

Coolidge was therefore privately critical of the Allied announcement on March 20 concerning the demarcation lines and neutrality zones between the Hungarians and their neighbors, which he thought part of a French scheme to force Allied intervention in Hungary to crush radicalism and which precipitated the Communist revolt in Budapest. He remained consistent throughout his life on this issue. In the Lowell Lectures he gave in 1920, he regretted that the new Hungary had the "old class . . . as aristocratic and reactionary" as before. The errors made in 1919 convinced him "that the Hungarians will not accept the present situation any longer than they absolutely have to." On December 13, 1927, a month before he died, he wrote to Hamilton Fish Armstrong: "I thought the Hungarians were badly treated at the time [1919]; I thought they were going to be before I went to Buda; I don't blame them for being very bitter. I did what I could for them."[47]

Reports from Vienna concerning boundaries for the new Czechoslovak state also had little impact in Paris. Coolidge forwarded full statements of the Czech and German communities and their leaders, as well as historical and statistical data both sides provided. The German communities in northern Bohemia and Moravia admitted the geographic and economic unity of Bohemia, but urged the Allies to follow the principles Wilson had outlined in the Fourteen Points and recognize their right of self-determination. The Czechs, on the other hand, emphasized historical claims and years of mistreatment under German rule. In his conversations with Coolidge in Prague, as in his earlier talks with Wilson in Washington, Masaryk urged assignment of these areas to Czechoslovakia as a matter of historical right and as a means of giving the new state a defensible military position.

Coolidge had recognized in 1893 that no solution for Bohemia satisfactory to both Germans and Czechs existed, because the Germans were "not intruders without rights" and had as strong a historical claim as the Czechs to areas in which both resided. At that time he supported the German position, because "the Germans have more at stake" and because assignment of Germans to a German state "seems needed to keep the peace." On the other hand, the essay published in 1915, "Nationality and the New Europe," recognized that the Czechs would resist creation of an independent state which would separate them "from frontier parts of their territory which have a German population."[48]

The 1919 reports observed that the Czechs in an "inconsistent but human fashion base their claims to the two halves of their territory on opposite principles": historic boundaries in the case of Bohemia and language and culture in other instances. Coolidge urged that the peacemakers keep the number of alien minorities in the new state to the absolute minimum, without jeopardizing the Czechoslovak economic and political position. Moreover, "a cause which is dear to millions and which is right and natural in itself is apt to triumph in the end, witness the resurrection of Poland." To prevent another injustice, a perhaps fatal "Alsace-Lorraine" for Czechoslovakia, he therefore suggested that "the so-called Sudetenland" be detached from Bohemia and Moravia, a proposal which Paris ignored.[49]

The dispute between the Czechs and the Poles concerning the 8,256 square miles of Teschen was just as complicated as that over the Sudetenland. Polish and Czech kings had disputed the territory from the ninth century, but the Austrian Silesian duchy had been a part of Bohemia since the fourteenth century. Three of the four districts were predominantly Polish, and the fourth heavily Czech. The Poles claimed Teschen on the basis of nationality while the Czechs argued that the previous five centuries supported their "unassailable" historical claim. To complicate things further, the only railroad connecting Bohemia and Slovakia ran through Teschen, and its Karvin area had several large coal mines. A preliminary agreement, made November 5, 1918, by the people who lived in the area, gave Poland ten of the thirty-four coal pits and the railroad.

The Czechs, who considered the area important because of the coal and the railroad, rejected the agreement and seized the Karvin area on January 24, 1919. In his review, Kerner urged that the area be divided, with the coal mines and the railroad going to the Czechs. Coolidge and the others concluded the Poles had a stronger claim, particularly because of the Czechs' use of force. Ultimately the Allies, pressed by the French, awarded three quarters of the area to Czechoslovakia, including the mines and the railroad, again violating one of the central elements of Wilson's Fourteen Points.[50]

The Czechs' actions in these instances damaged the image of Masaryk, whom Coolidge greatly admired, and of Czechoslovakia as a democratic state. They also weakened, if they did not destroy, the hopes of Masaryk and Polish Premier Ignace Paderewski for Polish-Czech cooperation. Czech successes in 1919 undermined Czechoslovakia in the 1930s, when Hitler ignited the dissatisfaction among the Germans under Czech rule and took advantage of Western division concerning assignment of the Sudetenland to Czechoslovakia. And Poland, in the confusion of the Munich crisis of October 1938, seized all of Teschen.

Ruthenia was another complicated area on which Paris rejected the facts and judgments the Vienna group produced. Coolidge, who had traveled in Ruthenia, had discussed this pivotal section and its people in his manuscript on the expansion of Russia almost two decades earlier, pointing out that the area was ethnically Ukrainian but had strong economic ties to Hungary, of which it had been part for a thousand years. In 1919 as in 1903, most of the inhabitants were "not in a position to know what they do want except peace, order and a certain respect for their individuality," because of their education and the general confusion. Czechoslovakia had "no tenable ground whatsoever" for acquiring the area, which Coolidge in 1919 described as a case of Slovak imperialism. Moreover, granting the territory to Czechoslovakia would add "to the dangers to which the new Czecho-Slovak state is exposed." Coolidge therefore urged that the Paris authorities give the territory to Hungary, which would reduce the dissatisfaction felt for other losses and thereby lessen the likelihood that an aggressive Hungarian nationalism would rise. However, the statesmen awarded Ruthenia to Czechoslovakia.[51]

Work in Paris from May through August 1919 continued Coolidge's Vienna labors and expanded his education. His main goal was to preserve as much territory for Austria, Hungary, and Bulgaria as possible and thereby lower the likelihood these states would become aggressively revisionist and launch another war. He emphasized safeguarding the rights of minorities in the new states, which might be as harsh with their minority groups as the Austro-Hungarian Empire had been. But the statesmen had already made the main decisions, leaving secondary boundary and other territorial disputes to second and third echelons, so his role was not significant. On the other hand, the so-called experts received little guidance from their political superiors, so they exercised some influence in defining some frontiers.

Coolidge was placed on the Committee on Czechoslovak Frontiers on May 24, replacing Charles Seymour, who in his work on the original draft treaty had ignored the facts and views Coolidge had presented and who instead had accepted Czechoslovak proposals concerning the boundaries of Bohemia, Teschen, and Ruthenia. Moreover, the experienced French diplomats who dominated this committee, and who were determined to create a large Czechoslovak state, told Coolidge that any changes in the agreements Seymour and others had accepted would upset a complicated series of treaties. Czechoslovakia on July 2, 1919, therefore received boundaries that included 3,124,000 Germans and 745,000 Magyars.[52]

On June 10, 1919, Coolidge was assigned to the Central Territorial Commission, replacing Haskins, and given responsibility for examining the Austrian response to Allied proposals and for helping to draft the Austrian and Hungarian treaties. In this and in his work on the Committees on New States and Protection of Minorities and on Greek Territorial Questions, he exercised some influence. He was particularly helpful in the 164 meetings of the latter committee in inserting provisions for minorities. In fact, the memorandum of February 19, which recommended the Allied Powers provide guarantees for the protection of minorities to "tranquillize" apprehension, persuaded American leaders to insert these principles in the treaties with Poland, Czechoslovakia, Germany, Austria, and the Balkan countries. His efforts to ensure the right of reciprocal and voluntary emigration without loss of property led to insertion of this right into the Greek-Bulgarian convention, signed on November 27, 1919. This helped reduce conflicts between Greece and Bulgaria over eastern Thrace, where Coolidge thought Greece's case was weak.[53]

Like other scholarly observers in 1919 and since, Coolidge thought the decisions on the Germans in Bohemia and the addition of Teschen and Ruthenia to Czechoslovakia mistaken and tragic. His estimates concerning the southern Tyrol, Fiume, Upper Silesia, Danzig, *Anschluss*, and the dismemberment of Hungary proved correct in the long run. Still, he thought that the peace conference had produced remarkably sound and sensible solutions. Statesmen had limited powers, because the Austro-Hungarian Empire had collapsed and the successor states had established new boundaries. Moreover, the conference could not decide all "rights" and could only try to determine the fairest boundaries, with special attention to those on the winning side.[54]

Coolidge's national and international reputation and the quality of his work with The Inquiry and in Vienna and Paris leads one to conjecture why his role in the peacemaking process was not more effective and why he did not emerge as the leading academic adviser to the president and to the Department of State on Russia and the new states of central Europe. He had friends in Paris in 1919 and in high positions throughout the Department of State in the 1920s, and he knew the president and the secretaries of state well enough to lunch with them on his trips to Washington. Yet Wilson did not place him on the Root mission to Russia in 1918, which had no effect but seemed important at the time. Much, if not most, of his advice from Vienna was ignored. When the Department of State sought an academic adviser on Soviet affairs after the war, it chose Samuel Harper of the University of Chicago, who lacked both Coolidge's comprehension of Russia and Eastern Europe and his standing as a scholar.

Coolidge had no party affiliations or connections. No one pressed him forward, as Charles R. Crane did his protegé, Samuel Harper. In addition, Coolidge lacked ambition and concern with power or helping establish policy. His decision to interest young men in diplomatic service, rather than in politics, is representative of his own concerns. He surely recognized that the most exciting and important post in 1919 would be in Paris, but he sought assignment in the Balkans, where he could help collect accurate information, identify the issues, and suggest alternative policies—the functions a scholar could best perform and those which would most increase his store of knowledge and understanding. Above all, his friends and associates, like Coolidge himself, recognized that Harvard was his deepest love and that government service was just a temporary obligation.

The work of scholars in The Inquiry and for the American diplomatic effort in Paris had less effect than its merits deserved, and many important decisions in Paris paid little attention to it. Nevertheless, the principles they raised and the detailed analyses they produced exercised some influence and helped educate the next generation of American leaders. Above all, the scholars acquired an understanding of the basic problems in Europe and of international politics which they could have achieved in no other way. Their experiences deepened their interest in the wider world in which the United States had to play a role and their universities had in general neglected. When they returned to campus, they carried increased knowledge and greater determination to transform American education. At Harvard alone, not only hundreds of undergraduates but dozens of graduate students and colleagues benefited when Coolidge, Haskins, Lord, and their colleagues returned to classes and faculty meetings. Clark, who taught at Michigan, Princeton, and Iowa; Lee, who carried on the Langer tradition at Clark for more than forty years; Nowak, who taught at Boston University from 1922 until 1965; Steiger, whose career at Simmons lasted three decades; and Sidney R. Packard, who taught at Smith College for forty-two years, are among the many alumni of The Inquiry and the American Commission to Negotiate Peace whose experience helped them contribute to the changes in American higher education after the war.

10. Educating the Informed Public: The Council on Foreign Relations and *Foreign Affairs*

THE REACTION OF THE American people and their representatives to World War I and the Treaty of Versailles removed the United States for about two decades from the active participation in world affairs which President Woodrow Wilson and many of his countrymen had envisaged during the months in which the United States participated in the war and in the 1919 negotiations. However, analyses of America's role in world politics between the wars which concentrate upon diplomatic history often exaggerate United States indifference to international affairs. The country played an increasing part in world political, economic and cultural life in the 1920s. It was active in many international activities, from the Washington Conference on naval armaments and East Asian questions to efforts to help resolve the reparations and foreign debt issues. Moreover, the United States in the 1920s became ever more involved in the world economy, as the effects of the stock market crash in 1929 demonstrate. American intellectual life became more entwined with that of Europe than before, and American music, art, and architecture began to acquire recognition throughout the world and, at the same time, absorb influences from other cultures. The rapid changes in transportation and communications that helped make the globe smaller drew Americans, including thousands of tourists, into increased interest in the world and helped create at least a vague realization that the United States was part of a larger community.

In the colleges and universities, the decade after the First World War witnessed a slow increase in the study of other countries and peoples as Coolidge and other scholars returned from participation in The Inquiry and the American Commission to Negotiate Peace and from service in the armed forces.

Journals whose readers included many of those who shaped opinion and policy, such as the *Nation,* the *Atlantic Monthly,* and the *Saturday Review of Literature,* in the 1920s began to devote increased attention to other parts of the world, as did the *National Geographic* and other popular magazines. Newspapers such as the *Times,* the *Herald,* and the *Evening Post* in New York and the Chicago *Tribune* supported correspondents abroad and gave increasing space to developments in other countries. Alfred A. Knopf was only the most prominent and successful of the publishers who multiplied the number of novels translated from other languages and the production of other books providing information and insight concerning foreign countries and international politics.

Coolidge's main interest was Harvard University, but improving the informed public's knowledge and understanding of the world and international affairs was a great concern. Public speaking was not his greatest talent or favorite undertaking because he was deeply conscious of his speech flaws. He often felt a sense of terror before he gave a lecture, even to a Harvard class. Moreover, he sought to preserve time for research and teaching and for other professional activities. Even so, he spoke willingly to meetings organized by the college, the graduate school, the summer school, undergraduate and graduate history organizations, and Harvard Clubs in Boston, New York, and Washington. Women's clubs in the Boston area and meetings of businessmen in Chicago invited him for addresses, and he presented papers before professional groups, such as the American Geographical Society and the Society of International Law. In the 1920s the Army War College and the Navy War College heard him speak on developments within the Soviet Union and on international affairs. He was the only one to give three sets of lectures at the Lowell Institute in Boston, and he presented series of talks at the University of Virginia, Northwestern, and Princeton in 1916 and 1917. Institutions from Cooper Union and Rochester in the East to Michigan in the Midwest and Berkeley on the West Coast invited him to lecture at a time when this practice was far less common than now.

Coolidge also helped widen the horizons of the American public through the press. The Harvard presidents under whom he served resolutely refused to hold press conferences or give interviews, but the Boston press, the Harvard *Crimson,* and the Yale undergraduate newspaper often interviewed Coolidge. Contributing reviews to professional quarterlies and to journals for the general public, such as the *Atlantic Monthly* and the *Saturday Review of Literature*, also enabled him to reach beyond the university.

For years he was an important contributor to the great liberal magazine, the *Nation*, a "Weekly Journal Devoted to Politics, Literature, Science, Drama, Music, Art, and Finance," founded in 1865 by E.L. Godkin, a Manchester liberal who used the London *Spectator* as his model in his effort to "reform" American journalism. It became the weekly edition of the New York *Evening Post* when Henry Villard purchased it in 1881. Many considered the *Nation* the leading American literary journal, and Lord James Bryce described it as "the best weekly not only in America but in the world."

The *Nation* provided informed analyses of national and international politics, was a center for literary criticism, tended to lean toward the Democrats in national elections, and had a deserved reputation as an independent journal that took "the moral view." From the end of the Civil War until 1914, it was the favorite magazine of American editors and teachers. It introduced Russian literature to the American public. Eugene Schuyler served as a contributor for twenty-five years, and Isabel Hapgood, probably the outstanding American translator of Russian literature from 1880 until 1930, was its St. Petersburg correspondent for twenty-two years.

Both the *Nation* and the New York *Evening Post* had strong Boston and Harvard connections. During the *Nation*'s early years, Francis Parkman, James Russell Lowell, Henry Adams, and William Dean Howells served as advisers and contributors. When Coolidge was an undergraduate and, later, a member of the Harvard faculty, Eliot and many eminent Harvard scholars contributed articles. Santayana, like many Harvard faculty members, subscribed and read it carefully.[1]

Coolidge began to provide articles and reviews to the *Nation* and the New York *Evening Post* as soon as he left Vienna in 1893. In the following decade he published thirty-one articles and sixty-two reviews of books dealing with Russia, the Balkans and Near East, Africa, and East Asia. Shortly after the First World War, he published twelve leading articles in the *Evening Post*. Half of these dealt with Central Europe, from which he had just returned.[2]

Coolidge's most important service toward educating the informed public concerning world affairs was helping found the

Council on Foreign Relations and editing its journal, *Foreign Affairs,* during its first six years. Created in 1921 to promote analysis and discussion of international affairs and American foreign policy, the Council sponsors *Foreign Affairs;* annual volumes (*Political Handbook of the World* and *The United States in World Affairs*); an annual collection of documents; and an increasing number of research studies of issues of current and future importance. From its first appearance, *Foreign Affairs* has been the most influential American quarterly devoted to informed analysis of world affairs. The Council, at least until the 1950s, was the most important private organization in the United States engaged in research and discussion of international issues, and it remains one of the most influential. It organizes research and study groups on critical subjects, such as Sino-Soviet relations, the Panama Canal, and the problems of the 1980s, which since 1927 have led to a flood of scholarly publications. The fruits of this research and the views of American specialists and a wide range of foreign statesmen and leaders reach the membership through late-afternoon meetings the Council arranges in its New York quarters two or three times each week.

Most members of the Council have been prominent bankers and lawyers from Wall Street and businesssmen, scholars, and officials, almost entirely from New York City and the East. The Council has been from its inception a center of the American elite. Its membership list, which numbered only 500 in 1936 and even in 1981 was less than 2,000, has been called "a Handbook of the Mighty" by both Marxist and extreme conservative critics.[3] Members of the Council's board of directors and of the board of editors of *Foreign Affairs* have been (or are) officials in government agencies, particularly the Department of State, the Department of Defense, the Department of the Treasury, and the Central Intelligence Agency. Late in the 1970s, in efforts to bring the knowledge and judgments of foreign and American statesmen and scholars to the growing number of members who are government officials or who work in other organizations in Washington, the Council organized occasional lectures and discussion groups in the capital. At the same time, it sought to become a more truly national organization by increasing the number of members beyond the East Coast and by encouraging the work of affiliate Committees on Foreign Relations (which it had helped found in earlier years) in major cities throughout the nation.

The Council on Foreign Relations was established on four

bases, and each was an effort to increase American understanding of and participation in world affairs. Two were New England attempts planned before the First World War, and one was active as early as 1910. The first of these was the *Journal of International Relations,* which Blakeslee edited at Clark University from 1910 until 1922. The second was the Institute of Politics at Williams College, a summer institute for discussion of international problems, conceived in 1913 and active from 1921 until 1932. The other two were a small band who took part in the American Commission to Negotiate Peace in Paris and a group of New Yorkers who formed an informal organization to discuss the war and to entertain foreign visitors in 1918 and 1919. Coolidge played an active role in the first three of these organizations and used the interest and momentum they represented to help establish the Council on Foreign Relations and its quarterly journal.

The *Journal of International Relations* and its conferences were among the first organized efforts to awaken American interest in the world. Blakeslee was concerned with relations between races as they affected domestic development and international politics. The first issue explained that the *Journal of Race Development* (its title until July 1919) was designed to present "the important facts which bear upon race progress, and the different theories as to the methods by which developed peoples may most effectively aid the progress of the undeveloped."[4] The quarterly's board of editors included scholars from universities throughout the United States and from Korea, India, and the Philippines. The journal concentrated on East Asia and Latin America, devoted some issues entirely to individual countries (such as Japan and China), and gave considerable attention to the Panama Canal and the Monroe Doctrine. Except for some junior diplomats, the contributors were university or college professors, including some from Europe and Asia and many former students of Coolidge. Between 1910 and the late 1920s, Blakeslee organized ten conferences and published six volumes of papers presented at these conferences, three on East Asia, one on the First World War, and two on Latin America and Central America.[5]

The *Journal of International Relations* and its conferences helped prepare the way for the Council on Foreign Relations and *Foreign Affairs.* When it became clear in 1920 that Clark University administrators would no longer provide the intellectual and financial sustenance the *Journal* required, Blakeslee agreed that the proposed new quarterly of the Council on Foreign

Relations absorb his journal. The transfer to *Foreign Affairs,* which Coolidge was to edit, was accomplished easily because Blakeslee had often turned to his old instructor for advice on editorial matters, for suggestions concerning potential contributors, and for participation in conferences. Stephen Duggan, head of the International Institute of Education and Blakeslee's assistant editor, was a founding member of the Council on Foreign Relations. Blakeslee, Duggan, and Leo Rowe of the Pan-American Union, members of the *Journal's* board, became members of the board of editors of *Foreign Affairs.* Two of the *Journal's* assistant editors, Harry Elmer Barnes and Denis P. Myers, joined the *Foreign Affairs* staff with responsibility for the book review and source material sections, respectively. Blakeslee contributed an essay to the first issue of the new journal, cementing the bridge from the Worcester enterprise to that in New York.[6]

The Institute of Politics at Williams College, which flourished throughout the 1920s, was a second New England effort to expand American knowledge of international problems and to nudge the United States into an informed role in the world.* Coolidge served as an immensely active member of its board of advisors from 1920 until his death, helping in particular to identify foreign and American lecturers of high quality. His knowledge of foreign statesmen and scholars was so vast and precise, and President Harry Garfield's respect for his judgment so high, that virtually all foreign visitors to the institute were those he had recommended or approved. Later, many of these men gave talks at meetings Coolidge helped organize at the Council on Foreign Relations in New York, and some contributed articles to *Foreign Affairs,* so that his activities in the institute, and all its work, contributed to the growth and ultimate success of the Council.[7]

Garfield, son of President James Garfield, became interested in international affairs from study at Oxford with Lord James

*The World Peace Foundation, established in Boston in 1910 and endowed by Edward Ginn, the publisher, was another illustration of the new concern with world politics. Blakeslee was president of this organization for sixteen years, Lowell was long a trustee, and Myers for a time was corresponding secretary and librarian. Coolidge did not join, perhaps because he was not a joiner, perhaps because he was interested in teaching, writing, and editing more than in what he called preaching, or perhaps because he thought the goals of the foundation impractical.

Bryce, teaching international law at Western Reserve University and Princeton and undertaking substantial travel. As president of Williams after 1908, he invited lecturers from Europe, particularly from the Balkans, to discuss international issues with the faculty and undergraduates. In 1913 the Williams board of trustees endorsed his proposal to establish a summer institute to provide a "more effective educational institution and one of greater social utility," raise the standards of undergraduate education, and give Williams faculty members additional intellectual contacts. When war broke out in 1914, nine members of a Williams faculty of fewer than fifty were traveling in Europe.

Garfield originally planned a program of summer lectures by scholars of international reputation to a select group of college teachers and graduate students. During the First World War he considered establishing courses "to diminish the animosities now existing between the great nations at war" and to help resolve the problems that would grow out of the war. By the time the institute opened, in the summer of 1921, Garfield had redefined its aims as "spreading throughout the length and breadth of the land an appreciation of the facts of our relationship to other nations and the consequent responsibilities we must assume."[8] His imaginative effort was a predecessor of the expansion of research and instruction concerning the so-called non-Western areas by American universities and colleges after the Second World War, a program to which the Ford and Rockefeller foundations and other private organizations contributed greatly. Later, the federal government, through the National Defense Education Act in 1958 and the National Endowment for the Humanities, began to support programs for educating young men and women and for retraining teachers concerning a greatly changing world.

Garfield established an informal four-week instructional program in August for approximately 300 teachers, graduate students, diplomats, bankers, and other interested and able men and women, all of whom lived in Williams dormitories and ate in the college dining room. Eight presidents and fifty-eight faculty members from forty-two colleges and universities in twenty-one states participated in the first session and eighty-six faculty members in the second. A third of the 2,365 active in the institute's first decade were faculty members, along with 594 people from business and the professions, 231 government officials and diplomats, and 325 journalists, writers, and lecturers.[9]

Garfield arranged that statesmen or scholars present lectures on particular areas or issues three mornings each week. Groups of thirty men and women met on the other mornings in "round tables" to discuss these problems. In the evening, one or two eminent statesmen or foreign scholars gave a series of six or eight lectures. The round table leaders prepared bibliographies and syllabi for the subjects under discussion each summer, and the college library established a reading room with copies of the principal works recommended.

The subjects included the danger spots of the world, principal problems facing American and other statesmen, and international issues of general concern. The Williams president was especially interested in Latin America, so the institute devoted at least one round table each year to that area. In nine of the twelve years, a round table concentrated upon East Asia, and India and Russia received attention on four occasions. Other principal subjects included the war settlements, reparations, disarmament, access to raw materials, the importance of oil and chemicals, aerial navigation, fertilizers, and the underlying causes of international conflict. The curriculum indeed was most impressive.

Garfield believed that having prominent men on his advisory group, and as lecturers and participants, would ensure success. The board of trustees therefore included four university presidents, Walter Lippmann, and other eminent men. Former President William Howard Taft presided at the first session in August 1921 and the speakers included Bryce, Elihu Root, and former Foreign Minister Tammasso Tittoni, president of the Italian senate.[10]

Convinced that bringing foreign statesmen, diplomats, and scholars together with eager but uninformed Americans would create an exciting intellectual program, the institute persuaded men from every country in Europe (except Albania), including the Soviet Union and most Latin American countries, and many Asian states to participate. In the first ten years alone, more than fifty foreigners lectured in Williamstown. The foreign statesmen who came to Williams for a month included General Jan Smuts from South Africa; Wellington Koo from China; Foreign Minister Edward Hansen from Norway; André Tardieu, Clemenceau's closest confidante, French High Commissioner to the United States in 1917 and 1918, and prominent politician and journalist; Masaryk and Benes from Czechoslovakia; Count Carlo Sforza, senator and former Italian foreign minister; Bryce and Lord Birkenhead from England; Count Alexander Skrzynski, foreign

minister of Poland; and Count Harry von Kessler, the first
German ambassador to Poland.* Hungary was represented so
often that the Theta Delta Chi fraternity house at Williams
became known as "the summer home of the Hungarian embassy."

Garfield sought to make the institute's impact national by
encouraging press interest and by publishing the lectures. The
personalities he invited attracted enormous attention. The Associated Press, the United Press, and newspapers such as the New
York *Times* and *Evening Post* sent correspondents, and the
institute in 1922 attracted 288 editorials. The Macmillan Company in New York and then the Yale University Press published
the evening lectures. Few of the thirty volumes sold more than a
thousand copies, but two books by Professor William E. Rappard,
of the University of Geneva and the League of Nations, and one by
André Siegfried, of Paris, were reprinted several times and enabled
the revolving fund to support the entire series. The success of
these volumes was considerable for that period. Even though
Walter Lippmann edited them, each of the first three annual
volumes on *The United States in World Affairs* of the Council on
Foreign Relations sold only three hundred copies.[11]

The Institute of Politics was successful in part because
wealthy men and women and foundations interested in education
and world affairs provided generous financing. In its twelve years,
the institute's total operating expenses amounted to $500,000,
three fourths of which came from such donors. Bernard Baruch in
December 1919 granted $100,000 for the first three years, and later
an additional $100,000. The Rockefeller Foundation and the
Carnegie Corporation each gave $10,000 for the succeeding five
years. Mrs. John D. Rockefeller, Jr., Charles R. Crane, and
Herbert Lehman, a wealthy Williams alumnus, New York
banker, and statesman, provided support for the last few years.
The teachers and others who attended contributed small fees and
paid for their residence in the dormitories.[12]

Garfield and his colleagues, naturally, encountered difficulties. Most participants proved unwilling to prepare for the

---

*Foreign scholars who participated included Josef Redlich from Austria,
Moritz Bonn and Otto Hoetzsch from Germany, Robert Michels from Switzer-
land, Paul Mantoux and Achille Viallate from France, Yusuke Tsurumi from
Japan, and George P. Gooch, Robert Seton-Watson, and Arnold Toynbee from
England. Most American specialists were from eastern universities.

meetings or to read the materials made available, and less than 10 percent attended more than one year. Many considered the institute "a pleasant, inexpensive vacation in a highbrow atmosphere." The Harding and Coolidge administrations saw the institute as a Democratic forum directed against a Republican administration. Others believed it a center for foreign propaganda. Creating a program that was evenhanded and fair, but not colorless, was demanding, particularly on issues such as naval disarmament. Few statesmen combined technical competence with ability to retain the attention of men and women of varied knowledge and interests. Moreover, Garfield's efforts to attract publicity made the discussions less frank and useful than he had hoped. The statesmen were impressed by the attention newspapers gave them; on the other hand, they were reluctant to speak candidly before the press on delicate issues involving their countries and other governments.

Garfield and his board, with the advice of Coolidge, in the early 1920s were able to lure eminent speakers from throughout the world by providing a month in a pleasant summer area, informal discussions with scholars and statesmen from other countries and with interested Americans, and honoraria from $750 to $1500, plus liberal travel expenses and their costs while they were in Williamstown. However, after the first few years attracting outstanding statesmen and specialists for a month became difficult. The institute did not excite the attention of the number of college teachers and graduate students Garfield had envisaged, and only nine college presidents attended in the final six years. Professors from New England institutions were eager to participate, especially when they received $750 (plus travel and expenses) as discussion leaders, but the institute's efforts to attract men and women from other parts of the country were ineffective.* Moreover, Williams College lacked renown as a national institution, and Garfield's effort to obtain an endowment was belated and ineffective. In the eyes of some critics, the institute became a "glorified summer circle, a sewing circle" that provided "adult education for the initiated, for those who were already interested" in international politics. By 1930, even the New England press gave it little attention. After the summer of 1932 it faded away,

---

*These payments were generous. Salaries at Williams, among the highest in the elite eastern colleges, in 1930 ranged from $3,000 to $6,000. Langer began as an assistant professor at Clark University in 1923 at a salary of $2,500.

although Garfield declared "the work of informing and educating public opinion is just as necessary today as it was in
1921."[13]

Even so, these "last shreds of the Puritan mantle" were an
important part of the effort to awaken American interest in world
affairs in the 1920s. The institute introduced a number of
important foreign statesmen and scholars to the United States and
increased their understanding of this country and some of its
leaders by providing an informal meeting place in circumstances
almost ideal.[14] Its sessions on reparations and on disarmament
exercised some influence on American and British policies. It
served to moderate isolationism and keep interest in the world and
in international affairs alive, particularly in the important small
colleges in New England. It stimulated more than a dozen other
educational institutions, especially in the South and Midwest, to
organize similar endeavors on a more modest level. Above all, it
introduced and strengthened efforts such as those of the Council
on Foreign Relations in New York and its journal to widen
American horizons.

The New York foundation for this effort to expand knowledge and understanding of the world was the New York Council
on Foreign Relations, a private organization of businessmen and
professional people established in 1918, which grew to more than
one hundred members, held fourteen seminars between June 1918
and April 1919, and then began to fade away.[15]

The last base was the group of American scholars and
diplomats who participated in the work of The Inquiry and the
American Commission to Negotiate Peace. Some of these men,
led by George Louis Beer and including Coolidge, met on May 30,
1919, in the Majestic Hotel in Paris with a number of British
colleagues to discuss common interests and establishment of a
joint organization. They agreed that "Right Public opinion was
mainly produced by a small number of people in real contact with
the facts who had thought out the issues involved." Paris had
brought them together and into contact with the realities.
Therefore, "when the Conference closed they would constitute
the most valuable factor in the production of sound public
opinion. But their value would deteriorate unless steps were taken
to keep them abreast of the facts and to enable them to think
[them] out by discussion, with each other."

At a second meeting, on June 17, the group decided to form
an Anglo-American organization "to keep its members in touch

with the international situation and to enable them to study the relation between national policies and the interests of society as a whole." Coolidge was one of a committee of eight named to establish a permanent joint committee, with a branch in each country, to maintain libraries, publish an annual register, and produce the six-volume *History of the Paris Peace Conference*, edited by Professor Harold W.V. Temperley of Cambridge University. This history, and continuing friendly personal relations, constituted the only joint actions to emerge from these sessions.[16]

After the Paris meetings, the American and British participants returned home, where other interests engaged them, and dreams of a cooperative organization faded. News that the British representatives in July 1920 had established their own institution, the Royal Institute of International Affairs, persuaded some Americans in New York and New England to establish an American equivalent. The New York Council on Foreign Relations was merged with some of the group who had participated in the peace conference and with those responsible for the *Journal of International Relations*. These men voted (on October 18, 1920) to establish an organization, and on July 29, 1921, incorporated the American Institute of International Affairs, which included sixty-six members from the New York Council and about thirty of the participants at Paris. Late in 1921 its name was changed to the Council on Foreign Relations. In the spring of 1922, when it decided to publish a quarterly journal, it had 182 members and $3,041.40 in its bank account.[17]

Coolidge was in Moscow with the American Relief Organization during those months in 1921 and 1922 when the Council on Foreign Relations began operations. However, his earlier work in Paris and his role in the discussions in New York in 1921 ensured that from the very beginning he was an active member of its board of directors. He participated in many meetings and dinners that the Council arranged, particularly those on Russia and the Balkans. He attended about three dinner sessions each year, even though his teaching schedule made travel to New York for evening events difficult. Above all, he helped found, then edited, the Council's journal.

In December 1921, the Council's committee on publications proposed that the Council publish a journal, absorbing Blakeslee's quarterly in the process. The executive committee a month later endorsed the proposals for "a really first-rate journal on foreign affairs" and that Coolidge be named editor, because it knew "no one [else] in the United States so fitted by equipment and contacts." Lowell thought Coolidge should decline, but he accepted "an unusual opportunity to do something worthwhile from the point of view of the public."[18] The success of *Foreign Affairs* was essential to the survival and growth of the Council and has above all contributed to the expansion of well-founded interest in international affairs among many leaders of American opinion, especially in the East.

Coolidge accepted the editorship on condition he be completely independent and that he have an assistant in New York. The board accepted these conditions and Coolidge quickly chose Hamilton Fish Armstrong as managing editor and executive director of the Council. A Princeton graduate in 1916, thirty years younger than Coolidge, Armstrong after army service became a reporter for the New York *Evening Post*, for which he wrote a weekly article, "Europe by the Week," until January 1924. He shared Coolidge's goals and tastes and contributed significantly to the journal's success, particularly through imaginative efforts in sales and in relations with the New York press. The two men corresponded almost every day, at a time when a letter mailed from New York or Boston at five in the afternoon was delivered in the other city before nine the following morning. They sent about 220 letters to each other every year, in addition to telephone calls and telegrams. Armstrong mailed Coolidge a postcard every day he did not have any news to communicate. Even in 1927, when he was desperately ill, Coolidge wrote 154 letters to Armstrong.

The editor gave substantial trust and freedom to his assistant, who proved an admirable successor from 1928 until his retirement after fifty years of distinguished service. Coolidge treated Armstrong as an equal in the formal but friendly relationship then common in academic life. Armstrong noted that Coolidge "did not trust my judgment, but he did trust me." Coolidge was generous in acknowledging Armstrong's contributions and in urging him to continue work outside the Council. Armstrong's salary from the Council in 1927 was higher than the total Coolidge received from the Council and Harvard, but Coolidge did not notice this.

The two men quickly agreed on the journal's title and selected the format, paper, and type face. The board of editors included the three members of the committee on publications and Garfield; Blakeslee; John W. Davis, president of the Council;

Rowe, of the Pan-American Union and the *Journal of International Relations;* and Alexander Legge, president of International Harvester Company in Chicago, the only member of the board not from the East (Legge resigned within a year). The Council opened its office at 25 West 43rd Street in New York on June 2, 1922. The first issue of *Foreign Affairs* was in the mail on September 13—a remarkable achievement, particularly when one considers the quality of the articles.[19]

Coolidge aimed to make the journal the "first authority in the United States on foreign policy," with the most able contributors available in the United States or abroad identifying and analyzing world problems that especially affected American national interests. Its "dominant purpose is to promote the discussion of current questions of international interest and to serve as the national medium for the expression of the best thought, not only of this country but of Europe."[20]

The editors wanted an evenhanded journal that would help the reader make up his own mind. Coolidge stayed aloof from politics, although he did not restrict Armstrong from serving as a trustee of the Woodrow Wilson Foundation or from open support of the Democratic party. He resolutely avoided expressing partisan views of his own in *Foreign Affairs* (or elsewhere) and was especially alert against efforts to use it for propaganda purposes. The policy he set in the first issue still prevails: *Foreign Affairs* "will not devote itself to the support of any one cause, however worthy.⁴... It will tolerate wide differences of opinion. Its articles will not represent any consensus of belief... but shall be competent and well-informed, representing honest opinions seriously held and convincingly expressed.... It does not accept responsibility for the views expressed in any article, signed or unsigned, which appears in its pages. What it does accept is the responsibility for giving them a chance to appear there."

Coolidge and Armstrong were fearful that *Foreign Affairs* would be considered an advocate of the League of Nations and an opponent of the Republican administration because "our crowd is overwhelmingly pro-League and pro-Woodrow Wilson." The quarterly therefore sought articles critical of the League and opposed to participation in it (or the World Court) by such men as Senator William E. Borah of Idaho. Similarly, after the October 1925 issue carried an article by Roberto Cantalupo, "Fascism in Italian History," described as "officially approved, as an expression of his views, by Signor Mussolini," the journal published one critical of Mussolini by Count Carlo Sforza. It obtained an essay on Hungarian foreign policy by Count Stephen Bethlen, Hungarian prime minister, and one critical of the Hungarian government by Oscar Jászi, a Hungarian radical who had become a professor at Oberlin College. After President Plutarco Elias Calles wrote an article critical of the role of the Catholic Church in Mexico, Coolidge invited Pietro Cardinal Gasparri to respond.[21]

Foreign Affairs aimed to publish essays on important international issues written accurately and succinctly by men and women of intellectual quality and technical competence who possessed "the sacred gift of terse, clear, and elegant expression or of well-turned epigram." It wanted no articles for specialists: each "instructive and informing" essay was to emphasize the basic factors in clear, factual, precise and unpretentious language an interested and informed American could comprehend. In particular, the journal sought "facts and reasons" and shunned "eloquence, generalities, and compliments."[22] Coolidge considered the journal an introduction to further study, so the magazine included a select annotated bibliography, book review articles, important documents, and maps.

The editor wanted an authoritative, dignified, judicious, and "high-toned publication" that had "identity and personality" in every aspect, including the form of the book notices. *Foreign Affairs* used official maps and current spelling. Coolidge's emphasis upon dignity was reflected in his insistence that the journal publish no brief articles and no letters to the editor. From its beginning, the quarterly accepted advertisements only from publishers, banks, and businesses engaged in dignified aspects of international trade. These advertisements appeared in the same formal and severe form as the rest of the journal.

Coolidge's main responsibilities were identifying significant subjects and selecting authors. He was especially eager to attract those whom he termed "headliners," outstanding statesmen and scholars from every country, and his proficiency in identifying and engaging them helped make the quarterly successful. The letter he wrote Bethlen on November 11, 1924, exemplified his genius: he sought "an exposition of the condition of Hungary at the present time, something authoritative and reliable, free from complaint or propaganda—something which would enable the public to appreciate the real state of the country," written by a man "whose name as well as whose words would carry conviction."

During its first six years *Foreign Affairs* published an article by at least one person from every European state (except Albania), and about a third of its contributors were foreign. Its authors included statesmen and scholars from Canada, Mexico, several Latin American states, and Japan, China, Australia, and India. Statesmen who wrote essays included Presidents Calles and T. Esquival Obregon of Mexico and Raymond Poincaré of France and Masaryk of Czechoslovakia. The foreign secretaries numbered Benes, Bethlen, Frank Kellogg, and Charles Evans Hughes. Other leaders included Hjalmer Branting of Sweden, George Brandes of Norway, Karl Kautsky of Germany, André Tardieu of France, and Remiro de Maetzger of Spain. Among foreign scholars were Redlich, Tsurumi, Aubert, Snouck Hurgronje from the Netherlands, Giovanni Gentile from Italy, and H.A.L. Fisher, Seton-Watson, and Toynbee from England, almost all of whom also participated in meetings of the Institute of Politics.

In identifying important contributors, Coolidge ignored his personal feelings, urging Stephen Bonsal to contribute an essay because he considered him well informed, although Coolidge thought him pretentious and Bonsal had been critical of Coolidge's reports from Vienna. He overcame Armstrong's reluctance to invite Lord Keynes: "I object vigorously to many of his views and the way he gets them over, but he is without question the most widely-read and influential writer on current economic and international questions. As such, he ought to have a place in our pages."[23]

Coolidge thought Armstrong and he, as editors, had a responsibility to contribute occasional articles, and he published nine essays on critical issues or areas in his customary evenhanded way and direct, spare style. He chose subjects in which he was interested and which others might find delicate or difficult, and limited himself to one essay on each issue. The variety of problems about which he wrote with good sense and authority and the wide range of knowledge reflect the mastery he had acquired on various parts of the world and on international politics.

Coolidge demonstrated remarkable knowledge and prescience in identifying issues of permanent international importance, not only in Europe, where the great conflict had left enormous problems, but in Latin America, the Middle East, Africa, and Asia, and in the wide sweep of international affairs. *Foreign Affairs* paid particular attention to America's neighbors, in its first six years publishing six articles on Canada and seven on

Mexico. The Philippines was a critical issue ("an American Ireland") so Coolidge accepted six articles on that country. The journal published essays on disarmament and the new air arm, the League of Nations and the World Court, socialism and fascism, the British Commonwealth, the potential power of Islam, the future of the Oecumenical Patriarchate, tariffs, relations between American agriculture and foreign policy, the future of radio communication and air transport, railroads in Manchuria, population movements and overpopulation, water control and floods, monopolies and cartels, smuggling, and race problems. The editors were particularly interested in the latter issue, in part because they were convinced these were critical and because of *Foreign Affairs'* inheritance from the *Journal of Race Development*. The new journal produced essays on Indians in Africa and on immigration problems. Coolidge was particularly impressed by the views of W.E.B. DuBois, and published five of DuBois's essays.

Foreign Affairs included pieces on such trouble spots of that time as Salonica, Cyprus, Ireland, Panama, Mosul, Tangier, and Manchuria, and it made available brief informational articles on population statistics and the size of national armed forces. It accepted a number of fascinating analyses of the importance of particular commodities in world trade and in international politics, which included oil, coal, copper, rubber, opium, wheat, tin, sugar, and fertilizers. Indeed, the reader in the 1980s of articles published in the 1920s can only marvel at Coolidge's foresight in identifying critical issues.

Foreign Affairs' attention to Russia illustrates recognition of its importance and its success in providing accurate information, views of important men, and balance. The editor wrote that "we must have plenty on Russia first and last." He searched widely for men of competence and authority to help satisfy his readers' keen interest in Russian affairs and in American policy toward the Soviet Union. The quarterly invited scholars and observers, such as Louis Eisenmann in Paris, to analyze French policy toward the Soviet Union and the Balkans, and Paul Scheffer, well-known German correspondent, to comment on the situation within the Soviet Union. The editors gave careful consideration to every essay that American, Soviet, and other scholars and statesmen submitted. Coolidge's comments were so tactfully cogent that William Henry Chamberlin continued to submit manuscripts even after *Foreign Affairs* had rejected five.[24]

In its first year, *Foreign Affairs* devoted six of its forty-nine articles to Russia. During the six years Coolidge was editor, the quarterly published twenty-three articles on Russia and even more on Eastern Europe. In its first forty-five years, it produced 248 articles on Russia and notes on approximately 2,000 books.[25] Appropriately and deliberately, the first of these articles was an anonymous one by Coolidge, "Russia after Genoa and The Hague," in the first issue in September 1922.

The editors especially sought contributions from Soviet leaders. Coolidge sent copies of *Foreign Affairs* to them through Golder, who spent many months in Moscow in the early 1920s for the American Relief Administration and the Hoover Institution. He repeatedly invited articles from Karl Radek, specialist on Soviet policy in Western Europe, whom he had met in the winter of 1921-22, directly and through Golder. Radek in February 1926 agreed to contribute an essay on Soviet policy in the Far East, but continued entreaties failed to procure the article. Coolidge encouraged Leo Krasin to comment on Soviet foreign trade policy, and in 1925 Krasin agreed—but again no manuscript arrived.[26] He was able to obtain a sober and uninspiring article from Christian Rakovsky, then Soviet ambassador in Paris, for the July 1926 issue.

One of the principal issues under discussion in the 1920s was American recognition of the Soviet government. Since Britain had reached its decision, *Foreign Affairs* turned to George A.B. DeWar, editor of the *Review of Reviews* in London, for "a clear, dispassionate, authoritative pronouncement of just what the Anglo-Russian treaty does signify, for what reasons it had been concluded, and what are the arguments for and against it."[27] DeWar's article in the December 1924 issue, "Britain's Recognition of Soviet Russia," was critical of British policy and approved American nonrecognition. Two years later Malcolm Davis, a member of the Council's administrative staff, who had been in Russia in 1919 and 1920, published an article favorable to recognition, titled "Soviet Recognition and Trade."

Coolidge believed that most of those whom he called liberals in the United States were favorable to the new Soviet system and would criticize *Foreign Affairs* for publishing articles by scholars who had left the Soviet Union and by anti-Communist political leaders, even though they constituted the largest group to whom the journal could turn for contributions. Still, *Foreign Affairs* sought out the critics to balance friendly articles. Coolidge considered Kerensky "a spent rocket,"[28] but Victor Chernov, head of the Social Revolutionaries and minister of agriculture in the Kerensky government, wrote three excellent articles from Berlin between September 1923 and January 1927. Chernov's colleague in the Social Revolutionary Party, Vladimir Zenzinov, in October 1925 contributed "Bolshevism and the Peasant," which saw bolshevism suffering one defeat after another. *Foreign Affairs* also printed two essays by Boris Bakhmetev, ambassador of the Provisional Government of Russia to Washington in 1917. The first, in March 1924, predicted the collapse of the Soviet Union, as did the second, ten years after establishment of the Soviet system.

Lenin and Mussolini both impressed the editor. Persuaded in 1923 "that there is more similarity in their theories than might appear at first sight and they have an equal respect for the goddess of liberty," he sought a scholar who would compare the two men and their new regimes.[29] Harold Laski of the London School of Economics in September 1923 completed a perceptive article that pointed out that the Soviet Union was the dictatorship of a party and the fascist state the dictatorship of a man, and that both reflected the violence of the age.

Providing brief and accurate summaries of a wide-ranging variety of recently published books was a simpler operation for *Foreign Affairs* than selecting issues and identifying authors, but this section again demonstrates the editors' interest in education and the intensity of their search for objectivity and balance. "Some Recent Books on International Affairs" included books published in French, German, Italian, Spanish, and Russian. It provided succinct summaries and analyses of about seventy-five volumes on international issues in the first issue, and about 125 by 1927. It not only listed memoirs and analyses of international politics, but defined the factors affecting world affairs in a broad way. For example, it noted the 1922 volume by Margaret Sanger, *The Pivot of Civilization,* one of the first modern proposals for artificial birth control. It provided brief summaries of volumes by Oswald Spengler, Charles Maurras, Maurice Barrès, and Julien Benda. It listed Soviet publications, the official documents of many governments, and the collected speeches of Mussolini.

The first book review editor of *Foreign Affairs* was Harry Elmer Barnes, who had served in that capacity for the *Journal of International Relations* and who later became a spectacular and often irresponsible *enfant terrible.* Barnes's successor in selecting and reviewing books was Langer, who with Armstrong in 1933 published *Foreign Affairs Bibliography, 1919-1932,* the first of a series of bibliographies the Council has published every ten years, which are of immense value to all those interested in world affairs and American foreign policy. Langer was an active member of the Council from 1925 until he died (in 1977), served on the editorial advisory board of *Foreign Affairs* for more than twenty-five years, and with Armstrong maintained a direct link between Coolidge and the work of the Council until almost 1980.

The quarterly benefited from the attention the New York press provided. The Council's board of directors in the 1920s included Edwin F. Gay, editor of the New York *Evening Post,* and John H. Finley, editor of the New York *Times.* Armstrong, who contributed a weekly article to the *Evening Post* through December 1923, was close to Finley and some of his associates and often lunched at the *Times.* He frequently succeeded in "planting" news stories in these newspapers. He also introduced some contributors to *Foreign Affairs* and some of the foreign speakers at Council meetings to *Times* editors at their lunches. This often led to articles in the next day's paper.[30]

Both the *Times* and the *Evening Post* published announcements of some issues and summaries of important articles, sometimes on the first page. They produced editorials on the most significant issues *Foreign Affairs* raised and published letters that the journal refused to print. This attention led other New York newspapers, such as the *World,* the *Herald,* the *American,* and the *Sun,* to follow their lead. Boston newspapers, particularly the *Christian Science Monitor,* the *Transcript,* and the *Herald,* also gave its most significant articles substantial publicity. One notice in the *Christian Science Monitor* so delighted Coolidge that he wrote he "would almost join the ranks of the faithful myself if I could get the organization to back up *Foreign Affairs* and prescribe it to all members."[31]

The quarterly also profited from the controversy some early articles attracted. The second issue (December 1922) contained an article by General Tasker H. Bliss on "Evolution of the Unified Command," an important subject because most observers thought that placing all armies on the western front under one command helped save the Allies from defeat and contributed significantly to winning the war. This essay displeased General Luigi Cadorna, who had been chief of staff of the Italian army and who published a long letter in the New York *Times,* to which Bliss responded. The following year Coolidge persuaded General Hermann von

Kuhl, who had been chief of staff of a German army and then of an army group, to contribute an essay on the command of the armies of the Central Powers.[32]

The March 1923 issue attracted even greater attention because an article, "The World Oil Situation" by E.C. Bedford, chairman of the board of Standard Oil of New Jersey, led to a decline in the price of oil shares on the stock market and to a substantial slump in the market itself. It produced responses from presidents of other oil companies in the pages of the New York press.[33]

Foreign newspapers and journals, such as *Figaro*, the *Economist*, the *Spectator*, and the *Review of Reviews*, helped *Foreign Affairs* by publishing comments on some of its essays. Coolidge wrote that European press attention "adds greatly to our international standing, and our reputation in Europe must react upon and affect our prestige here." The journal had 386 foreign subscribers by the time its second issue appeared. The editor rejoiced when a nephew wrote in 1926 that he had seen five copies in Liberia.[34]

Armstrong and Coolidge demonstrated skill and perception in organizing the subscription campaign. They lectured to groups of important businessmen. Coolidge obtained mailing lists from the American Historical Association and other professional groups, although he believed that professors were too poor to purchase subscriptions and would read *Foreign Affairs* in their libraries. So he attempted to persuade libraries to subscribe, even producing special reprints of the recent book and source material sections for distribution to libraries. By January 1923, 127 public libraries and 208 college and school libraries in the United States were subscribers. Seventeen foreign libraries had joined the list by June 1924.[35]

The editors were especially interested in placing *Foreign Affairs* in "pretty nearly every library and club that has quarters in America, likewise every know-it-all in New York, Boston, Washington, San Francisco, and Main Street." The reader they sought was ordinarily a club member. Armstrong mailed announcements to the Cosmos Club in Washington, the Century Association and the Knickerbocker Club in New York, and faculty clubs in all major universities. By early 1923, thirty-five American clubs were subscribers. For clubs in other countries, they obtained addresses from Baedeker volumes, Murray's *Guide for India and Ceylon*, and *The World Almanac*. In June 1924, when they learned that no British clubs subscribed, *Foreign Affairs* obtained a list of the clubs and their secretaries from David Boyle, secretary of the Prince of Wales, and mailed announcements. Coolidge acquired lists of clubs in Latin America from friends in embassies there and persuaded American banks to suggest others.[36]

Dismayed that only one congressman had subscribed by 1923, the editors sent announcements to the homes of members of the Senate and House Foreign Relations committees, and later to every member of both houses. In 1924 they mailed letters to delegates to the Republican and Democratic national conventions, pointing out that the summer issue carried essays by leaders of each party on the foreign-policy platforms. They wrote to the foreign missions in Washington and to consulates in New York and Los Angeles. They rejoiced that *Foreign Affairs* had received eighteen subscriptions from foreign legations by August 30, 1922, and that the first Soviet subscription arrived in June 1925. Later, the magazine sent letters to ministries of foreign affairs throughout the world with an issue which contained an article of special interest. Coolidge hoped that the Department of State would call it to the attention of its chiefs of missions, but decided that requesting or suggesting such action was improper.[37]

The editors' efforts to reach other elements of the informed public showed the same imagination. Coolidge decided that *Foreign Affairs* should be sold only by newsstands with a select clientele, such as the Back Bay railroad station in Boston. He was eager that important book stores, especially those abroad, should sell it, and was delighted to learn in June 1923 that Brentano's in Paris had sold twenty copies. Rejecting the proposal to send announcements to Rotary clubs and chambers of commerce, he agreed that interviews of Armstrong and eminent contributors on New York radio stations were acceptable. The journal obtained the mailing list of the *Yale Review* to help it identify potential readers in the Far West, and the Harvard University Press list was helpful. In 1925 *Foreign Affairs* mailed announcements to Harvard alumni, a select list from *Who's Who*, and members of the Summer Social register. Armstrong sent a sample copy to William of Hohenzollern in Doorn in the Netherlands, and Coolidge was pleased when his dentist in Cambridge filled out a subscription form. Armstrong urged subscribers to present Christmas gift subscriptions to friends; this tactic produced 118 subscriptions before Christmas 1922 and became an important base for *Foreign Affairs'* success in subsequent years.[38]

Foreign Affairs from the beginning was a remarkable success, in part because its founders established high standards but also because they were imaginative and alert in bringing it to the attention of potential readers. The Council in 1922 set a goal of 3,000 subscribers. The number rose quickly, from 900 on the first day of publication to 2,750 in November 1922, to 5,000 in January 1923, to 7,000 in November 1924, and to 11,200 in the summer of 1927. The journal was reaching important opinion makers throughout the United States and Western Europe as business-men, bankers, lawyers, government officials, diplomats, scholars, legislators, libraries, and clubs subscribed. In 1980 the number of subscribers exceeded 75,000.[39]

Thus the Council on Foreign Relations and *Foreign Affairs* became an important part of the effort to awaken Americans to the world and to the way in which their universe was "coming together." With its editor in Cambridge and an able confederate in New York, the journal had an eastern base and orientation. It concentrated on educating the prosperous and the best informed in "the liberal Eastern establishment," but the foundation of American education and interest in the world *was* in the East and in the group whose horizons and interests the editors sought to widen. From the beginning, *Foreign Affairs* established high standards, introduced large numbers of foreign statesmen and scholars and their views to an American audience, and created a sound base on which the Council on Foreign Relations and the journal together have had a significant impact on the American view of the world. If *Foreign Affairs* did not reach Main Street, it greatly advanced the process of widening American horizons in an age of isolationism. Coolidge's final success, it was a natural culmination of all his work.

Part 5:

Conclusion

11. Beginning a Continuing Revolution

FEW EXCITING AND SIGNIFICANT ideas have emerged in modern times from universities. Introducing change in the curricula and spirit of institutions of higher learning is especially difficult because educators, like generals, often conduct their work with strategies and tactics inherited from previous generations. Thus scholars and teachers, and the universities and colleges in which they live and work, have shown little more insight in comprehending the incredible series of changes which have overwhelmed the world in the past century in particular than have their less-well-educated fellows. In particular, they have been tardy in studying and describing other areas of the world, the way in which the world has shrunk, the degree to which lives of all peoples have been inextricably linked together. Even though the United States has made considerable progress in the last four decades and almost certainly devotes more attention to research and instruction concerning other parts of the world than does any other country, interest in and knowledge of the languages and histories of peoples beyond its boundaries and Western Europe remain shockingly low. Less than 5 percent of American schoolteachers know a foreign language or have studied materials which include significant information about other peoples or international affairs. Only about 10 percent of their students acquire any knowledge of another area of the world, fewer study (even briefly) one language, and the percentage of those who graduate from higher educational institutions after such study remains very low. The work of approximately 9,000 specialists in international studies (for almost 12 million students in colleges and universities!) and the dozens of books and articles these men and women produce have naturally widened and deepened knowledge and understanding among the educated public. The mass media, formal and informal organizations of citizens interested in world affairs or in particular areas of the world, and travel by millions to other parts of the globe have awakened interest and increased comprehension, but the problem remains and may be growing.

This volume has dealt with the realization of some Americans of the need to know and understand other peoples and world politics between the time when America began to emerge as a great power and the Great Depression. It concentrated upon the life and work of Archibald Cary Coolidge, who was one of the first to recognize this need and who contributed perhaps more than anyone else to laying the bases for enlarging knowledge and comprehension. The way in which he helped to reshape the structure and spirit of education at Harvard University, and then in many other colleges and universities; the qualities he stamped upon this great educational enterprise; and his achievements in establishing bases for reaching the informed public beyond the university identify him as a central figure in the evolution of American higher education.

Coolidge was a generalist, not a specialist, an able and productive scholar, but not one whose publications could command instant respect, as did those of Frederick Jackson Turner and Charles H. Haskins, whom he persuaded to come to Harvard from the University of Wisconsin. He was not a gifted teacher or commanding lecturer. He was modest, unpretentious, and indifferent to prestige and power, apparent handicaps in an age when strong personalities tended to lead and even to dominate in education, as well as in business and in politics. Moreover, colorful and dynamic characters, whether creative or not, attract the attention of historians. Coolidge was not an exciting or dramatic person; in fact, he was quite the reverse. He concentrated his time and energies upon his goals for Harvard and for the other professional circles in which he lived, rather than upon his personal life. This remained private, almost concealed, from all but his parents, his brothers and their families, and a handful of personal friends. For example, even the most imaginative and careful search of the immense amount of material available concerning his life and activities failed to provide information concerning his fiancée and their courtship, other than that she later married another Boston man. He deliberately chose his teaching and writing and living style, and his professional qualities became those through which we know him. He was not colorful, brilliant, or exciting, but his influence nevertheless was considerable.

Coolidge possessed and utilized considerable advantages. He was a Boston Brahmin and not a "court Jew." He possessed serene self-confidence and self-discipline. Family wealth enabled him to study and travel in comfort and to assist Harvard to make essential new appointments. He was, by birth and education, a member of the group which dominated Boston and New England intellectual life, and he worked within familiar institutions and traditions. However, he was not a dedicated "old boy," and he deliberately introduced changes which weakened the domination Harvard and New England had exercised over the American mind.

Though evenhanded and dispassionate in his approach to other countries and cultures, Coolidge reflected some of the parochialism of Boston and his region. Later generations would consider his views concerning the character and position of blacks and restricted immigration more civilized than those of many of his class and generation, but his positions reflected prejudices he was able to face but not eliminate. He recognized that history is more than past politics and emphasized that Americans should understand the histories of other peoples, but he saw only dimly the importance of ideas and of economic and social history. The socialism of the era barely attracted his attention. He was convinced that determining what had happened and describing it accurately and fairly was the goal—and should be the supreme accomplishment—of a historian, so he has not impressed scholars of a later age interested in political and philosophical interpretations of history. Moreover, he was basically a teacher and an institution builder, not an intellectual colossus or spectacular creator of new ideas. Consequently, he trained scholars, built a library, and produced a major expansion of the American definition of history, but created no new interpretations or theories. Indeed, for many who look upon his writing from the vantage point of later generations, his work may seem accurate and proper, but unsophisticated and simple. But he built wisely and well in an area of knowledge which still demands increasing attention.

The basic qualities in the years in which American study of other parts of the world began are even more important than the establishment of the foundations at such an early period. On the European continent, and to some degree in England, governments played a central role in beginning the study of Russia and other societies beyond Europe. Thus the Collège de France established a chair of Slavic studies in 1840, largely because the government of Louis Philippe sought support among friends of

Poland by creating a position for Adam Mickiewicz. The Third Republic's Ministry of Public Instruction sent Louis Leger to Moscow with a diplomatic passport in 1872 to learn about Russia because it foresaw a long-term shift in its foreign policy, from "Vive la Pologne!" to "Vive la Russie!", and needed an intellectual base for that change. Austrian and Prussian promotion of Russian studies in the 1840s and Germany activity in the 1890s (the first German chair in East European studies became permanent in 1902) sought increased knowledge of a rival and potential enemy. In these cases, governments were primarily responsible for launching and supporting educational enterprises. Oxford began instruction in Russian in 1849 and Cambridge in 1899, but the first Oxford professorship was established only in 1900. The efforts of Sir Bernard Pares, which led to the founding of the School of Slavonic and East European Studies in 1915, began just after the turn of the century. Pares always maintained a large group of government officials on his board of advisers. Both his school and the Institut d' Etudes Slaves in Paris benefited from financial support from East European governments, especially Poland and Czechoslovakia.

The American approach, like those of European countries, reflects and represents the society from which it came. First, individuals with a profound sense of *noblesse oblige* and then the university acted independently, with neither the state nor state purposes playing a role. Second, the goal was to increase knowledge and understanding of other peoples on as broad a base as possible, because educated people should have some knowledge of the entire universe. The American expansion of educational frontiers represented a sense of personal curiosity, imagination, and excitement which ensured vitality and reflected and guaranteed independence. It succeeded remarkably in beginning the adaptation of instruction and scholarship to America's role in international affairs as that role changed rapidly.

The third significant element in the foundations for the new studies was the emphasis on intellectual quality and high standards. Coolidge also pressed beyond political history toward an understanding of other societies, based on knowledge of such basic factors as the deep historical roots, geography, population, natural resources, and the regional, continental, and world framework of the country or culture under study. His work, that of his colleagues, and that of those whom he trained, helped give the study of history in the United States an international perspective, or at least an international flavor. These men, who awakened Americans to the study of other parts of the world, overcame the temptation which overwhelmed many scholars after the Second World War to emphasize recent or contemporary history or to train specialists on one country or culture, with little knowledge of their own country or other countries.

Just as he recognized no master and refused to acknowledge a "Father Professor" in Germany, or to allow others to make him one in America, Coolidge encouraged freedom and independence of thought among all with whom he worked. No "Coolidge doctrine" or "Coolidge school" emerged, in good part because he wanted every scholar, indeed every citizen, to reach his own decisions. He inculcated a careful, dispassionate, evenhanded approach. Integrity, sanity, and good sense prevented the appearance of partisan, doctrinaire positions and the creation of myths or legends in the form of "revolutionary heros" or "Slavic genius" or " Chinese incompetence." Blessed with a multinational mind in an age of growing nationalism and with the view that all cultures reflect particular pasts but are in effect equal, he was far removed from the arrogant national, political or racialist approaches to other cultures which sometimes mar scholarship. Similarly, his clear, spare style was designed to remove passion and carelessness from description and analysis.

The final stamp which Coolidge placed on the study of other areas at students' formative stage was insistence that they see each part of the world as a segment of the whole. This emphasis upon "the world," which ran counter to the contemporary priority given to rather narrow national history, reflected the large view he had acquired, which enabled him to see "the coming together of the world" and to impress that framework upon those he trained. This approach gave the study of other peoples fascinating breadth and sweep. It enabled him to understand some of the character of modern imperialism and the coming dominance of several great states. At the same time, his generation anticipated "the exploding desire for self-government," which has been of growing importance in the twentieth century and has helped to dismember the great empires.

Education deals with futures; so its work is never complete. Its products are knowledge and educated men and women, which are difficult to define or measure in any age. Between 1890 and 1930, American higher education made substantial progress in creating a base for the study of other peoples and of world affairs.

Indeed, its achievement was probably more substantial than that of any other country, even though the United States, at Coolidge's death, had produced only eighteen men with Ph.D.s in all areas of Russian studies and only twenty universities taught Russian and only thirty taught Russian history. By 1939, approximately 300 American men and women were teaching about Russia, whereas none did so in 1890, and only ten in 1910. Only four universities had departments of Slavic languages and literatures in 1939, and scarcely more than 200 men and women taught courses on other areas of the world. Yet, as the *American Historial Review* pointed out in April 1925, American historical journals devoted far more attention to other countries and cultures than did the most prestigious European journals. The most recent issues of the *English Historical Review* had devoted one page and seventeen lines to the United States, the *Historische Zeitschrift* two pages, and the *Revue historique* seven lines.

In expanding attention to other parts of Europe, the university led American intellectual life. Moreover, the change in the spirit and quality of higher education was carried beyond the walls of the university, from Harvard Yard to Fifth Avenue and, to some degree, to Main Streets all over the country. This continuing revolution contributed to "opening" American intellectual life by breaking down old parochialisms and awakening many to the richness and variety of other cultures. The "flowering of New England," represented in the work of Coolidge and his generation, thus produced pioneering work which helped transform the American view of the world.

The Boston Brahmins, Harvard, and New England demonstrated the responsible use of wealth and advantage and made the transition from an educational and intellectual life dominated by the Northeast to one to which more of the nation contributed and in which everyone shared. Much remains to be done, even after the great advances which followed the Second World War. But that is another story.

Notes

2. BOSTON, THE COOLIDGES, AND HARVARD

1. William W. Sweet review of Robert H. Lord, John E. Sexton, and Edward T. Harrington, *History of the Archdiocese of Boston in the Various Stages of Its Development, 1604-1943*, 3 vols. (New York, 1945), in *American Historical Review*, L (1944-1945), 543.

2. Barbara Solomon, *Ancestors and Immigrants: A Changing New England Tradition* (Cambridge, Mass., 1956), p. 53.

3. Henry Seidel Canby, *The Age of Confidence: Life in the Nineties* (New York, 1934), pp. 28-29; J. Joseph Huthmacher, *Massachusetts People and Politics, 1919-1933* (Cambridge, Mass., 1959), p. 7.

4. Walter Muir Whitehill, "Who Rules Here?" *New England Quarterly*, XLIII (1970), 21.

5. Edwin O'Connor, *The Last Hurrah* (Boston, 1956), p. 152.

6. George E. Peterson, *The New England College in the Age of the University* (Amherst, 1961), p. 149.

7. E. Digby Baltzell, *The Protestant Establishment: Aristocracy and Caste in America* (New York, 1964), pp. 194-195.

8. Arthur Mann, *Yankee Reformers in the Urban Age* (Cambridge, Mass., 1954), pp. 7, 236-237.

9. Ferris Greenslet, *The Lowells and Their Seven Worlds* (Boston, 1946), p. 322.

10. Charles Francis Adams, Jr., *Autobiography* (Boston, 1916) p. 205. See also Henry Cabot Lodge, *Early Memories* (New York, 1913).

11. Mann, *Yankee Reformers*, pp. 6-11, 236-237; Cleveland Amory, *The Proper Bostonians* (New York, 1947), p. 61.

12. Emma Downing Coolidge, *Descendants of John and Mary Coolidge of Watertown, Massachusetts, 1630* (Boston, 1930), pp. 341-342; Stephen C. Lockwood, *Augustine Heard and Company, 1858-1862: American Merchants in China* (Cambridge, Mass. 1971), pp. 5-9.

13. Robert Cruden, *James Ford Rhodes: The Man, the Historian, and His Work* (Cleveland, 1961), p. 56.

14. Thomas Jefferson Coolidge, "Remarks in Presenting a Large Collection of Jefferson Papers," *Massachusetts Historical Society Proceedings*, XII (1897-1899), 264-272; Coolidge, "Tribute to Lord Dufferin," *Massachusetts Historical*

Society Proceedings, XV (1901-1902), 497-500; John Torrey Morse, Jr., "Tribute to Thomas Jefferson Coolidge," *Massachusetts Historical Society Proceedings,* LIV (1920-1921), 141-149, especially 142; Horatio R. Storer, "Thomas Jefferson Coolidge," *Harvard Graduates' Magazine,* XXIX (1921), 408; Amory, *The Proper Bostonians,* pp. 67-68; Emma Coolidge, *Descendants,* pp. 351-352.

15. Louise Tharp, *Mrs. Jack: A Biography of Isabella Stewart Gardner* (Boston, 1965), pp. 21, 27, 33, 106, 216; Frank A. Gardner, *Gardner Memorial: A Biographical and Genealogical Record of the Descendants of Thomas Gardner, Planter* (Salem, Mass., 1933), p. 156.

16. Harvard University Archives (hereafter cited as HUA), Harvard College, "Class of 1883, Fiftieth Anniversary Report" (Cambridge, Mass., 1933), VII, 71-74; John F. Moors, "Joseph Randolph Coolidge," *Harvard Graduates' Magazine,* XXXVII (1928), 203-206; Coolidge, *Descendants,* p. 343.

17. John Gardner Coolidge, *Random Letters from Many Countries* (Boston, 1924), *passim,* especially pp. 7-8, 387, 392; Coolidge, *A War Diary in Paris, 1914-1917* (Cambridge, Mass. 1931); Richard D. Challener, *Admirals, Generals, and American Foreign Policy, 1894-1914* (Princeton, 1973), p. 169; John H. Ferguson, *American Diplomacy and the Boer War* (Philadelphia, 1939), pp. 94, 116; Isabel Anderson (editor), *Larz Anderson: Letters and Journals of a Diplomat* (London, 1940), *passim;* Coolidge, *Descendants,* p. 342.

18. HUA, Julian Coolidge, Diary, March 1900; Coolidge, *Descendants,* pp. 346-347.

19. William Bentinck-Smith, *Building a Great Library: The Coolidge Years at Harvard* (Cambridge, Mass. 1976), p. 13 n.

20. Ibid., pp. 6, 187.

21. Harold Jefferson Coolidge and Robert H. Lord, *Archibald Cary Coolidge: Life and Letters* (Boston, 1932), pp. 5-9; John Coolidge, *Random Letters,* foreword; Bentinck-Smith, *Building a Great Library,* pp. 5-10.

22. Amory, *The Proper Bostonians,* p. 19.

23. Baron Roman R. Rosen, *Forty Years of Diplomacy* (New York, 1922), I, 262.

24. Coolidge Old Farm Book, 4 vols., now in possession of Frederick M. Kimball of Boston, who married a niece of Professor Coolidge; W. Leroy White and others, *Twentieth Annual Excursion of the Sandwich Historical Society; Thursday, August 24, 1939* (Sandwich, N.H., 1939), pp. 15-22; Coolidge and Lord, *Coolidge,* p. 332; Bentinck-Smith, *Building a Great Library,* pp. 193-196.

25. HUA, Archibald Cary Coolidge, Diary, March 18, 1900; Council on Foreign Relations Archives (hereafter cited as CFRA), Archibald Cary Coolidge Letters to Hamilton Fish Armstrong, November 19, November 21, 1926; Archibald Cary Coolidge, "For Sister Universities of the East," in *University of Virginia in the Life of the Nation* (Charlottesville, 1905?), pp. 23-33; Coolidge, "Remarks at the Randolph Gathering at Tuckahoe," *Massachusetts Historical Society Proceedings,* XIV (1900-1), 205-209; John Coolidge, *Random Letters,* pp. 127-128; Coolidge and Lord, *Coolidge,* pp. 232, 327-331.

26. George Santayana, *Persons and Places* (New York, 1963), II, p. 163.

27. Arthur F. Beringause, *Brooks Adams: A Biography* (New York, 1955), p.

40; John A. Garraty, *Henry Cabot Lodge: A Biography* (New York, 1953), p. 24; Solomon, *Ancestors and Immigrants*, p. 89.

28. Hugh Hawkins, *Between Harvard and America: The Educational Leadership of Charles W. Eliot* (New York, 1972), p. 186. "Report No. 1 of the Secretary of the Harvard College Class of 1887" (Cambridge, 1887) reveals that no Jews were among the 112 of the 236 graduating members who indicated a religious belief; Sylvia Sprigge's *Berenson: A Biography* (Boston, 1960) declares that no other Jews were members of the class of 1887.

29. HUA, Harvard College class of 1887. "Report No. 1," pp. 4-38; *Harvard Crimson*, January 26, 1928; Roger B. Merriman, "Archibald Cary Coolidge," *Harvard Graduates' Magazine*, XXXVI (1928), 550-557.

30. Ernest Samuels, *Bernard Berenson: The Making of a Connoisseur* (Cambridge, Mass., 1979), pp. xi, 35, 49-50; Sprigge, *Berenson, passim.*

31. *American Historical Review*, LII (1946-1947), 798.

32. Luther V. Hendricks, *James Harvey Robinson, Teacher of History* (New York, 1946), pp. vii-viii, 1-108; Robert A. Skotheim, *American Intellectual Histories and Historians* (Princeton, 1966), pp. 68-82.

33. Bliss Perry, *And Gladly Teach: Reminiscenses* (Boston, 1935), pp. 88-89.

34. HUA, Archibald Cary Coolidge letter to Walter Lichtenstein, February 14, 1906; Eric F. Goldman, "Herman Eduard von Holst; Plumed Knight of American Historiography," *Mississippi Valley Historical Review*, XXIII (1937), 511-512, 516-532; Anna Haddow, *Political Science in American Colleges and Universities, 1636-1900* (New York, 1939), pp. 239-240; Edward A. Saveth, *American Historians and European Immigrants, 1875-1925* (New York, 1948), pp. 153-157; Jacob E. Cooke, *Frederick Bancroft, Historian* (Norman, Okla, 1957), pp. 28-35, 41.

35. HUA, Harvard College class of 1887. "Report No. 3" (Cambridge, 1893), p. 29; Coolidge and Lord, *Coolidge*, pp. 20, 38.

36. National Archives, Despatches from the United States Minister to Austria, 1883-1906, T 157, Roll 39. Coolidge letter to Secretary of State John W. Foster, January 12, 1893; Roll 40, Minister Frederick W. Grant to Foster, April 7, 1893; Roll 40, Coolidge letter to Foster, April 21, 1893.

37. Coolidge (translator), "Poems of Nekrasov and Lermontov," *Harvard Monthly*, XIX (1895), 131-135.

38. Bentinck-Smith, *Building a Great Library*, pp. 148, 320.

3. THE ETERNAL STUDENT AND SCHOLAR

1. HUA, Julian Coolidge, Diary, March 1900; George Santayana, *Persons and Places* (New York, 1963), II, 162.

2. HUA, Archibald Cary Coolidge letter to his father, August 10, 1905; Coolidge letter to Dexter Perkins, February 10, 1912; CFRA, Coolidge letter to Hamilton Fish Armstrong, July 16, 1927.

3. HUA, Coolidge letters to his mother, September 24, October 13,

November 13, December 19, 1908; Coolidge letters to his father, November 11, November 24, 1908; January 9, 1909; Coolidge letter to Henry Morse Stephens, September 24, 1908.

4. HUA, Coolidge letter to his father, November 29, 1921.

5. HUA, Coolidge, "Suleiman the Magnificent" (manuscript), VIII, 409; CFRA, Coolidge letters to Armstrong, February 21, 1924; January 26, 1926; Owen Lattimore, *Studies in Frontier History: Collected Papers, 1929-1958* (London, 1963), p. 24.

6. HUA, Coolidge letter to Harry Garfield, April 28, 1921; Coolidge letter to Louis Aubert, June 20, 1921; Coolidge letter to his mother, December 16, 1906; CFRA, Coolidge letters to Armstrong, November 10, 1923, June 16, 1924; Aubert letter to Coolidge, December 26, 1923; Lloyd C. Griscom, *Diplomatically Speaking* (Boston, 1940), pp. 277-278; *Harvard et la France* (Paris, 1936), p. 229; Harold Jefferson Coolidge and Robert H. Lord, *Archibald Cary Coolidge: Life and Letters* (Cambridge, Mass., 1932), p. 112.

7. Coolidge and Lord, *Coolidge*, p. 183 n.

8. Herbert Heaton, *A Scholar in Action: Edwin F. Gay* (Cambridge, Mass., 1952), p. 2.

9. HUA, Department of History meeting, February 16, 1928; Roger B. Merriman, "Archibald Cary Coolidge," *Harvard Graduates' Magazine*, XXXVI (1928), 554; Mark A. De Wolfe Howe review of Coolidge and Lord, *Coolidge*, in *American Historical Review*, XXXVIII (1933), 580; *The Economist*, March 26, 1977.

10. Hamilton Fish Armstrong, *Peace and Counterpeace: From Wilson to Hitler* (New York, 1971), p. 397.

11. HUA, Coolidge letters to his mother, October 7, 1906; January 15, 1915; Coolidge letter to Edwin V. Morgan, August 13, 1913.

12. HUA, Coolidge letters to his mother, December 6, 1906, January 20, 1914; Coolidge letter to Morgan, March 2, 1914; Coolidge letter to Walter Lichtenstein, February 28, 1914; R. B. Hobart letter to Harold J. Coolidge, July 15, 1931; Edith Wharton, *A Backward Glance* (New York, 1934), pp. 287-288.

13. CFRA, Armstrong letter to Tasker H. Bliss, January 28, 1928; Armstrong, *Peace and Counterpeace*, p. 395; Archibald Cary Coolidge, "Tacna and Arica," *Journal of the British Institute of International Affairs*, V (1926), 245-249.

14. HUA, Coolidge letter to George Lyman Kittredge, May 22, 1919; Coolidge letter to D'Arcy Paul, November 28, 1919; Coolidge and W. Harold Claflin (editors), Sir Edward Creasy, *Turkey* (Philadelphia, 1907), preface.

15. Juergen Herbst, *The German Historical School in American Scholarship: A Study in the Transfer of Culture* (Ithaca, 1965), pp. 100-104; Santayana, *Persons and Places*, II, 163.

16. HUA, Coolidge letter to Stephens, July 15, 1907; Coolidge letter to his father, July 22, 1897; Coolidge letter to his mother, March 17, 1912; Coolidge letter to Morgan, August 11, 1902; Coolidge and Lord, *Coolidge*, pp. 117-135.

17. Frederick Rudolph, *The American College and University* (New York, 1962), p. 499; W. Stull Holt, "Historical Scholarship," in Merle Curti (editor),

American Scholarship in the Twentieth Century (Cambridge, Mass., 1953), p. 89.

18. CFRA, Armstrong letter to Bliss, January 28, 1928; Bliss, "Archibald Cary Coolidge," *Foreign Affairs*, VI (1928), 354–355; Armstrong, *Peace and Counterpeace*, pp. 387–388.

19. CFRA, Coolidge letter to Harry Elmer Barnes, July 27, 1922.

20. Santayana, *Persons and Places*, II, 163.

21. HUA, Coolidge letter to Emil Ahlborn, February 4, 1915; Coolidge letter to Charles Evans Hughes, February 2, 1925; Coolidge, *Ten Years of War and Peace* (Cambridge, Mass., 1927), p. 44.

22. CFRA, Coolidge letters to Malcolm W. Davis, October 14 and 16, 1925.

23. CFRA, Coolidge letter to Armstrong, October 15, 1926.

24. Garrett Mattingly, "The Historian of the Spanish Empire," *American Historical Review*, LIV (1948), 42.

25. Coolidge and Lord, *Coolidge*, p. 8.

26. William S. Ferguson and others, "Archibald Cary Coolidge," *American Academy of Arts and Sciences Proceedings*, LXIV (1930), 515; Armstrong, *Peace and Counterpeace*, p. 397.

4. RUSSIA: ITS HISTORY AND ROLE

1. Peter Kropotkin, *Russian Literature* (Boston, 1905), p. 39.

2. Maxim Kovalevsky, "American Impressions," *Russian Review*, X (1951), 40.

3. HUA, Coolidge letter to his father, August 6, 1895; Gamaliel Bradford, *As God made Them: Portraits of Some Nineteenth Century Americans* (Port Washington, N.Y., 1969), pp. 205–206; Van Wyck Brooks, *New England: Indian Summer, 1865–1915* (New York, 1940), pp 32–34; Jeremiah Curtin, *Myths and Folk Tales of the Russians, Western Slavs, and Magyars* (Boston, 1890), p. 111; Isabel F. Hapgood, *The Epic Songs of Russia* (New York, 1886), preface, p. vii; *Dictionary of American Biography*, II, 66–67.

4. HUA, Coolidge, "The Expansion of Russia" (manuscript), p. 1; Henry May, *The End of American Innocence: A Study of the First Years of Our Own Time, 1912–1917* (New York, 1959), pp. 243–244.

5. HUA, Coolidge letter to his parents, January 26, 1890; Coolidge letter to Robert J. Kerner, June 10, 1926; Harvard College class of 1887. "Report No. 2" (Cambridge, Mass., 1890), p. 19; "Report No. 3" (Cambridge, Mass., 1893), p. 29.

6. HUA, Coolidge letter to Kerner, August 23, 1924; Coolidge letter to Dr. W.S. Thayer, January 14, 1925; Coolidge, "Nekrasov," *Johnson's Revised Universal Encyclopaedia* (New York, 1895), VI, 109–110; Coolidge, "Tiutchev," in ibid., VIII, 175; "Tolstoi, Alexei and Leo," in ibid., VIII, 180; "Turgenev," in ibid., VIII, 305; Coolidge, "Poems of Nekrasov and Lermontov," *Harvard Monthly*, XIX (1895), 131–135; Harvard *Daily News*, January 24, 1895.

7. Coolidge review of Isabel F. Hapgood, *Russian Rambles* (Boston, 1895),

in New York *Evening Post*, May 5, 1895; Anatole Leroy-Beaulieu preface to Coolidge, *Les Etats-Unis, puissance mondiale* (Paris, 1908), pp. vi–xv.

8. HUA, Coolidge, "Suleiman the Magnificent" (manuscript), bibliography, p. 2; Coolidge letter to Louis Aubert, June 20, 1921; Coolidge letter to Hamilton Fish Armstrong, June 16, 1924; Aubert letter to Coolidge, December 26, 1923; Coolidge letter to Harry Garfield, April 28, 1921; Coolidge, *The United States as a World Power* (New York, 1908), p. xv.

9. Coolidge, "A Plea for the Study of the History of Northern Europe," *American Historical Review*, II (1896), 34–38. This was reprinted in the American Historical Association *Annual Report 1895* (Washington, 1896), pp. 443–451.

10. Walter R. Batsell, *Soviet Rule in Russia* (New York, 1929), preface; HUA, George Grafton Wilson letter to Coolidge, February 9, 1927; Wilson letter to Batsell, February 11, 1927. The Coolidge Papers in the Harvard Archives include an immense number of letters concerning the institute in Prague between Coolidge and Lewis Einstein, American minister in Prague; Nicholas Murray Butler, president of Columbia University; William R. Castle, Jr., chief of the Division of Western European Affairs in the Department of State; and Stephen Duggan, president of the International Institute of Education. The records of the Division of Western European Affairs for 1924–1926 in the National Archives are also rich and full concerning this proposed institute. For detailed information concerning this imaginative proposal, see Robert F. Byrnes, "The American Institute for Slavic Studies in Prague: A Dream of the 1920's," in Alexander Fischer, Gunter Moltmann, and Klaus Schwabe (editors), *Russland-Deutschland-Amerika. Festschrift für Fritz T. Epstein zur 80 Geburtstag* (Wiesbaden, 1978), pp. 257–266.

11. HUA, Coolidge letter to his mother, July 22, 1895; Coolidge, "Across Siberia," *Nation*, LXI (1895), 238; Coolidge, "Ararat," *Nation*, LXVII (1898), 240; Coolidge review of M.M. Shoemaker, *The Great Siberian Railway* (New York, 1903), in *Nation*, LXXVI (1903), 318.

12. HUA, Coolidge, "Some Impressions of the Ninth Soviet Congress," pp. 1–3; Coolidge, "Liaison Work with the American Relief Administration in Russia, September 1921 to February 1922," pp. 1–9; J.C. Lehrs, "Memorandum of an Interview between Professor A.C. Coolidge and Mr. L.B. Kamenev, February 15, 1922, pp. 1–2; Coolidge letters to his father, September 25, October 1, October 19, October 23, November 3, November 15, November 26, 1921; January 4, January 11, January 25, January 31, 1922; Coolidge letters to Hiram Bingham, December 7, 1921; May 15, 1922; Bingham letter to Coolidge, December 30, 1922.

13. HUA, Coolidge, "The Expansion of Russia," XII, 13–24; Coolidge, *The United States as a World Power*, pp. 217–223.

14. HUA, Coolidge letter to Frank Golder, May 11, 1922; Golder letters to Coolidge, March 17, June 10, July 17, August 12, August 28, September 11, 1922; March 29, 1923; September 29, 1925; Hoover Institution, Records of the American Relief Administration, Russian Operations, "Statement by Prof. Archibald C. Coolidge Just Returned from Russia, March 13, 1922"; Coolidge

cablegrams to New York and London offices of American Relief Administration, February 16, February 20, March 22, 1922; Boston *Herald*, March 23, 1922; Harvard *Crimson*, March 23, 1922; Harold Jefferson Coolidge and Robert H. Lord, *Archibald Cary Coolidge: Life and Letters* (Boston, 1932), pp. 302-304; Hamilton Fish Armstrong, *Peace and Counterpeace: From Wilson to Hitler* (New York, 1971), pp. 192-194.

15. HUA, Sir Bernard Pares letters to Coolidge, July 14, 1923, March 2, May 11, 1924; Coolidge letter to Robert J. Kerner, January 30, 1915; CFRA, Coolidge letters to Hamilton Fish Armstrong, September 13, 1923, January 6, April 11, 1924; *Slavonic Review*, III (1924), 241-242.

16. HUA, Coolidge, "The Expansion of Russia," IV, 32-33; Coolidge and W. Harold Claflin (editors), Sir Edward Creasy, *Turkey* (Philadelphia, 1907), p. 7; Coolidge review of Hector H. Munro, *The Rise of the Russian Empire* (Boston, 1900), in *American Historical Review*, VII (1901), 138-140; Coolidge review of Edmund Noble, *Russia and the Russians* (Boston, 1900), in *American Historical Review*, VI (1901), 791-793; Coolidge reviews of George Frederick Wright, *Asiatic Russia* (New York, 1902), and John Foster Fraser, *The Real Siberia* (New York, 1902), in *Nation*, LXXV (1902), 407.

17. HUA, Coolidge, "The Expansion of Russia," XII, 35-42; Coolidge, "Recent Books about Russia in English," *American Historical Review*, X (1905), 455-456; Coolidge, *The United States as a World Power*, pp. 192, 217; Coolidge, "The British Commonwealth of Nations," in New York *Times* and New York *Journal of Commerce*, July 28, 1925, and in Providence *Journal*, July 29, 1925.

18. Coolidge, "Dispute between France and Siam," *Nation*, LVI (1893), 339; Coolidge review of E.F. Knight, *Where Three Empires Meet* (London, 1893), in *Nation*, LVI (1893), 460-461; Coolidge, "The British-Boer War," Boston *Globe*, January 21, 1900.

19. HUA, Coolidge, "Russia and the Present War"; "Prof. Coolidge Defends Russia," Boston *Herald*, March 24, 1904.

20. HUA, Coolidge, "The Expansion of Russia," XI, 24; Coolidge review of Munro, *The Rise of the Russian Empire*, p. 139.

21. HUA, Coolidge, "The Expansion of Russia," XIV, 62-167; XVI, 32-33; Coolidge, "The Expansion of Russia," in Andrew Lang (editor), *The Nineteenth Century: A Review of Progress* (New York, 1901), pp. 63-75; Coolidge, "Russia after Genoa and the Hague," *Foreign Affairs*, I (1922), 133-155.

22. HUA, Coolidge, "The Expansion of Russia," XII, 34-40.

23. HUA, Coolidge letter to Edwin Morgan, December 26, 1902; Albert Bushnell Hart letters to Coolidge, March 19, April 11, 1914; Coolidge letter to Allen Dulles, July 25, 1921; Coolidge, "The Peoples of the Peninsula," in Hamilton Fish Armstrong, *The New Balkans* (New York, 1926), pp. 2-3.

24. *American Historical Review*, VI (1901), 418; Coolidge, "Claimants to Constantinople," in Charles Downer Thayer and others, *Three Peace Congresses of the Nineteenth Century* (Cambridge, Mass., 1917), pp. 73-93; Coolidge, "Greece's Real Motive," New York *Evening Post*, March 22, 1893; Coolidge, "The Coup d'Etat in Servia," *Nation*, LVI (1893), 330-331; Coolidge,

"The Balkans," *Nation*, LVIII (1894), 421; Coolidge, "King Milan Returns to Servia," *Nation*, LVIII, (1894), 77; Coolidge, "In Montenegro," *Nation*, LXIX (1899), 239–240.

25. HUA, Coolidge, "The Expansion of Russia," pp. 16–17; George Parker Winship, "Archibald Cary Coolidge," *Harvard Library Notes*, no. 20 (1928), p. 157.

26. Coolidge, "King Milan Returns," p. 77.

27. HUA, Coolidge letter to Edwin V. Morgan, December 26, 1902; Coolidge, "The Expansion of Russia," pp. 63–75; Coolidge and Lord, *Coolidge*, p. 97.

28. HUA, Coolidge, "The Expansion of Russia," IV, 26; V, 11–15, 19–20; VII, 2; X, 30–35; XII, 4–6; XIV, 42–44; XVII, 21; Coolidge review of Knight, *Where Three Empires Meet*, pp. 460–461; Coolidge review of Vladimir, *Russia on the Pacific and the Siberian Railway* (London, 1899), *Nation*, LXX, (1900), 287; Coolidge, "Claimants," pp. 85–86.

29. HUA, Coolidge, "The Expansion of Russia," XIV, 57–61; Coolidge, "The Expansion of Russia," pp. 70–72.

30. HUA, Coolidge, "The Expansion of Russia," II, 8–13, 21–22; XIV, 58; XV, 18, 19; XVI, p. 21–28.

31. HUA, ibid., 4, XIV, 42–44; Coolidge, "The Expansion of Russia," p. 75; "Prof. Coolidge Defends Russia," Boston *Globe*, March 24, 1904.

32. Coolidge, "The Political Outlook in Europe," New York *Evening Post*, December 30, 1919, January 3, 1920; Coolidge, "Jefferson and the Problems of Today," *University of Virginia Alumni Bulletin*, XIV (1921), 53–58; Coolidge, "Dissatisfied Germany," *Foreign Affairs*, IV (1925), 35–46.

33. HUA, Coolidge letters to Charles Evans Hughes, October 9, November 20, 1921; Coolidge letter to Herbert H. Hoover, October 20, 1921; Coolidge letters to Henry Cabot Lodge, October 24, 1921; January 29, 1922; Lodge letters to Coolidge, November 14, 1921; February 11, 1922; Coolidge, "Liaison Work with the American Relief Administration in Russia," pp. 1–9; Lehrs, "Memorandum of an Interview between Coolidge and Kamenev"; Hoover Institution, "Records of the American Relief Administration, Russian Operations, Statement by Prof. Coolidge, March 13, 1922."

34. HUA, Coolidge letters to his father, November 22, December 25, 1921; Coolidge letter to Hughes, December 30, 1921; Coolidge letter to William R. Castle, Jr., September 25, 1921; Coolidge, "Some Impressions of the Ninth Soviet Congress"; Armstrong, *Peace and Counterpeace*, p. 193.

35. HUA, Coolidge letter to his father, January 31, 1922; Coolidge, "Some Impressions," pp. 1–3; Coolidge, "The Probable Future Orientation of Russia towards her Immediate Neighbors and Especially towards Poland and the Baltic Provinces," lecture delivered at Army War College, Washington Barracks, D.C., October 19, 1922, p. 12; Coolidge, "Russia after Genoa and the Hague," pp. 133–155, especially 134–136.

36. HUA, Coolidge, "The Probable Future Orientation of Russia," pp. 11, 22.

37. HUA, ibid., p. 14; Coolidge letter to Frank Golder, December 11, 1922;

CFRA, Coolidge letter to Hamilton Fish Armstrong, January 3, 1923; Coolidge, "Russia after Genoa," pp. 141-142, 152; Armstrong, *Peace and Counterpeace*, p. 194.

38. CFRA, Coolidge letter to George A.B. De War, September 30, 1924; De War, "Britain's Recognition of Soviet Russia," *Foreign Affairs*, III (1925), 313-319; Coolidge, "Two Years of American Foreign Policy," *Foreign Affairs*, I (1923), 1-24; Coolidge, "Ten Years of War and Peace," *Foreign Affairs*, III (1924), 1-21, especially pp. 17-19; Coolidge, "After the Election," III (1924), 171-182, especially pp. 175.

39. Coolidge, "Russia after Genoa," pp. 153-154.

5. "THE COMING TOGETHER OF THE WORLD"

1. William L. Langer, *The Diplomacy of Imperialism* (New York, 1935), I, 82-95.

2. HUA, Department of History Records, May 19, 1928; Coolidge and W. Harold Claflin (editors), Sir Edward Creasy, *Turkey* (Philadelphia, 1907), preface, *passim*; William S. Ferguson and others, "Archibald Cary Coolidge," *American Academy of Arts and Sciences Proceedings*, LXIV (1930), 514-518.

3. Langer, "Farewell to Empire," *Foreign Affairs*, XLI (1962), 130.

4. HUA, Coolidge, "The Probable Future Orientation of Russia towards Her Immediate Neighbors and Especially towards Poland and the Baltic Provinces," lecture delivered at Army War College, Washington Barracks, D.C., October 19, 1922, p. 14; Coolidge review of Captain Hamilton Bower, *Diary of a Journey across Tibet* (New York, 1894), in *Nation*, LIX (1895), 88; Coolidge, "The Position of China in World Politics," in George H. Blakeslee (editor), *China and the Far East* (New York, 1910), pp. 13-16; Coolidge, "Russia after Genoa and the Hague," *Foreign Affairs*, I (1922), 145-146; Coolidge, "Dissatisfied Germany," *Foreign Affairs*, IV (1925), 157-178; Coolidge, "The Achievements of Fascism," *Foreign Affairs* (1926), pp. 661-662.

5. HUA, Coolidge, "France as a World Power" (manuscript), I, 1-2, 11-14; Coolidge letter to Count Paul Teleki, April 2, 1925; Coolidge letter to Alonzo E. Taylor, May 21, 1925; Coolidge, *The United States as a World Power* (New York, 1908), pp. 12-13, 18-19.

6. HUA, Albert G. Waite (Harvard 1905), notes from Coolidge lecture in History 1, 1901.

7. HUA, "France as a World Power," VI, 1-35; Coolidge, "The Expansion of Russia," p. 2; Coolidge, *Theoretical and Foreign Elements in the Formation of the American Constitution* (Freiburg-im-Breisgau, 1892), pp. 5-9, 18-61; Coolidge, *The United States as a World Power*, pp. 8-9.

8. HUA, Coolidge, "France as a World Power," VI, 2, 9-35. Coolidge, *The United States as a World Power*, pp. 11-12.

9. Coolidge, *The United States as a World Power*, pp. 12-17.

10. HUA, Coolidge, memorandum for The Inquiry, October 29, 1918, pp.

1-6; Coolidge, "The New States of Central Europe," Lowell Lectures, 1920 (manuscript), VI: Coolidge, "Race Relations in the United States," talk given in Berlin, February 6, 1914 (manuscript), pp. 13-14; Coolidge, "Bohemia and Ireland," New York *Evening Post*, October 4, 1893; Coolidge, "British Treaty with Free Congo State," *Nation*, LVIII (1894), 479; Coolidge, "First Impressions of the Hawaiian Islands," *Nation*, LXV (1897), 258; Coolidge, "Nationalism and the New Europe," *Yale Review*, IV (1915), 447-461; Coolidge, *The United States as a World Power*, pp. 40-78.

11. Barbara Solomon, *Ancestors and Immigrants: A Changing New England Tradition* (Cambridge, Mass., 1956), especially pp. 50-58, 95-96, 233; E. Digby Baltzell, *The Protestant Establishment: Aristocracy and Caste in America* (New York, 1964), pp. 10, 47, 90-93, 383-384; Horace Scudder, *James Russell Lowell* (Boston, 1901), II, 302-335; Kenton J. Clymer, "Antisemitism in the Late Nineteenth Century: The Case of John Hay," *American Jewish Historical Quarterly*, LX (1971), 344-352.

12. HUA, Coolidge letter to Edwin V. Morgan, January 16, 1912; William R. Castle, Jr., letters to Coolidge, March 6, March 10, November 24, 1925; CFRA, Coolidge to Armstrong, March 10, 1923; University of California (Berkeley) Bancroft Library, Robert J. Kerner Papers, Kerner, "The German and Austrian Solutions" (memorandum for The Inquiry), pp. 17-18; John Gardner Coolidge, *Random Letters from Many Countries* (Boston, 1924), pp. 27, 65, 76, 110, 154, 166, 176, 366-367; Henry A. Yeomans, *Abbott Lawrence Lowell, 1856-1943* (Cambridge, Mass., 1948), pp. 175-177, 209-213; Lawrence E. Gelfand, *The Inquiry: American Preparations for Peace, 1917-1919* (New Haven, 1963), p. 201; Norbert Wiener, *Ex-Prodigy: My Childhood and Youth* (New York, 1953), pp. 241-243; John P. Marquand, *The Late George Apley: A Novel in the Form of a Memoir* (New York, 1940), pp. 289-290; *American Historical Review*, LXXXV (1980), 475-476.

13. HUA, Coolidge letter to James T. Shotwell, January 2, 1918; Hugh Hawkins, *Between Harvard and America: The Educational Leadership of Charles W. Eliot* (New York, 1972), pp. 186, 189; John Higham, *Strangers in the Land: Patterns of American Nativism, 1860-1925* (New Brunswick, N.J., 1955), pp. 272, 313; Dexter Perkins, *Yield of the Years: An Autobiography* (Boston, 1969), p. 28; Harold Jefferson Coolidge and Robert H. Lord, *Archibald Cary Coolidge: Life and Letters* (Boston, 1932), pp. 69-70; T. Lothrop Stoddard, *The French Revolution in San Domingo* (Westport, Conn., 1970), p. vii; Stoddard, *The Revolt against Civilization: The Menace of the Under-Man* (London, 1922), pp. 219-220; Stoddard, *The Rising Tide of Color against White World-Supremacy* (New York, 1920), pp. xxx-xxxi.

14. David Starr Jordan, *Imperial Democracy* (New York, 1899), pp. 9-12; Coolidge, "The British Commonwealth of Nations," New York *Times* and New York *Journal of Commerce*, July 28, 1925; Coolidge, *The United States as a World Power*, pp. 75-76. Coolidge differed in this from most American historians of his generation: see Edward A. Saveth, *American Historians and European Immigrants, 1875-1925* (New York, 1948), pp. 13-31, and Christopher Lasch, *The American Liberals and the Russian Revolution* (New York, 1962), pp. 1-2.

15. HUA, Coolidge, "Race Relations in the United States," p. 7; Coolidge, "The Expansion of Russia," XII, 27-29; Coolidge, "France as a World Power," III, 33-35; Coolidge, "The Probable Future Orientation of Russia," p. 3; Walter Lippmann letter to Coolidge, February 28, 1918; Coolidge letter to Lippmann, March 4, 1918; Coolidge, "The Ancient Capital of Poland, Cracow: July, 1896," *Nation*, LXIII (1896), 137-138; Coolidge, *The United States as a World Power*, pp. 51-52; Lewis S. Feuer, "Recollections of Henry Austryn Wolfson," *American Jewish Archives*, XXVIII (1976), 30; William Bentinck-Smith, *Building a Great Library: The Coolidge Years at Harvard* (Cambridge, Mass., 1976), p. 116; *American Historical Review*, XV (1910), 434.

16. HUA, Coolidge, "Race Relations in the United States," pp. 1-4, 8-10, 13-15, 18-22; Coolidge, "France as a World Power," VII, 12; Coolidge, *The United States as a World Power*, pp. 40-42, 62-73, especially 62-63; Coolidge, "Ten Years of War and Peace," *Foreign Affairs*, III (1924), 17.

17. Coolidge, *The United States as a World Power*, pp. 63-66.

18. CFRA, Coolidge letters to Hamilton Fish Armstrong, October 25, November 17, November 22, December 20, 1924; Coolidge, *The United States as a World Power*, pp. 279-280, 286; W.E.B. DuBois, "Worlds of Color," *Foreign Affairs*, III (1925), 423-444.

19. Coolidge, "The Position of China," p. 18; Saveth, *American Historians and European Immigrants*, pp. 48-49, 201-202; Ernest R. May, *Imperial Democracy: The Emergence of America as a Great Power* (New York, 1961), pp. 16, 25; Solomon, *Ancestors and Immigrants*, pp. 47-48, 82, 104, 118, 123, 140, 215; Yeomans, *Lowell*, p. 413; Higham, *Strangers in the Land*, pp. 302-303.

20. HUA, "Race Relations in the United States," pp. 23-29; Coolidge, *The United States as a World Power*, pp. 43-51, 63, 66-67, 329-340, 354.

21. HUA, Coolidge, Diary, March 1900; Coolidge, "The Expansion of Russia," IV, 21-22; VIII, 11-12, 36-41; X, 1-8; XVI, 16-31; Coolidge, "Suleiman the Magnificent" (manuscript), I, 5, 70; V, 331, 342; Coolidge, *Origins of the Triple Alliance* (New York, 1917), pp. 158-172, 207; Coolidge review of *The Memoirs of Count Witte* (New York, 1921), in *American Historical Review*, XXVI (1921), 790-792; Coolidge review of Tyler Dennett, *Roosevelt and the Russo-Japanese War* (New York, 1925), in *American Historical Review*, XXXI (1925), 156-158; Coolidge, "Busch's *Life of Bismarck*," Boston *Transcript*, October 5, 1898.

22. HUA, Coolidge, "The Expansion of Russia," X, 38.

23. HUA, Coolidge, "France as a World Power," I, 24, 38; X, 9-10; Coolidge, *The United States as a World Power*, pp. 23-24.

24. HUA, Coolidge, "The Expansion of Russia," VIII, 1, 41; Coolidge, "The Growth of Modern Drama in France," *Harvard Advocate*, XLII (1886), 27-29; Coolidge, "Ararat," *Nation*, LXVII (1898), 239-240.

25. HUA, Coolidge, "France as a World Power," VII, 17; Coolidge, "The Expansion of Russia," VII, 6-7; X, 19-20; XIV, 42-43, 63; Coolidge letter to Albert J. Beveridge, September 28, 1923; Coolidge letter to Frank G. Tyrrell, October 24, 1927; Coolidge, "The Expansion of Russia," in Andrew Lang (editor), *The Nineteenth Century: A Review of Progress* (New York, 1901), pp.

70–72; Coolidge, "Siam," *Nation*, LVII (1893), 93; Coolidge, "First Impressions of the Hawaiian Islands," p. 259; Coolidge, "A Candid Statement of the Hawaiian Annexation Question," Boston *Transcript*, October 2, 1897.

26. HUA, Coolidge, "France as a World Power," VI, 29; Coolidge, "America in the Pacific, 1908." (memorandum).

27. Coolidge, *The United States as a World Power*, pp. 6–9, 68–81.

28. HUA, Coolidge letter to his mother, September 1, 1905; Coolidge, *The United States as a World Power*, pp. 148–163, 166–170, 322–326, especially 149; May, *Imperial Democracy*, p. 28.

29. Coolidge, *The United States as a World Power*, pp. 244–280, 287–288; Coolidge, "The Grouping of Nations," *Foreign Affairs* V (1927), 185–186.

30. Coolidge, *The United States as a World Power*, p. 374.

31. Ibid., pp. 328–329; Coolidge, "Siam," p. 93; Coolidge, "Siam Today," *Nation*, LXXXII (1906), 219–221. This view was exceptional in the optimistic years before 1914. George H. Blakeslee, one of Coolidge's first students, who taught Asian history and politics at Clark University for almost half a century, in 1910 founded the *Journal of Race Development* to "deal with the problems connected with the attempts to extend Western civilization to peoples less highly developed." Blakeslee foresaw the spread of constitutional government throughout the world, "in accord with the natural law of political evolution, as is shown clearly by the history of Europe.... This world of ours every day more and more is a family of races." The United States had the obligation to assist the "race children" in the world family in their progress toward this form of government, just as it did the children in the cities of America. Blakeslee (editor), *China and the Far East* (New York, 1910), p. xi.

32. HUA, Coolidge, "France as a World Power," I, 12, 40; III, 23–24; Coolidge, "The Expansion of Russia," IX, 26; XI, 29–40; XII, 58; Coolidge letter to his mother, May 4, 1891; Coolidge, *The United States as a World Power*, p. 34; Coolidge, "In British East Africa," *Nation*, LXXXII (1906), 444.

33. Coolidge, "The Grouping of Nations," pp. 175–188.

34. Coolidge, *The United States as a World Power*, pp. 97, 100–120, 279–283, 298–312; Coolidge, "La Doctrine du Monroe," *Revue de Paris*, II (1907), 650–672, especially p. 652; Coolidge, "The Future of the Monroe Doctrine," *Foreign Affairs*, II (1924), 373–389; Coolidge, "The Grouping of Nations," pp. 182–183; Perkins, *Yield of the Years*, p. 119.

35. HUA, Coolidge, "France as a World Power," VII, 20–26; Coolidge, *The United States as a World Power*, pp. 13–14, 307–312; Coolidge, "The Grouping of Nations," pp. 187–189.

36. HUA, Coolidge letters to William R. Castle, Jr., July 1, 1922; June 29, 1926; Coolidge, "Jefferson and the Problems of Today," *University of Virginia Alumni Bulletin*, XIV (1921), 53–58; Coolidge, "Ten Years of War and Peace," *Foreign Affairs*, III (1924), 1–21; Coolidge, "After the Election," *Foreign Affairs*, III (1924), 171–182.

37. HUA, Coolidge, reports from A.C. Coolidge to American Commission to Negotiate Peace, "Report No. 210," on Ruthenia, April 11, 1919; Coolidge, "France as a World Power," III, 44; V, 23–26; VI, 8; VII, 38; XII, 17; Coolidge,

"Greece's Real Motive," New York *Evening Post*, March 22, 1893; Coolidge, "Ten Years," pp. 13-15; Coolidge, "Siam Today," p. 219; Coolidge, "The Grouping of Nations," p. 187.

38. Coolidge, "Ten Years," pp. 16-17.

39. HUA, Coolidge, "France as a World Power," V, 17; Coolidge letter to Count Paul Teleki, April 2, 1925; Coolidge letter to Raymond L. Buell, December 27, 1927; Coolidge, "Dissatisfied Germany," p. 45; Coolidge, "Siam Today," pp. 219-220.

6. "BROADENING THE UNIVERSITY'S HORIZONS"

1. Charles M. Flandrau's *The Diary of a Harvard Freshman* (New York, 1901) and Owen Wister's famous *Philosophy 4: A Story of Harvard University* (New York, 1903) describe the lives of particularly light-minded residents of the Gold Coast.

2. Henry Adams, *The Education of Henry Adams* (New York, 1934), p. 307; Ferris Greenslet, *The Lowells and Their Seven Worlds* (Boston, 1946), p. 309; Norman Hapgood, *The Changing Years: Reminiscences* (New York, 1930), p. 46; Leon Edel, *Henry James* (Philadelphia, 1953-1972), V, 260; Barbara Solomon, *Ancestors and Immigrants: A Changing New England Tradition* (Cambridge, Mass., 1956), pp. 14, 89.

3. Samuel Eliot Morison (editor), *The Development of Harvard University since the Inauguration of President Eliot, 1869-1929* (Cambridge, Mass., 1930), p. vii; Hugh Hawkins, *Between Harvard and America: The Educational Leadership of Charles W. Eliot* (New York, 1972), p. 78.

4. Samuel Eliot Morison, *Three Centuries of Harvard* (Cambridge, Mass., 1936), pp. 331-336, 419; Morison, *The Development of Harvard University*, p. vii.

5. Alfred Claghorn Potter, *The Changes at Harvard in Twenty-five Years, 1889-1914* (Cambridge, Mass., 1914), p. 13; Frederick Rudolph, *The American College and University* (New York, 1962), p. 290.

6. William C. De Vane, *Higher Education in Twentieth Century America* (Cambridge, Mass., 1965), p. 38; Morison, *The Development of Harvard University*, pp. xlvii-xlix; Hawkins, *Between Harvard and America*, p. 76; Rudolph, *The American College*, p. 304.

7. William Allan Neilson (editor), *Charles W. Eliot: The Man and His Beliefs* (New York, 1926), I, xii; Bliss Perry, *And Gladly Teach: Reminiscences* (Boston, 1935), pp. 223-227; Seymour Lipset and David Riesman, *Education and Politics at Harvard* (New York, 1975), p. 106; Edwin E. Slosson, *Great American Universities* (New York, 1910), pp. 1-2.

8. Van Wyck Brooks, *New England: Indian Summer, 1865-1915* (New York, 1940), p. 524; John Langstaff, *Harvard of Today, from the Undergraduate Point of View* (Cambridge, Mass., 1913), pp. 9-12; Morison, *The Development of Harvard University*, p. xc; Morison, *Three Centuries of Harvard*, pp. 346, 372; Rudolph, *The American College*, p. 395.

9. Henry A. Yeomans, *Abbott Lawrence Lowell, 1856-1943* (Cambridge, Mass., 1948), p. 249; William L. Lawrence, *Memories of a Happy Life* (Boston, 1926), p. 213; George Santayana, *Persons and Places* (New York, 1944), p. 1186; Oscar Handlin, "College and Community in 1900," *Harvard Library Bulletin*, XII (1958), 152-156; Morison, *The Development of Harvard University*, p. xli; Lipset and Riesman, *Education and Politics*, pp. 96-102.

10. Ernest Earnest, *Academic Procession: An Informal History of the American College, 1636 to 1953* (Indianapolis, 1953), pp. 153-155, 167, 204; Hawkins, *Between Harvard and America*, pp. 57-58; Slosson, *Great American Universities*, pp. 1-2.

11. Arthur M. Schlesinger, *In Retrospect: The History of a Historian* (New York, 1963), pp. 82-87; Henry May, *The End of American Innocence: A Study of the First Years of Our Own Time, 1912-1917* (New York, 1959), p. 57; Santayana, *Persons and Places* (New York, 1963), II, 162.

12. William James, *Memories and Studies* (London, 1911), p. 353; Laurence R. Veysey, *The Emergence of the American University* (Chicago, 1965), p. 288; Brooks, *Indian Summer*, p. 524.

13. May, *The End of American Innocence*, pp. 298-299, 322; Lipset and Riesman, *Education and Politics*, pp. 125-126; Brooks, *Indian Summer*, pp. 523-524.

14. Van Wyck Brooks, *An Autobiography* (New York, 1965), introduction, p. xx; Ernest Earnest, *Expatriates and Patriots: American Artists, Scholars, and Writers in Europe* (Durham, N.C., 1968), p. 255.

15. Samuel Eliot Morison, "Edward Channing: A Memoir," *Massachusetts Historical Society Proceedings*, LXIV (1931), 263; Ephraim Emerton and Samuel Eliot Morison, "History, 1838-1929," in Morison, *The Development of Harvard University*, pp. 154-155 n.

16. Samuel Eliot Morison, "A Memoir and Estimate of Albert Bushnell Hart," *Massachusetts Historical Society Proceedings*, LXXVII (1965), 31-33; Carol F. Baird, "Albert Bushnell Hart: The Rise of the Professional Historian," in Paul F. Buck (editor), *Social Sciences at Harvard, 1860-1920* (Cambridge, Mass., 1965), pp. 132-134.

17. Herbert B. Adams, *The Study of History in American Colleges and Universities* (Washington, 1887), pp. 12-41, 43, 49; Charles Kendall Adams, "Recent Historical Work in the Colleges and Universities of Europe and America," *American Historical Association Papers*, IV (1890), 41-46; Wallace Stegner, *The Uneasy Chair: A Biography of Bernard De Voto* (New York, 1974), pp. 12, 15; Emerton and Morison, "History," pp. 157, 165.

18. HUA, Albert G. Waite (Harvard 1905), notes from Coolidge lectures in History 15, "The History of Russia, 1904-1905"; Harvard Department of History and Government Records, May 1891-May 1901, pp. 33, 45, 52; October 1901-February 1910, p. 30; Harold Jefferson Coolidge and Robert H. Lord, *Archibald Cary Coolidge: Life and Letters* (Boston, 1932), pp. 40-41; Morison, *Three Centuries of Harvard*, p. 386; Emerton and Morison, "History," pp. 162-163, 166-168.

19. HUA, Harvard Department of History and Government Records, October 1901-February 1910, October 11, 1901; Coolidge letter to Charles H.

Haskins, January 27, 1902; Roger B. Merriman, "Archibald Cary Coolidge," *Harvard Graduates' Magazine*, XXXVI (1928), 551-552; Coolidge and Lord, *Coolidge*, pp. 40, 42, 50; Lipset and Riesman, *Education and Politics*, p. 128.

20. HUA, William C. Gerrish (Harvard 1899), notes from Coolidge lectures in History 1, 1895-1896; Wilhelm Segerblom (Harvard 1897), notes from Coolidge lectures in History 1, 1894-1895; Robert Morss Lovett, *All Our Years* (New York, 1948), p. 32; Roger B. Merriman, *Suleiman the Magnificent, 1520-1566* (Cambridge, Mass., 1944), preface; Hamilton Fish Armstrong, *Peace and Counterpeace: From Wilson to Hitler* (New York, 1971), p. 186; William Bentinck-Smith, *Building a Great Library: The Coolidge Years at Harvard* (Cambridge, Mass., 1976), pp. 8, 83, 234; Coolidge and Lord, *Coolidge*, p. 42; Morison, "Channing," pp. 268-269; *American Historical Review*, IV (1899), 413.

21. HUA, Coolidge, Diary, March 19, 1900, Coolidge's comments on term paper by G. Howland Shaw (Harvard 1915), "Relations between the French and English in Canada since 1840"; Frank Freidel, *Franklin D. Roosevelt: The Apprenticeship* (Boston, 1952), p. 53; George Parker Winship, "Archibald Cary Coolidge," *Harvard Library Notes*, no. 20 (1928), p. 158.

22. HUA, Harvard College Class of 1887, twenty-fifth anniversary (1887-1912), "Secretary's Report No. 7" (Boston, 1912), p. 48; Charles Jackson letter to Harold Jefferson Coolidge, May 7, 1931; Coolidge and Lord, *Coolidge*, pp. 62-63.

23. HUA, Coolidge, Diary, March 19, 1900; Coolidge letter to his mother, May 11, 1918; Coolidge letter to Henry Munroe, August 30, 1921; Coolidge letter to Harold Jefferson Coolidge, September 2, 1921; Coolidge letter to Tyler Dennett, June 20, 1927; Cass Canfield, *Up and Down and Around: A Publisher Recollects the Time of His Life* (New York, 1971), pp. 36-37; Bentinck-Smith, *Building a Great Library*, p. 45.

24. HUA, Bruce C. Hopper, "Archibald Cary Coolidge: The Olympian Teacher," talk given at Appleton Chapel, Harvard University, June 5, 1965; Hawkins, *Between Harvard and America*, pp. 108-110; Yeomans, *Lowell*, pp. 147-148; Coolidge and Lord, *Coolidge*, pp. 60-66.

25. HUA, Coolidge, Diary, march 20, 1900; Coolidge, "The Yard," undated memorandum; Coolidge letter to Charles W. Eliot, November 4, 1904; Coolidge, "Professional Coaches," from "Report of the Athletic Committee," *Harvard Graduates' Magazine*, XIV (1906), 392-395; Coolidge, "The Harvard Crew," New York *Evening Post*, June 15 and 24, 1897; Boston *Globe*, December 1, 1908; Coolidge and Lord, *Coolidge*, pp. 53-60.

26. Merriman, "Coolidge," pp. 551-552.

27. HUA, Harvard Department of History and Government Records, November 1910-March 14, 1922, pp. 221; Coolidge letter to Robert J. Kerner, August 23, 1924.

28. HUA, Harvard Department of History and Government Records, November 1910-March 14, 1922, pp. 8, 136; Albert G. Waite (Harvard 1905), notes from Coolidge lectures in History 18A, "The Expansion of Europe since 1815," 1904-1905.

29. HUA, Coolidge letter to Charles W. Eliot, January 23, 1907.

30. Garrett Mattingly, "The Historian of the Spanish Empire," *American Historical Review*, LIV (1948), 32-48.

31. HUA, Coolidge letter to Edwin V. Morgan, June 7, 1913; April 15, 1914; CFRA, Coolidge letter to Hamilton Fish Armstrong, January 4, 1924; Coolidge, *The United States as a World Power* (New York, 1908), p. 345; George W. Pierson, *Yale: The University College, 1921-1937* (New Haven, 1955), p. 389; Brooks, *Indian Summer*, pp. 367-368; Coolidge and Lord, *Coolidge*, p. 48.

32. HUA, Coolidge letter to Willard Strait, January 18, 1913; Strait letters to Coolidge, January 17, May 17, May 29, June 2, 1913; Coolidge, "Report of the Conference on Oriental History and Politics," *American Historical Association Annual Report, 1907* (Washington, 1908), pp. 71-78; Coolidge, "The Position of China in World Politics," in George H. Blakeslee (editor), *China and the Far East* (New York, 1910), pp. 1-19; Paula Cronin, "East Asian Studies at Harvard: A Scholarly Bridge between Two World," *Harvard Today* (Spring 1976), p. 7; Bentinck-Smith, *Building a Great Library*, pp. 161-162; *American Historical Review*, XIII (1908), 446-447.

33. HUA, Coolidge letter to Stanley K. Hornbeck, June 23, 1926; CFRA, Coolidge letter to Armstrong, September 11, 1925; Coolidge, "Oric Bates," *Harvard African Studies*, II (1915), preface; Harvard-Yenching Institute, *A Guide to the Chinese-Japanese Library of Harvard University* (Cambridge, Mass., 1932), pp. 5-9; Eugene P. Boardman (editor), *Asian Studies in Liberal Education* (Washington, D.C., 1959), p. 19; Cronin, "East Asian Studies at Harvard," pp. 7-8; Coolidge and Lord, *Coolidge*, pp. 47-48.

34. HUA, Edgar H. Wells letter to Coolidge, November 12, 1919; Coolidge letter to Wells, November 13, 1919; Ellery Sedgwick letter to Coolidge, November 25, 1924; Coolidge letter to Sedgwick, November 26, 1924; Ray Billington, *Frederick Jackson Turner* (New York, 1973), pp. 298-299, 310, 540 n.; Billington (editor), *Dear Lady: The Letters of Frederick Jackson Turner to Alice Forbes Perkins Hooper, 1910-1932* (San Marino, Calif., 1970), pp. 120, 359, 396-398; Schlesinger, *In Retrospect*, pp. 74-75.

35. HUA, Coolidge, "The New States of Central Europe," Lowell Lectures, 1920 (manuscript), VII; William L. Langer, *In and Out of the Ivory Tower* (New York, 1977), pp. 151-152; Lawrence E. Gelfand, *The Inquiry: American Preparations for Peace, 1917-1919* (New York, 1963), p. 208; Patricia A. Goler, "Robert Howard Lord and the Settlement of Polish Boundaries after World War I," 1957 Ph.D. thesis at Boston College, pp. 7-17, 52, 152.

36. HUA, Harvard Department of History Records, May 19, 1922-June 8, 1933, January 13, 1927; Boris A. Bakhmetev letter to Coolidge, January 9, 1925; Coolidge letter to Lewis Einstein, January 23, 1926; Einstein letter to Coolidge, February 1, 1927; Coolidge letters to Michael Karpovich, November 17, 1926; January 3, 1927; Karpovich letters to Coolidge, November 16, 1926; January 4, January 7, January 12, 1927; Coolidge letter to Sir Bernard Pares, March 22, 1927; Philip E. Mosely, "M.M. Karpovich, 1885-1959," *Russian Review*, XIX (1960), 56-60.

37. HUA, Coolidge letter to George H. Blakeslee, April 23, 1923; Langer, *In and Out of the Ivory Tower, passim*, especially pp. 104-121, 131-134, 145, 148,

162-168, 182, 189-197; Carl E. Schorske and Elizabeth Schorske (editors), William L. Langer, *Explorations in Crisis: Papers in International History* (Cambridge, Mass., 1969), xxvi-xxvii; Canfield, *Up and Down and Around*, pp. 130-131; Merriman, "Coolidge," p. 557.

38. George H. Williams (editor), *The Harvard Divinity School: Its Place in Harvard University and in American Culture* (Boston, 1954), pp. xvi, 203.

39. Robert Lee Wolff, "Robert Pierpont Blake, 1886-1950," *Dumbarton Oaks Papers*, no. 8 (1954), pp. 3-9; Bentinck-Smith, *Building a Great Library*, p. 202; Billington, *Dear Lady*, p. 405; *American Historical Review*, LVII (1950), 258.

40. HUA, William Coolidge Lane, Diary, May 17, November 11, November 15, 1898; Coolidge letter to Charles W. Eliot, November 6, 1903; Coolidge letter to Robert J. Kerner, August 23, 1924; Elias Schulman, "Introduction," in Leo Wiener, *The History of Yiddish Literature in the Nineteenth Century* (New York, 1972), pp. vi-viii, xxix-xxxii; Leo Wiener, "Songs of the Spanish Jews in the Balkan Peninsula," *Modern Philology*, I (1903), 205-206; Leo Wiener, "How I Educated My People at Home," in M.H. Weeks (editor), *Parents and Their Problems* (Washington, 1914), III, 305; Norbert Wiener, *Ex-Prodigy: My Childhood and Youth* (New York, 1953), pp. 8-30, 85, 122-125, 176, 234-238, 271-272, 290-292; Norbert Wiener, *I Am a Mathematician: The Later Life of a Prodigy* (Garden City, N.Y., 1956), pp. 44-47; Bentinck-Smith, *Building a Great Library*, pp. 11-12.

41. HUA, Coolidge letter to Sir Bernard Pares, June 9, 1924; Norbert Wiener, *Ex-Prodigy*, pp. 143-149; Norbert Wiener, *I Am a Mathematician*, p. 19; Schulman, "Introduction," pp. viii-xxii; Morison, *The Development of Harvard University*, p. 93; Albert Parry, *America Learns Russian: A History of the Teaching of the Russian Language in the United States* (Syracuse, 1967), pp. 50-52.

42. HUA, Coolidge letter to Samuel H. Cross, April 30, 1927; Cross letter to Coolidge, May 3, 1927; Coolidge letter to Robert J. Kerner, June 3, 1927; Ernest J. Simmons, "A Wayward Scholar" (manuscript), 12-14; Samuel H. Cross, "Pouchkine en Angleterre," *Revue de littérature comparée*, LXV (1937), 176; Cross, "Teaching College Russian," *American Slavic and East European Review*, III (1944), 39-41; David Bynum, "Child's Legacy Enlarged: Oral Studies at Harvard since 1856," *Harvard Library Bulletin*, XXII (1974), 250; Joseph Brozek, "Slavic Studies in America: The Present Status," *Journal of Higher Education*, XIV (1943), 296.

43. HUA, Coolidge letter to A. Lawrence Lowell, February 13, 1915; Coolidge letter to Harold Murdock, August 14, 1920; Coolidge letter to Beardsley Ruml, October 18, 1927; George Grafton Wilson letter to Helen Neill, April 2, 1930; Harvard University Bureau of International Research, *Report; July 1, 1929 to June 30, 1938* (Cambridge, Mass., 1938), pp. 3-6.

44. Melvin T. Copeland, *And Mark an Era: The Story of the Harvard Business School* (Boston, 1958), pp. 3-13; Wallace B. Donham and Esty Foster, "The Graduate School of Business Administration," in Morison, *The Development of Harvard University*, pp. 533-535; Morison, *Three Centuries of Harvard*,

p. 471; Hawkins, *Between Harvard and America*, pp. 220-221, 365; John W. Burgess, *Reminiscences of an American Scholar* (New York, 1934), pp. 191-200; Herbert Heaton, *A Scholar in Action: Edwin F. Gay* (Cambridge, Mass., 1952), p. 3.

45. HUA, Harvard Department of History and Government Records, May 1891-May 1901, pp. 134-135; Jerome D. Greene letter to Coolidge, July 25, 1906; Coolidge letter to his mother, December 31, 1906; Coolidge letters to Theodore F. Jones, April 17, May 1, May 8, May 11, June 1, June 10, June 14, 1907; *Harvard et la France* (Paris, 1936), pp. 229-232; André Siegfried, *America Comes of Age: A French Analysis* (London, 1927), pp. 149-151; R. Carlyle Buley, *The Equitable Life Insurance Company of the United States* (New York, 1959), pp. 86-88, 109-110, 128-129.

46. HUA, Harvard Department of History and Government Records, October 1901-February 1910, passim; Records, November 1910-March 14, 1922, pp. 127, 129, 147, 167, 171, 173, 201; Coolidge letter to Hiram Bingham, October 2, 1915; Coolidge letter to A. Lawrence Lowell, June 7, 1922; Coolidge letter to C.K. Webster, May 8, 1926; Coolidge letter to William L. Langer, March 29, 1927; Coolidge letters to Sir Bernard Pares, May 21, June 22, 1927; Emerton and Morison, "History," p. 175 n.; *American Historical Review*, XVII (1911), 205; XXXVII (1927), 678, 950.

7. "CIVILIZATION'S DIARY"

1. HUA, Coolidge letters to Charles H. Haskins, January 17, 1906, and undated; Coolidge letters to Walter Lichtenstein, September 17, 1905; January 18, February 14, April 29, May 2, 1906; Roger B. Merriman, "Archibald Cary Coolidge," *Harvard Graduates' Magazine*, XXXVI (1928), 553; William Bentinck-Smith, *Building a Great Library: The Coolidge Years at Harvard* (Cambridge, Mass., 1976), p. 22.

2. CFRA, Tasker H. Bliss letter to Hamilton Fish Armstrong, January 28, 1928.

3. Archibald Cary Coolidge, "The Harvard College Library," *Harvard Graduates' Magazine*, XXIV (1915), 23; William S. Ferguson and others, "Archibald Cary Coolidge," *American Academy of Arts and Sciences Proceedings*, LXIV (1930), 514-516; Charles A. Wagner, *Harvard: Four Centuries and Freedoms* (New York, 1950), p. 178.

4. HUA, Coolidge, "The Primacy of Harvard" (draft of 1915 speech).

5. Coolidge, "The Harvard College Library," p. 30.

6. HUA, William Coolidge Lane, Diary, November 5, November 12, November 26, December 14, December 16, 1909; January 31, 1910; Laurence R. Veysey, *The Emergence of the American University* (Chicago, 1965), p. 178; Bentinck-Smith, *Building a Great Library*, p. 10.

7. HUA, Coolidge, "Survey of the Library," (1910); Coolidge letter to Lichtenstein, January 31, 1910; Coolidge, "Crying Needs of the Library,"

Harvard Graduates' Magazine, XIX (1911), 410-411; Coolidge, "The Harvard College Library," pp. 26-28; Harvard University Committee Appointed to Study the Future Needs of the College Library, *Report Presented March 31, 1902* (Cambridge, Mass., 1902), pp. 3-10, 20-21; *Harvard University Library, 1636-1968* (Cambridge, Mass., 1969), pp. 13-14; William Coolidge Lane, "The Harvard College Library," in Samuel Eliot Morison (editor), *The Development of Harvard University since the Inauguration of President Eliot, 1869-1929* (Cambridge, Mass., 1930), p. 629; Bentinck-Smith, *Building a Great Library*, pp. 23-27, 170.

8. HUA, Coolidge to Lichtenstein, June 3, July 9, July 16, July 26, August 4, 1912; Ernest Cushing Richardson letter to William Coolidge Lane, April 16, 1928; Harvard University Medical School, Library Committee minute, 1928; Keyes D. Metcalf, *Report on the Harvard University Library: A Study of Present and Prospective Problems* (Cambridge, Mass., 1955), p. 49; Bentinck-Smith, *Building a Great Library*, pp. 148-151.

9. HUA, Coolidge letter to William R. Castle, Jr., December 18, 1912; Thomas Franklin Currier, "A Sheaf of Memories from the Cataloguers," *Harvard Library Notes*, no. 20 (April 1928), pp. 167-168; George Parker Winship, "Archibald Cary Coolidge," *Harvard Library Notes*, no. 20 (1928), p. 157; Bentinck-Smith, *Building a Great Library*, p. 34.

10. Coolidge, "The Objects of Cataloging," *Library Journal*, XLVI (1921), 735-739; Currier, "A Sheaf of Memories," p. 107.

11. HUA, Coolidge letters to Lichtenstein, January 2, February 1, 1911; Coolidge letter to Thomas F. Currier, December 22, 1927; Coolidge, "The Objects of Cataloging," pp. 735-737; Lane, "The Harvard College Library," pp. 618, 621; Bentinck-Smith, *Building a Great Library*, pp. 38-44.

12. HUA, Coolidge letter to Mrs. Hamilton Rice, August 19, 1920; Paul Buck, *Libraries and Universities: Addresses and Reports* (Cambridge, Mass., 1964), p. 74.

13. Coolidge, "Crying Needs of the Library," p. 411; Currier, "A Sheaf of Memories," p. 132; Bentinck-Smith, *Building a Great Library*, pp. 104-105.

14. HUA, Ernest Cushing Richardson letter to Lane, April 16, 1928; Coolidge letter to Lichtenstein, March 13, 1913; CFRA, Coolidge letter to Hamilton Fish Armstrong, February 16, 1925; *Harvard Library Notes*, no. 20 (April 1928), pp. 154-155; Currier, "A Sheaf of Memories," p. 132.

15. "Resources of American Libraries," *Annual Report of the American Historical Association for the Year 1922* (Washington, 1926), I, 243-245; Winifred Gregory (editor), *Union List of Serials in Libraries of the United States and Canada* (New York, 1927), preface.

16. Lucius M. Beebe, *Boston and the Boston Legend* (New York, 1935), p. 205.

17. Melville J. Ruggles, "Eastern European Publications in American Libraries," in Howard W. Winger (editor), *Iron Curtains and Scholarship: The Exchange of Knowledge in a Divided World* (Chicago, 1958), pp. 113-114; Paul L. Horecky, "The Slavic and East European Resources and Facilities of the Library of Congress," *Slavic Review*, XXIII (1964), 309-312; Frank Golder,

Russian Expansion on the Pacific, 1641-1850 (Cleveland, 1914), p. 340.

18. Phyllis Dain, *The New York Public Library: A History of Its Founding and Early Years* (New York, 1972), pp. 114-119; Avrahm Yarmolinsky, "The Slavonic Division: Recent Growth," *Bulletin of the New York Public Library*, XXX (1926), 71-77; Ruggles, "Eastern European Publications," p. 112; interview with Avrahm Yarmolinsky, January 6, 1973.

19. Herbert Hoover, *An American Epic* (Chicago, 1959-1964), I, 184-185, 327-328; III, 454-455; *Hoover Institution on War, Revolution, and Peace* (Stanford, 1963), pp. 1-3; Harold H. Fisher, *The Famine in Soviet Russia, 1919-1923: The Operations of the American Relief Administration* (New York, 1927), pp. 466, 563; Charles B. Burdick, *Ralph Lutz and the Hoover Institution* (Stanford, 1973), pp. 8-9, 23-32, 38, 45, 47, 80-83; Paul Miliukov, *Political Memoirs*, edited by Arthur P. Mendel, translated by Carl Goldberg (Ann Arbor, 1967), p. 198; *American Historical Review*, XXVI (1921), 622.

20. HUA, Lane, Diary, April 4, April 7, May 17, November 15, 1898; Otto Harrasowitz Buchhandlung and Antiquariat in Leipzig, *Antiquarischer Catalog 202. Slavica* (Leipzig, 1895); Dmitry Cizevsky, "The Slovak Collection of the Harvard College Library," *Harvard Library Bulletin*, VII (1953), 299-311; Ruggles, "Eastern European Publications," p. 112; Bentinck-Smith, *Building a Great Library*, p. 11.

21. HUA, Coolidge letters to his father, December 4, 1921, January 4, 1922; Coolidge letters to Frank Golder, October 2, 1922; May 1, 1923; Coolidge letters to Walter R. Batsell, February 8, 1924; February 14, 1925; Batsell letters to Coolidge, January 20, March 29, September 2, 1925; Coolidge letters to Robert J. Kerner, October 15, 1912; July 23, 1914; October 7, 1924; Michael Rostovtsev letter to Coolidge, January 24, 1927, Coolidge letter to Rostovtsev, January 25, 1927; "The Russian Books," *Harvard Library Notes* (November 9, 1922), pp. 203-208; Wilbur H. Siebert, "Collections of Materials in English and European History and Subsidiary Fields in the Libraries of the United States," *American Historical Association Annual Report, 1904* (Washington, D.C., 1905), pp. 693-694; Charles R. Gredler, "The Slavic Collection at Harvard," *Harvard Library Bulletin*, XVII (1969), 431; Bentinck-Smith, *Building a Great Library*, pp. 126-128, 156, 167.

22. HUA, Lane, Diary, April 5, April 10, September 29, October 2-6, 1899; Count Paul de Riant, *Catalogue de la bibliothèque de feu M. le comte Riant* (Paris, 1896-1899), vol. II, page opposite title page; Harold Jefferson Coolidge and Robert H. Lord, *Archibald Cary Coolidge: Life and Letters* (Boston, 1932), pp. 46-47; Bentinck-Smith, *Building a Great Library*, p. 13.

23. HUA, Lane, Diary, April 5, April 10, September 29, October 2-6, 1899; Albert H. Lybyer, *The Government of the Ottoman Empire in the Time of Suleiman the Magnificent* (Cambridge, Mass., 1913), p. 308; Stanford Shaw, "The Harvard College Library Collection of Books on Ottoman History and Literature" (Cambridge, Mass., 1959), typescript, preface; Labib Yamak, "Introduction: The Middle Eastern Collections of the Harvard Library," in Harvard University Library, *Catalogue of Arabic, Persian, and Ottoman Turkish Books* (Cambridge, Mass., 1968), I, vii-ix; Alfred Claghorn Potter, *The*

Library of Harvard University, fourth edition, (Cambridge, Mass., 1934), pp. 66, 118; Winship, "Coolidge," pp. 158–159.

24. HUA, Lane, Diary, February 20, 1905; Papers and other documents concerning Prof. Coolidge's Gift of the Hohenzollern Collection to the Harvard College Library and the opening of the Germanic Museum; Harvard University Library, Routine Records, Duplicates and Exchanges, "Katalog der bibliothek des verstorbenen Universität professors Konrad von Maurer"; Coolidge letter to Edwin V. Morgan, November 14, 1903; Coolidge letters to Lichtenstein, June 9, June 12, 1909; October 1, 1910; Lichtenstein letters to Coolidge, July 15, July 21, August 6, September 18, September 30, November 8, November 30, 1905; March 10, 1906; Kuno Francke letters to Coolidge, October 26, October 30, December 7, 1903; Walter R. Batsell letters to Coolidge, October 6, November 22, 1924; Coolidge letter to Batsell, December 8, 1924; Potter, *The Library*, pp. 88–90, 125; Winship, "Coolidge," p. 160; Washington *Times*, November 19, 1903; Boston *Transcript*, November 10–11, 1903; *American Historical Review*, XI (1905) 213–214.

25. HUA, Coolidge letter to Charles H. Haskins, January 17, 1906; Coolidge letters to Lichtenstein, March 28, 1908; November 28, 1910; Lichtenstein letters to Coolidge, August 27, 1907; March 28, 1908; August 26, 1910; Harvard University Library Chronological Miscellany, "W. Lichtenstein Report on Trip to Europe, 1905–1906"; "Report of W. Lichtenstein on European History Department, 1906–1907"; Lichtenstein, "Report on the Hohenzollern Collection of German History, October 1903–May 1905"; Lichtenstein, "Hohenzollern Collection, 1904–1914"; Lichtenstein, "Purchases on South American Trips, 1914"; Lichtenstein, "Report to the President of Northwestern University on the Results of a Trip to South America" (Evanston, Ill., 1915); Lichtenstein, "Statement about His Career and Especially His Relations with A.C. Coolidge and His Contribution to the Harvard Library, 27 June 1956," *passim*, especially pp. 1–4.

26. HUA, Coolidge letter to Haskins, January 17, 1906; Bentinck-Smith, *Building a Great Library*, pp. 133–135, 141.

27. HUA, Coolidge letter to Lane, February 8, 1907; Coolidge letter to Haskins, June 6, 1922; Philip M. Hamer (editor), *A Guide to Archives and Manuscripts in the United States* (New Haven, 1961), pp. 252–254; Potter, *The Library*, p. 86; Bentinck-Smith, *Building a Great Library*, pp. 18–19.

28. National Archives, Department of State Decimal File, 1910–1929, Coolidge letter to William B. Castle, Jr., February 19, 1924; HUA, Coolidge letter to Morgan, January 16, 1912; Bentinck-Smith, *Building a Great Library*, pp. 57–58, 142–143.

29. HUA, Coolidge letters to Lichtenstein, February 15, 1909; July 7, August 11, October 16, October 17, October 23, October 25, October 30, 1911; January 23, June 3, June 12, 1912; March 26, March 29, April 7, April 29, 1913; Lichtenstein letters to Coolidge, March 29, March 25, April 29, 1913; Coolidge letters to Morgan, September 27, 1910; July 13, 1912; December 25, 1914; April 27, 1916; Coolidge letters to Hiram Bingham, March 29, April 26, May 2, 1913; Bingham letters to Coolidge, May 1, May 5, 1913; November 8, November 15, 1915;

Lichtenstein letter to Bingham, May 2, 1913; Potter, *The Library*, pp. 105, 172; Bentinck-Smith, *Building a Great Library*, pp. 22, 114; *American Historical Review*, XV (1910), 472. The correspondence among Bingham, Coolidge, and Lichtenstein from April through June 1913 is voluminous.

30. HUA, Coolidge letter to W.S. Howe, September 18, 1925; Siebert, "Collections of Materials," pp. 622, 680; Coolidge and Lord, *Coolidge*, p. 47. Almost fifty years later, another member of the clan, Thomas Jefferson Coolidge, IV (Harvard 1954), headed a $20 million drive to strengthen the university's Asian collection and program, demonstrating the continued interest of the family in the library's resources on Asia. At that time, the Harvard-Yenching Institute Library contained more than 500,000 volumes. See Paula Cronin, "East Asian Studies at Harvard: A Scholarly Bridge between two Worlds," *Harvard Today* (Spring 1976), pp. 7–9, 13.

31. Ray Billington (editor), *Dear Lady: The Letters of Frederick Jackson Turner to Alice Forbes Perkins Hooper, 1910–1932* (San Marino, Calif. 1970), pp. 15–16, 20, 25–26, 53–69, 103, 118, 156–163, 210, 224, 304–305, 396, 423–424; Bentinck-Smith, *Building a Great Library*, pp. 115–120.

32. HUA, Lane, Diary, October 15, 1900; January 3, January 13, February 13, 1905; November 10, 1908; March 24, May 24, July 30, 1909; October 15, 1910; Coolidge letter to Lichtenstein, July 11, 1911; *The Letters of William Roscoe Thayer*, edited by Charles Downer Hazen (Boston, 1926), pp. 140–141; Coolidge and Lord, *Coolidge*, p. 87; Bentinck-Smith, *Building a Great Library*, pp. 108–109, 141–142, 157, 168–169, 204.

33. Winship, "Coolidge," pp. 162–164, 172–176; Bentinck-Smith, *Building a Great Library*, pp. 107–108, 120–122, 134, 177–180.

34. HUA, Coolidge letters to Morgan, February 10, 1901; December 25, 1914; April 27, 1916; Coolidge letters to Lichtenstein, May 15, August 10, 1914; Coolidge letters to J.P. Morgan, Jr., September 17, September 25, 1915; Coolidge letters to Robert Woods Bliss, October 23, 1920; October 27, 1922; September 16, 1924; Bliss letter to Coolidge, October 29, 1920; Coolidge letters to Castle, November 24, 1925; March 27, June 25, 1926; Charles L. Chandler letter to Harold Jefferson Coolidge, November 23, 1932; CFRA, Coolidge letters to Hamilton Fish Armstrong, October 10, 1922; May 6, 1927; Harvard University Library, *The Kilgour Collection of Russian Literature, 1750–1920* (Cambridge, Mass., 1959), preface, p. 201; Gredler, "The Slavic Collection," pp. 429–430; Winship, "Coolidge," p. 161; Bentinck-Smith, *Building a Great Library*, pp. 105, 129–133, 139–140.

35. HUA, Lane, Diary, February 11, 1907; Coolidge letters to Lichtenstein, November 19, 1905; January 17, 1912; Lichtenstein letters to Coolidge November 7, 1913; September 10, 1914; Ellis Dresel letters to Coolidge, December 12, 1919; October 2, 1920; April 12, 1921; Coolidge letter to Dresel, January 12, 1921; W. Cameron Forbes letter to Coolidge, March 16, 1922; John A. Gade, *All My Born Days* (New York, 1942), pp. 297–298; Morison, *The Development of Harvard University*, pp. 84–85.

36. HUA, Coolidge letter to Edwin V. Morgan, December 26, 1902; Coolidge letters to Kerner, July 13, July 23, 1914; Julius Klein letter to Coolidge, January

5, 1924; Mark A.D. Howe, *George von Lengerke Meyer: His Life and Public Services* (New York, 1920), pp. 5-6.

37. HUA, Coolidge letter to Edwin V. Morgan, August 14, 1912; Coolidge letters to Lichtenstein, May 24, June 3, July 16, 1912; Coolidge letter to Mrs. Hamilton Rice, August 19, 1920; Yeomans, *Lowell*, pp. 238-240; Bentinck-Smith, *Building a Great Library*, pp. 50-77.

8. TRANSFORMING AMERICAN HIGHER EDUCATION

1. Roger B. Merriman, "Archibald Cary Coolidge," *Harvard Graduates' Magazine*, XXVI (1928), 553.

2. HUA, Coolidge letters to Albert H. Lybyer, February 10, April 2, 1914; Harvard College Class of 1915, "Twenty-fifth Anniversary Report" (Cambridge, Mass., 1940), pp. 402-404; University of Illinois (Urbana) Archives, Albert H. Lybyer papers, "The Problem of Macedonia" (manuscript), August 28, 1918; William S. Ferguson and others, "Archibald Cary Coolidge," *American Academy of Arts and Sciences Proceedings*, LXIV (1930), 514; Dwight E. Lee, *Great Britain and the Cyprus Question of 1878* (Cambridge, Mass., 1934), preface, p. vii.

3. HUA, Coolidge letter to F.G. Cleveland, August 4, 1911; Coolidge letters to Robert J. Kerner, October 15, 1912, April 30, 1915; Coolidge letter to Lybyer, May 17, 1917; Coolidge letter to Dwight E. Lee, May 17, 1927; Bruce C. Hopper, "Archibald Cary Coolidge: The Olympian Teacher," talk given at Appleton Chapel, Harvard University, June 5, 1965, 4; CFRA, Coolidge letter to Hamilton Fish Armstrong, March 6, 1923; Dexter Perkins, *Yield of the Years: An Autobiography* (Boston, 1969), p. 29; George H. Rupp, *A Wavering Friendship: Russia and Austria, 1876-1878* (Cambridge, Mass., 1941), pp. vii-viii; William L. Langer, *The Franco-Russian Alliance, 1890-1894* (Cambridge, Mass., 1929), p. viii; Langer, *In and Out of the Ivory Tower* (New York, 1977), pp. 104-105, 131; Merriman, "Coolidge," pp. 555-556.

4. Harold Jefferson Coolidge and Robert H. Lord, *Archibald Cary Coolidge: Life and Letters* (Boston, 1932), p. 67; Perkins, *Yield of the Years*, pp. 28-32.

5. HUA, Coolidge letter to Laurence B. Packard, December 19, 1911; Coolidge letters to Kerner, March 10, March 20, April 26, 1913; March 21, March 31, July 23, 1914; CFRA, Coolidge letters to Armstrong, March 8, 1927; Langer, *In and Out of the Ivory Tower*, pp. 105, 111; *American Historical Review*, LXIII (1967), 679.

6. HUA, Coolidge letter to Packard, January 11, 1911; Coolidge letter to Kerner, March 10, 1913; University of Rochester Archives, Dexter Perkins Papers, Perkins letter to his father, April 18, 1912; Perkins, *Yield of the Years*, pp. 40-41, 118.

7. CFRA, Coolidge letter to Armstrong, March 6, 1923; Harvard University, *Doctors of Philosophy and Doctors of Science Who Have Received Their*

Degrees in Course from Harvard University, 1873–1926, with the Titles of Their Theses (Cambridge, Mass., 1926), pp. 79–96; Ephraim Emerton and Samuel Eliot Morison, "History, 1838–1929," in Samuel Eliot Morison (editor), *The Development of Harvard University since the Inauguration of President Eliot, 1869–1929* (Cambridge, Mass., 1930), pp. 164, 166.

8. William Henry Allison and others (editors), *A Guide to Historical Literature* (New York, 1931); Philip E. Mosely, "Some Vignettes of Soviet Life," *Survey*, no. 55 (1965), pp. 52–54; Emerton, "History," p. 170 n.

9. Williams College Archives, Richard A. Newhall Papers, letters of Newhall to Laurence B. Packard, July 27, 1930; September 22, 1931; December 9, 1941; August 20, 1951; May 1, October 2, December 18, 1952; Arthur P. Coleman, "Slavonic Studies in the United States, 1918–1938," *Slavonic and East European Review*, XVII (1938–39), 381; *American Historical Review*, LXXIX (1974), 924–925; Mrs. Sidney R. Packard letter to Robert F. Byrnes, May 18, 1978; Russell Bostert letter to Byrnes, July 24, 1978.

10. HUA, Coolidge letter to Lybyer, March 29, 1913; Amherst College Archives, Laurence B. Packard Papers, Packard letter to Mr. Fletcher, May 20, 1925; Packard letter to Frederick Barghoorn, May 30, 1945; Faculty Memorial to Laurence Bradford Packard; Alfred F. Havighurst, "Laurence Bradford Packard," *American Historical Review*, LXI (1956), 523; University of Rochester. *Catalogue, 1909–1910*, p. 120; *1914–1915*, p. 95; *1922–1923*, pp. 114–115; *1924–1925*, p. 123; New York *Times*, January 15, 1955.

11. HUA, Hopper, "Coolidge: The Olympian Teacher," p. 5; Hopper, *Pan-Sovietism* (Boston, 1931), pp. 12, 20, 24–25, 152–153; Hamilton Fish Armstrong, *Peace and Counterpeace: From Wilson to Hitler* (New York, 1971), pp. 411–412.

12. Arthur I. Andrews, "Instructors of Courses in Slavic or East European Languages in the Universities and Colleges of the United States of America," *Slavonic Review*, IX (1930), vi–xi.

13. National Archives, Inquiry Papers, Coolidge letter to James T. Shotwell, November 2, 1917; George H. Blakeslee, "An Historical Sketch of Clark University," in Wallace Atwood (editor), *The First Fifty Year* (Worcester, Mass., 1937), pp. 8–18; Blakeslee (editor), *Journal of Race Development*, I (1910), 2; Dwight E. Lee and George E. McReynolds (editors), *Essays in History and International Relations, in Honor of George Hubbard Blakeslee* (Worcester, 1949), p. 321; Joseph Clark Grew, *Turbulent Era: A Diplomatic Record of Forty Years, 1904–1945* (Boston, 1953), II, 1422; Lawrence E. Gelfand, *The Inquiry: American Preparations for Peace, 1917–1919* (New Haven, 1963), pp. 64–65; *American Historical Review*, LV (1949–50), 340–341; *American Historical Review*, LX (1954), 253–254.

14. University of Rochester Archives, Dexter Perkins letters to his parents, October 11, 1911–March 18, 1913; Perkins, *Yield of the Years, passim; Slavonic Review*, III (1924–25), vi–vii.

15. HUA, Coolidge letters to Lybyer, January 25, 1910; June 12, 1911; March 21, June 10, 1913; July 22, 1915; University of Illinois, Lybyer curriculum vitae; Lybyer letter to Dean Babcock, February 16, 1931; Lybyer, *The Government of the Ottoman Empire in the Time of Suleiman the Magnificent* (Cambridge,

Mass., 1913); Lybyer, "The Influence of the Rise of the Ottoman Turks upon the Routes of Oriental Trade," *American Historical Association Annual Report, 1914* (Washington, 1916), pp. 125-133; *American Historical Review*, LIV (1949), 985.

16. HUA, Coolidge letter to William Stearns Davis, August 28, 1912; Harvard College Class of 1907, "Fiftieth Anniversary Report" (Cambridge, Mass., 1957); William Stearns Davis, preface to Mason W. Tyler, *The European Powers and the Near East, 1875-1878* (Minneapolis, 1925), pp. v-vi; *American Historical Review*, XLVII (1924), 970-971; LXIII (1958), 860; LXV (1960), 1048; LXXXII (1977), 789-790.

17. Library of Congress, Manuscript Division, J. Franklin Jameson Papers, Frank Golder letters to Jameson, December 3, 1905; October 5, 1917; Golder letter to R.R. Smith of Macmillan Company, December 21, 1915; Golder, *Russian Expansion on the Pacific, 1641-1850* (Cleveland, 1914), pp. 13-16; Gelfand, *The Inquiry*, pp. 55-56, 68-69; Charles B. Burdick, *Ralph Lutz and the Hoover Institution* (Stanford, 1973), pp. 37-38; J. Franklin Jameson, *A Historian's World: Selections from the Correspondence of James Franklin Jameson* (Philadelphia, 1956), pp. 191-192; Paul Miliukov, *Political Memoirs, 1905-1907*, edited by Arthur P. Mendel, translated by Carl Goldberg (Ann Arbor, 1967), p. 198; *American Historical Review*, XXVI (1921), 62; Coolidge and Lord, *Coolidge*, p. 301.

18. HUA, Harvard College Class of 1894, "Third Report" (Cambridge, Mass., 1902), p. 88; "Fiftieth Anniversary Report" (Cambridge, 1944), pp. 394-398; Ernest J. Simmons, "A Wayward Scholar" (manuscript), pp. 4-9; George R. Noyes, "Teaching of Slavic Languages at the University of California," in Stephen N. Sestanovich (editor), *Slavs in California* (Oakland, 1937), pp. 34-37; Oleg A. Maslenikov, "Slavic Studies in America, 1939-1946," *Slavonic and East European Review*, XXV (1946-47), 528-537; Albert Parry, *America Learns Russian: A History of the Teaching of the Russian Language in the United States* (Syracuse, 1967), pp. 53-56.

19. HUA, Coolidge letter to his mother, July 8, 1905; Coolidge letters to Henry Morse Stephens, July 15, July 30, August 12, 1907; April 15, 1908; University of California, Berkeley, *Asiatic and Slavic Studies on the Berkeley Campus, 1896-1947*, p. 8; Luther V. Hendricks, *James Harvey Robinson, Teacher of History* (New York, 1946), pp. 75-76; John W. Caughey, *Hubert Howe Bancroft, Historian of the West* (Berkeley, 1946), pp. 395-396, 399; Morris Bishop, *A History of Cornell* (Ithaca, 1962), pp. 339-340; Henry A. Yeomans, *Abbott Lawrence Lowell, 1856-1943* (Cambridge, Mass., 1948), p. 95; *American Historical Review*, XXIV (1919-20), 747.

20. James Franklin Jameson, "The Meeting of the American Historical Association in California," *American Historical Review*, XXI (1915), 1-10; Caughey, *Bancroft*, pp. 357-365, 383, 393.

21. HUA, Coolidge letters to Kerner, February 26, April 2, 1910; Kerner letters to Coolidge, March 31, April 4, 1910; Coolidge letter to A.T. Olmstead, October 2, 1927; Kerner, "The Teaching of Slavic History at the University of California," in Sestanovich, *Slavs in California*, pp. 67-72; Kerner, "Slavonic

Studies in America," *Slavonic Review*, III (1924-25), 246-247; Josef Zacek, introduction to Kerner, *Bohemia in the Eighteenth Century* (Orono, Maine, 1969), pp. vii–x; Gelfand, *The Inquiry*, pp. 57-58, 337; *American Historical Review*, LXII (1957), 800-801.

22. Carl Berger, *The Writing of Canadian History: Aspects of English-Canadian Historical Writing, 1900-1970* (Toronto, 1976), pp. 145-146, 156; *American Historical Review*, XLVII (1941-42), 923-924; Montreal *Star*, April 26, 1941.

23. HUA, Coolidge letter to Lybyer, October 13, 1917; University of California (Berkeley), Bancroft Library, Julius Klein Papers; Klein, *The Mesta: A Study in Spanish Economic History, 1273-1836* (Cambridge, Mass., 1920), pp. ix–xi; Klein, *Frontiers of Trade* (New York, 1929); Klein and C. Court Treatt, *Black Cargo: Ethiopian War Drums* (Chicago, 1935), Joseph V. Fuller, *Bismarck's Diplomacy at Its Zenith* (Cambridge, Mass., 1922).

24. Waldo G. Leland, "Some Early Recollections of an Itinerant Historian," *American Antiquarian Society Proceedings*, LXI (1951), 268-271; *American Historical Review*, XXX (1925), 17, n; XXXIII (1928), 462; LXXI (1976), 292; LXXII (1977), 804.

25. John K. Wright, *Geography in the Making: The American Geographical Society, 1851-1951* (New York, 1952) pp. xviii, 221, 238-239; William Bentinck-Smith, *Building a Great Library: The Coolidge Years at Harvard* (Cambridge, Mass., 1976), pp. 190-191 n.

26. HUA, Coolidge letter to Waldo G. Leland, January 8, 1915; Leland letter to Coolidge, August 14, 1915; Coolidge, "Report of the Conference on Oriental History and Politics," *American Historical Association Annual Report, 1907* (Washington, 1908), pp. 70-75; "The Meeting of the American Historical Association at Indianapolis," *American Historical Review*, XVI (1911), 459-460; Waldo G. Leland, "Report on the Proceedings of the Twenty-sixth Annual Meeting of the American Historical Association," *Annual Report of the American Historical Association, 1910* (Washington, 1913), pp. 30, 36-51; *American Historical Review*, XVII (1913); *American Historical Review*, XVII (1913), 470; *American Historical Review*, XXIII (1918), 68; *American Historical Review*, XXV (1919), 112-117; Jameson, "Proceedings of the Forty-first Annual Meeting of the American Historical Association, Rochester, New York, December 28-30, 1926," *Annual Report of the American Historical Association for the year 1926* (Washington, 1930), pp. 30-51; Gelfand, *The Inquiry*, pp. 35-36.

27. HUA, Coolidge letter to Kerner, October 19, 1916; Coolidge, "A Plea for the Study of Northern Europe," *American Historical Review*, II (1896), 34-39; Coolidge, "Claimants to Constantinople," in Charles Downer Thayer and others, *Three Peace Congresses of the Nineteenth Century* (Cambridge, Mass., 1917), preface; Coolidge, "The Break-up of the Hapsburg Empire," in Coolidge, *Ten Years of War and Peace* (Cambridge, Mass., 1927), 241 n.; *American Historical Review*, II (1896), 201-202; Herbert B. Adams, "Report on the Proceedings of the Eleventh Annual Meeting of the American Historical Association," *Annual Report of the American Historical Association for the Year 1895* (Washington, 1896), p. 8; Adams, "Report of the Proceedings of the

Thirteenth Annual Meeting," *Annual Report . . . for 1897* (Washington, 1908), pp. 11-12; A. Howard Clark, "Report of the Proceedings of the Fifteenth Annual Meeting," *Annual Report . . . for 1899* (Washington, 1900), I, 42; Clark, "Report of Proceedings of the Sixteenth Annual Meeting," *Annual Report . . . for 1900* (Washington, 1901), pp. 5, 28; Leland, "Proceedings of the Twenty-fifth Annual Meeting," *Annual Report . . . for 1909* (Washington, 1911), p. 44; "Meeting of the American Historical Association in New York," *American Historical Association*, XV (1910), 494; "Meeting of the American Historical Association at Buffalo and Ithaca," *American Historical Review*, XVII (1912), 475; *American Historical Review*, XXVI (1921), 424.

28. HUA, Coolidge letter to Wallace S. Murray, May 3, 1921; Paul Miliukov, "The Chief Currents of Russian Historical Thought," *Annual Report . . . for 1904* (Washington, 1905), pp. 109-114; Pierre Caron," A French Cooperative Historical Enterprise," *American Historical Review*, XIII (1908), 501-509; Inazo Nitobé, "Anglo-Japanese Intercourse prior to the Advent of Perry," *Annual Report . . . for 1911* (Washington, 1913), pp. 129-140; Henri Pirenne, "The Stages in the Social History of Capitalism," *American Historical Review*, XIX (1914), 494-515; Inna Lubimenko, "The Correspondence of Queen Elizabeth with the Russian Czars," *American Historical Review*, XIX (1914), 525-542; Serge Gorianov, "The End of the Alliance of the Emperors," *American Historical Review*, XXIII (1918), 324-349; Michael Rostovtsev, "South Russia in the Prehistoric and Classical Period," *American Historical Review*, XXVI (1921), 203-224; Alexander Presniakov, "Historical Research in Russia during the Revolutionary Crisis," *American Historical Review*, XXVIII (1923), 248-257; Henryk Marczali, "The Papers of Count Tisza, 1914-1918," *American Historical Review*, XXIX (1924), 301-315; Harold Temperley, "Canning and the Conference of the Four Allied Governments at Paris, 1823-1826," *American Historical Review*, XXX (1924), 16-43; Michael Rostovtsev, "The Origin of the Russian State on the Dnieper," *Annual Report . . . for 1920* (Washington, 1925), pp. 165-170; Henri Sée, "Commerce between France and the United States, 1783-1784," *American Historical Review*, XXXI (1926), 732-751; Alexander A. Vasiliev, "Byzantine Studies in Russia, Past and Present," *American Historical Review*, XXXII (1929), 539-545; Harry Gay, "Communication: The International Congress of Historical Sciences," *American Historical Review*, VIII (1903), 808-812; Charles H. Haskins, "The International Historical Congress at Berlin," *American Historical Review*, XIV (1908), 1-8; *The Letters of William Roscoe Thayer*, edited by Charles Downer Hazen (Boston, 1926), pp. 120-122; *American Historical Review*, VIII (1903), 809-810; XV (1910), 475-476; XVII (1912), 45 n.; XVIII (1913), 680, 690; XIX (1914), 494-515.

29. HUA, Sir Bernard Pares letters to Coolidge, July 14, 1923; March 21, May 11, May 20, 1924; Coolidge letters to Pares, May 20, 1924; March 21, 1925; Arthur I. Andrews to Coolidge, May 22, 1924; Coolidge letters to Kerner, June 12, June 24, June 26, September 12, 1924; CFRA, Coolidge letters to Armstrong, December 4, December 8, December 23, 1924; Library of Congress Manuscript Division, J. Franklin Jameson Papers, Pares letters to Jameson, June 26, August 21, 1924; Pares, *A Wandering Student* (Syracuse, 1948), pp. 303-305; Clarence A.

Manning, *History of Slavic Studies in the United States* (Milwaukee, 1957), p. 54; Charles G. Abbot, "Proceedings of the Thirty-ninth Annual Meeting of the American Historical Association," *Annual Report...for 1924* (Washington, 1929), pp. 40, 55; *American Historical Review*, XXI (1916), 891; XXX (1925), 189, 410, 451–455, 458–459.

30. HUA, Sir Bernard Pares letters to Coolidge, June 20, August 27, 1925; April 29, July 12, 1926; Coolidge letter to Charles H. Haskins, September 29, 1924; Coolidge letters to Kerner, January 24, 1925; March 3, 1927; Kerner letter to Coolidge, January 8, 1927; CFRA, Armstrong letter to Coolidge, March 3, 1927; University of California Bancroft Library, Robert J. Kerner Papers, Kerner letter to Pares, January 6, 1925; Anglo-Russian Literary Society *Proceedings*, no. 35 (1903), p. 143; Kerner, "The Slavonic Conference at Richmond," *Slavonic Review*, III (1924–25), 684–693; Kerner, "Slavonic Studies in America," *Slavonic Review*, III (1924–25), 243–258; *American Historical Review*, XXX (1925), 189–90, 465.

9. THE SCHOLAR AND THE GOVERNMENT

1. Cited in John A. Garraty, *Henry Cabot Lodge: A Biography* (New York, 1953), p. 146.

2. Lloyd C. Griscom, *Diplomatically Speaking* (Boston, 1940), pp. 244–245; William Barnes and J.H. Morgan, *The Foreign Service of the United States: Origins, Development, and Functions* (Washington, 1961), pp. 146–147, 160; Ernest R. May, *Imperial Democracy: The Emergence of America as a Great Power* (New York, 1961), p. 5.

3. William B. Phillips, Jr., *Ventures in Diplomacy* (Boston, 1953), pp. 35–36, 49; Charles E. Bohlen, *Witness to History, 1929–1969* (New York, 1973), p. 7; Sister Rachel West, *The Department of State on the Eve of the First World War, 1913–1914* (Athens, Ga., 1978), pp. 1–6; Barnes and Morgan, *The Foreign Service*, pp. 127–131, 155–157, 159–160, 193–194.

4. Phillips, *Ventures in Diplomacy*, p. 36.

5. Barnes and Morgan, *The Foreign Service*, pp. 128–131, 155–157, 193–194.

6. Robert D. Schulzinger, *The Making of the Diplomatic Mind: The Training, Outlook, and Style of United States Foreign Service Officers, 1908–1931* (Middletown, Conn., 1975), pp. 3–7, 42–48; Lawrence E. Gelfand, *The Inquiry: American Preparations for Peace, 1917–1919* (New Haven, 1963), p. 35.

7. Waldo H. Heinrichs, Jr., *American Ambassador: Joseph C. Grew and the Development of the United States Diplomatic Tradition* (Boston, 1966), pp. 96–97; Edward Younger, *John A. Kasson: Politics and Diplomacy from Lincoln to McKinley* (Iowa City, Ia., 1955), pp. 283–284; Robert H. Wiebe, *The Search for Order, 1877–1920* (New York, 1967), p. 277; Griscom, *Diplomatically Speaking*, pp. 89–91; Barnes and Morgan, *The Foreign Service*, p. 139; *American Historical Review*, LXXXIV (1979), 577.

8. Martin Weil, *A Pretty Good Club: The Founding Fathers of the U.S. Foreign Service* (New York, 1978), p. 15; George W. Pierson, *Yale: A Short History* (New Haven, 1976), p. 88; Heinrichs, *American Ambassador*, pp. viii-ix, 18, 97-99; Schulzinger, *The Making of the Diplomatic Mind*, pp. 15-19.

9. Francis M. Huntington-Wilson, *Memoirs of an Ex-Diplomat* (Boston, 1945), pp. 38, 46-47, 167, 321; Richard Hume Werking, *The Master Architects: Building the United States Foreign Service, 1890-1913* (Lexington, Ky, 1977), pp. 126-129; Griscom, *Diplomatically Speaking*, pp. 26-28, 70; Barnes and Morgan, *The Foreign Service*, p. 184.

10. John Gardner Coolidge, *Random Letters from Many Countries* (Boston, 1924), pp. 27, 347; Emma Downing Coolidge, *Descendants of John and Mary Coolidge of Watertown, Massachusetts, 1630* (Boston, 1930), p. 342; Oscar Strauss, *Under Four Administrations* (Boston, 1922), p. 103; Phillips, *Ventures in Diplomacy*, pp. 7, 14, 16, 131; Griscom, *Diplomatically Speaking*, pp. 177, 195-197, 278, 284; Heinrichs, *American Ambassador*, pp. 16, 98; Werking, *The Master Architects*, pp. 126-131, 283; Barnes and Morgan, *The Foreign Service*, p. 201; West, *The Department of State*, pp. 15-17.

11. Katherine Crane, *Mr. Carr of State: Forty-seven Years in the Department of State* (New York, 1960), p. 261; Weil, *A Pretty Good Club*, p. 21; Barnes and Morgan, *The Foreign Service*, pp. 167, 201.

12. Barnes and Morgan, *The Foreign Service*, pp. 184, 210-212.

13. HUA, Julian Coolidge, Diary, March 21, March 29, 1900; Archibald Cary Coolidge, Diary, March 21, 1900; Coolidge letter to his mother, December 19, 1908; Coolidge letter to J.P. Moore, June 7, 1913; Coolidge letter to Walter Lichtenstein, August 13, 1913; Coolidge letter to Edwin V. Morgan, November 11, 1914; Coolidge letters to Hiram Bingham, November 19, 1920; Coolidge letter to Hugh Gibson, March 24, May 24, 1924; Coolidge letter to Ellis Dresel, February 12, 1925; Bruce C. Hopper, "Archibald Cary Coolidge: The Olympian Teacher," talk given at Appleton Chapel, Harvard University, June 5, 1965, p. 5; CFRA, Coolidge letter to Hamilton Fish Armstrong, January 7, 1924; Armstrong letters to Coolidge, October 13, 1922; May 6, September 16, 1924; William S. Ferguson and others, "Archibald Cary Coolidge," *American Academy of Arts and Sciences Proceedings*, LXIV (1930), 517-518; Harold Jefferson Coolidge and Robert H. Lord, *Archibald Cary Coolidge: Life and Letters* (Boston, 1932), p. 140.

14. HUA, Coolidge letter to Kerner, November 12, 1920; Coolidge letter to Harold J. Coolidge, Jr., November 29, 1926; Coolidge, *The United States as a World Power* (New York, 1908), pp. 85, 333; Coolidge and Lord, *Coolidge*, pp. 324-325.

15. HUA, Coolidge letter to Arthur I. Andrews, August 20, 1923; Andrews letter to Coolidge, August 22, 1923; Coolidge letter to Henry Wriston, May 5, 1924; Coolidge letter to Endicott Peabody, May 12, 1924; Coolidge letter to Franklin D. Roosevelt, May 28, 1924; CFRA, Coolidge letter to Armstrong, April 23, 1924; Heinrichs, *American Ambassador*, p. 9.

16. HUA, Coolidge letter to Edwin V. Morgan, February 10, 1911; Joseph Clark Grew letter to Coolidge, August 21, 1916; Coolidge letter to Nicholas

Roosevelt, September 29, 1927; CFRA, Coolidge letter to Armstrong, March 17, 1924; Joseph Clark Grew, *Turbulent Era: A Diplomatic Record of Forty Years, 1904-1945* (Boston, 1953), I, 9-12; Hugh Wilson, *Education of a Diplomat* (New York, 1938), p. 11; Nicholas Roosevelt, *A Front Row Seat* (Norman, Okla., 1953), pp. 66-68, 312; Heinrichs, *American Ambassador*, pp. 9-10, 22; New York *Times*, January 4, 1976.

17. HUA, Coolidge letters to Morgan, December 26, 1902; July 11, 1910; February 10, May 25, 1911; January 8, 1912; Coolidge letter to his mother, October 25, 1913; Harvard College Class of 1890, "Twenty-fifth Anniversary Report" (Norwood, 1915), pp. 156-160; Wilson, *Education of a Diplomat*, pp. vii, 18, 27, 110; Werking, *The Master Architects*, p. 246; Coolidge and Lord, *Coolidge*, p. 79.

18. HUA, Coolidge letters to Robert Woods Bliss, February 23, 1916; October 23, 1920; Coolidge letters to William R. Castle, Jr., March 27, June 25, 1926; CFRA, Coolidge letters to Armstrong, October 17, November 9, 1922; September 11, September 16, 1924; Walter Muir Whitehill, *Dumbarton Oaks: The History of a Georgetown House and Garden 1800-1966* (Cambridge, Mass., 1967); Heinrichs, *American Ambassador*, p. 97; Ephraim Emerton and Samuel Eliot Morison, "History, 1838-1929," in Samuel Eliot Morison (editor), *The Development of Harvard University since the Inauguration of President Eliot, 1869-1929* (Cambridge, Mass., 1930), p. 72.

19. HUA, Coolidge, Diary, March 9, 1900; Coolidge letters to Castle, January 30, 1918; July 8, 1922; December 2, 1924; November 24, 1925; May 26, 1927; Castle letters to Coolidge, January 29, May 3, May 13, 1918; March 10, 1920; December 5, 1924; March 6, November 28, 1925; "The Farm Book," *passim;* CFRA, Coolidge letters to Armstrong, May 29, June 1, November 20, 1923; September 18, 1924; May 28, 1925; February 18, May 12, 1927; Bohlen, *Witness to History*, pp. 4-8; Weil, *A Pretty Good Club*, p. 79; Coolidge and Lord, *Coolidge*, p. 320.

20. HUA, Coolidge letter to Morgan, December 25, 1914; Phillips, *Ventures in Diplomacy*, pp. 7, 14; *Letters of Louis D. Brandeis*, edited by Melvin I. Urovsky and David W. Levy (Albany, 1971-1973), III, 21, 382 nn.; Arthur M. Schlesinger, Jr., *The Crisis of the Old Order, 1913-1933* (Boston, 1957), pp. 357, 408; Schulzinger, *The Making of the Diplomatic Mind*, p. 159; Werking, *The Master Architects*, p. 144; Gelfand, *The Inquiry*, pp. 16-17.

21. Grew, *Turbulent Era*, I, xv-xxiv; Heinrichs, *American Ambassador*, pp. 3-19.

22. G. Howland Shaw, "The American Foreign Service," *Foreign Affairs*, XIV (1936), 323-333; Heinrichs, *American Ambassador*, pp. 147-149, 155, 160.

23. Trust Department of Riggs National Bank, Washington, D.C., Robert F. Kelley Papers; CFRA, Armstrong to Coolidge, August 21, 1924; John Charles Chalberg, "Samuel Harper and Russia under the Tsars and Soviets, 1905-1943," 1974 Ph.D. thesis at University of Minnesota, pp. 265-267; Boston *Evening Globe*, March 19, 1918; October 25, 1926; May 15, 1937.

24. Bohlen, *Witness to History*, pp. 39-42; Chalberg, "Samuel Harper," pp. 309-317, 402-413; New York *Times*, June 3, 1976; Department of State *Newsletter* (April 1977), pp. 4-5.

25. HUA, Harvard College Class of 1915, "Fiftieth Anniversary Report" (Cambridge, Mass., 1965), pp. 284–287; CFRA, Coolidge letter to Armstrong, August 21, 1924; George F. Kennan, *Memoirs, 1925–1950* (Boston, 1967), pp. 23–33, 73–84; Loy W. Henderson, "Robert F. Kelley," *American Historical Review*, LXXXII (1977), 237–238; Kelley, "New Economic Divisions of Russia: Notes and Maps," *Foreign Affairs*, IV (1926), 330–333; Kelley, "The Recent Russian Census," *Foreign Affairs*, VI (1928), 333–335; Chalberg, "Samuel Harper," p. 326; San Francisco *News Bulletin*, July 8, 1961.

26. HUA, Coolidge letter to Morgan, December 25, 1914; Coolidge letter to William Stearns Davis, October 2, 1914; May 25, 1915; Coolidge letter to Charles B. Beazley, February 15, 1915; Coolidge letter to J. Franklin Jameson, May 17, 1915; National Archives Enquiry Folder, minutes of National Board for Historical Service meetings, November 9, November 10, 1917; Newton D. Mereness, "American Historical Activities during the World War," *American Historical Association Annual Report, 1919* (Washington, 1923), I, 161, 173, 187; Coolidge and Lord, *Coolidge*, p. 158.

27. Coolidge, "Claimants to Constantinople," in Charles Downer Hazen and others, *Three Peace Congresses of the Nineteenth Century* (Cambridge, Mass., 1917), pp. 73–93; Coolidge, "The Break-up of the Hapsburg Empire," in Coolidge, *Ten Years of War and Peace* (Cambridge, Mass., 1927), pp. 241–268; Coolidge, "Nationality and the New Europe," *Yale Review*, IV (1915), p. 447–461.

28. Coolidge, "Claimants to Constantinople," p. 92; Hamilton Fish Armstrong, *Peace and Counterpeace: From Wilson to Hitler* (New York, 1971), pp. 126–127.

29. HUA, Coolidge letter to David Miller, February 19, 1918; National Archives, Department of State Decimal File, "1916–1929," p. 185, 212.3; Coolidge, "The New Frontiers in Former Austria-Hungary," memorandum for The Inquiry, March 10, 1918; Coolidge, "Nationality and the New Europe," pp. 447–449.

30. HUA, Coolidge letter to Edward M. House, January 14, 1918; "Coolidge Memorandum on Certain Frontier Questions," January, 1918; Coolidge letter to Walter Lippmann, March 19, 1918.

31. Ivo J. Lederer, *Yugoslavia at the Paris Peace Conference: A Study in Frontiermaking* (New Haven, 1963), pp. 135–136; Seth P. Tillman, *Anglo-American Relations at the Paris Peace Conference of 1919* (Princeton, 1961), pp. 17–19.

32. HUA, The Inquiry, "Report of A.C. Coolidge," January 15, 1918; Isaiah Bowman letter to Coolidge, October 30, 1917; Coolidge letter to A. Lawrence Lowell, October 30, 1917; Sidney E. Mezes letter to Coolidge, November 10, 1917; National Archives, Sandra K. Rangel *(compiler)*, recorder for The Inquiry, "Inventory of Group Records 256" (Washington, 1974), pp. 1–172, *passim;* Inquiry Document 102, correspondence of A.C. Coolidge; Harold Josephson, *James T. Shotwell and the Rise of Internationalism in America* (Rutherford, N.J., 1975), pp. 48–60, 70–75; Gladys M. Wrigley, "Isaiah Bowman," *Geographical Review*, XLI (1951), 21–23; Gelfand, *The Inquiry*, pp. xi, 37; Coolidge and Lord, *Coolidge*, pp. 192–193.

33. HUA, Coolidge letters to Shotwell, November 2, November 6, November 20, December 7, 1917; Coolidge letters to Mezes, November 28, 1917; October 30, 1918; Coolidge letters to Lippmann, January 26, 1918; February 14, February 16, March 8, March 14, April 4, 1918; Coolidge to Henry R. Shipman, February 11, 1918; National Archives, Rangel, "Records for The Inquiry," pp. 23, 33, 40, 46–47, 49–51, 63, 68, 70–72, 78–80, 86, 95, 102, 112; James T. Shotwell, *At the Paris Peace Conference* (New York, 1937), pp. 6–9, 78; Gelfand, *The Inquiry*, pp. 54–55, 64–65, 178, 337, 340, 342.

34. HUA, Harvard College Class of 1918, "Fiftieth Anniversary Report" (Cambridge, Mass., 1968); Coolidge letter to Mezes, November 28, 1917; Coolidge letter to Shotwell, December 7, 1917; Coolidge letters to Lippmann, February 16, February 22, March 19, 1918; National Archives, Rangel, "Records for The Inquiry," pp. 44, 46, 63, 78–79; Gelfand, *The Inquiry*, pp. 54–56, 340–342.

35. HUA, Coolidge, "Archangel and Murmansk," report for the War Trade Board; Coolidge, "Archangel," report to the Secretary of State, September 28, 1918; Felix Cole, "The Political Situation in Archangel before the Coup d'Etat," September 21, 1918; Coolidge letters to his mother, May 18, July 7, July 12, July 31, August 14, September 4, 1918; Coolidge letters to House, April 4, June 29, July 14, 1918; Coolidge letters to Lippmann, April 16, August 10, 1918; Lippmann letter to Coolidge, April 17, 1918; Coolidge letters to Mezes, April 19, May 13, July 31, 1918; Mezes letter to Coolidge, April 15, 1918; Shotwell letter to Coolidge, April 17, 1918; Coolidge letter to Vance McCormick, April 18, 1919; Coolidge letter to Tyler Dennett, June 20, 1917; National Archives, Department of State, Decimal File, "1910–1919," 10396.943, 1014 and 861.00 28991/2, cables from Whitehouse in Stockholm to War Trade Board, July 25, 1918; August 18, 1918; Coolidge cable to Secretary of State Lansing, September 28, 1918; Department of State, *Papers Relating to the Foreign Relations of the United States, 1918: Russia* (Washington, 1931–1932), III, 147, 150, 153, 164; John M. Thompson, *Russia, Bolshevism and the Versailles Peace* (Princeton, 1966), pp. 230, 288–289.

36. HUA, Coolidge letters to Morgan, May 31, 1918; February 1, 1919; Coolidge letter to Mrs. A.B. Randall, December 31, 1919; Department of State, *Paris Peace Conference*, II, 218–219; Dagmar Perman, *The Shaping of the Czechoslovak State: Diplomatic History of the Boundaries of Czechoslovakia, 1914–1920* (Leyden, 1962), p. 95 n.

37. HUA, Coolidge letter to Grew, April 21, 1919; Coolidge, American Commission to Negotiate the Peace, reports to Paris from Vienna, April 22, April 25, May 1, May 18, 1919; Philip M. Brown, "Foreign Relations of the Budapest Soviets in 1919: A Personal Narrative," *The Hungarian Quarterly*, III (1937), 56–69; Brown, *Foreigners in Turkey: Their Juridical Status* (Princeton, 1914); Griscom, *Diplomatically Speaking*, p. 158.

38. HUA, Coolidge, reports to Paris from Vienna, January 12, April 6, May 1, 1919; Nicholas Roosevelt letter to Allen Dulles, February 6, 1919; Department of State, *Paris Peace Conference*, XII, 259–260, 284–295; XIII, 245–247, 293–294; Lawrence Martin, "The Perfect Day of an Itinerant Peacemaker," in William W.

Bishop and Andrew Keogh (editors), *Essays Offered to Herbert Putnam* (New Haven, 1929), p. 341; Roosevelt, *A Front Row Seat*, pp. 96-99; *Das politische Tagebuch Josef Redlichs* (Graz-Cologne, 1953-1954), I, 329-330; II, 331-343; Alfred D. Low, *The Anschluss Movement 1918-1919 and the Paris Peace Conference* (Philadelphia, 1974), pp. 207-208; Robert Hoffman, "The British Military Representative in Vienna, 1919," *Slavonic and East European Review*, LII (1974), 255-271.

39. HUA, Dresel letter to Grew, March 20, 1919; University of California Bancroft Library, Kerner Papers, Kerner, "Bolshevism and the States of Central Europe," memorandum, March 5, 1919; National Archives, Rangel, "Records for The Inquiry," pp. 40, 50, 76, 82, 102; Department of State, *Paris Peace Conference*, XII, 345-350, 353-355; Gelfand, *The Inquiry* pp. 57-58, 201-202, 218-219, 237.

40. HUA, Coolidge letter to Morgan, February 1, 1919; Allen Dulles letter to Walter G. Davis, January 16, 1919; Davis letter to Charles Seymour, January 16, 1919; Coolidge, reports to Paris from Vienna, January 19, February 7, February 17, 1919.

41. National Archives, Department of State Decimal Files, "1910-1919," 840.48.2022. Paris to Secretary of State, April 18, 1919; William L. Langer, *Explorations in Crisis: Papers in International History*, edited by Carl E. Schorske and Elizabeth Schorske (Cambridge, Mass., 1969), p. 355; Joseph F. Harrington, Jr., "Upper Silesia and the Paris Peace Conference," *Polish Review*, XIX (1974), 28-29; Perman, *The Shaping of the Czechoslovak State*, p. 3.

42. Harold Nicolson, *Peacemaking 1919* (New York, 1939), p. 27; Stephen Bonsal, *Unfinished Business* (New York, 1944), p. 90; Perman, *The Shaping of the Czechoslovak State*, p. 92 n.; Kurt O. Rabl (editor), *Der nationale Anspruch der Sudetendeutschen. Die Coolidge-Berichte und andere Urkunden der amerikanischen Delegation bei den Friedensverhandlungen von 1918/1919* (Munich, 1957), pp. 3-6.

43. HUA, Coolidge reports to Paris from Vienna, February 10 through May 14, 1919, especially May 8, May 12, 1919; Department of State, *Paris Peace Conference*, II, 220-224, 254-256; XI, 74, 122; XII, 254-256, 260-264, 281, 287-293, 393-394; Coolidge, "The New Austria," in Harold W.V. Temperley (editor), *A History of the Peace Conference of Paris* (London, 1921), pp. 478-484; Armstrong, *Peace and Counterpeace*, pp. 64-65.

44. HUA, Coolidge reports to Paris from Vienna, January 20 through May 4, 1919, especially February 10, February 12; Department of State, *Paris Peace Conference*, XI, 57-64, 83, 88, 122, 226-228; XII, 468-475, 484-498, 521-523, 551-552; F.L. Carsten, *Revolution in Central Europe, 1918-1919* (Berkeley, 1972), pp. 280-289; Claudia Kromer, *Die Vereinigten Staten von Amerika und die Frage Kärnten, 1918-1920* (Klagenfurt, 1920), pp. 28-36; Victor S. Mamatey, *The United States and East Central Europe, 1914-1918; A Study in Wilsonian Diplomacy and Propaganda* (Princeton, 1957), p. 341; Lederer, *Yugoslavia at the Paris Peace Conference*, pp. 166-169, 220, 226-227.

45. HUA, Coolidge reports to Paris from Vienna, February 26, April 7, April

28, May 5, 1919; Coolidge, *Ten Years of War and Peace*, p. 5; Department of State, *Paris Peace Conference*, II, 225.

46. HUA, Coolidge reports to Paris from Vienna, May 13, May 14, 1919; Department of State, *Paris Peace Conference*, XI, 187–189; XII, 264–271; Low, *The Soviet Hungarian Republic and the Paris Peace Conference* (Philadelphia, 1963), p. 39 n.

47. HUA, Coolidge reports to Paris from Vienna, January 14 through April 25, 1919; Count Paul Teleki letter to Coolidge, September 25, 1919; Coolidge, "The New States of Central Europe," Lowell Lectures, 1920, (manuscript), II; Department of State, *Paris Peace Conference*, XI, 134–135, 231; XII, 289, 380–382, 385–388, 392–393, 404–405, 411–431, 437–442, 444–468; Charles H. Haskins and Robert H. Lord (editors), *Some Problems of the Paris Peace Conference* (Cambridge, Mass., 1920), pp. 248–260; Francis Deak, *Hungary at the Paris Peace Conference: The Diplomatic History of the Treaty of Trianon* (New York, 1942), pp. 15–20; Peter Pastor, *Hungary between Wilson and Lenin: The Hungarian Revolution of 1918–1919 and the Big Three* (New York, 1977), pp. 96–108; Low, *The Soviet Hungarian Republic*, pp. 57–58, 80; Low, "Soviet Hungary and the Paris Peace Conference," in Ivan Völgyes (editor), *Hungary in Revolution, 1918–1919* (Lincoln, Neb., 1971), pp. 137–157; Brown, "Foreign Relations of the Budapest Soviets," pp. 59–69; Roosevelt, *A Front Row Seat*, pp. 101–117; Armstrong, *Peace and Counterpeace*, pp. 74–75, 127–128.

48. HUA, Coolidge reports to Paris from Vienna, January 12, February 12, February 13, 1919; Coolidge, "The New States," VI; CFRA, Coolidge letter to Armstrong, June 25, 1927; Coolidge, "Bohemia and Ireland," New York *Evening Post*, October 4, 1893; Coolidge, "Nationality and the New Europe," pp. 447–461, especially 455; F. Gregory Campbell, *Confrontation in Central Europe: Weimar Germany and Czechoslovakia* (Chicago, 1975), p. 60; Perman, *The Shaping of the Czechoslovak State*, pp. 16, 92, n.; Rabl, *Der national Anspruch*, p. 3.

49. HUA, Coolidge reports to Paris from Vienna, January 12 through May 15, 1919; Department of State, *Paris Peace Conference*, XII, 337–346, 356–365.

50. HUA, Coolidge reports to Paris from Vienna, January 19 through March 23, 1919, especially February 5; Department of State, *Paris Peace Conference*, XII, 324–325, 327–332, 351, 359–360; Piotr S. Wandycz, *France and Her Eastern Allies, 1919–1925* (Minneapolis, 1962), pp. 82–84, 158; Perman, *The Shaping of the Czechoslovak State*, pp. 97–124, 133–134, 140–144, 165; Goler, "Robert Howard Lord and the Settlement of Polish Boundaries after World War I," 1957 Ph.D. thesis at Boston College, pp. 85–86.

51. Coolidge reports to Paris from Vienna, March 13 through April 11, 1919, especially April 11; Coolidge, "The Expansion of Russia" (manuscript), XII, 32; Castle letter to Coolidge, February 11, 1920; Coolidge letter to Castle, February 14, 1920; Department of State, *Paris Peace Conference*, XII, 395–404.

52. HUA, Coolidge letter to Morgan, June 30, 1919; Coolidge letter to Castle, February 14, 1920; Department of State, *Paris Peace Conference*, XI, 243–244, 248, 251–252, 265–266, 272, 453–454; Mamatey, *The United States and East Central Europe*, p. 383; Frank S. Marston, *The Peace Conference of 1919:*

Organization and Procedure (New York, 1944), pp. 111-114; Campbell, *Confrontation in Central Europe*, pp. 66-67, 73, 289, 291; Gelfand, *The Inquiry*, pp. 320-321; Perman, *The Shaping of the Czechoslovak State*, pp. 118-120, 141-142, 203-204, 230-233, 240-242, 255; Edward M. House and Charles Seymour (editors), *What Really Happened at Paris: The Story of the Peace Conference, 1918-1919, by American Delegates* (New York, 1921), p. 211; Coolidge and Lord, *Coolidge*, pp. 217-218.

53. HUA, Coolidge, "Memorandum on Certain Frontier Questions: The Balkan Peninsula"; Dulles letter to Coolidge, December 30, 1919; CFRA, Coolidge letter to Armstrong, June 19, 1926; Coolidge, *Ten Years of War and Peace*, pp. 6-8; *Das politische Tagebuch Redlichs*, II, 340; Coolidge and Lord, *Coolidge*, pp. 228-233.

54. Coolidge and Lord, *Coolidge*, p. 233.

10. EDUCATING THE INFORMED PUBLIC

1. George Santayana, *Persons and Places* (New York, 1963), II, 129; Henry A. Yeomans, *Abbott Lawrence Lowell, 1856-1943* (Cambridge, Mass., 1948), p. 200; Van Wyck Brooks, *New England: Indian Summer, 1865-1915* (New York, 1940), pp. 118-122; Royal A. Gettmann, *Turgenev in England and America* (Urbana, Ill. 1941), p. 118; Allen Nevins, *The Evening Post: A Century of Journalism* (New York, 1922), pp. 554-560; Gustave Pollack, *Fifty Years of American Idealism: The New York Nation, 1865-1915. Selections and Comments* (Boston, 1915), 22-25; Henry M. Christman (editor), *One Hundred Years of the* Nation: *A Centennial Anthology* (New York, 1965), pp. 15-22; Henry May, *The End of American Innocence: A Study of the First Years of Our Own Time, 1912-1917* (New York, 1959), pp. 72-73.

2. HUA, Edwin F. Gay letter to Coolidge, June 16, 1920; Coolidge letter to Gay, June 17, 1920.

3. Kent and Phoebe Courtney, *America's Unelected Rulers* (New Orleans, 1962); Lawrence H. Shoup and William Minter, *Imperial Brain Trust: The Council on Foreign Relations and United States Foreign Policy* (New York, 1977).

4. *Journal of Race Development*, I, no. 1 (July 1910), 2.

5. *Journal of International Relations*, vol. XII, no. 2 (October 1921), inside rear cover; Joseph Clark Grew, *Turbulent Era: A Diplomatic Record of Forty Years, 1904-1945* (Boston, 1953), II, 1422; George H. Blakeslee, "An Historical Sketch of Clark University," in Wallace Atwood (editor), *The First Fifty Years* (Worcester, Mass., 1937), pp. 8-19; *American Historical Review*, LX (1954), pp. 253-254.

6. Hamilton Fish Armstrong, *Peace and Counterpeace: From Wilson to Hitler* (New York, 1971), p. 161; Whitney S. Shepardson, *Early History of the Council on Foreign Relations* (Stamford, Conn., 1970), p. 15.

7. The Coolidge Papers in the Harvard University Archives and the Institute

of Politics collection at Williams College contain the voluminous correspondence between Coolidge and Garfield, and Coolidge and Professsor Walter W. McLaren of Williams College, who assisted Garfield.

8. Williams College Institute of Politics Archives (hereafter cited as WC), Edward Bok letter to Garfield; Arthur H. Buffinton, *The Institute of Politics at Williamstown, Massachusetts: Its First Decade* (Williamstown, Mass., 1931), passim; Eli Botsford (editor), *Fifty Years at Williams* (Pittsfield, Mass., 1928–1940), IV, 29–31; Lucretia Garfield Comer, *Harry Garfield's First Forty Years: Man of Action in a Troubled World* (New York, 1965), pp. 12, 65–116, 151, 213, 232.

9. WC, *Round-Table Conferences of the Institute of Politics at Its First Session, 1921* (New Haven, 1923), pp. 7–17, 419–439; Achille Viallate, *Impérialisme économique et les relations internationales pendant le dernier demi-siècle, 1870–1920* (Paris, 1923), pp. v–vii.

10. WC, *Preliminary Announcement* (Williamstown, 1921); Walter W. McClaren, "The Institute of Politics," in Botsford (editor), *Fifty Years at Williams*, IV, 163–164; Buffinton, *The Institute of Politics*, pp. 13–25.

11. WC, Donaldson (Yale University Press) to Walter W. McClaren, February 11, 1932; Coleman (Yale University Press) to McClaren, May 29, 1933; Lord Eustace Percy of Newcastle, *Maritime Trade in War* (New Haven, 1930), page opposite title page; George S. Counts, Luigi Villari, and Newton D. Baker, *Bolshevism, Fascism, and Capitalism: An Account of the Three Economic Systems* (New Haven, 1932); Armstrong, *Peace and Counterpeace*, p. 125; Buffinton, *The Institute of Politics*, pp. 17–18; McClaren, "The Institute of Politics," pp. 159–160.

12. HUA, Garfield letter to Coolidge, October 22, 1924; McLaren letters to Coolidge, October 28, December 22, 1924; Harry Garfield, *Lost Visions* (Boston, 1944), pp. ix–xi; Richard A. Newhall (editor), *Report of the Round Tables and General Conferences at the Ninth Session of the Institute of Politics, Williams College* (Williamstown, 1929), p. 5; McClaren, "The Institute of Politics," pp. 151–154; *Christian Science Monitor*, August 25, 1925.

13. HUA, Coolidge letter to Hiram Bingham, October 3, 1924; Coolidge letter to Garfield, December 11, 1924; WC, Stephen Duggan letter to Garfield, October 3, 1922; Garfield memorandum to board of advisers, August 23, 1932; Garfield letter to Lewis Perry, October 16, 1932; William Loeb, Jr., "Summer Sewing Circle: The Decline of Williamstown," *Outlook*, CLVI (1930), 207–209, 237–238; Buffinton, "The Institute of Politics," pp. 17–20, 41–43; Buffinton (editor), *Report of the Round Table and General Conferences at the Eleventh Session of the Institute of Politics, Williams College* (Williamstown, 1931), p. 5; McLaren, "The Institute of Politics," pp. 154–158; Armstrong, *Peace and Counterpeace*, p. 125.

14. Count Carlo Sforza wrote: "What Bayreuth is to music, The Hague to applied international law, Wall Street to international finance, Williamstown . . . is to discussions of international politics." He compared the Institute to Florence of the Quattrocento and termed it "an illustration of the moral elevation of the American ruling classes." "Williamstown: Impressions améri-

caines," *L'Esprit internationale,* I (1927), 519. Lord Bryce and Senator Tittoni were almost as effusive.

15. *Handbook of the Council on Foreign Relations* (New York, 1919), pp. 3-26.

16. HUA, minutes of meeting at Hotel Majestic, Friday, May 30, 1919; James T. Shotwell, *At the Paris Peace Conference* (New York, 1937), pp. 346, 356-357; Shepardson, *Early History of the Council,* pp. 3-7.

17. Council on Foreign Relations, *A Record of Fifteen Years* (New York, 1937), p. 10; Harold Jefferson Coolidge and Robert H. Lord, *Archibald Cary Coolidge: Life and Letters* (Boston, 1932), pp. 308-316; Shepardson, *Early History of the Council,* pp. 7-20.

18. HUA, Isaiah Bowman memorandum, December 14, 1921; Gay letter to Coolidge, January 22, 1922; Coolidge letter to Gay, March 19, 1922; Coolidge letter to A. Lawrence Lowell, June 14, 1922.

19. CFRA, Coolidge letters to Armstrong, September 13, 1922, November 10, 1926; Armstrong letter to Coolidge, June 24, 1922; Herbert Heaton, *A Scholar in Action: Edwin F. Gay* (Cambridge, Mass., 1952), pp. 204-218; Armstrong, *Peace and Counterpeace,* pp. 159-161, 181-182, 195.

20. Armstrong, *Peace and Counterpeace,* p. 159.

21. HUA, Coolidge letter to William R. Castle, Jr., July 1, 1922; Castle letter to Coolidge, January 10, 1927; CFRA, Coolidge letter to Father Aurelio Palmieri, June 22, 1923; Coolidge letter to William Phillips, July 9, 1923; Coolidge letter to Henry Cabot Lodge, March 18, 1924; Coolidge letter to T.E. Burton, May 16, 1924; Coolidge letter to William E. Borah, May 29, 1925; Coolidge letters to Pietro Cardinal Gasparri, November 10, 1926; February 12, 1927; Gasparri letter to Coolidge, December 30, 1926; Count Stephen Bethlen, "Hungary in the New Europe," *Foreign Affairs,* III (1925), 445-458; Oscar Jászi, "Dismembered Hungary and Peace in Central Europe," *Foreign Affairs,* II (1923), 270-281; Plutarco Elias Calles, "The Policies of Mexico Today," *Foreign Affairs,* V (1926), 1-5.

22. CFRA, Coolidge letters to Armstrong, January 9, April 12, 1924; Coolidge letters to Foster Rhea Dulles, May 10, 1924; October 14, 1925; Coolidge letter to Isaiah Bowman, July 15, 1927; Armstrong, *Peace and Counterpeace,* pp. 160, 192, 222-226.

23. CFRA, Coolidge letters to Armstrong, May 3, 1923; January 22, March 10, March 13, 1924; Armstrong letters to Coolidge, May 23, 1923; March 12, 1924.

24. CFRA, Coolidge letters to Armstrong, June 4, 1922, July 9, August 6, 1923; September 19, October 19, November 8, 1924; January 9, January 25, June 24, 1925; Armstrong letters to Coolidge, July 12, 1922; February 7, 1926; Coolidge letter to Lawrence Martin, July 19, 1923; Coolidge letter to Malcolm W. Davis, October 6, 1925; Frank Golder letter to Coolidge, December 11, 1922; Armstrong, *Peace and Counterpeace,* p. 192.

25. CFRA, Coolidge letter to Armstrong, May 13, 1924; Armstrong, *Peace and Counterpeace,* pp. 143-145, 159-160. More than one-fifth of all the meetings the Council held during its first decade were devoted to the Soviet Union and Eastern Europe, including eight dinner sessions during its first six years.

26. CFRA, Coolidge letter to Golder, October 2, 1922; Coolidge letters to Armstrong, July 11, September 9, September 26, September 29, 1922; January 3, March 9, March 19, April 16, 1923; February 1, 1926; Armstrong letter to Coolidge, December 13, 1922; Coolidge letters to Karl Radek, March 22, March 23, September 12, 1927; Armstrong, *Peace and Counterpeace*, pp. 192, 403, 411–412.

27. CFRA, Coolidge letter to George A.B. Dewar, September 30, 1924; Coolidge letter to Armstrong, September 16, 1924.

28. CFRA, Coolidge letter to Armstrong, March 31, 1921.

29. CFRA, Coolidge letters to Armstrong, October 28, 1922; April 2, April 4, 1923; March 22, 1924.

30. CFRA, Coolidge letters to Armstrong, October 28, 1922; March 6, March 16, August 21, 1923; January 2, 1924; Armstrong letters to Coolidge, July 14, 1923; January 4, March 15, September 17, 24, 1924; May 29, June 16, June 18, June 29, December 1, December 16, 1925; Coolidge letter to George H. Blakeslee, March 20, 1923.

31. CFRA, Coolidge letter to Armstrong, March 13, 1923.

32. CFRA, Coolidge letter to Tasker H. Bliss, March 2, 1923; Coolidge letter to Armstrong, April 27, 1923; Bliss letter to Armstrong, March 5, 1923; Armstrong letters to Coolidge, March 2, March 5, 1923. Tasker H. Bliss, "The Evolution of the Unified Command," *Foreign Affairs*, I (1922), 1–20; Hermann von Kuhl, "Unity of Command among the Central Powers," *Foreign Affairs*, II (1923), 130–146.

33. CFRA, Coolidge letter to E.C. Bedford, December 30, 1922; Armstrong letters to Coolidge, March 16, March 17, 1923; Coolidge letter to Blakeslee, March 20, 1923.

34. CFRA, Coolidge letters to Armstrong, October 28, November 18, 1922; October 11, October 21, November 30, December 9, 1926; January 27, 1927; Armstrong letters to Coolidge, June 25, July 19, 1923; October 4, 1924; February 18, June 25, 1925; October 14, 1926.

35. CFRA, Coolidge letters to Armstrong, July 14, July 18, July 20, October 22, November 29, December 11, 1922; Armstrong letters to Coolidge, November 1, 1922; August 21, 1923; Foster Rhea Dulles letter to Coolidge, July 11, 1924.

36. HUA, Coolidge letter to Charles Lynn Chandler, August 29, 1922; CFRA, Coolidge letters to Armstrong, September 11, September 25, 1922; January 29, April 9, May 22, November 17, 1924; Armstrong letters to Coolidge, August 26, August 30, 1922; April 9, 1923; September 17, 1924; Dulles letter to Coolidge, July 14, 1924; Coolidge letters to David Boyle, October 16, 1924; January 21, 1925.

37. CFRA, Coolidge letters to Armstrong, September 22, 1922; March 2, September 26, 1923; Armstrong letters to Coolidge, June 22, July 27, 1922; July 5, July 20, 1923.

38. CFRA, Coolidge's letters to Armstrong, July 21, September 16, 1922; January 3, July 5, July 20, July 23, September 9, September 14, 1923; Armstrong letters to Coolidge, September 16, November 1, 1922; February 10, 1923.

39. CFRA, Coolidge letter to Armstrong, October 11, 1926; Armstrong letters to Coolidge, September 13, November 29, 1922; May 24, September 18, December 11, 1923; September 29, November 29, 1924; December 5, 1925; January 7, August 30, 1926.

Bibliographical Essay and Bibliography

THE RICH PRIMARY AND secondary materials on which this study rests are well organized and readily available. Indeed, only scholars who have engaged in research in such countries as the Soviet Union can fully appreciate the advantages which those interested in American history enjoy.

All those interested in scholarship and learning appreciate that no law guides one in organizing a bibliography, because assigning books and articles to appropriate headings defies easy definition and explanation. Coolidge's life involved so many parts of the world and such varied activities that an imaginative search for primary and secondary sources identified a variety of materials difficult to arrange in clear and precise categories. In addition, many sources provided material concerning a wide number of Coolidge's interests, so that assigning them to particular headings seemed nonsensical. The arrangements I have chosen seem most logical and orderly.

The bibliography includes all the published sources I have cited, as well as some that are not listed or quoted but nevertheless contributed to my understanding of this subject. They would help anyone interested in American higher education, in expanding knowledge of other peoples and cultures, and in the United States' role in world affairs.

PRIMARY SOURCES

A. Archives

1. Harvard University

The publications of Coolidge and those whom he helped train are at the heart of this volume, but splendid archival and manuscript collections are of almost equal importance. The Harvard University Archives constitute the most important collection.

Professor Coolidge and his family, because of their sense of history and because of his professional interest in history, preserved his professional and personal papers in an admirable way and then presented them to Harvard. The university's archives possess his four unpublished manuscripts, "The Expansion of Russia," "France as a World Power," "Suleiman the Magnificent," and "The New States of Central Europe." They also contain manuscripts of talks he gave, such as his lectures in Berlin, especially that on "Race Relations in the

United States" on Febrary 6, 1914, and one at the Army War College in Washington on October 19, 1922, "The Probable Future Orientation of Russia." Coolidge preserved other invaluable professional materials: copies of most of his articles and even drafts, lecture notes, book reviews, summaries of public lectures, newspaper interviews and clippings about his lectures, a diary, and scrapbooks of the planning, construction and dedication of Widener Library as well as the Hohenzollern collection. His family also deposited at Harvard full information concerning his funeral, including many obituaries and letters from friends and associates.

Harvard also possesses personal letters and other papers concerning Coolidge's work in various American ministries abroad in the 1890s. The materials are particularly rich concerning the period 1917 through 1922, because they include his official memoranda, papers, and reports for the period when he was engaged in The Inquiry, the War Trade Board, the American Commission to Negotiate Peace, and the American Relief Administration in the Soviet Union. The National Archives in Washington have most, but not all of the materials for the first three activities, and the Hoover Institution most of those for the ARA. I have generally cited the Harvard University Archives because I used these materials at Harvard and because they are most readily available. His letters to his family and colleagues, his private accounts of meetings with Soviet officials, and copies of other reports, such as those of Felix Cole (American consul in Murmansk in 1918), are especially valuable for this period.

Coolidge's correspondence was voluminous, and the Harvard University Archives possess much of it. His letters to his parents over more than thirty years are a rich resource. His letters to several who studied with him as undergraduates, such as Walter R. Batsell, Richard B. Hobart, Franklin B. Parker, Jr., and Franklin D. Roosevelt, provide insight concerning Coolidge as a teacher. Correspondence with many scholars whom he helped educate contributes information concerning his ideas and their spread through the educational system, and his letters with men who became diplomats are equally valuable. Coolidge also preserved some of his correspondence with Harvard colleagues, with other historians, and with many others prominent in public life, such as Philip M. Brown, Charles R. Crane, Stephen Duggan, Harry Garfield, Hugh Gibson, Herbert Hoover, Edward M. House, Charles Evans Hughes, Walter Lippmann, Lawrence Martin, Sidney Mezes, Beardsley Ruml, and Henry Wriston. Foreigners with whom he exchanged letters were Louis Aubert, Richard Fester, Michael Karolyi, Sir Bernard Pares, Alfred Pribham, Josef Redlich, and C.K. Webster.

The Harvard archival material concerning Coolidge as a teacher is most valuable. It includes examinations Coolidge wrote as an undergraduate, the course outlines he used for History 1 and other courses, notes that ten different undergraduates kept of History 1 and advanced lecture courses, papers which students wrote for him, and two sets of tutoring notes for History 1. The archives also contain the theses Coolidge directed or on which he gave advice. Data concerning his activities as a member of the faculty are also helpful; they include the minutes and records of the Department of History and Government and the Athletics Committee.

The reports of Harvard class secretaries, not only for Coolidge's 1887 class but also for those of his brothers, friends, students, and colleagues, are immensely important.

Quite naturally, the Harvard University Archives materials concerning the library are especially full. They provide magnificent detail concerning the collections which Coolidge purchased and presented to the library, many reflective and policy papers concerning the library, his correspondence as director, the reports and correspondence of Walter Lichtenstein for 1905 until 1919, and the papers and diaries of William C. Lane, librarian of Harvard College before 1910 and a colleague of Coolidge during the latter's years as director. Finally, the archives contain the voluminous papers of Presidents Eliot and Lowell, as well as the less important but interesting files of Coolidge friends and colleagues on the faculty.

2. National Archives

These invaluable materials include the voluminous files of The Inquiry, the War Trade Board, and the American Commission to Negotiate Peace, repetitions of the materials the Coolidge family gave the Harvard University Archives, except for correspondence and reports by others than Coolidge who engaged in these activities. The National Archives also possess other useful collections: Diplomatic Instructions of the Department of State, 1801–1906; Dispatches from the United States Ministers of Austria, 1883–1906; Dispatches from the United States Consuls in Moscow, 1859–1906; Dispatches from the United States Ministers to Russia, 1808–1896; Records for the Russian Division, 1918–1923, the Division of Eastern European Affairs, 1927–1937, and the Division of European Affairs, 1937–1941; and Records Relating to Internal Affairs of Russia and the Soviet Union, 1918–1929.

3. Council on Foreign Relations

The files of the Council include the complete correspondence between Coolidge and Hamilton Fish Armstrong from 1922 through 1927, almost a daily record of their work together, as well as the correspondence between Coolidge, dozens of contributors and potential contributors to the journal, and officers and staff members of the Council. The Coolidge-Armstrong letters are particularly valuable because Coolidge incorporated material concerning his entire career. The Council also possesses the large correspondence of Armstrong and the records of its discussion groups and meetings.

4. Hoover Institution, Stanford University

This library contains the full records of the American Relief Administration and the Russian Operation, as well as the papers of Hugh Gibson, Frank Golder, Herbert Hoover, and others engaged in the ARA's work, all well organized.

5. Library of Congress Manuscript Division

This repository holds the papers of the American Historical Association and of some historians with whom Coolidge worked closely, such as Albert Beveridge, J. Franklin Jameson, and Waldo G. Leland. The papers of other men with whom he was associated are also in the Manuscript Division. These include Ambassador Leland Harrison, Sidney Mezes of The Inquiry, David Hunter Miller of the American Commission to Negotiate Peace, and General Tasker H. Bliss, who was much involved in the work of the Council on Foreign Relations.

6. Williams College

The Williams College Library possesses several filing cabinets of documents concerning the Institute of Politics that provide a unique picture of its effort to expand knowledge and understanding of the world and of international politics among the informed public. These records not only supplement the information Coolidge's papers contribute concerning his role in the institute, but also provide perspective concerning the strengths and weaknesses of campaigns to awaken interest in other peoples. The papers of Professor Richard Newhall at Williams illuminate the career of one of those whom Coolidge helped train for expanding research and instruction concerning modern history and other cultures and of one who was active in the Institute of Politics.

7. University of California, Berkeley, Bancroft Library

This library contains the papers of Robert J. Kerner, a remarkably complete collection, beginning with Kerner's letters to Coolidge, when he was first interested in graduate study, and continuing until just before Coolidge died. Henry Morse Stephens, a close friend of Coolidge, and Julius Klein, a graduate student, who went on to a striking career in government and in the motion picture industry, also deposited their papers at the Bancroft Library.

8. University of Illinois, Champaign-Urbana

Professor Albert H. Lybyer, who received his graduate training with Coolidge, left a remarkably complete collection of papers to the University of Illinois, in which he taught for more than thirty years. They include course outlines and years of correspondence with Coolidge. The outlines provide a particularly clear illustration of the way in which young men who completed their graduate work at Harvard introduced Coolidge's ideas into other educational institutions.

9. Yale University

This collection includes the papers of Hiram Bingham and materials concerning The Inquiry, particularly those of members who played an important role: Clive Day, Walter G. Davis, Edward M. House, and Charles Seymour.

10. Institute of Current World Affairs

This research organization, founded by Charles R. Crane, possesses the memoirs and other papers of Crane, as well as many of the private papers of Samuel Harper of the University of Chicago.

11. Other Colleges and Universities

The archives of many colleges and universities throughout the country provide fundamental data concerning the activites of those whom Coolidge helped train, in some cases as complete as the materials left by Kerner and Lybyer and of Coolidge himself. Among the many institutions to which I am under heavy obligation for access to manuscripts and other materials are Amherst College, Boston College, Boston University, Bowdoin College, Brown University, Bryn Mawr College, Clark University, the University of Colorado, Cornell University, De Pauw University, Dickinson College, Dumbarton Oaks, Dartmouth College, Haverford College, the University of Idaho, McGill University, Miami University, the University of Minnesota, New York University, Northwestern University, Princeton University, Queens University, Reed College, the University of Rochester, Simmons College, Smith College, Tufts University, Washington State University, Widener College (formerly Pennsylvania Military College), William and Mary College, the University of Wisconsin at Madison, and the University of Wyoming.

The alumni offices of the University of California at Berkeley, the University of Colorado, Findlay College, and Queens University were helpful, as were the Division of History of the Department of State, the Trust Department of Riggs National Bank in Washington, D.C. (which has the Robert F. Kelley papers), and the Royal Institute of International Affairs.

B. Published Documents: Department of State

Papers Relating to the Foreign Relations of the United States transmitted to Congress with the Annual Message of the President, December 9, 1891 (Washington, 1892).

Papers Relating to the Foreign Relations of the United States, 1918. Russia (Washington, 1931-1932), three vols.

Papers Relating to the Foreign Relations of the United States, 1919. The Paris Peace Conference (Washington, 1932-1947), thirteen vols.

C. Journals

For the years in which Coolidge was actively involved in their work, the *American Historical Review* (New York, 1895–1930), the *Journal of International Relations* (Baltimore, 1910–1922), and *Foreign Affairs* (1922–1930) were of course essential sources, as were (to a lesser degree) the *Nation* and the New York *Evening Post*. The *American Historical Review* and the annual reports of the American Historical Association together provided full accounts of the annual meetings of the association and its executive committee.

D. Publications of Archibald Cary Coolidge

1. Books

Origins of the Triple Alliance: Three Lectures (New York, 1917). Second edition, 1926.
Ten Years of War and Peace (Cambridge, Mass., 1927). Several articles reprinted from *Foreign Affairs*, two from the *American Historical Review*, and one from the *Yale Review*.
Theoretical and Foreign Elements in the Formation of the American Constitution (Freiburg-im-Breisgau, 1892).
The United States as a World Power (New York, 1908). This was reprinted in 1909, 1910, 1912, 1916, 1919, 1921, 1927, and 1971. A French translation was published in Paris in 1908, a German translation in Berlin in the same year, and a Japanese translation in Tokyo in 1913.

2a. Articles and Essays: General

"Americo en el Pacifico," *First Pan-American Scientific Congress, Santiago de Chile, 1908–1919* (Santiago de Chile, 1912), XX, 91–98.
"Annals of an Epoch," *Literary Review*, IV (1923), 121–122.
"Oric Bates," *Harvard African Studies*, II (1918), preface.
"The Break-up of the Hapsburg Empire," in Coolidge, *Ten Years of War and Peace* (Cambridge, Mass., 1927), pp. 241–268.
"Claimants to Constantinople," in Charles Downer Thayer and others, *Three Peace Congresses of the Nineteenth Century* (Cambridge, Mass., 1917), pp. 73–93.
"Crying Needs of the Library," *Harvard Graduates' Magazine*, XIX (1911), 410–411.
"La Doctrine de Monroe," *Revue de Paris*, II (1907), 650–672.
"Les Etats-Unis comme puissance mondiale," *Revue Economique Internationale*, I (1907), 60–83.
"The European Reconquest of North Africa," *American Historical Review*, XVII (1912), 723–734.
"The Expansion of Russia," in Andrew Lang (editor), *The Nineteenth Century: A Review of Progress* (New York, 1901), pp. 63–75.

"For Sister Universities of the East," in *The University of Virginia in the Life of the Nation* (Charlottesville, 1905?), pp. 23-33.

"The Growth of Modern Drama in France," *Harvard Advocate*, XLII (1886), 27-29.

"The Harvard College Library," *Harvard Graduates' Magazine*, XXIV (1915), 23-31.

"Jefferson and the Problems of Today," *University of Virginia Alumni Bulletin*, XIV (1921), 53-58.

"Nationality and the New Europe," *Yale Review*, IV (1915), 447-461.

"Nekrasov," *Johnson's Revised Universal Encyclopaedia* (New York, 1895), VI, 109-110.

"The New Austria," in Harold W.V. Temperley (editor), *A History of the Peace Conference of Paris* (London, 1921), IV, 462-484.

"The Objects of Cataloging," *Library Journal*, XLVI (1921), 735-739.

"The Peoples of the Peninsula," in Hamilton Fish Armstrong, *The New Balkans* (New York, 1926), pp. 1-16.

"A Plea for the Study of the History of Northern Europe," *American Historical Review*, II (1896), 34-39. Reprinted in *American Historical Association Annual Report. 1895* (Washington, 1896), pp. 443-451.

"The Position of China in World Politics," in George H. Blakeslee (editor), *China and the Far East* (New York, 1910), pp. 1-19.

"Preface," in Alexander I. Petrunkevich and others, *The Russian Revolution* (Cambridge, Mass., 1918), pp. iii-iv.

"Professional Coaches. From Report of the Athletic Committee," *Harvard Graduates' Magazine*, XIV (1906), 392-395.

"Remarks at the Randolph Gathering at Tuckahoe," *Massachusetts Historical Society Proceedings*, XIV (1900-1901), 205-209.

"Report of the Conference on Oriental History and Politics," *American Historical Association Annual Report. 1907* (Washington, 1908), pp. 71-78.

"Should Recent European History Have a Place in the College Curriculum?" *American Historical Association Annual Report. 1899* (Washington, 1900), pp. 537-538.

"Tacna and Arica," *Journal of the British Institute of International Affairs*, V (1926), 245-249.

"Tiutchev," *Johnson's Revised Universal Encyclopaedia* (New York, 1895), VIII, 175.

"Tolstoi, Aleksei and Leo," in ibid., VIII, 180.

"Turgenev," in ibid., VIII, 305.

2b. Articles and Essays: Foreign Affairs*

*All of these essays except "A Quarter Century of Franco-British Relations" are reprinted in *Ten Years of War and Peace* (Cambridge, Mass., 1927).

"The Achievements of Fascism," IV (1926), 661-676. Signed F.

"After the Election," III (1924), 171-182. Signed E.

"Dissatisfied Germany," IV (1925), 35–46.
"The Future of the Monroe Doctrine," II (1924), 373–389. Signed C.
"The Grouping of Nations," V (1927), 175–188.
"A Quarter Century of Franco-British Relations," VI (1927), 1–13.
"Russia after Genoa and The Hague," I (1922), 133–155. Signed K.
"Ten Years of War and Peace," III (1924), 1–21.
"Two Years of American Foreign Policy," I (1923), 1–24. Signed A.

2c. *Articles and Essays:* Nation

Many of these were also published in the New York *Evening Post.*
"Across Siberia," LXI (1895), 165–166, 203–204, 238. Omsk, Tomsk, Tiumen.
"The Ancient Capital of Poland. Cracow. July, 1896," LXIII (1896), 137–138.
"Ararat," LXVII (1898), 239–240.
"The Balkans," LVIII (1894), 431.
"British Treaty with Congo Free State," LVIII (1894), 479.
"Controversy between France and Siam," LXVII (1893), 101.
"The Coup d'Etat in Servia," LVI (1893), 330–331.
"Dahomey," LVI (1893), 339.
"Dispute between France and Siam," LVI (1893), 339.
"First Impressions of the Hawaiian Islands," LXV (1897), 259.
"In British East Africa," LXXXII (1906), 444–446.
"In Montenegro," LXIX (1899), 239–240.
"Italian Defeat in Abyssinia," LXI (1895), 439.
"King Milan Returns to Servia," LVIII (1894), 77.
"League for the Intellectual Culture of the Rumanians," LVIII (1894), 450.
"Madagascar," LVII (1893), 441.
"New Port in Tunis," LVI (1893), 413.
"Pekin Two Years after the Siege," LXXV (1902), 261–262.
"A Polish Summer Resort, Zakopane, Galicia. August 25, 1896," LXIII (1896),
    268–269.
"Quarrel between France and Britain," LVIII (1894), 461.
"The Ruins of Angkor," LXXXII (1906), 136–138.
"Siam," LVII (1893), 93.
"Siam Today," LXXXII (1906), 219–221.
"A Trip in Daghestan," LXVII (1898), 164–165.
"With the Rush to the Klondike," LXV (1897), 125.

2d. *Articles and Essays: New York* Evening Post

"Anglo-French Relations," June 23 and 25, 1920.
"Constantinople and the Straits," February 19, 1920.
"Bohemia and Ireland," October 4, 1893.
"Greece's Real Motive," March 22, 1893.
"The Harvard Crew," June 15 and 24, 1897.

"The Italians in Erythrea," January 24, 1895.
"The Origins of the War," July 16 and 19, 1920.
"Peace with the Ottoman Empire," February 19 and 25, 1920.
"The Political Outlook in Europe," December 30, 1919 and January 3, 1920.
"The Question of Fiume," December 8 and 10, 1919.
"Questions between England and France," November 4, 1920.
"Secret Treaties Brought to Light," January 24, 31, and February 6, 1920.
"The Situation in the Near East," September 1 and 23, 1920.
"Spanish Morocco," August 12, 1921.
"Tomsk," October 7, 1895.
"A Trip in Daghestan," September 3, 1898.
"The Turks and the Turkish Empire," June 14 and 18, 1920.

2e. Articles and Essays: Other Newspapers

"The British Commonwealth of Nations," New York *Times* and New York
    Journal of Commerce, July 28, 1925.
"The British-Boer War," *Boston Globe*, January 21, 1900.
"A Candid Statement of the Hawaiian Annexation Question," Boston *Tran-
    script*, October 2, 1897.
"Prof. Coolidge Defends Russia," Boston *Herald*, March 24, 1904.

3. Edited Works

The Barrington-Bernard Correspondence and Illustrative Matter, 1760–1770
    (Cambridge, Mass., 1912). With Edward Channing.
Alfred Francis Pribram, *The Secret Treaties of Austria-Hungary, 1879–1914*
    (Cambridge, Mass., 1920–1921), two vols. Reprinted in New York, 1967.
Sir Edward S. Creasy, *Turkey*. Revised and edited by Archibald Cary Coolidge
    and W. Harold Claflin (Philadelphia, 1907). Revised and reprinted in 1916,
    1928, 1932, 1936, and 1939.

4. Translations

"Poems of Nekrasov and Lermontov," *Harvard Monthly*, XIX (1895), 131–135.
    Reprinted in Leo Wiener, *Anthology of Russian Literature from the
    Earliest Period to the Present Time* (Boston, 1902–1903), II, 170–171,
    359–360.
"Translations from the Russian," Anglo-Russian Literary Society *Proceedings*,
    no. 14 (1896), pp. 35–38 and no. 15 (1896), p. 97.
"The Demon," *Slavonic Review*, IV (1925), 278–307.

5a. Book Reviews: General

"Busch's *Life of Bismarck.*" *Boston Transcript*, October 5, 1898.
"A Self-Appointed Diplomat." Will Rogers, *Letters of a Self-Made Diplomat to His President* (New York, 1926). *Saturday Review of Literature*, December 25, 1926, p. 465.

5b. Book Reviews: American Historical Review

Count Julius Andrassy, *The Development of Hungarian Constitutional Liberty* (London, 1908). XV (1910), 359–361.

A. de Bertha, *La Hongrie moderne de 1849 à 1901. Etude historique* (Paris, 1901). VIII (1903), 578–580.

Tyler Dennett, *Roosevelt and the Russo-Japanese War* (New York, 1925). XXXI (1925), 156–158.

Botschafsrat A.D. Hermann Freiherrn v. Eckardstein, *Lebenserinnerungen und Politische Denkwürdigkeiten* (Leipzig, 1919), two vols., XXVI (1921), 517–519.

Comte Fédor Golovkine, *La Cour et le Règne de Paul I* (Paris, 1904). XI (1905), 198–199.

Otto Hammann, *Der Neue Kurs: Erinnerungen* (Berlin, 1918) and *Zur Vorgeschichte des Weltkrieges: Erinnerungen aus dem Jahren 1879–1906* (Berlin, 1919). XXV (1920), 718–719.

Dr. H.F. Halmolt (editor), *The History of the World: A Survey of Man's Record. V. South Eastern and Eastern Europe* (New York, 1907). XIV (1908), 97–99.

Alexander Kornilov, *Modern Russian History* (New York, 1917), two vols. XXIII (1917), 148–149.

Maxime Kovalevsky, *Russian Political Institutions* (Chicago, 1902), and W.R. Morfill, *A History of Russia from Peter the Great to Nicholas II* (New York, 1901). VIII (1902), 131–134.

Alexis Krause, *Russia in Asia: A Record and a Study, 1588–1899* (New York, 1899). V (1900), 345–347.

Ludwig Kulczycki, *Geschichte der Russischen Revolution*, Band I (Gotha, 1910). XVI (1911), 819–820.

———. Band II. XVII (1912), 378–379.

Jean Larmeroux, *La Politique extérieure de l'Autriche-Hongrie, 1875–1914* (Paris, 1918), two vols. XXIV (1919), 510–511.

Hector H. Munro, *The Rise of the Russian Empire* (Boston, 1900). VII (1901), 138–140.

Edmund Noble, *Russia and the Russians* (Boston, 1900). VI (1901), 791–793.

"Recent Books about Russia in English." X (1905), 455–457.

Sir Horace Rumbold, *Francis Joseph and His Times* (New York, 1909). XV (1910), 654.

Theodor Schiemann, *Die Ermordung Pauls und die Thronbesteigung Nicholas I* (Berlin, 1902). VII (1903), 576–578.

――――. *Geschichte Russlands unter Kaiser Nikolaus I.* Band I (Berlin, 1904). X (1905), 898–900.

Frances H. Skrine, *The Expansion of Russia, 1815 to 1900* (New York, 1903). IX (1904), 617–618.

Alexandre A.C. Sturdza, *La Terre et la Race Roumaines* (Paris, 1904). X (1905), 912–913.

The Memoirs of Count Witte, translated by Abraham Yarmolinsky (Garden City, N.Y., 1921). XXVI (1921), 790–792.

5c. Book Reviews: Nation

Albert J. Beveridge, *The Russian Advance* (New York, 1903). LXXVIII (1904), 135.

Poultney Bigelow, *White Man's Africa* (New York. 1898). LXVII (1898), 111.

Clive Bingham, *A Ride through Western Asia* (New York, 1897). LXV (1897), 247–248.

Alan Boisragon, *The Benin Massacre* (London, 1898). LXVII (1898), 111.

Pierre Bonnassieux, *Les Grandes Compagnies de Commerce* (Paris, 1892). LVII (1893), 84.

John W. Bookwalter, *Siberia and Central Asia* (Springfield, O., 1899). LXIX (1899), 176–177.

Captain Hamilton Bower, *Diary of a Journey across Tibet* (New York, 1894). LIX (1895), 88.

Noah Brooks, *The Mediterranean Trip* (New York, 1895). LXII (1896), 179.

Edward G. Browne, *A Year Among the Persians* (New York, 1893). LVIII (1894), 317–318.

Ellen H. Browning, *A Girl's Wandering in Hungary* (London, 1896). LXIV (1897), 421–422.

Isabelle Burton, *Life of Sir Richard Burton* (New York, 1893), two vols. LVII (1893), 177–178.

――――, *The Romance of Isabelle Lady Burton: The Story of Her Life* (New York, 1896). LXV (1897), 190–191.

Léon Cahun, *Introduction à l'Histoire de l'Asie, Turcs et Mongols des Origines à 1405* (Paris, 1895). LXII (1895), 495–496.

Colonel Sir Henry Colville, *The Land of the Nile Springs* (New York, 1895). LXII (1896), 204–205.

Captain Cool, *With the Dutch in the East* (London, 1897), LXV (1897), 279.

Rev. W.E. Cousins, *Madagascar of Today* (New York, 1895). LXI (1895) 193–194.

George M. Dawson and Alexander Sutherland, *Elementary Geography of the British Colonies* (London, 1893). LVII (1893), 120.

Courtenay de Kalb, *Nicaragua* (Irvington-on-Hudson, N.Y., 1893). LVII (1893), 65.

Geoffrey Drage, *Russian Affairs* (New York, 1904) and Wolf von Schierbrand,

Russia: Her Strength and Her Weakness (New York, 1904). LXXIX (1904), 399.

Pompiliu Eliade, *De l'Influence française sur l'Esprit public en Roumanie: Les Origines* (Paris, 1899). LXIX (1899), 110.

Alexander Platonovich Engelhardt, *A Russian Province of the North* (New York, 1900). LXX (1900), 282.

John Foreman, *The Philippine Islands* (New York, 1893). LVII (1893), 357.

Hugo Ganz, *The Land of Riddles: Russia of Today* (New York, 1904). LXXX (1905), 180.

Wirt Gerrare, *Greater Russia* (New York, 1903). LXXVI (1903), 500-501.

Rev. William Parr Gresevell, *Outlines of British Colonisation* (London, 1893). LVI (1893), 409.

Mrs. Ernest Hart, *Picturesque Burma, Past and Present* (Philadelphia, 1898). LXVII (1898), 111.

Rev. George H. Hepworth, *Through Armenia on Horseback* (New York, 1899). LXIX (1899), 110.

Edward Jenks, *The History of the Australasian Colonies* (London, 1896). LXII (1896), 384-385.

Memoirs of the Prince of Joinville, (London, 1895). LXI (1895), 175.

J. Scott Keltie, *The Partition of Africa* (London, 1893). LVII (1893), 48-49.

E.F. Knight, *Where Three Empires Meet* (London, 1893). LVI (1893), 460-461.

Henry Lansdell, *Chinese Central Asia* (New York, 1895), two vols. LXI (1895), 87.

Jules Legras, *En Sibérie* (Paris, 1899). LXIX (1899), 112.

Jules Liorel, *Kabylie du Jurjura* (Paris, 1893). LVII (1893), 46.

C.P. Lucas, *South and East Africa* (New York, 1897). LXV (1897), 211-212.

Francis Macnab, *On Veldt and Farm* (London, 1897). LXV (1897), 115-116.

G. Montbard, *Among the Moors* (New York, 1894). LVIII (1894), 475.

T. Douglas Murray and A. Silva White, *Sir Samuel Baker: A Memoir* (London, 1895). LXI (1895), 262.

H. Nobert, *Das deutsche Sprachgebiet in Europe* (Stuttgart, 1893). LVII (1893), 194-195.

On India's Frontier, or Nepal, the Gurkhas' Mysterious Land (London, 1895). LX (1895), 361.

Elizabeth Robbins Pennell, *To Gypsy Land* (New York, 1893). LVII (1893), 348-349.

William Woodville Rockhill, *Diary of a Journey through Mongolia and Tibet* (Washington, 1895). LXII (1896), 158.

R.H. Russell, *On the Edge of the Orient* (New York, 1896). LXIV (1897), 224.

M.M. Shoemaker, *The Great Siberian Railway* (New York, 1903). LXXVI (1930), 318.

_____, *Trans-Caspia: The Sealed Provinces of the Tsar* (Cincinnati, 1894). LX (1895), 300.

Rev. James Sibree, *Madagascar before the Conquest* (New York, 1887). LXIV (1897), 378.

Francis H. Skrine, *The Expansion of Russia, 1815-1900* (New York, 1903). LXXVIII (1904), 135.

Maxwell Sommerville, *Siam on the Meinam* (Philadelphia, 1897). LXV (1897), 383.

E.R. Stidmore, *Java, the Garden of the East* (New York, 1898). LXVII (1898), 99.

Georgiana M. Stistead, *The True Life of Capt. Sir R.F. Burton* (New York, 1897). LXIV (1897), 230-231.

Ellen C. Sykes, *Through Persia on a Side-Saddle* (Philadelphia, 1899). LXIX (1899), 169.

Herbert Vivian, *Servia, the Poor Man's Paradise* (London, 1898). LXVII (1898), 59-60.

Vladimir, *Russia on the Pacific and the Siberian Railway* (New York, 1899). LXX (1900), 287.

Major Otto von Wachs, *The Future of the West Indies and the Nicaraguan Canal.* LVII (1894), 448.

Edwin Lord Weeks, *From the Black Sea through Russia and India* (New York, 1896). LXII (1896), 276.

A. Wilmott, *The Story of the Expansion of South Africa* (New York, 1895). LXI (1895), 195-196.

Hartley Withers, *The English and Dutch in South Africa* (London, 1896). LXIII (1896), 290.

Fanny Bullock Workman and William Hunter Workman, *Algerian Memories* (New York, 1895). LXI (1895), 448.

George Frederick Wright, *Asiatic Russia* (New York, 1902), two vols., and John Foster Fraser, *The Real Siberia* (New York, 1902), LXXV (1902), 407.

Captain Younghusband, *Heart of a Continent* (New York, 1896). LXIII (1896), 290.

5d. Book Reviews: New York Evening Post

Allen and Sachtleben, *Across Asia on a Bicycle* (New York, 1895). April 3, 1895.

The Kaiser vs. Bismarck: Suppressed Letters by the Kaiser and New Chapters from the Autobiography of the Iron Chancellor (New York, 1921). April 2, 1921.

Archibald Forbes, *Czar and Sultan* (New York, 1894). May 1, 1895.

Joseph Goricar and Lyman Beecher Stowe, *The Inside Story of Austro-German Intrigue* (New York, 1920). May 15, 1920.

F.D. Greene, *The Armenian Crisis in Turkey* (New York, 1895). May 5, 1895.

Isabel F. Hapgood, *Russian Rambles* (New York, 1895). May 5, 1895.

Charles à Court Repington, *After the War* (New York, 1922). June 10, 1922.

Ferdinand Schevill, *The History of the Balkan Peninsula* (New York, 1922). October 13, 1922.

E. Theses Coolidge Directed and Helped Direct.*

*Theses Coolidge directed are preceded by an asterisk (*).

*Andrews, Arthur I., "The Campaign of the Emperor Charles V Against Tunis and Kheir-ed-Din Barbarossa," 1905.

Arragon, Reginald F., "The Congress of Panama of 1826," 1923. Two vols.

Artz, Frederick B., "The Polignac Ministry," 1924. Two vols.

*Bingham, Hiram, "The Scots Darien Company," 1905.

*Blake, Robert, "Studies in the Religious Policies of Constantine the Great and His Successors," 1916.

Blakeslee, George H., "The History of the Anti-Masonic Party," 1903.

*Claflin, Walter H., "The Prussian Campaign of Gustavus Adolphus, 1626–1629: A Military Study," 1908.

Clark, Chester W., "Austria and the Origins of the War of 1866," 1931.

Davis, William Stearns, "Stephen Gardiner, Bishop of Winchester," 1905.

*Fay, Sidney B., "The *Fürstenbund* of 1785: A Study in German History," 1900.

Fryer, Charles E., "English Church Disestablishment," 1906.

*Fuller, Joseph V., "The Transformation of Bismarck's European System," 1921.

George, Robert H., "The Relations of England and Flanders, 1066–1154," 1916.

*Golder, Frank, "Russian Voyages in the North Pacific Ocean to Determine the Relations between Asia and America," 1909.

Goodykoontz, Colin B., "The Home Missionary Movement and the West, 1798–1861," 1921.

Gray, Howard L., "A Contribution to the Study of Anglo-Saxon Settlement," 1907.

Grose, Clyde L., "A Study of Anglo-French Relations under Charles II," 1918.

*Hopper, Bruce," Soviet Economic Statecraft," 1930.

*Jones, Theodore F., "Venice and the Porte, 1520–1542," 1910.

*Kerner, Robert J., "Bohemia under Leopold II, 1790–1792," 1914.

*Klein, Julius, "The Mesta: A Study in Spanish Economic History 1273–1836," 1915.

Langer, William L., "European Alliances during the Chancellorship of Caprivi," 1923.

Leach, Henry Goddard, "The Relations between England and Scandinavia in History and Literature from 1066 to 1399," 1908.

*Lee, Dwight E., "British Policy in the Eastern Question, 1878," 1928.

*Lichtenstein, Walter, "The Turkish Peril and the German Reformation," 1907.

*Lord, Robert H., "Austrian Policy and the Second Partition of Poland," 1910.

Lunt, William E., "The Financial Relations between the Papacy and England during the Reigns of Edward I and Edward II," 1908.

*Lybyer, Albert H., "The Government of the Ottoman Empire under Suleiman the Magnificent," 1909.

Newhall, Richard A., "The English in Normandy, 1416-1424," 1917.
*Nowak, Frank, "The Foreign Policy of Poland under King Stephen," 1924.
*Packard, Laurence B., "Some Antecedents of the Conseil du Commerce of 1790," 1921.
Packard, Sidney R., "The Administration of Normandy under Richard and John, 1198-1204," 1921.
*Perkins, Dexter, "The Reception of the Monroe Doctrine in Europe, 1823-1824," 1914.
Read, Conyers, "The Life of Sir Francis Walsingham to 1578," 1908.
*Rupp, George H., "Russia and Austria, 1876-1878," 1934.
*Shipman, Henry R., "Russian Foreign Policy under Catherine I," 1904.
*Steefel, Lawrence, "The Schleswig-Holstein Question, 1863-1864," 1923.
*Steiner, George N., "The Origins and Development of the Boxer Movement," 1923.
*Stoddard, T. Lothrop, "The French Revolution in San Domingo," 1914.
*Trotter, Reginald G., "On the Federation of the Dominion of Canada," 1921.
*Tyler, Mason Whiting, "Anglo-French Relations under James II," 1911.
Varrell, Henry M., "The Early History of Ecclesiastical Jurisdiction in England," 1912.
Wright, John K., "Geographical Knowledge in Western Europe, 1100-1250 A.D.," 1922.

F. Selected Works of Coolidge Students

Batsell, Walter R. *Soviet Rule in Russia* (New York, 1929).
Bingham, Hiram, *The Possibilities of South American History and Politics as a Field for Research* (Washington, 1908).
Blakeslee, George H. (editor), *China and the Far East* (New York, 1910).
———, "An Historical Sketch of Clark University," in Wallace Atwood (editor), *The First Fifty Years* (Worcester, Mass., 1937), pp. 1-22.
———, (editor), *Mexico and the Caribbean* (New York, 1920).
———, *The Recent Foreign Policy of the United States: Problems in American Cooperation with Other Powers* (New York, 1925).
Chekrezi, Constantine A., *Albania, Past and Present* (New York, 1919).
———, *Chekrezi's English-Albanian Dictionary* (Boston, 1923).
Claflin, Walter H., *History of Persia* (Philadelphia, 1906).
Clark, Chester W., *Franz Joseph and Bismarck: The Diplomacy of Austria before the War of 1866* (Cambridge, Mass., 1934).
Davis, William Stearns, *A Day in Old Athens: A Picture of Athenian Life* (Boston, 1914).
———, *Europe since Waterloo* (New York, 1926).
———, *A Short History of the Near East from the Founding of Constantinople* (New York, 1922).
Fay, Sidney B., *The Origins of the World War* (New York, 1930), two vols.
———, *A Syllabus of European History, 378-1900* (Hanover, N.H., 1912). Fourth edition.

Fuller, Joseph V., *Bismarck's Diplomacy at Its Zenith* (Cambridge, Mass., 1922).

Golder, Frank (editor), *Bering's Voyages* (New York, 1922-1925), two vols.

_____, (editor), *Documents of Russian History, 1914-1917* (New York, 1927).

_____, *Guide to Materials for American History in Russian Archives* (Washington, 1917).

_____, *Russian Expansion on the Pacific, 1641-1850* (Cleveland, 1914).

_____, and Lincoln Hutchinson, *On the Trail of the Russian Famine* (Stanford, 1927).

Hopper, Bruce, *Pan-Sovietism* (Boston, 1931).

_____, "Soviet Economy in a New Phase," *Foreign Affairs*, X (1932), 453-464.

Jones, Theodore F. (editor), *New York University, 1832-1932* (New York, 1933).

Kelley, Robert F., "New Economic Divisions of Russia: Notes and Maps," *Foreign Affairs*, IV (1925), 330-333.

_____, "The Recent Russian Census," *Foreign Affairs*, VI (1928), 333-335.

_____, "Soviet Policy on the European Border," *Foreign Affairs*, III (1924), 90-98.

Kerner, Robert J., *Bohemia in the Eighteenth Century* (New York, 1932). Reprinted in 1969.

_____, *Slavic Europe* (Cambridge, Mass., 1918).

_____, *Social Sciences in the Balkans and in Turkey* (Berkeley, 1930).

Klein, Julius, "The Making of the Treaty of Guadalupe Hidalgo, on February 2, 1848," (Berkeley, 1905), typescript.

_____, *The Mesta: A Study in Spanish Economic History, 1273-1836* (Cambridge, Mass., 1920). Published in a Spanish translation in Madrid in 1936.

Langer, William L., *The Diplomacy of Imperialism* (New York, 1935), two vols. Second edition, 1951.

_____ (compiler and editor), *An Encyclopedia of World History, Ancient, Medieval and Modern* (Boston, 1940). Four editions appeared by 1972.

_____, *European Alliances and Alignments, 1871-1890* (New York, 1931). A second editon was published in 1950.

_____, *Explorations in Crisis: Papers in International History.* Edited by Carl E. Schorske and Elizabeth Schorske (Cambridge, Mass., 1969).

_____, *The Franco-Russian Alliance, 1890-1894* (Cambridge, Mass., 1929).

_____, *Gas and Flame in World War I* (New York, 1965). Reprint of 1919 edition, titled *With "E" of the First Gas.*

_____, *In and Out of the Ivory Tower: The Autobiography of William L. Langer* (New York, 1977).

_____ and others, *Conyers Read, 1881-1959* (Fairfax, Calif., 1963).

Leach, Henry Goddard, *Angevin Britain and Scandinavia* (Cambridge, Mass., 1921).

_____, *My Last Seventy Years* (New York, 1956).

Lee, Dwight E., *Great Britain and the Cyprus Question of 1878* (Cambridge, Mass., 1934).

_____ and George E. McReynolds (editors), *Essays in History and International Relations, in Honor of George Hubbard Blakeslee* (Worcester, Mass., 1949).

Leland, Waldo G., "The Anglo-American Conference of Historians, London, July 12-16, 1926," *American Historical Review*, XXXII (1926), 56-61.

———, "Some Early Recollections of an Itinerant Historian," *American Antiquarian Society Proceedings*, LXI (1951), 267–296.

Lord, Robert H., "Bismarck and Russia in 1863," *American Historical Review*, XXIX (1923), 24–48.

———, *The Second Partition of Poland* (Cambridge, Mass., 1915). This was published in a Polish translation in Warsaw in 1973.

Lybyer, Albert H., *The Government of the Ottoman Empire in the Time of Suleiman the Magnificent* (Cambridge, Mass., 1913). Reprinted in New York in 1966.

———, "The Influence of the Rise of the Ottoman Turks upon the Routes of Oriental Trade," *American Historical Association Annual Report. 1914* (Washington, 1916), pp. 125–133.

———, *The Question of the Near East* (New York, 1921).

Newhall, Richard A., *The English Conquest of Normandy, 1416–1424* (New Haven, Conn., 1924).

Packard, Laurence B., *The Age of Louis XIV* (New York, 1938).

———, *The Commercial Revolution* (New York, 1927).

———, *Constantinople and Byzantine Civilization, 300–1200* (Ann Arbor, Mich., 1925).

Packard, Sidney R., *12th Century Europe. An Interpretive Essay* (Amherst, Mass., 1973).

Perkins, Dexter, *The Monroe Doctrine 1823–1826* (Cambridge, Mass., 1927). Reprinted in 1932 and 1965.

———, *The Monroe Doctrine, 1867–1907* (Baltimore, 1937).

———, *Yield of the Years. An Autobiography* (Boston, 1969).

Rupp, George H., "The Reichstadt Agreement," *American Historical Review*, XXX (1925), 503–510.

———. *A Wavering Friendship: Russia and Austria, 1876–1878* (Cambridge, Mass., 1941).

Steefel, Lawrence, *The Schleswig-Holstein Question* (Cambridge, Mass., 1932).

Steiger, George N., *China and the Occident: The Origin and Development of the Boxer Movement* (New Haven, Conn., 1927). Reprinted in 1966.

Stoddard, T. Lothrop, *Clashing Tides of Colour* (New York, 1935).

———, *The French Revolution in San Domingo* (Westport, Conn., 1970).

———, *The New World of Islam* (New York, 1921).

———, *Racial Realities in Europe* (London, 1924).

———, *The Revolt against Civilization: The Menace of the Under-Man* (London, 1922). This was published in Spanish and German translations in 1923 and 1925, respectively.

———, *The Rising Tide of Color against White World-Supremacy* (New York, 1920). Reprinted in 1969 and 1971.

Trotter, Reginald G., *Canadian Federation: Its Origins and Achievement* (Toronto, 1924).

Tyler, Mason W., *The European Powers and the Near East, 1875–1878* (Minneapolis, 1925).

Wright, John K., *The Geographical Basis of European History* (New York, 1928).

———, *Geography in the Making: The American Geographical Society, 1851–1951* (New York, 1952).

SECONDARY SOURCES

A. Higher Education in the United States

1. General

Allmendinger, D., *Paupers and Scholars: The Transformation of Student Life in Nineteenth Century New England* (New York, 1975).

Atwood, Wallace, *The First Fifty Years: An Administrative Report* (Worcester, Mass., 1937).

Bishop, Morris, *A History of Cornell* (Ithaca, N.Y., 1962).

Canby, Henry Seidel, *Alma Mater: The Gothic Age of the American College* (New York, 1936).

_____, *American Memoir* (Boston, 1947).

Carnegie Foundation for the Advancement of Teaching, *The Financial Status of the Professor in America and in Germany* (New York, 1908).

Coubertin, Pierre de, *Les Universités transatlantiques* (Paris, 1890).

_____, *Les Universités des deux mondes* (Paris, 1896).

Cross, Wilbur, L., *Connecticut Yankee: An Autobiography* (New Haven, Conn., 1943).

Curti, Merle, *The Social Ideas of American Educators* (New York, 1935).

DeVane, William C., *Higher Education in Twentieth Century America* (Cambridge, Mass., 1965).

Earnest, Ernest, *Academic Procession: An Informal History of the American College, 1636-1953* (Indianapolis, 1953).

Gilman, Daniel K., *University Problems in the United States* (New York, 1898). Reprinted in 1969.

Hofstadter, Richard, and C. DeWitt Hardy, *The Development and Scope of Higher Education in the United States* (New York, 1952).

Johnson, Owen, *Stover at Yale* (New York, 1910). Reprinted in 1940.

Moore, John. H., "Football's Ugly Decades, 1893-1913," *Smithsonian Journal of History*, II (1967), 49-68.

Patton, Cornelius H., and W.T. Field, *Eight O'Clock Chapel: A Study of New England College Life in the Eighties* (Boston, 1927).

Peterson, George E., *The New England College in the Age of the University* (Amherst, Mass., 1964).

Pierson, George W., *The Education of American Leaders: Comparative Contributions of U.S. Colleges and Universities* (New York, 1969).

_____, "The University and American Society," in Michael Mooney and Florian Stuber (editors), *Small Comforts for Hard Times: Humanists on Public Policy* (New York, 1977), pp. 263-276.

_____, *Yale: A Short History* (New Haven, Conn., 1976).

_____, *Yale: The University College, 1921-1937* (New Haven, Conn., 1955).

_____, *Yale College: An Educational History, 1871-1921* (New Haven, Conn., 1952).

Rudolph, Frederick, *The American College and University* (New York, 1962).

_____, *Curriculum: A History of the American Undergraduate Course of Study since 1636* (San Francisco, 1977).

Schmidt, George P., *The Liberal Arts College: A Chapter in American Cultural History* (New Brunswick, N.J., 1958).

Sedgwick, Ellery, *The Happy Profession* (Boston, 1946).

Slosson, Edwin E., *Great American Universities* (New York, 1910).

Snow, Louis F., *The College Curriculum in the United States* (New York, 1909).

Veysey, Laurence R., *The Emergence of the American University* (Chicago, 1965).

2. *Research and Instruction Concerning Other Parts of the World*

Andrews, Arthur I., "Instructors of Courses in Slavic or East European Subjects in the Universities and Colleges of the United States of America," *Slavonic Review*, IX (1930), i-xvi.

———, "Slavic Courses in the United States," *Slavonic and East European Review*, XI (1932), 210.

———, "Slavonic Studies in America," *Slavonic Review*, III (1925), v-viii.

———, "University Courses Given in the United States of America on Slavic and Other Eastern European History, Languages and Literatures," *Slavonic and East European Review*, XV (1936), appendix, 1-23.

Babey, Anna Mary, *Americans in Russia, 1776-1917: A Study of the American Travelers in Russia from the American Revolution to the Russian Revolution* (New York, 1938).

Black, Cyril E., and John M. Thompson (editors), *American Teaching about Russia* (Bloomington, Ind., 1959).

Boardman, Eugene P. (editor), *Asian Studies in Liberal Education: The Teaching of Asian History and Civilization to Undergraduates* (Washington, 1959).

Brozek, Joseph, "Slavic Studies in America: The Present Status," *Journal of Higher Education*, XIV (1943), 293-296, 342.

Burdick, Charles A., *Ralph Lutz and the Hoover Institution* (Stanford, 1973).

Byrnes, Robert F., "The American Institute for Slavic Studies in Prague: A Dream of the 1920's," in Alexander Fischer and others (editors), *Russland-Deutschland-Amerika: Festschrift für Fritz T. Epstein zur 80 Geburtstag* (Wiesbaden, 1978), pp. 257-266.

———, "Russian Studies in the United States before the First World War," *Forschungen zur osteuropaischen Geschichte*, XXV (1978), 35-46.

University of California (Berkeley), *Asiatic and Slavic Studies on the Berkeley Campus, 1896-1947* (Berkeley, 1957).

Chalberg, John Charles, "Samuel Harper and Russia under the Tsars and Soviets, 1905-1943," 1974 Ph.D. thesis at the University of Minnesota.

Coleman, Arthur P., "Slavonic Studies in the United States, 1918-1938," *Slavonic and East European Review*, XVII (1938-39), 372-388.

Curtin, Jeremiah, *Myths and Folk Tales of the Russians, Western Slavs, and Magyars* (Boston, 1890). Reprinted in 1971.

Filene, Peter G. (editor), *American Views of Soviet Russia, 1917-1965* (Homewood, Ill., 1968).

Fisher, Harold H. (editor), *American Research on Russia* (Bloomington, Ind., 1959).

Gettman, Royal A., *Turgenev in England and America* (Urbana, Ill, 1941).

Hapgood, Isabel, *The Epic Songs of Russia*, with introductory note by Francis J. Child (New York, 1885). Reprinted in 1886, 1916, 1969, and 1970.

Harper, Paul V. (editor), *The Russia I Believe In: The Memoirs of Samuel N. Harper, 1902-1941* (Chicago, 1945).

Hoover Institution on War, Revolution, and Peace (Stanford, 1963).

Horecky,Paul L., "The Slavic and East European Resources and Facilities of the

Hucker, Charles O., *The Association for Asian Studies: An Interpretative History* (Seattle, 1973).

Jelavich, Charles (editor), *Language and Area Studies: East Central and Southeastern Europe. A Survey* (Chicago, 1969).

Kovalevsky, Maxim, "American Impressions," *Russian Review*, X (1951), 37-45, 106-117, 176-184.

Kerner, Robert J., "The Slavonic Conference at Richmond," *Slavonic Review*, III (1924-1925), 684-693.

———, "Slavonic Studies in America," *Slavonic Review*, III (1924-25), 243-258.

———, "The Teaching of Slavic History at the University of California," in Stephen N. Sestanovich (editor), *Slavs in California* (Oakland, 1937), pp. 67-72.

Library of Congress," *Slavic Review*, XXIII (1964), 309-327.

Manning, Clarence A., *History of Slavic Studies in the United States* (Milwaukee, 1957).

Maslenikov, Oleg A., "Slavic Studies in America, 1939-1946," *Slavonic and East European Review*, XXV (1946-47), 528-537.

Mosely, Philip E., "Some Vignettes of Soviet Life," *Survey*, no. 55 (1965), pp. 52-63.

Noyes, George R., "Slavic Languages at the University of California," *Slavonic and East European Review*, XXII (1944), 53-60.

———, "Teaching of Slavic Languages at the University of California," in Stephen N. Sestanovich (editor), *Slavs in California* (Oakland, 1937), pp. 29-37.

Parry, Albert, *America Learns Russian: A History of the Teaching of the Russian Language in the United States* (Syracuse, 1967).

Petrovich, Michael B., "Eugene Schuyler and Bulgaria, 1876-1878," *Bulgarian Historical Review*, VII (1979), 51-69.

———, "Pioneers, O Pioneers." Manuscript of talk given in Detroit, March 29, 1968.

Ruggles, Melville J., "Eastern European Publications in American Libraries," in Howard W. Winger (editor), *Iron Curtains and Scholarship: The Exchange of Knowledge in a Divided World* (Chicago, 1958), pp. 111-123.

Sestanovich, Stephen N., *Slavs in California* (Oakland, 1937). Reprinted in 1968.

Simmons, Ernest J., "An American Institute for Slavic Studies," New York *Herald Tribune*, December 30, 1944.

3. Research and Instruction in Other Countries concerning Other Parts of the World

Cooley, Martha Helms, "Nineteenth Century French Historical Research on Russia: Louis Leger, Alfred Rambaud, Anatole Leroy-Beaulieu," 1971 Ph.D. thesis at Indiana University.

Cronia, Arturo, "Slavonic Studies in Italy," *Slavonic and East European Review*, XXVI (1947-48), 197-208.

Eisenmann, Louis, "Ernest Denis, 1849-1921," *Revue des études Slaves*, I (1921), 138-143.

Galton, Dorothy, "The Anglo-Russian Literary Society," *Slavonic and East European Review*, XLVIII (1970), 272-282.

_____, "Sir Bernard Pares and Slavonic Studies in London University, 1919-1939," *Slavonic and East European Review*, XLVI (1968), 481-491.

Hollingsworth, Barry, "The Society of Friends of Russian Freedom: English Liberals and Russian Socialists," *Oxford Slavonic Papers*, III (1970), 45-64.

Ito, Takaiuki, "Slavianovedenie v IAponii: Istoriia, Uchrezhdeniia i Problemy," *Slavic Studies* (Hokkaido), no. 25 (1980), pp. 127-147.

Jagić, Vatroslav, "A Survey of Slavistic Studies," *Slavonic Review*, I (1922-23), 11-58, 523-524.

Josson, N.B., "The School of Slavonic and East European Studies, I, 1922-1937," *Slavonic and East European Review*, XLIV (1966), 1-7.

Kiga, Kenzo, "Soviet Studies in Japan," *ICSEES International Newsletter*, no. 7 (1978), annex, pp. i-v.

Meyer, Klaus, *Theodor Schiemann als politischer Publizist* (Frankfurt-am-Main, 1956).

Palme, Anton, "The Progress of Russian Studies in Germany," *Russian Review*, III (1914), 131-136.

Pares, Sir Bernard, *A Wandering Student* (Syracuse, 1948).

Rose, William J., *Cradle Days of Slavic Studies: Some Reflections* (Winnipeg, 1955).

_____, *The Polish Memoirs of William John Rose*, edited by Daniel F. Stone (Toronto, 1975).

The Russian Review (London, 1912-1914).

Seton-Watson, Robert W., "Slavonic Studies in Germany," *Slavonic Review*, I (1922), 494-496.

Simmons, J.S.G., "Slavonic Studies at Oxford, I: The Proposed Slavonic Chair at the Taylor Institution, 1844," *Oxford Slavonic Papers*, III (1952), 125-152.

Voigt, Gerd, *Otto Hoetzsch, 1876-1946. Eine biographischer Beitrag zur Geschichte der Deutschen Osteuropakunde* (Halle, 1967), two vols.

_____, *Otto Hoetzsch, 1876-1946. Wissenschaft und Politik im Leben eines deutschen Historiker* (East Berlin, 1978).

B. Boston

Abrams, Richard M., *Conservatism in a Progressive Era: Massachusetts Politics, 1900-1912* (Cambridge, Mass., 1964).

Adams, Charles Francis, Jr., *Autobiography* (Boston, 1916).

Adams, Henry, *The Education of Henry Adams* (New York, 1934).

_____, *Letters*, edited by Worthington Chauncey Ford (Boston, 1930-1938), two vols.

Allen, Frederick, *Only Yesterday* (New York, 1931).

Amory, Cleveland, *The Proper Bostonians* (New York, 1947).

_____, *Who Killed Society?* (New York, 1960).

Beebe, Lucius, *Boston and the Boston Legend* (New York, 1935).

Beringause, Arthur F., *Brooks Adams: A Biography* (New York, 1955).

Letters of Louis D. Brandeis, edited by Melvin I. Urovsky and David W. Levy (Albany, 1971-1973), three vols.

Brooks, Van Wyck, *An Autobiography* (New York, 1965).

_____, *The Confident Years, 1885-1915* (New York, 1955).

_____, *New England: Indian Summer, 1865-1915* (New York, 1940).

Donovan, Timothy, *Henry and Brooks Adams: The Education of Two American Historians* (Norman, Okla., 1961).

Duberman, Martin, *Charles Francis Adams, 1807-1886* (Boston, 1961).

_____, *James Russell Lowell* (Boston, 1966).

Edel, Leon, *Henry James* (Philadelphia, 1953-1972), five vols.

Edelstein, Tilden G., *Strange Enthusiasm: A Life of Thomas Wentworth Higginson* (New Haven, Conn., 1968).

Garraty, John A., *Henry Cabot Lodge: A Biography* (New York, 1953).

Greenslet, Ferris, *James Russell Lowell: His Life and Work* (Boston, 1905).

_____, *The Lowells and Their Seven Worlds* (Boston, 1946).

_____, *Under the Bridge: An Autobiography* (Boston, 1943).

Griffin, Solomon B., *People and Politics Observed by a Massachusetts Editor* (Boston, 1923).

Hennesey, Michael E., *Four Decades of Massachusetts Politics, 1890-1935* (Norwood, Mass., 1935).

Howe, Helen, *The Gentle Americans, 1864-1960: Biography of a Breed* (New York, 1965).

_____, *We Happy Few* (New York, 1946).

_____, *A Venture in Remembrance* (Boston, 1941).

Howells, William Dean, *The Rise of Silas Lapham* (New York, 1962).

Huthmacher, J. Joseph, *Massachusetts People and Politics, 1919-1933* (Cambridge, Mass., 1959).

James, Henry, *Autobiography* (New York, 1956).

Lawrence, William L., *Memories of a Happy Life* (Boston, 1926).

Lockwood, Stephen C., *Augustine Heard and Company, 1858-1862: American Merchants in China* (Cambridge, Mass., 1971).

Lodge, Henry Cabot, *Early Memories* (New York, 1913).
_____, "Some Impressions of Russia," *Scribner's Magazine*, XXXI (1902), 570–580.
McKibbin, David, *Sargent's Boston* (Boston, 1956).
Mann, Arthur, *Yankee Reformers in the Urban Age* (Cambridge, Mass., 1954).
Marquand, John P., *The Late George Apley: A Novel in the Form of a Memoir* (New York, 1940).
Morison, Samuel Eliot, *One Boy's Boston, 1887–1901* (Boston, 1962).
O'Connor, Edwin, *The Last Hurrah* (Boston, 1956).
Scudder, Horace, *James Russell Lowell* (Boston, 1901), two vols.
Shattuck, George C., *A Memoir: Frederick Cheever Shattuck, 1847–1929* (Boston, 1967).
Solomon, Barbara, *Ancestors and Immigrants: A Changing New England Tradition* (Cambridge, Mass., 1956).
Thernstrom, Stephen, *The Other Bostonians: Poverty and Progress in the American Metropolis, 1800–1970* (Cambridge, Mass., 1973).
Warner, Sam Bass, *Streetcar Suburbs: The Process of Growth in Boston, 1870–1900* (Cambridge, Mass., 1978).
Weeks, Edward, *My Green Age* (Boston, 1974).
Wells, Anna Mary, *Dear Preceptor: The Life and Times of Thomas Wentworth Higgins* (Boston, 1963).
Whitehill, Walter Muir, *Analecta Biographica: A Handful of New England Portraits* (Brattleboro, Vt., 1969).
_____, *Boston: A Topographical History* (Cambridge, Mass., 1959).
_____, *Boston in the Age of John Fitzgerald Kennedy* (Norman, Okla., 1966).
_____, "Who Rules Here?" *New England Quarterly*, XLIII (1970), 434–449.

C. The Coolidge Family

Coburn, Frederick W., "Isabella S. Gardner," *Dictionary of American Biography* (London, 1931), VII, 142–143.
Coolidge, Alice B., *Random Thoughts* (Boston, 1927).
Coolidge, Emma Downing, *Descendants of John and Mary Coolidge of Watertown, Massachusetts, 1630* (Boston, 1930).
Coolidge, Harold Jefferson, *Thoughts on Thomas Jefferson, or What Jefferson Was Not* (Boston, 1936).
Coolidge, John Gardner, *Random Letters from Many Countries* (Boston, 1924).
_____, *A War Diary in Paris, 1914–1917* (Cambridge, Mass., 1931).
Coolidge, J. Randolph, "Achievement through Conviction," *Library Journal*, XLV (1920), 103–104.
Coolidge, Julian Lowell, "Harvard Thirty Years After," *Harvard Graduates' Magazine*, XXXIV (1925), 46–52.
_____, "When Old Men Dream Dreams," *Harvard Graduates' Magazine*, XXXIV (1925), 185–193.

Coolidge, T. Jefferson, *The Autobiography of T. Jefferson Coolidge, 1831-1920* (Boston. 1923).

———, "Remarks in Presenting a Large Collection of Jefferson Papers," *Massachusetts Historical Society Proceedings*, XII (1897-1899), 264-272.

———, "Tribute to Lord Dufferin," *Massachusetts Historical Society Proceedings*, XV (1901-02), 497-503.

Gardner, Frank A. *Gardner Memorial: A Biographical and Genealogical Record of the Descendants of Thomas Gardner, Planter* (Salem, Mass., 1933).

Moors, John F., "Joseph Randolph Coolidge," *Harvard Graduates' Magazine*, XXXVII (1928), 203-206.

Morse, John Torrey, Jr., "Tribute to Thomas Jefferson Coolidge," *Massachusetts Historical Society Proceedings*, LIV (1920-21), 141-149.

Storer, Horatio R., "Thomas Jefferson Coolidge," *Harvard Graduates' Magazine*, XXIX (1921), 402-412.

Tharp, Louise, *Mrs. Jack: A Biography of Isabella Stewart Gardner* (Boston, 1965).

White, W. Leroy, and others, *Twentieth Annual Excursion of the Sandwich Historical Society, Thursday, August 24, 1939* (Sandwich, N.H., 1939).

D. Studies of Archibald Cary Coolidge

Armstrong, Hamilton Fish, "Archibald Cary Coolidge," *Le Monde Slave*, VI (1928), 94-98.

Bentinck-Smith, William, *Building a Great Library: The Coolidge Years at Harvard* (Cambridge, Mass., 1976). The substance of this volume appeared earlier in a series of articles in *Harvard Library Bulletin*, vols. XXI-XXII (1973 and 1974).

Bliss, Tasker H., "Archibald Cary Coolidge," *Foreign Affairs*, VI (1928), 353-355.

Bolton, Charles, "Archibald Cary Coolidge—Historian, Teacher, Writer," Boston *Evening Transcript*, January 18, 1928.

Coolidge, Harold Jefferson, and Robert H. Lord, *Archibald Cary Coolidge: Life and Letters* (Boston, 1932).

Emerton, Ephraim, "Archibald Cary Coolidge," *Dictionary of American Biography* (New York, 1946), IV, 393-395.

Ferguson, William S., and others, "Archibald Cary Coolidge," *American Academy of Arts and Sciences Proceedings*, LXIV (1930), 514-518.

Merriman, Roger B., "Archibald Cary Coolidge," *Harvard Graduates' Magazine*, XXXVI (1928), 550-557.

———, "Archibald Cary Coolidge, a Memoir," *Massachusetts Historical Society Proceedings*, LXIV (1932), 394-403.

Pares, Sir Bernard, "Archibald Cary Coolidge," *Slavonic and East European Review*, XI (1932), 607-616.

Schmitt, Bernadotte E., "Archibald Cary Coolidge," *Slavonic Review*, VI (1928), 671-674.

E. Harvard University

1. General

Adams, James D., *Copey of Harvard: A Biography of Charles Townsend Copeland* (Boston, 1960).

Baird, Carol F., "Albert Bushnell Hart: The Rise of the Professional Historian," in Paul Buck (editor), *Social Sciences at Harvard, 1860-1920* (Cambridge, Mass., 1965), pp. 129-174.

Bealle, Morris A., *The History of Football at Harvard, 1874-1948* (Washington, 1948).

Billington, Ray (editor), *Dear Lady: The Letters of Frederick Jackson Turner to Alice Forbes Perkins Hooper, 1910-1932* (San Marino, Calif., 1970).

_____, *Frederick Jackson Turner* (New York, 1973).

_____, "Frederick Jackson Turner Comes to Harvard," *Massachusetts Historical Society Proceedings*, LXXIV (1962), 51-84.

Blanchard, John A. (editor), *The H Book of Harvard Athletics, 1852-1922* (Cambridge, Mass., 1923).

Bradford, Gamaliel, *As God Made Them: Portraits of Some Nineteenth Century Americans* (Port Washington, N.Y., 1969).

Brown, Rollo W., *Dean Briggs* (New York, 1900).

_____, *Harvard Yard in the Golden Age* (New York, 1948).

Buck, Paul, *Social Sciences at Harvard, 1860-1920: From Inculcation to the Open Mind* (Cambridge, Mass., 1965).

Bynum, David, "Child's Legacy Enlarged: Oral Literary Studies at Harvard since 1856," *Harvard Library Bulletin*, XXII (1974), 237-267.

Canfield, Cass, *Up and Down and Around: A Publisher Recollects the Time of His Life* (New York, 1971).

Copeland, Melvin T., *And Mark an Era: The Story of the Harvard Business School* (Boston, 1958).

Cross, Samuel Hazzard, "The Contributions of G.F. Müller to Russian Historiography, with Some Considerations of A.L. Schlözer," 1916 Ph.D. thesis at Harvard University.

_____, *Lectures on the Russian Drama and Theater for Slavic 7, 1938-1939* (Cambridge, Mass., 1939).

_____, "On Teaching Contemporary Russian Civilization," *American Slavic and East European Review*, III (1944), 93-101.

_____, "Pouchkine en Angleterre," *Revue de littérature comparée*, LXV (1937), 163-181.

_____, "Teaching College Russian," *American Slavic and East European Review*, III (1944), 39-52.

_____, and Ernest J. Simmons (editors), *Centennial Essays for Pushkin* (Cambridge, Mass., 1937).

Donham, Wallace B., and Esty Foster, "The Graduate School of Business Administration," in Samuel Eliot Morison (editor), *The Development of*

Harvard University since the Inauguration of President Eliot, 1869-1929 (Cambridge, Mass., 1930), 533-548.

Eliot, Charles William, *Harvard Memories* (Cambridge, Mass., 1923).

Emerton, Ephraim, and Samuel Eliot Morison, "History, 1838-1929," in Morison, *The Development of Harvard University*, pp. 150-177.

Feuer, Lewis S., "Recollections of Henry Austryn Wolfson," *American Jewish Archives*, XXVIII (1976), 25-51.

Flandrau, Charles M., *The Diary of a Harvard Freshman* (New York, 1901).

Freidel, Frank B., *Franklin D. Roosevelt: The Apprenticeship* (Boston, 1952).

Grant, Robert, *Fourscore: An Autobiography* (Boston, 1934).

Hägler, Ernest, *Harvard Inside-Out* (Boston, 1916).

Handlin, Oscar, "College and Community in 1900," *Harvard Library Bulletin*, XII (1958), 149-160.

Hapgood, Norman, *The Changing Years: Reminiscences* (New York, 1930).

Hart, Albert Bushnell, "Government, 1874-1929," in Morison, *The Development of Harvard University*, pp. 178-186.

Harvard et la France (Paris, 1936).

Harvard University, Bureau of International Research, *Report: July 1, 1929 to June 30, 1938* (Cambridge, Mass., 1938).

_____, *Researches, 1924-1929* (Cambridge, Mass., 1929).

Harvard University, *Doctors of Philosophy and Doctors of Science Who Have Received Their Degrees in Course from Harvard University, 1873-1926, with the Titles of Their Theses* (Cambridge, Mass., 1926).

_____, Department of History, *List of References in History 1, 1910* (Cambridge, Mass., 1910).

Haskins, Charles H., "The Graduate School of Arts and Sciences, 1872-1929," in Morison, *The Development of Harvard University*, pp. 451-462.

_____, *The Historical Curriculum in College* (New York, 1904).

Hawkins, Hugh, *Between Harvard and America: The Educational Leadership of Charles W. Eliot* (New York, 1972).

Heaton, Herbert, *A Scholar in Action: Edwin F. Gay* (Cambridge, Mass., 1952).

Hicks, Granville, *John Reed: The Making of a Revolutionary* (New York, 1936).

Hill, George B., *Harvard College, by an Oxonian* (New York, 1895).

Hindus, Maurice, *A Traveler in Two Worlds* (Garden City, N.Y., 1971).

Howe, Mark A. De Wolfe, *Barrett Wendell and His Letters* (Boston, 1924).

_____. (editor), *The Scholar-Friends: Letters of Francis James Child and James Russell Lowell* (Cambridge, Mass., 1953).

Hyder, Clyde K., *George Lyman Kittredge: Teacher and Scholar* (Lawrence, Kan., 1962).

James, Henry, *Charles W. Eliot, President of Harvard University, 1869-1909* (Boston, 1930), two vols.

James, William, *Memories and Studies* (London, 1911).

Joyce, David D., *Edward Channing and the Great Work* (The Hague, 1974).

Langstaff, John, *Harvard of Today, from the Undergraduate Point of View* (Cambridge, Mass., 1913).

Lipset, Seymour, and David Riesman, *Education and Politics at Harvard* (New York, 1975).

Lovett, Robert Morss, *All Our Years* (New York, 1948).

Lowell, A. Lawrence, *What a University President Has Learned* (New York, 1938).

Merriman, Roger B., *Suleiman the Magnificent, 1520-1566* (Cambridge, Mass., 1944).

Morison, Samuel Eliot, "Edward Channing: A Memoir," *Massachusetts Historical Society Proceedings*, LXIV (1931), 250-284.

————. (editor), *The Development of Harvard University since the Inauguration of President Eliot, 1869-1929* (Cambridge, Mass., 1930).

————, "A Memoir and Estimate of Albert Bushnell Hart," *Massachusetts Historical Society Proceedings*, LXXVII (1965), 28-52.

————, *Three Centuries of Harvard, 1636-1936* (Cambridge, Mass., 1936).

Morse, William G., *Pardon My Harvard Accent* (New York, 1941).

Mosely, Philip E., "M.M. Karpovich, 1885-1959," *Russian Review*, XIX (1960), 56-60.

————, "Professor Michael Karpovich," in Hugh McLean and others (editors), *Russian Thought and Politics* (Cambridge, Mass., 1957), pp. 1-13.

Munsterberg, Margaret, *Hugo Münsterberg: His Life and Work* (New York, 1932).

Neilson, William Allan (editor), *Charles W. Eliot: The Man and His Beliefs* (New York, 1926), two vols.

Pease, Arthur Stanley, *Sequestered Vales of Life* (Cambridge, Mass., 1946).

Perry, Bliss, *And Gladly Teach: Reminiscences* (Boston, 1935).

————, *Life and Letters of Henry Lee Higginson* (Boston, 1921).

Perry, Ralph Barton, "Charles W. Eliot," *Dictionary of American Biography* (London, 1931), VI, 71-78.

Potter, Alfred Claghorn, *The Changes at Harvard in Twenty-Five Years, 1889-1914* (Cambridge, Mass., 1914).

Powicke, F.M., "Charles Homer Haskins," *English Historical Review*, LII (1937), 649-656.

Robinson, George W., *Bibliography of Edward Channing* (Cambridge, Mass., 1920).

Samuels, Ernest, *Bernard Berenson: The Making of a Connoisseur* (Cambridge, Mass., 1979).

Santayana, George, *Persons and Places* (New York, 1963), three vols. in one.

Schlesinger, Arthur M., *In Retrospect: The History of a Historian* (New York, 1963).

Schulman, Elias, Introduction to Leo Wiener, *The History of Yiddish Literature in the Nineteenth Century* (New York, 1972), pp. vii-xxvii.

Secrest, Meryle, *Being Bernard Berenson* (New York, 1979).

Self, Robert T., *Barrett Wendell* (Boston, 1975).

Sprigge, Sylvia, *Berenson: A Biography* (Boston, 1960).

Stearns, Frank P., *Cambridge Sketches* (Philadelphia, 1905).

Stegner, Wallace, *The Uneasy Chair: A Biography of Bernard De Voto* (New York, 1974).

Strakhovsky, Leonid I., "In Memoriam—Samuel Hazzard Cross," *American Slavic and East European Review*, V (1946), vii–viii.

Sutherland, Arthur E., *The Law at Harvard: A History of Ideas and Men, 1817–1967* (Cambridge, Mass., 1967).

The Letters of William Roscoe Thayer, edited by Charles Downer Hazen (Boston, 1926).

Thorndike, Lynn, "Charles Homer Haskins," *Isis*, XXVIII (1938), 53–56.

Thorpe, James E. (comp.), *A Bibliography of the Writings of George Lyman Kittredge* (Cambridge, Mass., 1948).

Tunis, John, *Was College Worth While?* (New York, 1936).

Vanderbilt, Kermit, *Charles Eliot Norton: Apostle of Culture in a Democracy* (Cambridge, Mass., 1959).

Wagner, Charles A., *Harvard: Four Centuries and Freedoms* (New York, 1950).

Wendell, Barrett, "Social Life at Harvard," *Lippincott's Monthly Magazine*, XXXIX (1887), 152–159.

Wiener, Leo (comp.), *Anthology of Russian Literature from the Earliest Period to the Present Time* (New York, 1923). Reprinted in 1967.

———, *The History of Yiddish Literature in the Nineteenth Century* (New York, 1899). Reprinted in 1972.

———, "How I Educated My People at Home," in M.H. Weeks (editor), *Parents and Their Problems* (Washington, D.C., 1914), III, 305–312.

———, *An Interpretation of the Russian People* (New York, 1915).

———, "Songs of the Spanish Jews in the Balkan Peninsula," *Modern Philology*, I (1903), 205–216, 259–274.

———. (translator), Count Leo N. Tolstoy, *Complete Works* (New York, 1904–1905), twenty-four vols.

Wiener, Norbert, *Ex-Prodigy: My Childhood and Youth* (New York, 1953).

———, *I Am a Mathematician: The Later Life of a Prodigy* (Garden City, N.Y., 1956).

Williams, George H. (editor), *The Harvard Divinity School: Its Place in Harvard University and in American Culture* (Boston, 1954).

Wister, Owen, *Philosophy 4: A Story of Harvard University* (New York, 1903).

Wolff, Robert Lee, "Robert Pierpont Blake, 1886–1950," *Dumbarton Oaks Papers*, No. 8 (1954), pp. 1-9.

Yeomans, Henry A., "A Russian Historian at Harvard," *Russian Review*, XVII (1958), 292–300.

2. Harvard University Library

Buck, Paul, *Libraries and Universities: Addresses and Reports* (Cambridge, Mass., 1964).

Cizevsky, Dmitry, "The Slovak Collection of the Harvard College Library," *Harvard Library Bulletin*, VII (1953), 299–311.

Cronin, Paula, "East Asian Studies at Harvard: A Scholarly Bridge between two Worlds," *Harvard Today* (Spring 1976), pp. 7-9, 13.

Currier, Thomas Franklin, "Archibald Cary Coolidge," *Library Journal*, LIII (1928), 131–133.

————, "A Sheaf of Memories from the Cataloguers," *Harvard Library Notes*, no. 20 (April, 1928), pp. 165-171.

Dain, Phyllis, *The New York Public Library: A History of Its Founding and Early Years* (New York, 1972).

Dorn, Richard W., "Otto Harrassowitz, Buchhandlung-Verlag-Antiquariat: The First Century," *Harvard Library Bulletin*, XXI (1973), 365-374.

Gredler, Charles R., "The Slavic Collection at Harvard," *Harvard Library Bulletin*, XVII (1969), 425-433.

Gregory, Winifred (editor), *Union List of Serials in Libraries of the United States and Canada* (New York, 1927). A two-volume supplement was published in 1932, and later editions in 1943 and 1965.

Harrassowitz, Hans, *Otto Harrassowitz und seine Firma* (Leipzig, 1932).

"Otto Harrassowitz Buchhandlung und Antiquariat in Leipzig," *Antiquarischer Catalog 202. Slavica* (Leipzig, 1895).

Harvard Library Bulletin (1947-1960, 1966-1979).

Harvard University Committee Appointed to Study the Future Needs of the College Library, *Report Presented March 31, 1902* (Cambridge, Mass., 1902).

Harvard University Library, *Catalogue of Arabic, Persian, and Ottoman Turkish Books* (Cambridge, Mass., 1968), five vols.

————, *Dictionary Catalogue of the Byzantine Collection of the Dumbarton Oaks Research Library* (Boston, 1975), twelve vols.

————, *Finnish and Baltic History and Literatures* (Cambridge, Mass., 1972).

————, *Harvard University Library, 1638-1968* (Cambridge, Mass., 1969).

————. *"The Harvard University Library, 1966-1976: Report of a Planning Study,"* (Cambridge, Mass., 1966), typescript.

————, *The Kilgour Collection of Russian Literature, 1750-1920* (Cambridge, Mass., 1959).

————, *Slavic History and Literature: Widener Library Shelflist, Numbers 18-31* (Cambridge, Mass., 1971), four vols.

Harvard-Yenching Institute, *A Guide to the Chinese-Japanese Library of Harvard University* (Cambridge, Mass., 1932).

Lane, William Coolidge, "Certain Plain Facts about the Harvard Library," *Harvard Graduates' Magazine*, VII (1899), 168-176.

————, "The Harvard College Library," in Morison, *The Development of Harvard University*, pp. 608-632.

Lydenberg, Harry M., *History of the New York Public Library* (New York, 1923). Reprinted in Boston in 1972.

Metcalf, Keyes D., *Report of the Harvard University Library: A Study of Present and Prospective Problems* (Cambridge, Mass., 1955).

Palha, Fernando, *Catalogue de la bibliothèque de M. Fernando Palha* (Lisbon, 1896), four vols. in two.

Potter, Alfred Claghorn, *The Library of Harvard University* (Cambridge, Mass., 1934), fourth edition.

Riant, Count Paul de, *Catalogue de la bibliothèque de feu M. le comte Riant* (Paris, 1896-1899), three vols. in two.

"The Russian Books," *Harvard Library Notes*, no. 9 (1922), pp. 203-208.

Shaw, Stanford, "The Harvard College Library Collection of Books on Ottoman History and Literature," (Cambridge, Mass., 1959), typescript.

Siebert, Wilbur H., "Collections of Materials in English and European History and Subsidiary Fields in the Libraries of the United States," *American Historical Association Annual Report. 1904* (Washington, 1905), pp. 651-696.

Stetson, John B., Jr., *The John B. Stetson, Jr. Collection of Hispanic and Other Americana* (New York, 1953), three vols.

_____, *The Oscar Wilde Collection of John B. Stetson Jr.* (New York, 1920).

_____, *Romances of Chivalry, European Literature, French Books with Engravings, Rare Americana from the Library of John B. Stetson, Jr.* (New York, 1935).

Whitehill, Walter Muir, *Dumbarton Oaks: The History of a Georgetown House and Garden, 1800-1966* (Cambridge, Mass., 1967).

Winship, George Parker, "Archibald Cary Coolidge," *Harvard Library Notes*, no. 20 (1928), pp. 157-164.

Yamak, Labib, "Introduction: The Middle Eastern Collections of the Harvard Library," in Harvard University Library, *Catalogue of Arabic, Persian, and Ottoman Turkish Books* (Cambridge, Mass., 1968), I, vii-xiii.

Yarmolinsky, Avrahm, "The Slavonic Division: Recent Growth," *Bulletin of the New York Public Library*, XXX (1926), 71-79.

F. Historical Scholarship

Adams, Charles Kendall, "Recent Historical Work in the Colleges and Universities of Europe and America," *American Historical Association Papers*, IV (1890), 39-65.

Adams, Herbert B., *The Study of History in American Colleges and Universities* (Washington, 1887).

_____, "The Teaching of History," *American Historical Association Annual Report, 1896* (Washington, 1897), I, 243-258.

Allison, William H. and others (editors), *A Guide to Historical Literature* (New York, 1931).

American Historical Association, Committee on the Planning of Research, *Historical Scholarship in America: Needs and Opportunities* (New York, 1932).

_____. Committee of Five, *The Study of History in Secondary Schools* (New York, 1912).

_____, Committee of Seven, *The Study of History in Schools* (New York, 1894).

_____, Committee of Ten, *Report on Secondary School Studies* (New York, 1894).

American-Scandinavian Foundation, *Scandinavian Studies: Essays Presented to Dr. Henry Goddard Leach on the Occasion of His Eighty-Fifth Birthday* (Seattle, 1965).

Andrews, Charles M., "These Forty Years," *American Historical Review*, XXX (1925), 225-250.

Barnes, Harry Elmer, *A History of Historical Writing* (Norman, Okla., 1937). A second revised edition was published in 1962.

———, "James Harvey Robinson," in Howard W. Odum (editor), *American Masters of Social Science* (New York, 1927), pp. 321-408.

Berger, Carl, *The Writing of Canadian History: Aspects of English-Canadian Historical Writing, 1900-1970* (Toronto, 1976).

Billington, Ray Allen, "Tempest in Clio's Teapot: The American Historical Association's Rebellion of 1915," *American Historical Review*, LXXVIII (1973), 348-369.

Broderick, Francis L., *W.E.B. DuBois: Negro Leader in Time of Crisis* (Stanford, 1959).

Bundy, William P., "William Leonard Langer, 1896-1977," *Foreign Affairs*, LVI (1978), 473-475.

Burgess, John W., *Reminiscences of an American Scholar* (New York, 1934).

Callcott, George H., *History in the United States, 1800-1860* (Baltimore, 1970).

Caughey, John W., *Hubert Howe Bancroft: Historian of the West* (Berkeley, 1946).

Cohen, Warren, *The American Revisionists: The Lessons of Intervention in World War I* (Chicago, 1967).

Cooke, Jacob E., *Frederic Bancroft, Historian* (Norman Okla., 1957).

Cruden, Robert, *James Ford Rhodes: The Man, the Historian, and His Work* (Cleveland, 1961).

Cunliffe, Marcus, and Robin Winks (editors), *Pastmasters: Some Essays on American Historians* (New York, 1975).

Curti, Merle (editor), *American Scholarship in the Twentieth Century* (Cambridge, Mass., 1953). Reprinted in New York in 1967.

Diehl, Carl, *Americans and German Scholarship, 1770-1870* (New York 1978).

DuBois, W.E.B., *The Autobiography of W.E.B. DuBois* (New York, 1968).

———. "Worlds of Color," *Foreign Affairs*, III (1825), 423-444.

Eisenstadt, A.S., *Charles McLean Andrews: A Study in American Historical Writing* (New York, 1956).

Essays in Intellectual History, Dedicated to James Harvey Robinson by his Former Seminar Students (New York, 1929).

Fisher, Ruth Anna and William Lloyd Fox, *J. Franklin Jameson: A Tribute* (Washington, 1966).

Fox, Dixon, R. (editor), *A Quarter Century of Learning, 1904-1929* (New York, 1931).

Gay, Harry N., "Communication: The International Congress of Historical Sciences," *American Historical Review*, VIII (1903), 809-812.

Goddard, Arthur (editor), *Harry Elmer Barnes, Learned Crusader: The New History in Action* (Colorado Springs, Colo., 1968).

Goldman, Eric, *John Bach McMaster, American Historian* (Philadelphia, 1943).

———, "Herman Eduard von Holst: Plumed Knight of American Historiography," *Mississippi Valley Historical Review*, XXIII (1937), 511-532.

Grob, Gerald N. (editor), *Statesmen and Statecraft of the Modern West: Essays in Honor of Dwight E. Lee and H. Donaldson Jordan* (Barre, Vt., 1967).

Gruber, Carol S., *Mars and Minerva: World War I and the Uses of Higher Learning in America* (Baton Rouge, 1976).

Haddow, Anna, *Political Science in American Colleges and Universities, 1636-1900* (New York, 1939).

Hall, G. Stanley (editor), *Methods of Teaching History* (Boston, 1884). Reprinted in 1902.

Hart, Albert Bushnell, "The Historical Opportunity in America," *American Historical Review*, IV (1898), 1-20.

Haskins, Charles H., "European History and American Scholarship," *American Historical Review*, XXVIII (1923), 215-227.

_____, "The International Historical Congress at Berlin," *American Historical Review*, XIV (1908), 1-8.

Havighurst, Alfred F., "Laurence Bradford Packard," *American Historical Review*, LXI (1956), 523.

Hendricks, Luther V., *James Harvey Robinson, Teacher of History* (New York, 1966).

Herbst, Juergen, *The German Historical School in American Scholarship: A Study in the Transfer of Culture* (Ithaca, N.Y., 1965).

Hofstadter, Richard, *The Progressive Historians: Turner, Beard, Parrington* (New York, 1968).

_____, *Social Darwinism in American Thought* (Philadelphia, 1945).

Holt, W. Stull (editor), *Historical Scholarship in the United States, 1876-1901, as Revealed in the Correspondence of Herbert B. Adams* (Baltimore, 1938.)

_____, *Historical Scholarship in the United States and Other Essays* (Seattle, 1967).

_____, "Historical Scholarship," in Merle Curti (editor), *American Scholarship in the Twentieth Century* (Cambridge, Mass., 1953), pp. 83-110.

Howe, Mark A. DeWolfe, *James Ford Rhodes: American Historian* (New York, 1929).

Hughes, Arthur J., "Carleton J.H. Hayes: Teacher and Historian," 1970 Ph.D. thesis at Columbia University.

Jameson, J. Franklin, "The American Historical Association, 1884-1909," *American Historical Review*, XV (1909), 1-20.

_____, *A Historian's World: Selections from the Correspondence of James Franklin Jameson* (Philadelphia, 1956).

_____, "The International Congress of Historical Sciences, Held at London," *American Historical Review*, XVIII (1913), 679-691.

_____, "List of Doctoral Dissertations in History Now in Progress at the Chief American Universities, December 1914," *American Historical Review*, XX (1915), 484-502.

Johnson, Henry, *Teaching of History in Elementary and Secondary Schools* (New York, 1915). A revised edition was published in 1940.

Josephson, Harold, *James T. Shotwell and the Rise of Internationalism in America* (Rutherford, N.J., 1975).

McCoy, Donald R., "Eighty Years On: A Review of the *American Historical Review*," *Maryland Historian* (1975), pp. 127–136.

Mattingly, Garrett, "The Historian of the Spanish Empire," *American Historical Review*, LIV (1948), 32–48.

Mereness, Newton D., "American Historical Activities during the World War," *American Historical Association Annual Report. 1919* (Washington, 1923), I, 139–293.

Pinkney, David H., and Theodore Ropp (editors), *A Festschrift for Frederick B. Artz* (Durham, N.C., 1964).

Robinson, James Harvey, *The German Bundesrath: A Study in Comparative Constitutional Law* (Philadelphia, 1891).

———, *The Humanizing of Knowledge* (New York, 1924). Reprinted in 1971.

———, *Mind in the Making* (New York, 1921).

———, *The New History* (New York, 1913). Reprinted in 1965.

———, "The Teaching of European History in the College," *American Historical Association Annual Report. 1896* (Washington, 1897), I, 265–278.

Saveth, Edward A., *American Historians and European Immigrants, 1875–1925* (New York, 1948).

Schapiro, J. Salwyn, "James Harvey Robinson, 1863–1936," *Journal of Social Philosophy*, I (1936), 278–281.

Shotwell, James T., *The Autobiography of James T. Shotwell* (Indianapolis, 1961).

Skotheim, Robert A., *American Intellectual Histories and Historians* (Princeton, 1966).

Stephens, Henry Morse, *Revolutionary Europe, 1789–1815* (London, 1959). Sixth edition.

Strout, Cushing, *The Pragmatic Revolt in American History: Carl Becker and Charles Beard* (New Haven, Conn., 1958).

Van Tassel, David D., *Recording America's Past: An Interpretation of the Development of Historical Studies in America, 1607–1884* (Chicago, 1960).

G. Economic and Social History

Baltzell, E. Digby, *Philadelphia Gentleman: The Making of a National Upper Class* (Glencoe, Ill., 1958).

———, *The Protestant Establishment: Aristocracy and Caste in America* (New York, 1964).

———, *Puritan Boston and Quaker Philadelphia: Two Protestant Ethics and the Spirit of Class Authority and Leadership* (New York, 1980).

Canby, Henry Seidel, *The Age of Confidence: Life in the Nineties* (New York, 1934).

Christman, Henry M. (editor), *One Hundred Years of the "Nation": A Centennial Anthology* (New York, 1965).

Clymer, Kenton J., "Antisemitism in the Late Nineteenth Century: The Case of John Hay," *American Jewish Historical Quarterly*, LX (1971), 344–354.

Handlin, Oscar, *Race and Nationality in American Life* (Boston, 1957).

Higham, John, "Anti-semitism in the Gilded Age: A Reinterpretation," *Mississippi Valley Historical Review*, XLIII (1957), 559-578.

———, *Strangers in the Land: Patterns of American Nativism, 1860-1925* (New Brunswick, N.J., 1955). A second edition was published in 1965.

Kirkland, Edward C., *Industry Comes of Age: Business, Labor, and Public Policy, 1860-1897* (New York, 1961).

———, *Men, Cities, and Transportation: A Study in New England History, 1820-1900* (Cambridge, Mass., 1948), two vols.

Kolko, Gabriel, *Railroads and Regulation, 1877-1916* (Princeton, 1965).

Lasch, Christopher, *New Radicalism in America, 1889-1963: The Intellectual as a Social Type* (New York, 1965).

May, Henry, *The End of American Innocence: A Study of the First Years of Our Own Time, 1912-1917* (New York, 1959).

Nevins, Allen, *The Evening Post: A Century of Journalism* (New York, 1922).

Pollak, Gustave (editor), *Fifty Years of American Idealism: The New York Nation, 1869-1915, Selections and Comments* (Boston, 1915).

Schlesinger, Arthur M., Jr., *The Crisis of the Old Order, 1913-1933* (Boston, 1957).

H. International Relations

Barnes, Harry Elmer, *The Genesis of the World War: An Introduction to the Problem of War Guilt* (New York, 1929).

Beisner, Henry L., *Twelve against Empire: The Anti-Imperialists, 1898-1900* (New York, 1968).

Challener, Richard D., *Admirals, Generals, and American Foreign Policy, 1898-1914* (Princeton, 1973).

Feis, Herbert, *The Diplomacy of the Dollar: First Era, 1919-1932* (Baltimore, 1960).

Ferguson, John H., *American Diplomacy and the Boer War* (Philadelphia, 1939).

Filene, Peter G., *Americans and the Soviet Experiment, 1917-1933* (Cambridge, Mass., 1967).

Grenville, John A.S., and George B. Young, *Politics, Strategy, and American Diplomacy: Studies in American Foreign Policy, 1873-1917* (New Haven, Conn., 1966).

Jordan, David Starr, *Imperial Democracy* (New York, 1899). Reprinted with a new introduction in New York in 1972.

La Feber, Walter, *The New Empire: An Interpretation of American Expansion, 1860-1898* (Ithaca, N.Y., 1963).

Latané, John H., *America as a World Power, 1897-1907* (New York, 1907).

May, Ernest R., *Imperial Democracy: The Emergence of America as a Great Power* (New York, 1961).

Mayer, Arno J., *Wilson vs. Lenin: Political Origins of the New Diplomacy, 1917-1918* (Cleveland, 1959). Reprinted in 1964.

Parrini, Carl P., *Heir to Empire: United States Economic Diplomacy, 1916-1923* (Pittsburgh, 1969).

Plesur, Milton, *America's Outward Thrust: Approaches to Foreign Affairs, 1865-1890* (De Kalb, Ill., 1971).

Pratt, Julius W., *Challenge and Rejection: The United States and World Leadership, 1900-1921* (New York, 1961).

Reinsch, Paul S., *Colonial Administration* (New York, 1905).

———, *Colonial Government: An Introduction to the Study of Colonial Institutions* (New York, 1911).

———, *World Politics at the End of the Nineteenth Century* (New York, 1900).

Rosen, Baron Roman R., *Forty Years of Diplomacy* (New York, 1922), two vols.

Wiebe, Robert H., *The Search for Order, 1877-1920* (New York, 1967).

Williams, William Appleman, *The Roots of the Modern American Empire* (New York, 1969).

Young, Marilyn B., *The Rhetoric of Empire: American China Policy, 1895-1901* (Cambridge, Mass., 1968).

I. The Department of State and American Diplomats

Anderson, Isabel (editor), *Larz Anderson: Letters and Journals of a Diplomat* (London, 1940).

Barnes, William, and J.H. Morgan, *The Foreign Service of the United States: Origins, Development, and Functions* (Washington, 1961).

Beaulac, William L., *Career Diplomat: A Career in the Foreign Service of the United States* (New York, 1964).

Bohlen, Charles E., *Witness to History, 1929-1969* (New York, 1973).

Bullitt, Orville H. (editor), *For the President, Personal and Secret: Correspondence between Frankin D. Roosevelt and William C. Bullitt* (Boston, 1972).

Campbell, John F., *The Foreign Affairs Fudge Factory* (New York, 1971).

Clymer, Kenton J., *John Hay: The Gentleman as Diplomat* (Ann Arbor, Mich., 1975).

Cohen, Naomi W., *A Dual Heritage: The Public Career of Oscar S. Strauss* (Philadelphia, 1969).

Crane, Katherine, *Mr. Carr of State: Forty-seven Years in the Department of State* (New York, 1960).

Dallek, Robert, *Democrat and Diplomat: The Life of William E. Dodd* (New York, 1968).

Einstein, Lewis, *A Diplomat Looks Back*, edited by Lawrence Gelfand (New Haven, Conn., 1968).

Farnsworth, Beatrice, *William C. Bullitt and the Soviet Union* (Bloomington, Ind., 1967).

Gade, John A., *All My Born Days* (New York, 1942).

Gerard, James W., *My Four Years in Germany* (New York, 1917).

Grew, Joseph Clark, *Turbulent Era: A Diplomatic Record of Forty Years, 1904-1945* (Boston, 1953), two vols.

Griscom, Lloyd C., *Diplomatically Speaking* (Boston, 1940).

Harr, John E., *The Professional Diplomat* (Princeton, 1969).

Heinrichs, Waldo H., Jr., *American Ambassador: Joseph C. Grew and the Development of the United States Diplomatic Tradition* (Boston, 1966).

Henderson, Loy W., "Robert F. Kelley," *American Historical Review*, LXXXII (1977), 237-238.

Howe, Mark A.D., *George von Lengerke Meyer: His Life and Public Services* (New York, 1920).

Huntington-Wilson, Francis M., *Memoirs of an Ex-Diplomat* (Boston, 1935).

Ilchman, Warren F., *Professional Diplomacy in the United States, 1779-1939: A Study in Administrative History* (Chicago, 1961).

Jessup, Philip C., *Elihu Root* (New York, 1938), two vols.

Kennan, George F., *Memoirs, 1925-1950* (Boston, 1967).

Parsons, J. Graham, "From Wall Street to the Ginza," *Foreign Service Journal*, LVI (1979), 9, 35-37.

Phillips, William B., *Ventures in Diplomacy* (Boston, 1953).

Schulzinger, Robert D., *The Making of the Diplomatic Mind: The Training, Outlook, and Style of United States Foreign Service Officers, 1908-1931* (Middletown, Conn., 1975).

Shaw, G. Howland, "The American Foreign Service," *Foreign Affairs*, XIV (1936), 323-333.

Strauss, Oscar, *Under Four Administrations* (Boston, 1922).

Varg, Paul A., *Open Door Diplomat: The Life of W.W. Rockhill* (Urbana, Ill., 1952).

Weil, Martin, *A Pretty Good Club: The Founding Fathers of the U.S. Foreign Service* (New York, 1978).

Welles, Sumner, *Naboth's Vineyard: The Dominican Republic, 1844-1924* (New York, 1928), two vols.

Werking, Richard Hume, *The Master Architects: Building the United States Foreign Service, 1890-1913* (Lexington, Ky., 1977).

West, Sister Rachel, *The Department of State on the Eve of the First World War, 1913-1914* (Athens, Ga., 1978).

Wilson, Hugh, *Diplomat between Wars* (New York, 1941).

————, *Education of a Diplomat* (New York, 1938).

Younger, Edward, *John A. Kasson: Politics and Diplomacy from Lincoln to McKinley* (Iowa City, Ia., 1955).

J. The United States in World Politics, 1917-1922

Albrecht-Carrié, René, *Italy at the Paris Peace Conference* (New York, 1938).

Almond, Nina, and Ralph H. Lutz (comps.), *The Treaty of St. Germain* (Stanford, 1935).

Baernreither, Joseph M., *Fragments of a Political Diary*, edited and introduction by Joseph Redlich (London, 1930).

Baker, Ray Stannard, *American Chronicle: The Autobiography of Ray Stannard Baker* (New York, 1945).

Bane, Suda L., and Ralph H. Lutz (editors), *Organization of Relief in Europe, 1918-1919* (Stanford, 1943).

Bartlett, Ruhl J., *The League to Enforce Peace* (Chapel Hill, N.C., 1944).

Blakey, George, *Historians on the Homefront: American Propagandists for the Great War* (Lexington, Ky., 1972).

Bonsal, Stephen, *Unfinished Business* (New York, 1944).

Brown, Philip M., "Foreign Relations of the Budapest Soviets in 1919: A Personal Narrative," *Hungarian Quarterly*, III (1937), 56-69.

————, *Foreigners in Turkey: Their Juridical Status* (Princeton, 1914).

————, *International Realities* (New York, 1917).

Bullard, Arthur, *The Russian Pendulum: Autocracy—Democracy—Bolshevism* (New York, 1919).

Calder, Kenneth J., *Britain and the Origins of the New Europe, 1915-1918* (Cambridge, England, 1976).

Campbell, F. Gregory, *Confrontation in Central Europe: Weimar Germany and Czechoslovakia* (Chicago, 1975).

Carsten, F.L., *Revolution in Central Europe, 1918-1919* (Berkeley, 1972).

Cuninghame, Thomas, "Between the War and Peace Treaties: A Contemporary Narrative," *Hungarian Quarterly*, V (1939), 410-424.

Czakó, Istvan, *How the Hungarian Problem was Created* (Budapest, 1934).

Dam, Hari N., *The Intellectual Odyssey of Walter Lippmann: A Study of His Protean Thought* (New York, 1973).

David, Donald E., and Eugene P. Trani, "The American YMCA and the Russian Revolution," *Slavic Review*, XXXIII (1974), 492-514.

Deak, Francis, *Hungary at the Paris Peace Conference: The Diplomatic History of the Treaty of Trianon* (New York, 1942).

Deak, Istvan, "Budapest and the Hungarian Revolutions of 1918-1919," *Slavonic and East European Review*, no. 106 (1968), pp. 129-140.

Fisher, Harold H., *The Famine in Soviet Russia, 1919-1923. The Operations of the American Relief Administration* (New York, 1927).

Floto, Ingra, *Colonel House in Paris: A Study of American Policy at the Paris Peace Conference, 1919* (Aarhus, Denmark, 1973).

Fräss-Ehrfeld, Claudia, "Die Berichte des Miles-Mission. Bezüglich der entgültgen Grenze in Kärnten," *Carinthia*, I (1975), 255-266.

Fry, Michael G., *Illusions of Security: North Atlantic Diplomacy, 1918-1922* (Toronto, 1932).

Gay, George I., and Harold H. Fisher (comps.), *Public Relations of the Commission for the Relief in Belgium: Documents* (Stanford, 1929), two vols.

Gelfand, Lawrence E., *The Inquiry: American Preparations for Peace, 1917-1919* (New Haven, Conn., 1963).

Goler, Patricia A., "Robert Howard Lord and the Settlement of Polish Boundaries after World War I," 1957 Ph.D. thesis at Boston College.

Goodman, Melvin A., "The Diplomacy of Nonrecognition: Soviet-American Relations, 1917-1933," 1972 Ph.D. thesis at Indiana University.

Hanak, Harry, *Great Britain and Austria-Hungary during the First World War: A Study in the Formation of Public Opinion* (New York, 1962).

Harrington, Joseph F., Jr., "Upper Silesia and the Paris Peace Conference," *Polish Review*, XIX (1974), 25-45.

Haskins, Charles H., and Robert H. Lord (editors), *Some Problems of the Paris Peace Conference* (Cambridge, Mass., 1920).

Helmreich, Paul C., *From Paris to Sèvres: The Partition of the Ottoman Empire at the Peace Conference of 1919-1920* (Columbus, O., 1974).

Hoffman, Robert, "The British Military Representative in Vienna, 1919," *Slavonic and East European Review*, LII (1974), 252-271.

Hoover, Herbert, *An American Epic* (Chicago, 1959-1964), four vols.

Hopkins, George W., "The Politics of Food: United States and Soviet Hungary, March-August, 1919," *Mid-America*, LV (1973), 245-270.

von Hofmannsthal, Hugo, and Josef Redlich, *Briefwechsel* (Frankfurt-am-Main, 1971).

House, Edward M., *The Intimate Papers of Colonel House* (Boston, 1926-1928), four vols.

———, and Charles Seymour (editors), *What Really Happened at Paris: The Story of the Peace Conference, 1918-1919, by American Delegates* (New York, 1921).

Jareb, Jarome (editor), "Le Roy King's Reports from Croatia, March to May 1919," *Journal of Croatian Studies*, I (1960), 75-168.

———, "Sherman Miles' Reports from Croatia, March to April 1919," *Journal of Croatian Studies*, III-IV (1962-1963), 121-165.

Jászi, Oszkar, *Revolution and Counter-Revolution in Hungary* (London, 1924).

Kennan, George, *Soviet-American Relations, 1917-1920* (Princeton, 1956-1958), two vols.

Kromer, Claudia, *Die Vereinigten Staaten von Amerika und die Frage Kärnten, 1918-1920* (Klagenfurt, 1920).

Kusielewicz, Eugene, "New Light on the Curzon Line," *Polish Review*, I (1956), 82-88.

Lasch, Christopher, *The American Liberals and the Russian Revolution* (New York, 1962).

Lederer, Ivo J., *Yugoslavia at the Paris Peace Conference: A Study in Frontiermaking* (New Haven, Conn., 1963).

Low, Alfred D., *The Anschluss Movement, 1918-1919, and the Paris Peace Conference* (Philadelphia, 1974).

———, *The Soviet Hungarian Republic and the Paris Peace Conference* (Philadelphia, 1963).

———, "Soviet Hungary and the Paris Peace Conference," in Ivan Völgyes (editor), *Hungary in Revolution, 1918-1919* (Lincoln, Neb., 1971), 137-157.

McCormick, Vance C., *Report of the War Trade Board, June 15, 1917-June 30, 1919* (Washington, 1920).

Mamatey, Victor S., *The United States and East Central Europe, 1914-1918: A Study in Wilsonian Diplomacy and Propaganda* (Princeton, 1957).

Marston, Frank S., *The Peace Conference of 1919: Organization and Procedure* (New York, 1944).

Martin, Geoffrey, J., *Mark Jefferson: Geographer* (Ypsilanti, Mich., 1968).

Martin, Lawrence, "The Perfect Day of an Itinerant Peacemaker," in William

W. Bishop and Andrew Keogh (editors), *Essays Offered to Herbert Putnam* (New Haven, Conn., 1929), pp. 333–350.

Miller, David Hunter, "The Adriatic Negotiations at Paris," *Atlantic Monthly*, CXXVI (1921), 267–277.

———, *My Diary at the Conference of Paris with Documents* (New York, 1924), twenty-one vols.

Nicolson, Harold, *Peacemaking 1919* (New York, 1939).

Pastor, Peter, *Hungary between Wilson and Lenin: The Hungarian Revolution of 1918–1919 and the Big Three* (New York, 1977).

Perman, Dagmar, *The Shaping of the Czechoslovak State: Diplomatic History of the Boundaries of Czechoslovakia, 1914–1920* (Leyden, 1962).

———, "President Wilson and Charles Crane: Russia and the U.S. Declaration of War," *Peace and Change*, II (1974), 18–28.

Rabl, Kurt O. (editor), *Der nationale Anspruch der Sudetendeutschen. Die Coolidge-Berichte und andere Urkunden der amerikanischen Delegation bei den Friedensverhandlungen von 1918/19* (Munich, 1957).

Das politische Tagebuch Josef Redlichs (Graz-Cologne, 1953–1954), two vols.

Roosevelt, Nicholas, *A Front Row Seat* (Norman, Okla., 1953).

Schmid, Georg E., "Die Coolidge-Mission in Österreich 1919. Zur Österreich-politik der USA wahrend der Pariser Friedenskonferenz," *Mitteilungen des Österreichischen Staatsarchivs*, XXIV (1971), 433–467.

Shotwell, James T., *At the Paris Peace Conference* (New York, 1937).

Silverlight, John, *The Victor's Dilemma: Allied Intervention in the Russian Civil War* (New York, 1970).

Spector, Sherman D., *Rumania at the Paris Peace Conference: A Study of the Diplomacy of Ioan I.C. Bratianu* (New York, 1963).

Temperley, Harold W.V. (editor), *A History of the Peace Conference of Paris* (London, 1920–1924), six vols.

Tillman, Seth P., *Anglo-American Relations at the Paris Peace Conference of 1919* (Princeton, 1961).

Thompson, John M., *Russia, Bolshevism, and the Versailles Peace* (Princeton, 1966).

Tökes, Rudolf, *Bela Kun and the Hungarian Soviet Republic: The Origin and Role of the Communist Party of Hungary in the Revolution of 1918–1919* (New York, 1967).

Trask, David F., *General Tasker Howard Bliss and the "Sessions of the World"* (Philadelphia, 1966).

———, *The United States in the Supreme War Council: American War Aims and Inter-Allied Strategy, 1917–1918* (Middletown, Conn., 1961).

Ullman, Richard H., *Anglo-Soviet Relations, 1917–1921* (Princeton, 1961–1972), three vols.

Völgyes, Ivan (editor), *Hungary in Revolution, 1918–1919* (Lincoln, Neb., 1971).

Wandycz, Piotr S., *France and Her Eastern Allies, 1919–1925* (Minneapolis, 1962).

———, *Soviet-Polish Relations, 1917–1921* (Cambridge, Mass., 1969).

Weissman, Benjamin M., *Herbert Hoover and Famine Relief to Soviet Russia: 1921–1923* (Stanford, 1974).

Williams, William Appleman, "American Intervention in Russia, 1917-1920," *Studies on the Left*, III (1963), 24-48; IV (1964), 39-57.

Willis, Edward F., *Herbert Hoover and the Russian Prisoners of World War I: A Study in Diplomacy and Relief* (Stanford, 1951).

Wrigley, Gladys M., "Isaiah Bowman," *Geographical Review*, XLI (1951), 7-65.

Zivozinović, Dragan R., *America, Italy and the Birth of Yugoslavia, 1917-1919* (New York, 1972).

K. The Institute of Politics

Bonn, Moritz J., *Wandering Scholar* (New York, 1948).

Botsford, Eli (editor), *Fifty Years at Williams under the Administrations of Presidents Chadbourne, Carter, Hewitt, Hopkins, and Garfield* (Pittsfield, Mass., 1928-1940). Four vols.

Buffington, Arthur H., "The Institute of Politics," in Harry A. Garfield, *Lost Visions* (Boston, 1944), 245-277. Published originally as a booklet, *The Institute of Politics at Williamstown, Massachusetts. Its First Decade* (Williamstown, Mass., 1931).

————. (editor), *Report of the Round Tables and General Conferences of the Eleventh Session of the Institute of Politics, Williams College* (Williamstown, Mass., 1931).

Comer, Lucretia Garfield, *Harry Garfield's First Forty Years: Man of Action in a Troubled World* (New York, 1965).

————, *Strands from the Weaving* (New York, 1959).

Counts, George, Luigi Villari, and Newton D. Baker, *Bolshevism, Fascism, and Capitalism: An Account of the Three Economic Systems* (New Haven, Conn., 1932).

Garfield, Harry, "The Institute of Politics: Its Origin and Underlying Idea: Problems Considered, Functioning, Accomplishments, and Future Possibilities," 1930 memorandum.

————, *Lost Visions* (Boston, 1944).

Loeb, William Jr., "Summer Sewing Circle: The Decline of Williamstown," *Outlook*, CLVI (1930), 205-207, 237-238.

McClaren, Walter W., "The Institute of Politics," in Botsford, *Fifty Years at Williams*, IV, 149-163.

Martindale, Bruce, "The Institute of Politics at Williamstown, Massachusetts, 1921-1932," 1967 undergraduate honors thesis at Williams College.

Newhall, Richard A. (editor), *Report of the Round Tables and General Conferences at the Ninth Session of the Institute of Politics, Williams College* (Williamstown, Mass., 1929).

Lord Eustace Percy of Newcastle, *Maritime Trade in War: Lectures on the Freedom of the Seas* (New Haven, Conn., 1930).

Sforza, Count Carlo, "Williamstown: Impressions américaines," *L'Esprit internationale*, I (1927), 519-524.

Viallate, Achille, *Economic Imperialism and International Relations during the Last Fifty Years* (New York, 1923).

Williams College, Institute of Politics, *Roundtable Conferences of the Institute of Politics at Its First Session, 1921* (New Haven, Conn., 1923). "World Relations as Seen from Williamstown," *Review of Reviews,* LXIV (1921), 272-274.

L. The Council on Foreign Relations and *Foreign Affairs*

Armstrong, Hamilton Fish (editor), *The Foreign Affairs Reader* (New York, 1947).

_____, *Peace and Counterpeace: From Wilson to Hitler* (New York, 1971).

_____, *Those Days* (New York, 1963).

The Council on Foreign Relations, *A Record of Fifteen Years* (New York, 1937).

Courtney, Kent, and Phoebe Courtney, *America's Unelected Rulers* (New Orleans, 1962).

Fox, Victor J., (pseud.) *The Welfare Staters* (New York, 1962).

Handbook of the Council on Foreign Relations (New York, 1919).

Harbaugh, William H., *Lawyer's Lawyer: The Life of John W. Davis* (New York, 1973).

Langer, William L., "Hamilton Fish Armstrong," *Foreign Affairs,* vol. LI (1973), unpaged.

Lucas, J. Anthony, "The Council on Foreign Relations, Is It a Club? Seminar? Presidium? 'Invisible' Government?" New York *Times Sunday Magazine,* November 21, 1971.

Shepardson, Whitney S., *Early History of the Council on Foreign Relations* (Stamford, Conn., 1970).

Shoup, Laurence H., and William Minter, *Imperial Brain Trust: The Council on Foreign Relations and United States Foreign Policy* (New York, 1977).

M. Miscellaneous

Baedeker, Karl, *West und Mittel Russland. Handbuch für Reisende* (Leipzig, 1882). This was printed in six editions by 1904. A French translation was published in Leipzig in 1893 and reprinted in 1897 and 1903. English editions were published in 1912 and 1914.

_____, *Russland: europäisches Russland. Eisenbahnen in Russ.-Asien, Teheran, Peking. Handbuch für Reisende* (Leipzig, 1888). This was printed in seven editions by 1913.

Bryce, Lord James, *The American Commonwealth* (New York, 1899), two vols, third edition.

Buley, R. Carlyle, *The Equitable Life Insurance Company of the United States* (New York, 1959).

Davis, Richard Harding, *With Both Armies in South Africa* (New York, 1900).

Hamer, Philip M. (editor), *A Guide to Archives and Manuscripts in the United States,* compiled for the National Historical Publications Commission (New Haven, Conn., 1961).

Lattimore, Owen, *Studies in Frontier History: Collected Papers, 1928-1958* (London, 1963).
Morrison, Elting (editor), *The Letters of Theodore Roosevelt* (Cambridge, Mass., 1951-1954), eight vols.
Wharton, Edith, *A Backward Glance* (New York, 1943).

Because of the nature of this study, biographical aids and indices to newspapers and to journals were especially important. I made intensive use of the *Dictionary of American Biography* and its supplements, the *Dictionary of American Scholars*, the *Dictionary of National Biography*, the *Encyclopedia Americana*, the *Canadian Who's Who, Who's Who in America, Who's Who in American Education, Who's Who in Canada, Who's Who in the Central States, Who's Who in the East, Who's Who in the Midwest, Who's Who in New England, Who's Who in the West*, the *United States Department of State Biographical Register*, and Richardson Dougal and Mary Patricia Chapman, *United States Chiefs of Mission* (Washington, 1973).

Index

293